NOT GUILTY

Not Guilty

REPORT OF THE COMMISSION OF INQUIRY INTO THE CHARGES MADE AGAINST LEON TROTSKY IN THE MOSCOW TRIALS

Pathfinder

NEW YORK   LONDON   MONTREAL   SYDNEY

ISBN 978-0-87348-847-1
Library of Congress Catalog Card Number 72-87928
Manufactured in Canada

First edition, 1938
Second edition, 1972
First paperback edition, 2008

The cover painting, "Portrait of Lev Trotsky" (1937) by Dorothy Eisner
is reprinted by permission of Christie McDonald and of the Houghton
Library, Harvard University (call number *59Z-4).

Back cover photo: Dewey Commission hearings, April 1937. Left to right
around table: Jean van Heijenoort, Leon Trotsky, Jan Frankel (behind him in
corner, Natalia Sedova), Otto Ruehle, Carleton Beals, John Dewey, Suzanne
La Follette, Benjamin Stolberg, John Finerty, Albert Glotzer, Albert
Goldman. At far right, standing with sketchbook, is artist Dorothy Eisner.
(Beinecke Library, Yale University)

Pathfinder
www.pathfinderpress.com
E-mail: pathfinder@pathfinderpress.com

Contents

Introduction to the 1972 edition

Not Guilty is the full report of the findings of the "International Commission of Inquiry into the Charges Made Against Leon Trotsky in the Moscow Trials." The Commission is generally referred to as the Dewey Commission after John Dewey, the noted American philosopher and educator, who served as its chairman.

The Dewey Commission was formed in 1937 to review the charges made against Trotsky and his son Leon Sedov, a leader of the Left Opposition in his own right, and to determine whether the "guilty" verdicts returned against them in the Moscow Trials had a basis in fact.

The Commission was to determine this by examining the transcripts of the Moscow Trials, taking testimony from Trotsky, Sedov and any witnesses they could produce in their defense and examining such documents pertaining to the case as Trotsky, Sedov, the witnesses and the Soviet authorities would provide.

Originally published by Harper&Brothers in a limited edition in 1938, *Not Guilty* has long been out of print. The decision to reprint it at this time testifies to the renewed interest in the issues raised by the Moscow Trials and in the political struggles in the Soviet Union in the 1920s and 1930s which formed their backdrop.

In all, four major trials from 1936 to 1938 were collectively known as the Moscow Trials. The defendants, who were charged with such crimes as organizing a terrorist apparatus to assassinate Soviet leaders, plotting the restoration of capitalism, conspiring with the leaders of Nazi Germany against the Soviet Union and other "crimes against the Soviet state," included all the surviving members of Lenin's Politburo with the exception of Stalin.

There were sixteen defendants in the first trial, which took place in August 1936. Among them were Gregory Zinoviev, Leon Kamenev, and Leon Trotsky.

In the 1937 trials, Pyatakov and Radek were among the seventeen brought to trial. Following their conviction, Marshal Tukhachevsky, the Deputy Commissar of Defense and actual commander of the Red Army, and a number of other top Red Army generals were tried in secret and executed.

In March 1938, Bukharin, Rykov, and Yagoda, who as the former head of the secret police had himself been an organizer of the earlier trials, were among those found guilty and executed for their "crimes against the Soviet state."

A glance at the "Biographical Index of the Accused" (Appendix II of this volume) indicates the caliber of those tried and executed in the first trials. Many observers found it preposterous that so many leaders of the Russian Communist Party, such as Kamenev, Zinoviev, Trotsky, Smirnov, Sokolnikov, Serebryakov, Muralov, Pyatakov, Radek, Bukharin and Tomsky, who had devoted their lives to the Communist movement and had played key roles in the victory of the October Revolution and the consolidation of the new Soviet state, were now accused of being traitors conspiring with German fascism to overthrow the Soviet Union and restore capitalism.

Defenders of Stalin were able to point, however, to the fact that all of the defendants with the exception of Trotsky and Sedov, the only two not in the Soviet Union, had confessed their "crimes" and had demanded harsh punishment or had committed suicide before their trials took place.

Much speculation has taken place about why all the prisoners in the dock made confessions that the Dewey Commission showed to be so patently untrue. Leon Sedov believed that the confessions were the result of physical torture. He argued that "with their self-accusatory statements based on no facts and no evidence, with their literal repetition of the Prosecutor's pronouncements, and with their zeal for self-defamation, the defendants were in effect saying to the world: 'Don't believe us, don't you see that all this is a lie, a lie from beginning to end!'"

In recent years, more specific information about the methods used to extract such "confessions" has come to light. Nikita Khrushchev, in his "secret speech" to the Twentieth Congress of the CPSU in 1956, confirmed that confessions were fabricated "through the crudest kind of pressure . . . by physical means." "Confessions of guilt" he stated, "were gained with the help of cruel and inhuman tortures."

In *The Confession*, Artur London, a former leader of the Czech Communist regime, describes the methods employed by the Czech secret police to force him and his thirteen co-defendants, eleven of whom were subsequently executed, to denounce each other and confess to a multitude of crimes they had not and could not have committed.

The Moscow Trials, which were aimed at Stalin's best known and most influential political opponents, were only the tip of the iceberg of arrests, purges, executions, and other forms of political repression which swept the Soviet Union during Stalin's years in power. How many Soviet citizens were swept up in the terror has never been disclosed by Soviet authorities. But an example of the scope of the purges can be seen in information cited by Khrushchev at the Twentieth Congress where he said that "of the 139 members and candidates of the party's Central Committee who were elected at the seventeenth congress [January, 1934], ninety-eight persons, i.e. 70 per cent, were arrested and shot (mostly in 1937–1938)" and that of the 1,966 delegates at that congress, 1,108 were ultimately arrested on charges of "anti-revolutionary crimes." More than 80 per cent of these delegates had been longtime members of the Communist Party, having joined before the revolution or during the Civil War.

Using the confessions of the other defendants as evidence, the Soviet court found Trotsky and Sedov guilty in absentia of "having directly prepared and personally directed the organization in the U.S.S.R. of terroristic acts" and stated that they were "subject, in the event of their being discovered on the territory of the U.S.S.R., to immediate arrest. . . ."

When the verdicts were announced, Trotsky, from his exile in Norway, challenged Stalin to demand his extradition, hoping in this way to be able to present his case before the Norwegian tribunal which would have to decide if extradition was justified. Stalin, however, wanted no scrutiny of the case by any tribunal not directly controlled by him.

The Soviet government resorted, instead, to putting major pressure on the Norwegian government both directly and through the important Norwegian shipping industry, to silence Trotsky. These efforts were successful and prevented Trotsky from defending himself fully while the trials were still fresh in the public mind.

One day after the verdicts in the first trial were announced, the Norwegian government ruled that Trotsky had violated the terms of his asylum by denouncing the trial, despite the fact that he was a major figure in it. The Norwegian police furthermore demanded that he sign a statement promising to refrain from interfering "directly or indirectly, orally and in writing, in political questions current in other countries." They also demanded that as an author, Trotsky "strictly limit his activity to historical works and general theoretical observations not directed towards any specific country."

Trotsky refused to sign such an agreement, arguing that it would then be impossible to defend himself against the trial which had just branded him an accomplice of Hitler and ringleader of a terrorist organization with plans to assassinate seven major Soviet leaders.

In retaliation for Trotsky's refusal to sign, the Norwegian government placed him under house arrest. They posted guards at his door and forbade him to make any statements for publication. These measures were soon followed by even more stringent internment and by the deportation of his secretaries.

The effect of these measures was, of course, to gag Trotsky and prevent him from publicly defending himself. The Soviet government used this enforced silence to give credence to the charges. In fact the Soviet prosecutor cynically pointed to Trotsky's silence as a tacit admission of guilt.

As a result of Trotsky's internment, it fell to Leon Sedov to shoulder the main burden of defending himself and his father for the first half year after the initial trial. It was Sedov who collected most of the documents and prepared most of the defense material which would ultimately be submitted to the Dewey Commission for examination.

Not until six months after the close of the first trial, when Trotsky had been granted asylum in Mexico and was thus free from the restrictions the Norwegians had put on him, was he able to begin his own public defense in a vigorous way. Upon his arrival in Mexico, Trotsky called for the creation of an International Commission of Inquiry to examine the records of the Moscow Trials, evaluate the defense against the charges by Trotsky and Sedov, and determine whether they were in fact guilty of the crimes they had been convicted of in absentia. Trotsky announced, in advance, that he would abide by the verdict of such a commission, composed of people whose integrity was recognized around the world, and would, if found guilty, deliver himself to Soviet authorities for execution.

The establishment of such an impartial commission was to prove harder than one might expect from the vantage point of 1972. It is difficult now to imagine the barrage of hostile propaganda against the proposed commission and the tremendous pressure put on individuals not to become a part of it. John Dewey, for example, found himself isolated from long-time friends and associates. The *New Republic*, of which he had been a founder, opposed his participation and forced his resignation from its editorial board.

A manifesto urging a boycott of the Commission of Inquiry was published widely in the United States. It warned "all men of good will" not to assist the Commission. Critics of the Moscow Trials were, according to the manifesto, interfering in domestic Soviet affairs, giving aid and comfort to fascism, and "dealing a blow to the forces of progress." Among the many professors, writers, and artists who signed it were Theodore Dreiser, Granville Hicks, Corliss Lamont, Max Lerner, Anna Louise Strong, Paul Sweezy, and Nathanael West. Similar expressions of opposition to such a commission were voiced all over the world.

An International Commission of Inquiry was, nonetheless, formed and its subcommission began hearings in Coyoacan, Mexico, in March 1937. In addition to its chairman, John Dewey, the Commission's members were John Chamberlain, then an associate editor of the *Saturday Review of Literature*; Alfred Rosmer, a member of the Executive Committee of the Communist International from 1920–1921 and the former editor of the French Communist Party's organ *l'Humanité*; Edward A. Ross, professor emeritus of sociology at the University of Wisconsin and an authority on the history of the Russian revolution; Otto Ruehle, Karl Marx's biographer, who, alone with Karl Liebknecht voted in the Reichstag against war credits in 1914–1915; Benjamin Stolberg, an American journalist; Wendelin Thomas, leader of the sailors' revolt in Wilhelmshaven, Germany, in November 1918 and later a Communist Party member of the Reichstag; Carlo Tresca, an internationally known anarchist leader who had been active in the defense of Sacco and Vanzetti; Francisco Zamora, a Latin American journalist and former member of the national committee of the Mexican Federation of Workers; Suzanne La Follette, an American journalist and former editor of *The Freeman* and *The New Freeman*. The counsel for the Commission was the noted civil liberties lawyer John F. Finerty, who had been a defense lawyer for Sacco and Vanzetti and Tom Mooney.

The members of the Commission represented a broad political spectrum, including Marxists and anti-Marxists, liberals and radicals. None was a follower of Trotsky, although Alfred Rosmer had been earlier in his career.

The Dewey Commission's findings were published in 1938 in two volumes. The first, *The Case of Leon Trotsky*, was a report of the hearings held by the Preliminary Commission in Mexico City and the verbatim record of the proceedings including Trotsky's testimony there. *The Case of Leon Trotsky* was reprinted in 1969 by Merit Publishers.

The present volume contains the report of the Commission's analysis of the evidence presented at the Moscow Trials themselves and the evidence, exhibits, and documents presented at the Dewey Commission hearings. Its conclusions are summed up in the following words:

> "We therefore find the Moscow trials to be frameups.
> We therefore find Trotsky and Sedov not guilty."

The historic importance of the Dewey Commission's findings, republished in this volume, lies in the fact that this was the first major blow struck against the show trials in the Soviet Union in the mid 1930s and against the wholesale falsification of history by Stalin and his followers.

The Dewey Commission's findings were vindicated in Nikita Khrushchev's 1956 speech to the Twentieth Congress of the CPSU when he too admitted that many of the Stalinist trials had been frame-ups. Since that time there have been limited moves within the Soviet Union to correct the record of the Moscow Trials. A number of the main defendants have been partially and posthumously "rehabilitated."

But this process has not been extended to Trotsky or Sedov. The characterization of them as terrorists, agents of German fascism, and the like remains unexpunged. For that reason, the documents of the Dewey Commission retain their relevance and topicality, and will continue to do so at least until such time as Trotsky's true role is again acknowledged within the Soviet Union.

Will Reissner

The commissioners

John Dewey: Educator and author. Professor Emeritus of Philosophy, Columbia University. Founder of Progressive Education in the United States. Leader of American Pragmatism. Member of Sacco-Vanzetti and Tom Mooney Defense Committees. Author of numerous books on philosophy, psychology, education and social problems.

John P. Chamberlain: Author and journalist. Former literary critic, *New York Times.* Former lecturer, School of Journalism, Columbia University, and associate editor, *Saturday Review of Literature.*

Alfred Rosmer: Author and labor journalist. Member of Executive Committee of the Communist International, 1920–21; member of Praesidium, Second Congress of the C.I., 1920. Editor-in-chief of *l'Humanité,* 1923–1924.

Edward Alsworth Ross: Educator and author. Professor Emeritus of Sociology, University of Wisconsin. Author of numerous volumes on economics, sociology and politics, including "The Russian Bolshevik Revolution" and "The Russian Soviet Republic."

Otto Ruehle: Author, biographer of Karl Marx. Former Social Democratic member of the German Reichstag. Leader of the Saxon revolution, November, 1918.

Benjamin Stolberg: Author and journalist. Former editor of labor and literary journals. Writer for many years on American Labor.

Wendelin Thomas: Leader of the Wilhelmshaven revolt, November 7, 1918. Independent Socialist and later Communist member of the German Reichstag, 1920–24. Editor, daily *Volkswille* (Augsburg), 1919–22. Later editor of and contributor to other party and union papers.

Carlo Tresca: Anarcho-Syndicalist leader. Editor of *Il Martello* (New York). Leader in Mesabi Range, Lawrence, and Paterson strikes. Active in Sacco-Vanzetti Defense.

Francisco Zamora: Latin American left publicist. Editorial writer, *El Universal* (Mexico City). Former member, National Committee of the *Confederacion de Trabajadores de Mexico.*

Suzanne La Follette: Author and journalist. Former editor, *The Freeman* and *The New Freeman.*

COUNSEL FOR THE COMMISSION

John F. Finerty: Former counsel for Sacco and Vanzetti, and counsel for Tom Mooney.

Preface

The Commission of Inquiry, at its session of September 21, 1937, drew up and signed the findings which appear as the Introduction to this volume. It appointed an editorial committee—John Dewey, Suzanne La Follette, and Benjamin Stolberg—to write its final Report in accordance with these findings. The Report which forms the present volume of its publications has been approved by all the ten members of the Commission.

The actual writing of this Report, and most of the painstaking research required in verifying the wealth of documentary material and other evidence submitted to the Commission and in weighing these against the charges and testimony in the trial records, has been done by Suzanne La Follette.

We, as the other members of the editorial committee, wish to express our deep sense of indebtedness to Miss La Follette. And we do so the more gladly because we believe that in acknowledging our own obligation to her we speak for all those who want to know the truth and are not afraid of it.

The importance of this task, it seems to us, can hardly be exaggerated. And to its performance Miss La Follette has brought unwearied industry and rare intellectual integrity.

John Dewey
Benjamin Stolberg

Explanatory note

In this volume, the records of the hearings of sub-commissions are, except for that of the Preliminary Commission, quoted from the unpublished transcripts. The records of sub-commissions and the documents in the case will be published in a subsequent volume.

The records of our sub-commissions are referred to as follows:

Preliminary Commission: PC
Commission Rogatoire: CR
New York Sub-Commission: NY

The Preliminary Commission, the *Commission Rogatoire,* and the Commission received documents in evidence. Several exhibits contain many documents, divided into categories determined by their bearing upon the subject-matter of those exhibits. These categories are indicated by Roman numerals, and the documents within these sub-divisions by Arabic numerals—e.g., PC Exh. 18, III/1. Where a document is in more than one part, or where several documents are closely related, the several parts or documents carry the same number, with letters added—e.g., PC Exh. 19, II/4, a. Documents submitted to the Commission which logically belong in exhibits submitted to the Preliminary Commission have been added to those exhibits, and identified as supplementary by the addition of the letter S—e.g., PC Exh. 18, S VIII/26. The listing indicates that document number 26 is a supplementary document in category VIII of Exhibit 18 of the Preliminary Commission.

In referring to the records of the trials of August, 1936, and January, 1937, we have used the initials of the popular titles, as follows:

Zinoviev-Kamenev trial (August, 1936): ZK
Pyatakov-Radek trial (January, 1937): PR

Following is a list of other abbreviations used in the report:

C.P.S.U.: Communist Party of the Soviet Union

C.C.: Central Committee of the Communist Party of the Soviet Union

C.C.C.: Central Control Commission of the Communist Party of the Soviet Union

C.E.C.: Central Executive Committee of the Soviet Union

C.I., Comintern: The Communist International

E.C.C.I.: Executive Committee of the Communist International

GPU: The Soviet Secret Police

Summary of findings

CONDUCT OF THE TRIALS

Independent of extrinsic evidence, the Commission finds:

(1) That the conduct of the Moscow trials was such as to convince any unprejudiced person that no effort was made to ascertain the truth.

(2) While confessions are necessarily entitled to the most serious consideration, the confessions themselves contain such inherent improbabilities as to convince the Commission that they do not represent the truth, irrespective of any means used to obtain them.

THE CHARGES

(3) On the basis of all the evidence, we find that Trotsky never gave Smirnov any terrorist instructions through Sedov or anybody else.

(4) On the basis of all the evidence, we find that Trotsky never gave Dreitzer terrorist instructions through Sedov or anybody else.

(5) On the basis of all the evidence, we find that Holtzman never acted as go-between for Smirnov on the one hand and Sedov on the other for the purposes of any terrorist conspiracy.

(6) We find that Holtzman never met Sedov in Copenhagen; that he never went with Sedov to see Trotsky; that Sedov

was not in Copenhagen during Trotsky's sojourn in that city; that Holtzman never saw Trotsky in Copenhagen.

(7) We find that Olberg never went to Russia with terrorist instructions from Trotsky or Sedov.

(8) We find that Berman-Yurin never received terrorist instructions from Trotsky in Copenhagen, and that Berman-Yurin never saw Trotsky in Copenhagen.

(9) We find that David never received terrorist instructions from Trotsky in Copenhagen, and that David never saw Trotsky in Copenhagen.

(10) We find no basis whatever for the attempt to link Moissei Lurye and Nathan Lurye with an alleged Trotskyist conspiracy.

(11) We find that Trotsky never met Vladimir Romm in the Bois de Boulogne; that he transmitted no messages through Romm to Radek. We find that Trotsky and Sedov never had any connection with Vladimir Romm.

(12) We find that Pyatakov did not fly to Oslo in December, 1935; he did not, as charged, see Trotsky; he did not receive from Trotsky any instructions of any kind. We find that the disproof of Pyatakov's testimony on this crucial point renders his whole confession worthless.

(13) We find that the disproof of the testimony of the defendant Pyatakov completely invalidates the testimony of the witness Bukhartsev.

(14) We find that the disproof of Vladimir Romm's testimony and that of Pyatakov completely invalidates the testimony of the defendant Radek.

(15) We find that the disproof of the confessions of Smirnov, Pyatakov and Radek completely invalidates the confessions of Shestov and Muralov.

(16) We are convinced that the alleged letters in which Trotsky conveyed alleged conspiratorial instructions to the various defendants in the Moscow trials never existed; and that the testimony concerning them is sheer fabrication.

(17) We find that Trotsky throughout his whole career has always been a consistent opponent of individual terror. The Commission further finds that Trotsky never instructed any of the defendants or witnesses in the Moscow trials to assassinate any political opponent.

(18) We find that Trotsky never instructed the defendants or witnesses in the Moscow trials to engage in sabotage, wrecking, and diversion. On the contrary, he has always been a consistent advocate of the building up of socialist industry and agriculture in the Soviet Union and has criticized the present régime on the basis that its activities were harmful to the building up of socialist economy in Russia. He is not in favor of sabotage as a method of opposition to any political régime.

(19) We find that Trotsky never instructed any of the accused or witnesses in the Moscow trials to enter into agreements with foreign powers against the Soviet Union. On the contrary, he has always uncompromisingly advocated the defense of the U.S.S.R. He has also been a most forthright ideological opponent of the fascism represented by the foreign powers with which he is accused of having conspired.

(20) On the basis of all the evidence we find that Trotsky never recommended, plotted, or attempted the restoration of capitalism in the U.S.S.R. On the contrary, he has always uncompromisingly opposed the restoration of capitalism in the Soviet Union and its existence anywhere else.

(21) We find that the Prosecutor fantastically falsified Trotsky's rôle before, during and after the October Revolution.

CONCLUSIONS

(22) We therefore find the Moscow trials to be frame-ups.

(23) We therefore find Trotsky and Sedov not guilty.

John Dewey, Chairman
John R. Chamberlain
Alfred Rosmer
E.A. Ross
Otto Ruehle
Benjamin Stolberg
Wendelin Thomas
Carlo Tresca
F. Zamora
Suzanne La Follette, Secretary
John F. Finerty, Counsel, Concurring.

NEW YORK, SEPTEMBER 21, 1937.

Part 1

The Commission of Inquiry

1

Reasons for a commission

§ 1. This Commission of Inquiry into the Charges made against Leon Trotsky in the Moscow Trials was initiated in March, 1937, by the American Committee for the Defense of Leon Trotsky, acting for its own nation-wide membership and under mandates from the French *Comité pour l'Enquête sur le Procès de Moscou,* the English Committee for the Defense of Leon Trotsky, and the Czechoslovak *Internationales Komitee für Recht und Wahrheit.* Since that time it has acted as an independent body, controlling its own membership and finances, authorizing sub-commissions to take testimony, and conducting its inquiry in pursuance of those methods which its members regarded as best calculated to further the purpose for which it was created.

§ 2. The reasons for its formation are generally known, and therefore need be stated only briefly. In the Moscow trials of August, 1936, and January, 1937, Leon Trotsky and his son Leon Sedov had been accused of serious crimes against the Soviet state and its leaders, and declared convicted without having been offered any opportunity to be heard. They had denied their guilt through the world press and in their turn accused the Soviet government of having based their "conviction" on framed-up evidence. At the time of the August trial, Trotsky had challenged the Soviet government to request his extradition from Norway, where he was living in exile from the Soviet Union, a procedure which would automatically have brought his case before a Norwegian court. He repeated this challenge from his Mexican asylum at the time of the January trial. In the absence of any attempt by the Soviet government to secure their extradition, and in the consequent absence of opportunity to answer the charges against them before any legally constituted court, Trotsky and Sedov had called for the formation of an international commission of inquiry to take their testimony and to consider documentary proofs of their innocence which they declared themselves ready to submit.

The August trial had precipitated a worldwide controversy, which the January trial had further embittered. There was widespread suspicion of political persecution in juridical form. An investigation was, therefore, justified and necessary in the interest of historic truth. The members of this Commission, holding widely divergent political and social opinions, and none of them being a political adherent of Leon Trotsky, have united solely for the purpose of investigating this issue and establishing the facts.

§ 3. The importance of its task and the gravity of its responsibility to public opinion have grown immeasurably during the months it has been at work. The continuing arrests and executions of Soviet officials and other citizens on charges of terrorism, wrecking, sabotage, "Trotskyism," etc., have strengthened the suspicion of thousands of genuine friends of the Russian people that the present régime is seeking to identify political opposition to itself with criminal activity against the Soviet Union and people. Even outside Russia, charges of this nature have become a formula by which the ranks of labor everywhere have been divided. For example, in Spain Andres Nin, one of the leaders of the Workers' Party of Marxist Unity (POUM), was arrested and later kidnapped and murdered, with others, in consequence of this division. Other leaders of the POUM are in jail. In China, oppositionists to the policies of the official Communist Party are accused in terms identical with those used against the so-called Trotskyites in Spain. The issue, even more than those involved in such historic cases as that of Dreyfus, Sacco-Vanzetti, or Dimitrov-Torgler, must therefore be regarded as international. It imperils countless human lives and compromises those standards of justice which mankind has painfully established to safeguard the individual against governmental oppression.

The Commission therefore submits its report to public opinion in all countries, with a profound awareness of the historic and contemporary significance of the issue with which it has had to deal, and in the hope that this result of many months of painstaking investigation will clarify that issue.

2

Procedure of the Commission

§ 4. The procedure of this Commission has been similar to that of such bodies as Senate investigating committees, the National Labor Relations Board, and the unofficial international commission which investigated the Reichstag Fire case. Its sole purpose having been to ascertain the truth concerning the charges made against Leon Trotsky and Leon Sedov, it has been concerned with bringing to light all available facts in the case, whether favorable or unfavorable to Trotsky and Sedov. In accepting evidence it has been guided by the so-called "best evidence rule," under which it has received only the best evidence which the circumstances made available. The action of the Soviet government in executing twenty-nine of the thirty-three defendants in the two Moscow trials has made it forever impossible to obtain through cross-examination the best evidence of the truth of their alleged confessions; and the Soviet government's attitude of non-cooperation precludes the cross-examination of those four defendants who were sentenced to terms of imprisonment. This attitude also makes impossible an examination of the records of the investigations preliminary to the trials, or any of the secret documentary evidence which is allegedly in the possession of the prosecution. Other direct evidence, such as police records of Trotsky's movements, is in the possession of foreign governments, and repeated efforts on behalf of the Commission to obtain access to it have failed. Nevertheless we have been able to amass a wealth of direct evidence and of corroborating indirect evidence. In view of the reiterated assertions made by partisan critics of the Commission, to the effect that no original documents were available to it, we emphatically assert here that we are in possession of a very large number of *original* and important documents submitted in evidence.

§ 5. Our inquiry has been furthered by three sub-commissions, the names of whose members are listed in Appendix No. 1 to this report. The first, generally known as the Preliminary Commission, held thirteen hearings in Coyoacan, D.F., Mexico, from April 10 to April 17, 1937, during which it took Trotsky's testimony and that of his secretary, Jan Frankel, cross-examined both witnesses, heard Trotsky's argument in which he answered the charges against him and made counter-charges against the Soviet government, and accepted, subject to verification, such documentary evidence as he had to introduce. Its report and the record of its sessions, in a volume of 617 pages, have been published by Harper & Brothers under the title, "The Case of Leon Trotsky." A rogatory commission *(Commission Rogatoire)*, created by the French *Comité pour l'Enquête sur le Procès de Moscou*, held eleven sessions from May 12 to June 22, 1937, in Paris, taking the testimony of Leon Sedov and four other witnesses, and accepting such documentary evidence as Leon Sedov had to submit. A sub-commission in New York held five hearings on July 26 and 27, 1937, three in public and two in closed session, during which it took the testimony of eleven witnesses. The records of all sub-commissions have been accepted by the Commission and included in the materials which form the basis of this report.

§ 6. Both the Preliminary Commission of Inquiry and the *Commission Rogatoire* invited the Soviet government, through its diplomatic representatives, to be represented at their hearings with the right to cross-examine witnesses and offer evidence in rebuttal of their testimony. The Preliminary Commission also requested that the Soviet government make available to its members the records of hearings preliminary to the two Moscow trials. The invitations and the request were ignored (PC, App. 3, p. 594; CR, Exh. 6). The Preliminary Commission also invited the Communist Party of the U.S., the Communist Party of Mexico, the well-known Communist lawyer of New York, Mr. Joseph Brodsky, and Mr. Lombardo Toledano, General Secretary of the *Confederacion de Trabajadores de Mexico* and outstanding opponent of Trotsky, to participate in its inquiry. The invitations were ignored or declined (PC, App. 3, pp. 594–5, 600–2). The *Commission Rogatoire* extended the same invitation to the French Communist Party, the Friends of the U.S.S.R., and the League for the Rights of Man, with the same results (CR, Exhs. 5, 7, 8, 11, 12).

In the absence of any representative of the prosecution, an increased burden of cross-examining witnesses fell upon the members of the sub-commissions and their counsel.

§ 7. The preliminary work of investigation having been completed, and the reports of all sub-commissions and documents submitted either to the sub-commissions or the Commission being in our hands, the Commission has met in New York City, and examined the evidence. Its final report follows.

Part 2

The basis of inquiry

3

Scope

§ 8. As the Preliminary Commission pointed out in its report (PC xv), the scope and content of the inquiry is necessarily determined by the proceedings in the Moscow trials. According to the Prosecutor, A.Y. Vyshinsky, the evidence was of two kinds:

> First, there is the historical connection which confirms the theses of the indictment on the basis of the Trotskyites' past activity. We have also in mind the testimony of the accused, which in itself represents enormous importance as proof. (PR 513.)

The Commission's inquiry, accordingly, required the examination not only of factual material relating to the definitive charges against Leon Trotsky and Leon Sedov, but also of the alleged evidence of "historical connection" introduced in the speeches of the Prosecutor or the confessions of the accused. We have been obliged to consult the relevant his-

torical sources, and to evaluate the alleged "historical connection" in the light of the facts as revealed therein. This
procedure has involved a study of Leon Trotsky's biography,
with special reference to his past relations with the accused
in the Moscow trials, his relations with Lenin, his rôle in
the October Revolution and the building of the Soviet state,
and in the struggle of the Opposition against the majority
of the Communist Party of the U.S.S.R. It has also required
a study of his writings, with special reference to their bearing upon the credibility of the accusations, the confessions
and the summations in the Moscow trials.

4

Materials

§ 9. In view of the failure of the Soviet government to cooperate with the Commission by producing records of the hearings preliminary to the Moscow trials and the documentary evidence allegedly in its possession, and by delegating representatives to cross-examine witnesses and offer evidence in rebuttal of their testimony, the published records of the trials embody the case for the prosecution. Since these documents are official it may be assumed, even in the case of the first, which is a summary of only 180 pages, that the Soviet Commissariat of Justice, in presenting them to the world, considers that they sufficiently represent the case for the prosecution and justify the verdicts of the court. We shall proceed on this assumption in considering the prosecution's side of the case.*

§ 10. The case for Leon Trotsky and Leon Sedov is to be

---

* The Commission has used the official records as published in English by The People's Commissariat of Justice of the U.S.S.R.

found in the following materials:

(1) The official reports of the trials in so far as they engender doubt because of omissions, contradictions, falsifications, and questionable procedure.

(2) Proceedings and reports of sub-commissions.

(3) Affidavits of witnesses, letters, telegrams, passports and other official documents, press reports and other materials submitted by Leon Trotsky and Leon Sedov either directly to the Commission or to its sub-commissions.

(4) The testimony of Tarov and Dr. Anton Ciliga, taken by the *Comité pour l'Enquête sur le Procès de Moscou,* and transmitted to the Commission.

(5) The published writings of Leon Trotsky, Leon Sedov, Lenin, Stalin, Radek, Zinoviev and others, offered in evidence before the Commission or its sub-commissions. Also other historical materials bearing upon the charges and confessions and upon the "historical connection" alleged by the Prosecutor.

(6) The archives of Leon Trotsky, consisting of several thousand documents, to which this Commission has had unhampered access.

5

Certification of documents

§ 11. The documents accepted by the Commission fall into the following categories:

(1) Documents, or photostats of documents, which are official.

(2) Holograph documents or photostats thereof, which, under Civil Law, are accepted as authentic without requirement of attestation by subscribing witnesses, notarial seal, etc. The Commission, as an international body bound by no specific legal procedure, has followed the Civil Law in accepting such documents as authentic, demanding no other attestation than reliable evidence of their source.

(3) Documents which have been, for a reasonable length of time, matters of public record, and whose authenticity has not been challenged.

(4) Press clippings; also extracts from newspapers, magazines, etc., which are readily verifiable by consultation of the originals. Such extracts as are cited in this report have been so verified.

(5) Notarized affidavits, or other notarized documents.

(6) Depositions of witnesses whose signatures were authenticated by a Special Committee created by the *Comité pour l'Enquête sur le Procès de Moscou* (cf. PC 301). The members of this Special Committee were Alfred Rosmer, Fernand Charbit, and André Breton.

(7) Depositions of witnesses whose signatures were authenticated by mayors or police commissioners, or by official labor organizations.

(8) Depositions of witnesses whose signatures were authenticated by one or more members of this Commission. Also other documents certified by one or more members of this Commission.

(9) Documents certified by the *Comité pour l'Enquête sur le Procès de Moscou,* or the *Internationales Komitee für Recht und Wahrheit.*

(10) Originals, photostats or certified copies of letters, articles, or other documents furnished to the Commission from the archives of Trotsky, Sedov, or other witnesses.

§ 12. The Commission wishes to emphasize that acceptance of a document as authentic implies no judgment of its relevance or of its value as evidence. In judging the relevance and evidential value of each document, the Commission has been guided by accepted rules of evidence, such as: its bearing upon the case; whether it constituted direct or hearsay evidence; and the circumstances under which it was obtained.

Part 3

The Moscow trials

6

General nature of the charges

§ 13. The accused in the first trial were charged with having organized and conducted a Trotskyite-Zinovievite terrorist center for the purpose of assassinating the leaders of the Communist Party of the Soviet Union and the Soviet state, with the object of seizing power; and specifically with having organized the assassination, on December 1, 1934, of Commissar S.M. Kirov (ZK 37).

§ 14. The accused in the second trial were charged with having organized and conducted a reserve or parallel center,

> the object of which was to direct criminal anti-Soviet, espionage, diversive and terrorist activities for the purpose of undermining the military power of the U.S.S.R., accelerating an armed attack on the U.S.S.R., assisting foreign aggressors to seize territory of the U.S.S.R. and to dismember it and of overthrowing the Soviet Power and restoring capitalism and the rule of the bourgeoisie in the Soviet Union. (PR 18.)

They were specifically accused of having conducted treasonable negotiations with representatives of foreign states; of having engaged in espionage on behalf of those states; of having organized and carried out wrecking and "diversive" acts; and of having organized and attempted to carry out terrorist acts against the leaders of the Communist Party and the Soviet government (PR 18).

§ 15. In both indictments Leon Trotsky and his son, Leon Sedov, are definitely accused of having instigated and led the criminal activities with which the defendants were charged. In the "Report of Court Proceedings: The Case of the Trotskyite-Zinovievite Center,"* this accusation is stated as follows in the Definition of the Charge:

> L. Trotsky and his son L.L. Sedov, both of whom are abroad, having been exposed by the materials in the present case as having directly prepared and personally guided the work of organizing in the U.S.S.R. terroristic acts against the leaders of the C.P.S.U. and of the Soviet State, in the event of their being discovered on the territory of the U.S.S.R., are subject to immediate arrest and trial by the Military Collegium of the Supreme Court of the U.S.S.R. (ZK 39.)

In the "Report of Court Proceedings in the Case of the Anti-Soviet Trotskyite Center,"† it is stated as follows in the Definition of the Charge:

> L. Trotsky, and his son, L.L. Sedov, now in emigration, once again convicted by the materials in the pres-

---

* Published by the People's Commissariat of Justice of the U.S.S.R., Moscow, 1936.

† Published by the People's Commissariat of Justice of the U.S.S.R., Moscow, 1937.

ent case as the direct leaders of the treasonable activities of the Trotskyite centre, in the event of their being discovered on the territory of the U.S.S.R. are subject to immediate arrest and trial by the Military Collegium of the Supreme Court of the U.S.S.R. (PR 19.)

7

Procedure of the Soviet court

§ 16. The argument most generally advanced in defense of
the conduct of the Moscow trials is that they conformed to
Soviet legal procedure; and that any impression of unfairness
which they may have created abroad is due to differences
between Soviet procedure and that of other countries.

In the opinion of the Commission, adherence to a given
legal procedure is not the basic criterion in judging any trial.
The basic criterion is fairness and honesty in the attempt to
ascertain the truth. It is quite possible, as history has proved,
for accused persons to be falsely convicted without departure
from the letter of the law governing criminal trials. This
question can be approached only in the light of what must
be the theory of criminal procedure in any system of jurisprudence, namely: that its purpose is to enable the establishment of the ascertainable truth in any given case. Only
in so far as any procedure fulfills this purpose is it justifiable; and only in so far as prosecutor and court conform to
the spirit as well as the letter of a justifiable procedure can

they be held to safeguard the right of accused persons to be convicted or acquitted on the basis of the truth concerning the charges against them.

§ 17. If the procedure in the Moscow trials had in fact conformed to Soviet law, the conclusion would in our opinion be inescapable that Soviet procedure is not designed to develop the ascertainable truth. In fact, however, the conduct of the trials violated Soviet law on criminal procedure in every important point.

(1) The accused were convicted on the basis of their own confessions and those of self-inculpating witnesses, uncorroborated by any important documentary evidence.

The value theoretically attached to confessions in Soviet law is stated as follows by Professor M.S. Strogovich in a book entitled "Criminal Trials, a Textbook for Law Schools and Juridical Courses,"* edited by the State Prosecutor, A.Y. Vyshinsky, who conducted the case for the prosecution in each of the trials under review:

> Under the system of formal proofs the admission of guilt by the accused was considered "the best proof extant," "the sovereign proof of proofs." Nowadays faith in the absolute correctness of the defendant's admission has been in a large measure destroyed. The accused might be pleading guilty falsely (for example, in a desire to shield another person or, by pleading guilty to a minor crime, to evade the accusation of a grave crime). Therefore, the admission of the accused, like any other evidence, is subject to verification and evaluation in the sum total of the circumstances in the case.
>
> The main significance of the testimonies of the accused consists in this, that they are the explanations of the accused

---

* Third edition, corrected and amplified, 132 pages. Published by OGIZ, Moscow, 1936.

regarding the facts and circumstances of the case investigated, and considered by the court explanations which are subject to verification and evaluation in accordance with the sum total of all the circumstances of the case.

In no measure whatever does it correspond to the principles of the Soviet criminal trial to re-evaluate the evidential significance of the testimony of the accused, to depend on it as the fundamental and most important proof. Such significance the testimony of the accused in a Soviet trial does not and cannot possess; the testimony of the accused, in particular his admission of guilt, like every other piece of evidence, is subject to verification and careful evaluation as a result of juxtaposing it with all the other evidence gathered in the case.

As was pointed out above (p. 36) the Fascist criminal trial fixes its course upon the admission of guilt by the accused, extorting this admission by all sorts of violence or torture (p. 44).

Not only did the case for the prosecution in both trials depend upon the testimony of the accused as the "fundamental and most important proof," but the records of the trials abound in instances of that re-evaluation of this testimony which, according to Strogovich-Vyshinsky, in no measure corresponds to the principles of Soviet criminal trial. We cite the following examples:

RADEK: With regard to some of [the "Trotskyite" leaders] I was convinced from the very beginning that they had something in the back of their minds when they returned and, moreover, something was already apparent from certain symptoms. For instance, once when I was walking home from the offices of the *Izvestia*, I saw Smirnov on the Tverskaya with his former, if one may so express it, "Chief of Staff"—Ginsburg. Observing me, they turned down the Gnezdnikovsky Pereulok. And I immediately realized that something was in preparation, that something was brewing. But they did not come to me, and did not speak to me openly.

VYSHINSKY: In a word, you already at that period noticed that they were engaged in some underground preparatory work?

RADEK: I noticed that something was thickening, that sentiments were leading somewhere. But they did not speak openly, because, since the split with Trotsky in 1929 was connected with a great straining of personal relations between me and Trotsky, who regarded me as responsible, or one of those most responsible for the split of the Trotskyites, they feared to address me themselves and considered that this could be overcome only by relations between Trotsky and myself. And to all appearances they informed Trotsky, and, knowing of my frame of mind, requested him to take the first step so as to make it easier for them to approach me.

VYSHINSKY: Consequently, it may be formulated in this way: after you had noticed that something was brewing with Mrachkovsky and Smirnov, they in their turn noticed that something was brewing with you?

RADEK: They sensed that I was in a depressed frame of mind and that this frame of mind might crystallize into definite actions.

VYSHINSKY: That is, in other words, that you too, to some extent, represented soil for action of some sort?

RADEK: Yes.

VYSHINSKY: Now it is clear why your correspondence with Trotsky arose. (PR 86.)

On page 427 of the same record appears the following remarkable colloquy between the Prosecutor and the accused Hrasche:

VYSHINSKY: Tell the Court about your Trotskyism.

HRASCHE: I have never had anything to do with Trotskyism.

VYSHINSKY: Never had anything to do with it?

HRASCHE: I came in contact with it on the basis of my espionage and wrecking activities.

VYSHINSKY: Ah!, I see! From espionage to Trotskyism, then, and not the other way about.

(2) We have remarked that such witnesses as were summoned to testify against the accused inculpated themselves by their testimony. Indeed, they were persons who themselves were already under arrest, who were brought into court under guard and might, one would think, more properly have been occupying seats in the defendants' box. Under these circumstances it would be extremely difficult to preclude a suspicion of duress. And in these circumstances the following quotation from Strogovich-Vyshinsky under the chapter heading "Testimony of Witnesses" has a special significance:

> The testimony of witnesses constitutes the principal evidence-material in the overwhelming majority of criminal cases. The specific weight of other proofs is considerably lower. Together with this, the evaluation of the testimony of witnesses presents the greatest difficulty.
>
> In the bourgeois juridical theory for a long time complete credence was placed in the testimony of witnesses, bound by an oath, while the "inner conviction" of the judges was deemed an adequate guarantee against mistakes in the evaluation of testimony of witnesses. But life has to a considerable degree shattered this credence and practice has quite patently shown how frequently untruths are spoken, while even more frequently the witnesses who "merit confidence" are in error. (p. 39.)

... Often to be met with in court practice are instances of appraising the evidence of a witness according to the impression which the witness makes upon the court. Impressions are a basis which is quite flimsy and deceptive. A conscientious and honest witness may become confused and contradict himself in his testimony inasmuch as he becomes embarrassed and loses his head in the strange environment of a court, while a false witness who has learned his rôle by heart can give very seductive testimony because of its categorical and lucid character. (p. 40.)

(3) Even if corroboration of the testimony of one accused by that of other accused or of self-inculpating witnesses had sufficiently established the fact of conspiracy in the cases of those men who were actually tried, it would still be of dubious value as concerns the alleged rôles of Trotsky and Sedov. That this is true not only in the jurisprudence of so-called democratic countries, but also in that of the Soviet Union, is evident in the following further quotation from Strogovich-Vyshinsky:

A special form of testimony by the accused is constituted by the so-called denunciation. That is to say, testimony by one of the defendants implicating another defendant or extraneous individuals and by virtue of this very thing mitigating the responsibility of the defendant himself. In the nature of things this is evidence of a witness inasmuch as in these instances the defendant gives evidence not against himself but with respect to actions of other parties. This form of evidence is the least meritorious. The low evidential value of denunciation flows from the fact that the accused, in denouncing another party, acts usually on motives of personal interest, desirous of shifting a share of his

guilt upon another and thereby mitigating his own responsibility. (p. 45.)

In both trials the accused and witnesses who testified
against Leon Trotsky and Leon Sedov denounced them as
the alleged instigators and directors of the alleged conspiracy.
Since no other evidence than these confessions was introduced
against Trotsky and Sedov—except the Prosecutor's alleged
evidence of a confirmative "historical connection"—it is clear,
in the light of the passage quoted above, that the testimony
on which they were convicted belongs in that category which
is held, under Soviet law, to be "least meritorious."

(4) In view of the foregoing quotations the failure of the
prosecution to introduce any important documentary evidence takes on special significance. We quote again from
Strogovich-Vyshinsky:

> . . . As we have already pointed out above (p. 44) the
> testimony of the accused is not the principal and central
> evidence in the case, and the general direction of the in-
> vestigation must proceed along the line of collecting ob-
> jective evidence, not at all orienting upon the testimony
> of the accused and not concentrating upon it. (p. 73.)

Moreover, the Prosecutor, in handling such documentary evidence as he did introduce showed very little regard
for the principles of Soviet law governing material proofs
as stated by Strogovich-Vyshinsky:

> We shall not dwell here in detail on material proofs . . .
> we shall merely point out that this or another object to be
> used as material proof, like any other piece of evidence,
> must be given a formulation according to court practice.
> It must be described in detail, the conditions and circum-
> stances of obtaining it must be set down. . . . (p. 47.)

a. In the first trial, the Prosecutor presented to the accused Olberg, for identification, the Honduran passport with which Olberg had, according to his testimony, entered the Soviet Union (ZK 89). The "conditions and circumstances of obtaining it" were not set down in the published record. There is nothing to show whether it was attached to the record; but the indictment states that it "figures as an exhibit in the present case" (ZK 25). In his final speech Vyshinsky refers to an "Open Letter" of 1932 in which Trotsky,

in a fit of counter-revolutionary fury . . . burst out . . . with an appeal to "put Stalin out of the way." (ZK 127.)

This letter, the Prosecutor says, "figured as an exhibit in this case." He tells how it was obtained ("found between the double walls of Holtzman's suitcase"); but the letter was not produced in court.

The passport of the accused Olberg proved nothing except that he had entered the U.S.S.R. as a Honduran citizen. It constituted no corroboration of his testimony that he was Trotsky's emissary for terrorist purposes. As for Trotsky's Open Letter, it is discussed in Chapter XXII of this report. It suffices here to state that it had been published outside the Soviet Union, in many countries and languages.

b. In the second trial several documents were produced in connection with minor defendants:

A notebook of the accused Stroilov containing the telephone number of one von Berg was shown him for identification of book and entry (PR 270, 271). There is nothing to show how the Prosecutor obtained it, or whether it was attached to the record. A statement from the Hotel Savoy (city not specified; presumably Moscow) was attached to the record, certifying that von Berg, a German merchant, had stayed at that hotel, December 1–15, 1930, and giving his telephone number (PR 271, 276). A book in a dark red binding was identified by Stroilov as his, and the address of one Wüster identified as his entry (PR 271). (Stroilov testified that he got in touch with Wüster at the end of March, 1931.—PR 265.) There is nothing to show how Vyshinsky obtained this book, or whether it was attached to the record. A black book which Stroilov identified as his diary, kept abroad in 1930–31, containing references to Berg, Wüster and one Sommeregger, was identified by him. The record does not show under what conditions it was obtained; but the Prosecutor states that it has been attached to the files as material evidence. (PR 272–3.)

A telephone and address directory of the German Reich containing Wüster's Berlin address was attached to the record. (PR 272, 276.)

Four entry-permit files, recording the entry and place of residence of certain Germans, were attached to the record. (PR 276–7.) The dates of entry, as read by the Court, were, October 24, 1929, November 30, 1930, September 11, 1930 or 1931, June, 1931, November, 1932, and April, 1935.

Twenty photographs were shown to the accused Stroilov and the accused Shestov, and ten to the accused Rataichak and the accused Hrasche, who identified certain Germans mentioned in their testimony. There is nothing to show whether or not these photographs were attached to the record.

Vyshinsky presented to the accused Knyazev a photostat of a letter from a Mr. X. Knyazev admitted that he had received this letter in August 1936, and that it had disappeared from his desk. Vyshinsky's questions and Knyazev's answers indicate that the letter informed Knyazev that Mr. X was coming to Moscow to work in a certain institution of his government, and would like to see him. (PR 382–3.) Vyshinsky did not state the conditions under which he obtained the photostat, and there is nothing to show whether or not it was attached to the record. The same is true of an original letter which Vyshinsky showed to Knyazev, and which the latter identified as a letter received from Mr. X in 1931. In this letter Mr. X apparently asked Knyazev to send him something. (PR 383.)

Vyshinsky showed to the accused Hrasche for identification a Czechoslovak passport of 1919; also a statement from the Austro-Hungarian Soviet of War Prisoners at Kiev, 1919, to the effect that Hrasche was an Austro-Hungarian subject; also a statement from the mobilization commission, 1919, saying that he was unfit for military service. The conditions under which they were obtained are not specified, nor is it apparent whether or not they were attached to the record. (PR 423–4.)

Vyshinsky also asked the Court to include in the findings of the case a report (source not indicated) about a train wreck at Shumikha station (date not specified; presumably October 27, 1935) which Knyazev had testified was caused by the "Trotskyist" organization (PR 369).

An official statement from the Commissariat of Foreign Affairs was put into the record, to the effect that the Kjellere (Kjeller) airdrome near Oslo is open to foreign planes the year round and that arrivals and departures are possible in the winter months (PR 443). (See §§ 135, 141.)

Such is the documentation in the case of the "Anti-Soviet Trotskyite Center." It has little bearing on the case. The documents indicating Stroilov's contact with certain Germans antedate the formation of the alleged parallel center and even the alleged main center. They also antedate Stroilov's alleged enlistment by Shestov for "Trotskyite" wrecking work at the end of 1931, after Shestov's return from abroad (PR 243, 246). The same may be said of Mr. X's letter of 1931 to Knyazev, who, according to his testimony, joined the alleged conspiracy in 1934 (PR 359–62). Both this letter and that of 1936 might be taken, assuming their genuineness, to corroborate Knyazev's statements that he was in touch with Japanese agents; but they constitute no corroboration of his testimony to connection with an alleged Trotskyite conspiracy. The passport and other two documents shown to the accused Hrasche antedated the alleged conspiracy by some thirteen years. Moreover it should be noted that Hrasche stated that he had never had anything to do with Trotskyism (PR 427).

None of this documentary material is worth anything so far as concerns the existence of a "Trotskyite" conspiracy, or the alleged connection of these accused with such a conspiracy. And indeed no documentation supporting the charge of conspiracy was either shown to any accused for identification or attached to the records. Yet the accused, according to the testimony, had not hesitated to write and send at considerable risk of exposure letters concerning the most compromising of their alleged criminal activities. We may cite the alleged letter containing Trotsky's terrorist instructions to Radek which, according to the witness Vladimir Romm, was mailed to him by Sedov at the office of the Soviet News Agency (Tass) in Paris (PR 138)—at the risk of its being opened by some substitute of the addressee. Also Smirnov's admission that he communicated with Sedov by mail (ZK 83). Surely a conspiracy involving hundreds of people in the Soviet Union and abroad who freely exchanged letters concerning their criminal activities, must have yielded some conspiratorial document to a vigilant secret police. This assumption takes on weight from the statement of the Prosecutor that the "Trotskyites"

> . . . again penetrated into Soviet offices . . . concealing for a time, as has now been established beyond a shadow of doubt, their old Trotskyite, anti-Soviet wares in their secret apartments, together with arms, codes, passwords, connections and cadres. (PR 464.)

Moreover, although the Prosecutor argued that in cases of conspiracy material evidence cannot be demanded, he was at pains to state that the prosecution had a number of documents to prove its case (PR 513). If this was so, it is strange that he did not produce them, since he was at such pains to produce documentary evidence of doubtful relevance to the cases of certain minor defendants—evidence which only serves to emphasize the total absence of any important or even highly relevant documentation.

(5) In the absence of material proofs, the Prosecutor was obliged to fall back upon what Strogovich-Vyshinsky call the "bourgeois" theory of "inner conviction." In his summation in the second trial, he said:

> In order to distinguish truth from falsehood in court, judicial experience is, of course, sufficient; and every judge, every procurator, and every counsel for defence who has taken part in scores of trials knows when an accused is speaking the truth and when he departs from the truth for some purpose or other. (PR 513.)

Yet Professor Strogovich in a book edited by the Prosecutor himself says:

> . . . the theory of inner conviction of a bourgeois trial is in no way applicable to a Soviet criminal trial. The subjective, individualistic and idealistic character of the classic bourgeois theory of evidence runs sharply counter to the principles of the Soviet criminal trial. These principles can only be materialistic and dialectic. (p. 36.) [See also (2) above.]

(6) The failure of the prosecution to summon important witnesses was also in contravention of Soviet law as defined by Strogovich-Vyshinsky:

. . . 1) that to the court sessions must be called to give testimony witnesses indicting the accused or mitigating his guilt, also those witnesses who exonerate the accused, who speak in his favor; 2) that to the court sessions must be called witnesses whose testimony is contradictory to each other or to the testimony of the accused; 3) that to the court sessions must be called witnesses upon whose testimony was based the indictment presented to the accused. (p. 107.)

a. In the Zinoviev-Kamenev trial Paul Olberg is quoted in the indictment as having testified against his brother, Valentine Olberg (ZK 25). Paul Olberg was not called to the court sessions. N.A. Karev was quoted as having testified against Bakayev (ZK 33); Karev was not called to the court sessions. N.M. Matorin, "formerly Zinoviev's private secretary," was quoted as having testified against Zinoviev (ZK 34); Matorin was not called to the court sessions. In his summation the Prosecutor, addressing the accused Smirnov, said:

. . . You denied that you had received any instructions on terrorism, but you were exposed on this matter by Gaven, and you confessed; . . . (ZK 158.)

The witness Yuri Gaven, obviously, from this passage, one of "the witnesses upon whose testimony was based the indictment presented to the accused" Smirnov, was not called to the court sessions.

b. In the Pyatakov-Radek trial the accused Radek answered in the affirmative Vyshinsky's question whether he was confronted with Tivel, the former manager of his bureau, in the preliminary examination, and said:

He said partly what was true and partly what was not true, but I denied everything. (PR 134.)

Tivel was not called to the court sessions. Testifying about Prigozhin, whose terrorist activities he admitted having directed, Radek said:

> His statement that he saw me in 1935 is untrue, . . .
> (PR 97.)

Apparently Prigozhin also testified against Radek. Prigozhin was not called to the court sessions. Sokolnikov admitted that he was confronted with Kamenev (PR 167). The accused Kamenev was not called as a witness to the court sessions in the second trial. He had been shot, although the Soviet authorities were patently aware that they were shooting an important witness against the alleged "Trotskyite" center.

And so on. Radek, Serebryakov, and Sokolnikov, who were tried in January, had been accused in the August trial, in the published testimony, by Kamenev, Zinoviev, Evdokimov, and Reingold; Serebryakov and Radek by Kamenev. At the evening session of August 21, Vyshinsky stated that these three men, and Pyatakov also, were among those implicated by Zinoviev, Kamenev and Reingold (ZK 115). The accused in the first trial who had first implicated these principal defendants in the second were not called to the court sessions. They had all been shot immediately after the August trial.

§ 18. We cite the following further examples of what seem to us to have been wholly unnecessary defects in the conduct of the trials:

(1) The failure of the prosecution to make any attempt, so far as the records show, and so far as public knowledge goes, to obtain the appearance in court of the two alleged directors of the treasonable conspiracies described in the indictments and the confessions, namely, Leon Trotsky and Leon Sedov, and its further failure to take into account evidence made public by Leon Trotsky through the world press, purporting to disprove the charges in so far as they concerned

himself and Sedov, and the list of questions which Trotsky posed, also through the world press, to be put to the accused Pyatakov in connection with his testimony concerning his alleged flight to Oslo and his interview at Weksal, Norway, with Leon Trotsky.

(2) The failure of the prosecution to obtain from the governments of those countries in which Trotsky lived or sojourned, and to produce in court, the official records of his whereabouts and activities at those periods when certain accused, and the witness Vladimir Romm, alleged they saw him. Since Trotsky, during his exile, has been under constant police surveillance, such records undoubtedly exist and could presumably have been obtained upon request by the Soviet government. Also the failure of the prosecution to obtain and produce in court official records of the movements of those accused who testified that they had travelled from one country to another in order to visit Trotsky. These records would include: 1) the Danish police-record of Trotsky's movements during his stay in Copenhagen, November–December, 1932; 2) the records of entry into Denmark of those accused who testified that they travelled from Berlin to Copenhagen to see him; 3) the French police-record of Trotsky's movements at the end of July, 1933, when he was alleged to have met Vladimir Romm in the Bois de Boulogne; 4) the official record of Pyatakov's alleged entry into Norway in December, 1935, and that of the arrival and departure of the special airplane which allegedly took him there.

(3) The failure of the Prosecutor to confront the accused Pyatakov, at the January trial, with Konrad Knudsen's telegram informing the Prosecutor of official denials that any foreign plane landed in Norway in December, 1935; also that as Trotsky's host he could state that no interview had taken place between Trotsky and Pyatakov.

(4) The failure of the Prosecutor and the Court to call the attention of the accused and witnesses to contradictions in

their own testimony, or between their testimony and facts of general knowledge, or between their testimony and that of other accused or witnesses, on matters of great importance to the credibility of the alleged conspiracy. To be sure, witnesses are notoriously capable of making mistakes concerning dates, names, etc. But since in these cases establishment of the alleged fact of conspiracy rested wholly upon the confessions of the accused and witnesses, and since the interests of the accused were not safeguarded by counsel (the cases of those three accused who did avail themselves of their right to counsel can hardly be called exceptions), it would seem to have been the duty of the Prosecutor and the judges to ask questions which might have prevented that evidence, in the aggregate, from taking on an appearance of absurdity. The contradictions are extremely numerous, as we shall have frequent occasion to note. We refer our readers especially to Chapters IX and XVI of this report, on the two alleged centers. In our opinion, the contradictions dealt with in these two chapters alone refute, when taken together with the complete absence of relevant material proofs, the Prosecutor's claim in the January trial that

> In the course of the trial when one of the proofs was the evidence of the accused themselves, we did not confine ourselves merely to the Court hearing the statements of the accused; we did all we possibly could to verify these statements. And I must say that we did this here with all impartial conscientiousness, and with all possible care. (PR 513.)

(5) The Prosecutor's systematic falsification of universally known facts of history for the purposes of his case against the accused and Leon Trotsky; also his editing, for the same purposes, of quotations which he cited as evidence. This report notes many instances of these methods. We refer our

readers especially to Chapter XXV. Here we confine ourselves, in illustration, to one edited quotation:

In an article published during the Zinoviev-Kamenev trial
(*Izvestia*, August 21, 1936), Radek said:

> ... In 1929, he, Trotsky, having persuaded the Trots-
> kyist Blumkin to organize the transport of propaganda
> matter into the U.S.S.R., sent to his hotel his son Sedov
> with the mission to organize assaults on Soviet Trade
> Missions abroad to obtain the money needed by Trotsky
> for anti-Soviet work ... (PC, Exh. 11.)

Vyshinsky, in summing up during the second trial, quoted
this passage, substituting for the words "sent to his hotel
his son Sedov" the words "sent his son Sedov to Radek's
hotel." (PR 485–6.) The change is senseless, of course, since
Trotsky and Sedov saw Blumkin in Turkey, whereas Radek
was, presumably, either in Siberian exile or in Moscow. But
it enabled the Prosecutor to accuse Radek of having freely
admitted receiving from Trotsky instructions to "organize
assaults on Soviet Trade Missions abroad," and to say:

> I think we cannot disbelieve this authoritative admis-
> sion made before Soviet public opinion, not from the
> prisoners' dock, but in the Soviet press. (PR 486.)

It is not without a significant bearing on the general nature
of the trial that the defendant Radek did not defend himself
against this falsification of his words by Vyshinsky.

§ 19. Because of all the foregoing considerations, we find
that the records of the trials, far from establishing the guilt
of Leon Trotsky and Leon Sedov, inspire the gravest doubt.
This doubt can be resolved only through an examination
of the charges against them in the light of all available evidence.

8

The 'capitulators'

§ 20. In both trials the Prosecutor imputed an evidential significance to the former political relations between Leon Trotsky and the principal accused. And indeed Trotsky's past relations with these men, and his attitude toward them during the years of the alleged conspiracy, have an important bearing upon the credibility of the charges against him. We shall have occasion to discuss his relations with certain individual accused in examining the definitive charges against him. But since the most important of the accused in both trials belonged, with the exception of Sokolnikov (§ 24), in the political category known among Trotsky's tendency as "capitulators," it becomes necessary to examine his attitude, and that of his followers, toward the "capitulators" in general.

In the first place this political category must be defined; and this can best be done through a brief résumé of political alignments in Russia since 1922.

§ 21. During Lenin's first illness in 1922, Stalin, Zinoviev, and Kamenev formed, in the Political Bureau (Politburo), the most important executive organ of the Central Committee of the Communist Party of the Soviet Union (C.P.S.U.), a bloc which was known as the *Troïka*. From Lenin's second illness, in 1923, this *Troïka* became an openly recognized institution, and the controlling group of the Party. It was formed in opposition to Trotsky and his sympathizers. The struggle of Trotsky's tendency, known as the Left Opposition or "Bolshevik-Leninists," against the ruling majority of the Party dates from this period. The *Troïka* lasted until the 14th Congress of the C.P.S.U., in December, 1925. After that Congress Zinoviev and Kamenev broke with Stalin and formed a bloc with the Left Opposition. At the 15th Party Congress, in December, 1927, the Left Opposition, Trotskyist and Zinovievist, was expelled from the Party. The Zinoviev-Kamenev group "capitulated" to the ruling majority in the so-called Statement of the Twenty-Three, on December 18, but did not avoid expulsion. Some six months after the Congress, Zinoviev, Kamenev and their followers "capitulated" once more, renounced the Opposition program, acknowledged that they had been wrong and Stalin right, and were readmitted to the Party. Those former Trotskyist leaders who were tried in August, 1936 and January, 1937, had also "capitulated" and been reinstated, except Muralov, who had left the Opposition without formally renouncing it.

§ 22. It was contended by the prosecution in both trials that the "capitulators" had not been sincere in their declarations. Summing up in the first trial, Vyshinsky said:

> . . . these people put masks on their faces, adopted the pose of repentant sinners who had broken with the past, who had abandoned their old erring ways and mistakes which grew into crime. (ZK 133.)

Summing up in the second trial, he said:

The Trotskyites went underground, they donned the mask of repentance and pretended that they had disarmed. Obeying the instructions of Trotsky, Pyatakov and the other leaders of this gang of criminals, pursuing a policy of duplicity, camouflaging themselves, they again penetrated into the Party, again penetrated into Soviet offices, here and there they even managed to creep into responsible positions of state, concealing for a time, as has now been established beyond a shadow of a doubt, their old Trotskyite, anti-Soviet wares in their secret apartments, together with arms, codes, passwords, connections and cadres. (PR 464.)

§ 23. These statements of the Prosecutor were warranted by some of the testimony. The accused Zinoviev is thus reported in the record of the first trial:

"Our differences with Trotsky after the Fifteenth Congress," says Zinoviev, "when Trotsky used the word 'treachery' in relation to me and Kamenev, were really slight zig-zags, petty disagreements. We committed no treachery whatever against Trotsky at that time, but committed one more act of treachery against the Bolshevik Party to which we belonged."

But it was precisely at that moment, says Zinoviev, continuing his testimony, that we were completely adopting, as our main line, double-dealing to which we had already resorted previously, which we had practised in 1926 and in 1927. . . . (ZK 71.)

The accused Reingold testified that Zinoviev and Kamenev

insisted upon every advantage being taken of legal possibilities for the purpose of "crawling on the belly into the Party" . . . and of winning the confidence of the Party,

particularly of Stalin. After this confidence had been restored, strictly secret terrorist work was to be carried on
parallel with open work. . . . (ZK 56–7.)

The witness Loginov, in the second trial, said:

> It was agreed with Pyatakov that if the struggle should
> assume a protracted character he himself would submit
> a statement to the effect that he had broken with the
> opposition and this was to be the signal for the filing of
> similar statements by us in the provinces. That is what
> we did; . . . (PR 177.)

Pyatakov confirmed this statement "as regards the facts,"
but denied a policy of "deliberate duplicity."
The accused Boguslavsky attributed this policy of deliberate duplicity to Trotsky:

> . . . In 1929 Smirnov had transmitted Trotsky's directive
> to us, to the effect that while not laying down our arms,
> while not disarming ideologically, we were to disarm
> organizationally, to declare that we would put a stop to
> factional work, and return to the Party, while preserving
> in our declarations, as far as possible, something of the
> old Trotskyite ideas—which is what I.N. Smirnov and I
> actually did. . . . (PR 195.)

§ 24. Leon Trotsky testified that of the nineteen accused
in the two trials who were known to him, two, Sokolnikov
and Holtzman, never belonged to the Left Opposition, although Holtzman was a sympathizer in 1926–27. Sokolnikov
had declared at the Fifteenth Congress that he had no differences with the Party, and was elected to the Central Committee by that Congress, which expelled the Left Opposition.
Sixteen had belonged to the Left Opposition bloc and had

been expelled.* Six of these—Zinoviev, Kamenev, Reingold, Bakayev, Pickel, Evdokimov—were of the Zinoviev faction. Two—Drobnis and Boguslavsky—adhered to an ultra-Left (Sapronov) group. Radek joined the Left Opposition only in 1926. (PC 75–127.)

He testified that these people had been his adversaries for years before the trials (PC 75). He denied that he had ever discussed with anyone, after the break-up of his bloc with Zinoviev and Kamenev, the possibility of organizing a united center between his followers and theirs, saying:

> . . . My articles show that it is absolutely impossible. My appreciation of them, my total contempt after the capitulation, my hostility to them and their hostility to me, excluded that absolutely. (PC 88.)

Pages 75–134 of the record of the Preliminary Commission deal in detail with Trotsky's previous relations with those of the accused in the Moscow trials who were known to him, and with his enmity toward the "capitulators" in general. In this testimony Trotsky maintained that since their capitulations he had had no communication with any of the "capitulators" among the accused, and that he, and the Left Opposition in general, had regarded them as enemies and had fought them consistently and publicly. He said:

> . . . When friends are split, the antagonism is more bitter than between the ruling group and the Opposition as a whole. It is a historical and political law that the relationship between the Oppositionists and the capitulators was all these years more bitter than the relation between the Opposition and the Stalinists (PC 132.)

_____

* For Trotsky's testimony concerning the nineteenth accused who was known to him, V. Olberg, see Chapter XIII.

§ 25. In support of this testimony he introduced in evidence a mass of material (PC Exhs. 7, 12, 14, Com. Exh. 3). Exhibit 7 is a list of eighty-four articles concerning the capitulations which appeared in *The Militant* (New York) from December 15, 1928, to June 6, 1936, and twelve books and pamphlets in which the same subject is dealt with, introduced under the general title, "The Struggle Against the Capitulators." Excerpts from the articles in this list were read into the record of the Preliminary Commission. We have examined the materials listed, and find them as represented. The following further quotations will suffice to illustrate their general tone with regard to the "capitulators":

> The second point we wish to speak of here deals with the capitulators. The declaration establishes, with perfect justice and pitilessly, that these people have lost "any right at all to the confidence of the Party and the working class." (Introduction to the Declaration of the Russian Bolshevik-Leninists. *The Militant*, New York, January 15, 1931.)
>
> If one leaves aside the absolutely demoralized part of the capitulators of the type of Radek and Pyatakov, who, as journalists or functionaries, will continue to serve every victorious faction (under the pretext of serving socialism), then the capitulators taken as a political group represent in themselves moderate intra-Party "liberals" who, at a given moment, rushed too far to the Left (or to the Right) and who subsequently took to the road of coming to terms with the ruling bureaucracy. ("The Expulsion of Zinoviev." *The Militant*, New York, November 26, 1932.)
>
> And so they have capitulated again. The Soviet press carries triumphant notices of it while the Tass spreads the news of the capitulation over the whole world. Yet it would be difficult to imagine a fact which would more

cruelly compromise not only the capitulators themselves but also a régime which requires such sacrificial offerings. . . .

During the first capitulation, they might have still cherished illusions: "work in the Party," "rapprochement with the Party," "influence on the masses." Today not a trace has remained of these illusions. Zinoviev and Kamenev are returning to the Party not from the Opposition but only—from exile to Moscow. Their return is needed by Stalin for the selfsame goal as the appearance of Bukharin and Rykov on the tribune during the May 1st demonstration: while the void around the "leader" is not filled up thereby it is at least masked. ("On Zinoviev and Kamenev," May 23, 1933. *Bulletin of the Opposition*, No. 35, July, 1933; *The Militant*, New York, June 10, 1933.)

§ 26. The hostility of the Opposition to Radek appears from this and other material before us to have been particularly intense. According to Trotsky, this was due to the contempt of the Opposition for Radek's character; and particularly to Radek's having denounced and thereby caused the execution of a former Oppositionist, Blumkin, who had visited Trotsky in Constantinople. Trotsky stated that Blumkin, who had confidence in Radek, had informed him of his visit to Trotsky and that Radek had immediately denounced Blumkin to the GPU; whereupon Blumkin was shot. (PC 105–6.) We quote from a letter dated December 25, 1929, which appeared in *The Militant*, February 22, 1930:

. . . When Blumkin arrived in Moscow, his first act was to hunt up Radek . . . whom he looked upon as a leader of the Opposition. . . . He could not yet bring himself to the realization that in Radek the Opposition already had an implacable foe, who, having lost the last vestige of moral balance, did not stop at any abomination. . . . Blumkin told Radek of the thoughts and plans of L.D. [Trotsky] concerning the necessity of secret struggle for their ideas. In reply, Radek, according to his own words, demanded of Blumkin that *he immediately appear before the GPU and tell everything.* Several comrades say that Radek threatened Blumkin with immediate denunciation if he did not do this. This is quite likely, considering the actual statements of this hysterical mass of putty. . . . Following this, according to the official version, Blumkin "repented," presented himself to the GPU, and turned over the letter from Comrade Trotsky which he had upon his person. Not only that, *he even demanded his own shooting.*

In July, 1932, Trotsky replied in the *Bulletin of the Opposition*, No. 28, to an article by Radek which had appeared in the German newspaper, *Berliner Tageblatt.* The sub-title of Trotsky's article is "A Light-Minded Man on a Serious Question." We quote:

Lenin gave it to be understood quite unequivocally that serious statements might come from Radek only accidentally in the guise of rarest exceptions. With the passing years, matters have in nowise improved on this score. There is less hair on the head but there is more light-mindedness inside.

As further evidence of the mutual enmity between Trotsky and Radek after Radek's capitulation, we have a letter (copy) written by Leon Trotsky on October 3, 1933, to the editor of the daily paper, *Adelante,* in Barcelona. Trotsky says:

I have received from Spain the announcement of the appearance of *Adelante* among whose contributors my

name is cited along with those of Karl Radek and Preobrazhensky. Now absolutely no one has invited me to
contribute to *Adelante*, and consequently I could not
have given anyone my consent. As for Preobrazhensky,
who is in exile, a misuse of his name can only hurt him.
The not very respectable name of Karl Radek gives to
this list an entirely fantastic and inexplicable character.
In view of the above facts, I am obliged to request you to
discontinue the misuse of my name. (Com. Exh. 3, 2.)

We have also a clipping from the newspaper *Adelante*
containing a telegram to its editors, dated Moscow, November 3, 1933, and signed by Karl Radek and Preobrazhensky.
It reads:

> In No. 165 of October 5 of the paper *La Batalla* ap-
> peared an announcement of the publication of the daily
> *Adelante* in which our names figure in the list of con-
> tributors. The mention of our names as contributors to
> the daily *Adelante* was made without our knowledge
> and without our permission. We can never consent to
> contribute to a paper along with such renegades of com-
> munism as Brandler, Thalheimer, Trotsky, Souvarin,
> etc. . . . (*Ibid.* 3.)

Exhibit 12 of the Preliminary Commission, a post-card
received from Russia by Leon Trotsky, tells of a group of
Oppositionist exiles who met Radek at a Siberian railway
station on his way back to Moscow after his renunciation of
the Opposition, in 1929. (PC 527–8). In this post-card Radek
is reported as saying of Trotsky:

> I have completely broken with L.D. From now on we
> are political adversaries. . . . With the collaborator of Lord
> Beaverbrook we can have nothing in common.

Other quotations illustrating the relations between Radek and the Left Opposition will be found in the record of the Preliminary Commission (pp. 522–534).

We shall have occasion in Chapter XVIII to revert to Radek's relations with the Left Opposition. We have dwelt upon the subject here because of the crucial importance of his testimony in the January trial, and because of the Prosecutor's contention that

> Radek is one of the most outstanding and, to do him justice, one of the most able and persistent Trotskyites. . . . He is one of the men most trusted by and intimate with the big chief of this gang, Trotsky. (PR 477–8.)

§ 27. The attitude of Zinoviev and Kamenev toward Trotsky after their capitulation is illustrated by a declaration made by them to the Central Committee of the Communist Party of the Soviet Union and to the Control Commission, February 13, 1932, which was read into the record of the Preliminary Commission:

> Comrades Yaroslavsky and Shkiriatov have brought to our attention a document of L. Trotsky dated January 4, 1932, which is an ignoble invention on Trotsky's part, pretending that we discussed with Comrade Stalin in 1924–25 the opportunity for a terrorist act against Trotsky, and that subsequently, when we went over to the Opposition, we told him of this discussion. All this is a perfidious lie, with the evident purpose of compromising our Party. Only a diseased mentality like Trotsky's, thoroughly empoisoned with the thirst of making a sensation before bourgeois audiences and always ready to come out with the dribble and hate of the past of our Party, is capable of imagining such an ignoble lie. It is beyond question that never could we have discussed such

a question, nor even made an allusion to it in the Party circles, and we never said any such thing to Trotsky. All this has been invented by him from beginning to end, and that is one of the methods adopted in the infamous struggle that he is carrying on against the party of Lenin and its leadership, in the past as at present, for the profit and pleasure of counter-revolution. The statement from Trotsky pretending that in our Bolshevik Party one can be forced to make lying statements on this subject is the established procedure of a master blackmailer. (PC 113.)

§ 28. The question arises, of course, whether all these expressions of mutual enmity might not have been published for the purpose of cloaking the alleged conspiracy. In fairness, however, it must be taken into account that several of the above quotations from Trotsky appeared in his paper, the *Bulletin of the Opposition,* which, according to his own testimony, he made every effort to introduce into Russia. (PC 130, 265–6.) His testimony on this point is corroborated by other evidence in our possession, among it four photostatic copies of the *Bulletin,* greatly reduced in size for illegal introduction into the Soviet Union. One of the above quotations, that from the *Bulletin* No. 35, July, 1933, is from his article, "On Zinoviev and Kamenev," which appears in one of these reduced copies. (Com. Exh. 4, 1.) It is at least questionable whether Trotsky would have considered it politically expedient to undermine the prestige in Russia of men in whose company he expected again to come to power. It should also be remarked that Trotsky's public enmity to the "capitulators" considerably antedates the "new line" on terrorism alleged to have been proposed to Smirnov by Leon Sedov in 1931.

§ 29. Trotsky's testimony concerning the enmity which existed between his tendency and the "capitulators" is corroborated by material presented to the Preliminary Commission showing the enmity of the Opposition within the Soviet Union toward their comrades who had yielded to the régime (PC 107–8, 119–20, 132; Exhs. 12, 14). It is also corroborated in the testimony of Dr. Anton Ciliga and A. Tarov.

Dr. Ciliga (former member of the Politburo of the Jugoslav Communist Party—PC 131) testifies that he joined the Russian Opposition in the summer of 1928, after the break-up of the Trotskyist-Zinovievist bloc, and adhered to it until the latter part of 1932, when he left it with a group of comrades belonging to a more radical faction. He testifies in part as follows on the relations between the Trotskyists and the Zinovievists:

> From the summer of 1928 until my arrest in 1930 I had several talks with Zinovievists among my acquaintances. Although they capitulated, they believed that Stalin was carrying out in essence the Opposition's policy, in which they saw a justification for their capitulation. At the same time they took an extremely negative attitude towards Trotsky. . . . In spite of all their disagreements with the Stalinists, they considered both themselves and the Stalinists real "Leninists"; they did not have that opinion of the Trotskyist group. From all my observations in Russia I got a definite impression that for all the undoubted nearness of the Zinovievists and Trotskyists there existed between them a mutual distrust and hostility. (Com. Exh. 5, 1.)

The "capitulators," says Ciliga, could be divided into four categories: (1) Those who surrendered completely, even at the price of becoming GPU provocateurs; (2) those who definitely went over to Stalin but who refused to become provocateurs; (3) those who continued to maintain an interest in the ideological life of the Opposition, but refused to do any

active opposition work (this group was the most numerous);
(4) those who, to one degree or another, returned to Oppositionist activity. *(Ibid.)*

§ 30. A. Tarov (real name in our possession) testifies that he was born on November 7, 1898, the son of a mason; that he was a mechanic by trade; that he joined the Bolshevik Party in 1917 and took part in the Civil War; that in 1923 the Party sent him to the Transcaucasian Communist University, from which he was expelled in 1925 as a Left Oppositionist; that in 1927 he was expelled from the Party for Oppositionist activities; that on September 19, 1928, he was arrested for Oppositionist work and after three months in prison was deported to Siberia. On January 22, 1931, he was again arrested, in exile, and sentenced to three years imprisonment, which he served in the isolator of Verkhne-Uralsk. At the end of his sentence he was deported to Andijan in Central Asia, and after five months escaped to Persia, where he was twice arrested and sent the first time to prison and the second time to Amadan, deep in the interior. He succeeded in escaping to Europe in 1937.

Tarov states that the Oppositionists who capitulated were called upon to betray their comrades, and were told that unless they did so, they would be accused of crimes, handed over to the GPU and executed.

> In 1927, in Erivan, after such threats from Tatian, the secretary of the control commission, the capitulator Tonov (I do not remember his name exactly) went home and blew out his brains. (Com. Exh. 6.)

The incident, says Tarov, was published in the newspaper *Kharurdeit-Ayastan,* in an article by Tatian himself; but the issue was suppressed after about half the copies had been sold.

Tarov says that

> . . . the great majority of the capitulators abandoned the
> Opposition because they could not endure the bestial
> repressions of the GPU. . . . All the capitulators, without
> exception, in the beginning did not wish to slander the
> Opposition or to consider their convictions erroneous,
> "counter-revolutionary," etc. They all began by pledging
> no longer to carry on factional work. Unemployment, ar-
> rests, deportations, executions, concentration camps, tor-
> tures in prison, were all applied to the Bolshevik-Leninist
> Oppositionists by the GPU agencies in the cruelest form,
> in accordance with the special orders issued by the head
> of the Central Committee. *(Ibid.)*

This pressure upon Oppositionists to capitulate, and upon
"capitulators" to betray their fellow-Oppositionists had, says
Tarov, the following result:

> In the face of such cruel repression on the part of the
> GPU, the Opposition obviously could not tolerate the
> slightest wavering among its members. . . . The Oppo-
> sition broke off all relations with the capitulators even
> before the latter decided to inform the GPU of their
> abandonment of the Opposition. . . . In the isolators we
> treated the capitulators still more firmly. At the slight-
> est sign of vacillation we immediately expelled them . . .
> from the common cells, and we requested that they be
> excluded from our daily exercises. *(Ibid.)*

The "capitulators," Tarov testifies, were not released from
jail at once. They were required to declare that the tenets of
the Opposition were counter-revolutionary, anti-Communist,
Menshevist, and that Trotsky was an "agent of the counter-
revolutionary bourgeoisie." They were even kept in prison
after their sentences had expired, forced to write dozens of
statements, and subjected to repeated questioning.

The capitulators returned to their cells in a state of nervous collapse, cursing the GPU, cursing themselves, but finding no way out. For them there was no road back to the Opposition. The Opposition would invariably look upon them as spies and agents of the GPU and never tolerate living with them in a common cell. . . . Finally, his backbone was broken and the firm Oppositionist of yesterday was transformed in the hands of the GPU into a tool against the Opposition of the Bolshevik-Leninists. *(Ibid.)*

Tarov cites his own case in illustration of his statements that the GPU attempted to force "capitulators" to become informers and that the Opposition definitively broke with them. In 1934 he subscribed to Rakovsky's telegram calling for the unity of all proletarian, Communist, and revolutionary forces against fascist aggression. He believed, he said, that in the face of the fascist menace the Central Committee would at least go halfway to meet Rakovsky's telegram. But the GPU at once demanded that Tarov declare his convictions counter-revolutionary. When he refused he was dismissed from his job. The GPU demanded that he name the comrades with whom he had worked in the Opposition. When he still refused he was kept under constant surveillance by the GPU and deprived of correspondence with his wife and friends. The Oppositionists, on their part, would have nothing to do with him. He decided that the only way out of his situation lay in escape; and this he finally achieved. *(Ibid.)*

§ 31. In view of the fact that Trotsky had formed a bloc with Zinoviev and Kamenev after the break-up of their bloc with Stalin against him, it seems reasonable to assume that he might have joined them again in political opposition, had they renewed their opposition along a line in agreement with his own. But between an open political opposition and a secret terrorist conspiracy there is a world of difference.

For the risky purposes of the latter, it is necessary to find accomplices upon whose loyalty one can place absolute reliance. And Trotsky, who had been fought by Zinoviev and Kamenev during the period of the *Troïka*, and repudiated by them at the 15th Congress, would appear to have had very little reason to trust them in an alliance as dangerous as an underground conspiracy. The same thing is true of such men as Radek, Pyatakov, and the other former Trotskyists who had also repudiated the Left Opposition.

If, on the other hand, one accept the testimony quoted above, and the contention of the Prosecutor, that the "capitulators" had returned to the Party in pursuance of Trotsky's orders, the question arises, Why did several of the most important among them hold out against capitulation on pain of exile and imprisonment? Why did Rakovsky, one of Trotsky's oldest friends, who was implicated in the January trial, hold out until 1934? Why did Muralov, Trotsky's friend and one of the accused in the January trial, abandon the Opposition without formally capitulating? As a participant in the alleged anti-Soviet plot, Muralov would surely have found it advantageous to obey Trotsky's alleged orders, and to cloak his anti-Soviet work, as his co-conspirators allegedly did, with the mantle of Party membership. Moreover, if Trotsky had really given such orders, why did not all his followers in Russia re-enter the Party, where they would certainly have been much more useful to him than in exile or in the political prisons of the GPU? If one assume that this order was known only to the leaders, then it would appear that Trotsky was deceiving not only the Party but his own followers, and thus senselessly wasting a great deal of potentially useful devotion to his cause. Such an assumption also implies what the confessions in both trials contradict: that the Trotskyist "leaders" of the conspiracy were attempting to carry out an extensive program of terrorism and sabotage without any rank-and-file support—unless one adopt another hypothesis which is also contradicted by the confessions: that the numerous terrorist and wrecking organizations all over the U.S.S.R were composed entirely of non-Trotskyite terrorists and wreckers.

Thus the contention that those Trotskyists who returned to the Party did so in pursuance of a deliberate policy of duplicity inaugurated by Trotsky himself is borne out neither by the evidence nor by any tenable theory. On the other hand, the evidence introduced in rebuttal indicates that capitulations were often due to repressions by the GPU; that "capitulators" were systematically pressed to become informers against the Opposition; and that Oppositionists were therefore obliged for the sake of their own safety to abstain from all relations with them and to regard them as enemies. It also indicates that mutual distrust existed between the Trotskyists and Zinovievists, even in exile and in political prisons, and constitutes a legitimate basis for doubting the probability of a new "Trotskyist-Zinovievist" bloc for the purposes of a terrorist conspiracy. We find that all this evidence warrants due consideration, in weighing the charges and confessions in the two Moscow trials, of Trotsky's contention that he had regarded the "capitulators" in those trials as his political enemies from the time of their capitulations.

9

The 'Trotskyite-Zinovievite Terrorist Center'

§ 32. Of the sixteen accused in the trial of the alleged Trotskyite-Zinovievite Terrorist Center, five were in no way connected in the proceedings with the formation of the center, and only one of these claimed the slightest connection with its activity. Indeed, the indictment explicitly states:

> The investigation has established that after the smash-up of the Trotskyite-Zinovievite center in connection with the murder of Comrade *Kirov, L. Trotsky* himself assumed the leadership of terroristic activities in the U.S.S.R. and began strongly to press forward the organization of the assassinations of Comrades *Stalin* and *Voroshilov*. For this purpose he took steps to restore the terrorist groups in the U.S.S.R. and to stimulate their activity by sending a number of his tried agents to the U.S.S.R. from abroad and also by using for this purpose persons belonging to underground Trotskyite organiza-

tions in the U.S.S.R. who went abroad ostensibly on official business.

> The investigation has established that at various times the following accused persons were sent from Berlin to Moscow as such agents: *V. Olberg, Berman-Yurin, Fritz David (Kruglyansky), Moissei Lurye, Nathan Lurye* and several others. . . . (ZK 23.)

This statement, clearly implying that no organization was left in the U.S.S.R. to direct the alleged terrorist work, is remarkable in view of a passage in the testimony of the accused Kamenev:

> Knowing that we [the united center] might be discovered, we designated a small group to continue our terroristic activities. For this purpose we designated Sokolnikov. It seemed to us that on the side of the Trotskyites this role could be successfully performed by Serebryakov and Radek. (ZK 67.)

It might be assumed, of course, that Trotsky did not know about the existence of the "reserve center"; but it seems unlikely that the main center would have kept its alleged instigator and director in ignorance of a precautionary measure so important as the formation of a directorate to continue its terrorist activities in case its own members were exposed. The indictment in the January trial alleged that the reserve center was formed "on the direct instructions of L.D. Trotsky" (PR 5). If this were so, then Trotsky must surely have considered that the "terrorist groups in the U.S.S.R." could be much more easily "restored" by such well-known revolutionary figures as Radek, Sokolnikov and Serebryakov than by five obscure foreigners. To be sure, although the indictment says that these five people were sent "as such agents" (to "restore the terrorist groups in the U.S.S.R. and to stimulate their activity") it also goes on to state that they had received instructions from Trotsky and Sedov to organize the assassinations of Soviet leaders. The latter instructions, of course, would not preclude the former, but the dates on which these five accused allegedly arrived in the Soviet Union would seem to do so.

The Kirov assassination took place on December 1, 1934 (ZK 11); and according to the indictment the smash-up of the Trotskyite-Zinovievite terrorist center followed this event. Yet the five people whom Trotsky allegedly sent to "restore the terrorist groups" after this smash-up all arrived in Russia well before that date. Olberg, David, and Berman-Yurin all testified that they received in 1932 instructions from Trotsky to go to Russia on terrorist missions, and left for Moscow in March, 1933 (ZK 87–8, 95–6, 113–14). In other words, they received these instructions from Trotsky at the very time that the alleged united center was formed according to the indictment. M. Lurye said that he also left Berlin for Moscow on March 4, 1933, with instructions from Maslow and Ruth Fischer to speed up the organization of terrorist acts against the leaders of the C.P.S.U. and the Soviet government (ZK 105–6). N. Lurye stated that he went to the U.S.S.R. on instructions from Moissei Lurye in April, 1932, for the purpose of carrying on terroristic work with the Trotskyites he had known in Germany (ZK 102). That is, he went there some months before the alleged formation of the united center. None of these defendants testified that he had any instructions to "restore terrorist groups." Indeed, two of them, Fritz David and Berman-Yurin, expressly stated that Trotsky instructed them to work independently without contacts with other Trotskyites (ZK 95, 113). The one who testified to connection with the alleged center was M. Lurye, who said that he saw Zinoviev (ZK 106), and that from April, 1933,

Nathan Lurye's group, which was organized by the fascist Franz Weitz, worked with the knowledge and indisputably with the consent of the center, and of Zinoviev personally. (ZK 107.)

§ 33. Of the other eleven accused, only three claimed to have had any direct communication with either Leon Trotsky or Leon Sedov. The accused Smirnov confessed that in 1931 he had an interview with Sedov in Berlin in which Sedov expressed his "personal opinion" that only the removal of the leaders of the C.P.S.U. and the Soviet government could change conditions in the U.S.S.R. (ZK 17, 45, 79–80, 85), and that in 1932 he received terrorist instructions from Trotsky through Yuri Gaven (ZK 17, 42, 44, 80–85). The accused Dreitzer confessed that in the autumn of 1931 he had two conversations with Sedov in Berlin, having been instructed by Smirnov to ascertain Trotsky's attitude on the formation of a bloc with the Zinovievites (ZK 51–52); and that in October, 1934, he received from Trotsky a letter in invisible ink, containing instructions on terrorism and defeatism (ZK 22, 52). The accused Holtzman testified that he delivered to Sedov in 1932 a report and a secret code from Smirnov; that he had several conversations with Sedov and at his suggestion went in November, 1932, to see Trotsky in Copenhagen where he received from him verbal instructions to the effect that Stalin must be killed, and that

> for this purpose it was necessary to choose cadres of responsible people fit for this task. (ZK 101.)

Such is the evidence of these three accused against Trotsky and Sedov. There is nothing in it indicating the attitude of either toward the formation of the alleged terrorist center. The record does not tell us how Trotsky answered Dreitzer's queries on the subject of a bloc; we learn only that

> Sedov then told him that Trotsky's instructions would be sent on later. (ZK 52.)

Nor does the record make clear the exact contents of the letter allegedly sent to Smirnov by Trotsky through Yuri Gaven, or how Gaven came by this letter. In the examination of Mrachkovsky, who claimed no direct communication with Trotsky or Sedov, it is stated that Trotsky in this letter (allegedly received in the autumn of 1932) approved the decision to unite with the Zinovievites, and that

> it was also at that time that he conveyed to them through his emissary, Gaven, that union must take place on the basis of terrorism. (ZK 42.)

The Prosecutor, curiously, did not ask Smirnov to corroborate this "approval of the decision to unite with the Zinovievites." Instead he asked:

> VYSHINSKY: Do you corroborate the testimony of Mrachkovsky that in 1932 you received a reply from Trotsky through Gaven?
> SMIRNOV: I received a reply from Trotsky through Gaven. . . .
> VYSHINSKY: You, Smirnov, confirm before the Supreme Court that in 1932 you received from Gaven the direction from Trotsky to commit acts of terrorism?
> SMIRNOV: Yes. (ZK 42.)

Again, on page 82, Smirnov answers in the affirmative the following question by the Prosecutor about the alleged instructions through Gaven:

Did these instructions contain direct reference to the necessity of embarking on a terroristic struggle against the leadership of the Party?

There is nothing here about Trotsky's attitude toward the formation of a united center. On page 83 of the record it is stated:

> From the testimony of the accused it appears, however, that . . . these negotiations for the organization of the *bloc* were conducted on the basis of the first instructions on terror received by Smirnov from Trotsky through Sedov in 1931.

Since, however, according to Smirnov, these instructions consisted only of Sedov's "personal opinion" that terrorism was necessary, negotiations based on them can hardly be taken as indicating any direct and personal participation of Trotsky or Sedov in the formation of the bloc.

Thus there is, as we have said, no direct evidence of the attitude of either Sedov or Trotsky toward the formation of the bloc, or concerning their rôle, if any, in its formation. Therefore, the evidence which we quote below in discussing the formation of the alleged center is, in so far as it concerns Trotsky or Sedov, hearsay, uncorroborated by any direct evidence whatever.

§ 34. The date of the formation of the united center is given without exception in vague words, such as "summer" and "autumn" and "at the end of 1932." Nevertheless, there is a fundamental contradiction in the testimony on this important point. The indictment explicitly states that it was formed "at the end of 1932" (ZK 11). Mrachkovsky said the same thing (ZK 42). The witness Yakovlev placed its formation in the "autumn of 1932" (ZK 70). The accused Dreitzer stated that in the autumn of 1932 Smirnov informed him that the bloc had been formed. However, according to Dreitzer's testimony, Smirnov had sent him as early as the autumn of 1931 to ask Sedov in Berlin Trotsky's opinion about the formation of a bloc. (ZK 51–52.) Mrachkovsky said that the question of the necessity of uniting with the Zinovievites was raised in the second half of 1932 by Smirnov, and that Smirnov sent a letter to Trotsky through Holtzman at that time, putting before him the question of uniting. (Neither Smirnov nor Holtzman corroborated this testimony.) In the autumn, he stated, Trotsky's letter approving this union was received. (ZK 41–42.) Ter-Vaganyan set two dates for the beginning of negotiations for the bloc and his own alleged instructions from Smirnov to act as his intermediary in these negotiations. In the morning session of August 21, he said that these negotiations began in the autumn of 1931 (ZK 110–11), after having already testified during the morning session of August 19 that they began "as far back as June, 1932" (ZK 45).

Zinoviev set the beginning of negotiations for the formation of the bloc, "on Trotsky's instruction," in the autumn of 1931 (ZK 72), and its actual formation in the summer of 1932 (ZK 44). Kamenev stated that at a meeting of the Zinovievite center in "our villa," in the summer of 1932, Zinoviev reported that the union with the Trotskyites "was an accomplished fact" (ZK 66).

§ 35. From this welter of contradictions one may glean that the bloc was formed at two quite distinct periods: the summer of 1932 and the end of 1932. Naturally, the question arises, Why these two periods, and why did Prosecutor and Court accept both without question? The formation and activity of the alleged center is the central theme of the whole trial; certainly, therefore, precision on these points was of great importance in establishing proof that it existed; indeed, it would have afforded a more convincing refutation of Smirnov's repeated denials that there was a center than the mere affirmations of other accused. How the contradiction

weakens the record becomes evident when one considers the
fantastic absurdity of the activity attributed in the various
confessions to the accused Smirnov, whom the defendants
accused of having been the prime mover in the conspiracy
and "Trotsky's principal representative and even deputy in
the U.S.S.R." (ZK 72.) We summarize this testimony:

In the autumn of 1931, after having received terrorist instructions from Sedov in Berlin, Smirnov began, "on Trotsky's instructions," negotiations with Zinoviev and others for
the formation of a bloc with the Zinovievites and "Leftists"
(ZK 72, 110–11), and sent Dreitzer to Berlin with instructions to see Sedov and ascertain Trotsky's attitude on the
question of such a bloc. Dreitzer was told that Trotsky's instructions would be sent on later (ZK 51–52). In the same
period Smirnov instructed Ter-Vaganyan to begin negotiations for a bloc (ZK 110–11). In June of 1932, negotiations
were begun for the formation of a bloc, with Ter-Vaganyan
acting as intermediary between Smirnov and Zinoviev, and
Kamenev and Lominadze (ZK 45). In the summer of 1932,
at a meeting in Kamenev's villa, Zinoviev announced that
the bloc was an accomplished fact (ZK 66). Yet in the second half of 1932, Smirnov posed to the leading trio of the
Trotskyite organization the question of a bloc with the Zinovievites and Leftists, and sent a letter to Sedov through
Holtzman, asking Trotsky's opinion on this question (ZK
21, 41–2). In the autumn of 1932, a letter was received from
Trotsky approving the decision to unite, and at the same
time Trotsky sent word through his emissary Gaven that
the union must be on the basis of terrorism. After having
received these instructions Smirnov instructed Ter-Vaganyan
to bring about the formation of a bloc. (ZK 42.) The bloc
was formed for the second time at the end of 1932 (ZK 11,
42). On January 1, 1933, Smirnov was arrested and sent to
prison, whence, according to the Prosecutor, he continued
to communicate with the Trotskyites by code (ZK 152–3),

possibly on the question whether or not it would be advisable to form a Trotskyite-Zinovievite bloc, and whether or not Trotsky could be persuaded to sanction it.

§ 36. It may be noted here that if the bloc was organized at the end of 1932 it must have been without the participation of Zinoviev and Kamenev, while Smirnov would barely have had time to participate in its organization before his arrest and his imprisonment which continued up to the time of the August trial. Zinoviev and Kamenev were expelled from the Communist Party of the Soviet Union in October, 1932, and exiled in November—Kamenev to Minussinsk and Zinoviev to Kustunay, Siberia. If they participated in the organization of the alleged united center, it must have been formed before their exile. It was Zinoviev and Kamenev who stated that it was formed in the summer of 1932. On the other hand, there is no direct evidence to connect Trotsky personally with the alleged "terrorist line" before his trip to Copenhagen in November, 1932.* Holtzman, on the other hand, allegedly saw Trotsky—at about the time of, or possibly a little after, the exile of Zinoviev and Kamenev. It may be noted that he was the only one of the eleven who made this claim. Yet in his testimony there is nothing about Trotsky's attitude toward the proposed Trotskyite-Zinovievite bloc, which, assuming that it was about to be formed at that time, must, one would think, have been uppermost in his own mind and that of Trotsky. The record does not show whether or not Holtzman knew the contents of the letter he conveyed to Sedov from Smirnov, which, according to Mrachkovsky, put to Trotsky the question of a bloc. If he did know, then assuming that its contents were as Mrachkovsky represented them, it might certainly be supposed that he would have spoken to Trotsky about the matter. Yet

---

* For discussion of the letter allegedly sent by Trotsky to Smirnov through Yuri Gaven in the autumn of 1932, see § 47.

according to his account, the interview consisted of a verbal instruction from Trotsky to be conveyed to Smirnov, to the effect that Stalin must be removed by terrorist means and that responsible cadres should be chosen for the task—an instruction which, according to various accused, Smirnov had already received from Sedov more than a year before, and had been diligently carrying out ever since. It seems hardly worth the trip from Berlin to Copenhagen.

§ 37. The record is also contradictory concerning the duration of the center's activities and of the period of suspension to which several accused testified. If one is to believe the indictment, it smashed up in connection with the Kirov assassination (ZK 23). Zinoviev, on the other hand, said that it functioned "actually up to 1936." The defendant Reingold said that

> there was an interruption in our terroristic activities between the autumn of 1932 and the summer of 1933 caused by the fact that Zinoviev and Kamenev were compromised in connection with the Ryutin case. In connection with that, in the beginning of 1933 . . . Evdokimov passed on the instruction in the name of the united center to suspend terroristic work until Zinoviev and Kamenev had returned from exile, until they had declared their repentance, were reinstated in the Party and had gained a certain amount of confidence. (ZK 56.)

Yet according to the record,

> In the spring of 1933 Mrachkovsky repeated to Dreitzer the instructions of the Trotskyite-Zinovievite center to expedite the acts of terror. . . . (ZK 52.)

Bakayev testified that after the exile of Zinoviev and Kamenev it was resolved to suspend terroristic activities for a time. In the autumn of 1934 they were resumed. (ZK 60.)

Zinoviev said:

> After our return from exile the first steps we took were directed toward liquidating, if one may so express it, the breakdown of our terroristic activities, the fiasco of the conspirators, and toward restoring confidence in order to be able to continue our terroristic activities later on. (ZK 73–74.)

Kamenev said:

> The exile of myself and Zinoviev somewhat held up the execution of our terroristic plans. (ZK 66.)

If one accept Mrachkovsky's testimony concerning the formation of the center, and Bakayev's concerning its suspension, it would appear that immediately after, or possibly even a little before, its formation its activities were suspended, and that very shortly after they were resumed the center, according to the indictment, smashed up. On the other hand, if one accept the summer of 1932 for its formation and the summer of 1933 for resumption of activities, it could have been active for three or four months in 1932 and for approximately eighteen months after the summer of 1933. The student of the trial may combine the various versions to taste, without much concern to accommodate them to any specific crime, since the only actual crime attributed to the center was the assassination of Kirov on December 1, 1934. He will be more concerned about their bearing upon the credibility of the confessions in general, and upon the conduct of the trial.

THE ZINOVIEV-KAMENEV TRIAL: DEFINITIVE CHARGES AGAINST TROTSKY AND SEDOV

10

The testimony of I.N. Smirnov

§ 38. The first basis of the charge against Leon Trotsky and Leon Sedov in the trial of August, 1936, was the confession of the accused I.N. Smirnov that in 1931, while in Berlin on official business, he accidentally met Sedov and had an interview with him in which Sedov advanced the view that

> it was necessary to change the old methods of struggle against the party and that the time had arrived to adopt terroristic methods of struggle . . . (ZK 79);

that upon his return to Moscow he passed on this opinion to the Trotskyites; that in 1932 he received from Trotsky instructions on terrorism through Yuri Gaven, and though not in agreement with them communicated them to the Zinovievites through the accused Ter-Vaganyan, and also to the Trotskyites (ZK 85–6); that he wrote a letter to Trotsky and received a reply from him (ZK 84); and that "there was communication by mail with Trotsky's son" (ZK 83). He did not state the nature of these alleged communications by mail, and the Prosecutor asked no questions about them.

§ 39. The accused Holtzman testified that in 1932, before his departure for Berlin, Smirnov gave him a report to be delivered to Sedov for Trotsky, a telephone number by which he might ring up Sedov, and a password which was: "I have brought greetings from Galya." According to the record,

> As Smirnov and Holtzman both admit, this report was to have been handed to Sedov personally for delivery to Trotsky. (ZK 99.)

The record, however, does not show that either Smirnov or Holtzman stated the contents of this report, or that Vyshinsky questioned either of them on that point. The record also states that

> Further evidence establishes the fact that Smirnov also gave Holtzman a secret code for corresponding with Trotsky, for which purpose certain pages from the "Arabian Nights" were used. (ZK 99.)

§ 40. Leon Trotsky, testifying before the Preliminary Commission, stated that Smirnov had been his friend, and a member of the Opposition, had been expelled from the Party with the Opposition at the Fifteenth Congress, and had capitulated in November, 1929; and that he, Trotsky, had commented on this capitulation in the *Bulletin of the Opposition* in an article beginning, "On November 3rd there was printed in *Pravda* a miserable article by Smirnov and Boguslavsky" (No. 7, November–December, 1929). He further testified that after Smirnov's capitulation he had had no direct communication with him, but that his son, Sedov, had met Smirnov on the street in Berlin in 1931. Trotsky

said that his son thereafter wrote him that Smirnov was un-
happy and without political orientation, and had given him
information about old friends. (PC 88–9.) Trotsky denied
that he had communicated with Smirnov through Gaven,
whom he had not seen since 1926 (PC 225–6).

§ 41. Sedov testified before the *Commission Rogatoire* that
from his adolescence he had known Smirnov, who was on
friendly terms with his family, and that he had been closely
connected with him in Opposition work; that after Smirnov
capitulated in 1929 he had regarded him as a political adversary and had had no communication with him; that he did
meet Smirnov accidentally in Berlin in July, 1931; that he
did subsequently have an interview with him at Smirnov's
apartment during which he gave him two addresses and a
telephone number, and suggested that Smirnov should take
advantage of the trips of comrades to send him information
on conditions in the Soviet Union; that Smirnov said jokingly
that if anyone came to find Sedov he would present himself
in the name of Galya, the little girl who had accompanied
Smirnov at their first meeting. (CR 4.) Sedov's testimony,
and Smirnov's, to the accidental nature of this meeting is
confirmed by the deposition of Sedov's wife, Jeanne Martin
des Pallières, who, according to her own testimony and that
of Sedov, was with her husband at the time of the meeting
(PC Exh. 16, 1/18; CR 6). Sedov further affirmed that the
defendant Holtzman did get in touch with him in Berlin
around the end of September or the beginning of October,
1932, that in presenting himself he stated that he brought
greetings from Galya, and that he brought a document for
Trotsky from Smirnov which he had carried in a spectacle
case (CR 16–18). He further testified that he saw Holtzman
several times (CR 19).

§ 42. Thus there is agreement between Sedov on the one
hand and Smirnov or Holtzman on the other, on the following points:

(1) The accidental meeting of Sedov and Smirnov in 1931, a second meeting at Smirnov's lodgings, and the exchange of addresses and a telephone number on Sedov's side and a password on the side of Smirnov;

(2) the meeting of Holtzman and Sedov in Berlin in 1932 and the delivery to Sedov by Holtzman of a communication for Trotsky; also several subsequent meetings.

On the nature of the conversation between Smirnov and Sedov there is complete disagreement. According to Sedov, this conversation dealt largely with economic conditions in the U.S.S.R. Certain political matters were also discussed, such as the defeat of the Right Opposition and the part played by Radek in the denunciation and subsequent execution of Blumkin. Sedov also testified that Smirnov missed no opportunity to emphasize his own complete lack of accord with the Left Opposition. (CR 6–7.)

Sedov further testified that the document delivered to him by Holtzman was an unsigned report on economic conditions in the Soviet Union, which he, Sedov, published in the *Bulletin of the Opposition*, No. 31, of November, 1932, p. 20 (CR 17). Neither Smirnov nor Holtzman, as we have already noted, testified on the contents of this report. Sedov said that in publishing it he affixed as a signature the syllable "Ko" which was an allusion to Trotsky's having compared Smirnov, in polemicizing with him, to a bell-ringer (from *kolokol*—"bell") (CR 17). We have examined this article and find it as represented. Sedov also testified that Holtzman in their conversations gave him information concerning the state of agriculture and industry in the Soviet Union and

also discussed facts and events bearing upon specific individuals, such as Ryutin, a Right-winger, and Zinoviev and Kamenev, who, he said, were no longer doing anything at all and were generally scorned. (CR 17.)

He called attention to the fact that the published record of the trial is silent on the subject of his discussions with Holtzman, and declared that the failure of the Prosecutor to question Holtzman concerning these conversations justified the assumption that Holtzman could say nothing in support of the accusations against him. He denied that he ever received from Holtzman the key to a cipher, and stated that the document which Holtzman delivered to him was written in holograph. (CR 18.)

§ 43. It is precisely as regards the accused Smirnov that the summarized record of the August trial is most unsatisfactory. Since Smirnov, even in the summarized report of his own testimony and that of other accused against him, appears to have been a most refractory witness, and since the rôle attributed to him is, as we shall see, of crucial importance to the claim that a conspiracy existed and that Trotsky was its instigator, it is precisely through a verbatim report of this testimony that the record would have gained most in the appearance of honesty. As it stands, the record shows that Smirnov repeatedly denied or attempted to deny the most important allegations of the prosecution—even those allegations which he had himself previously admitted. For example, on page 45 he denies Mrachkovsky's testimony that he, Smirnov, had conveyed Trotsky's instructions on terrorism to the Moscow Trotskyite center, and he repeats this denial on page 77. On page 80, he denies having anticipated that the center would take his information concerning his conversation with Sedov as Trotsky's instructions. On page 84, he again denies having passed on these alleged instructions to the Trotskyite group. On page 81, he denies that the center existed, saying

I did not intend to resign. There was nothing to resign from.

On page 82, he denies having been the leader of the alleged Trotskyite organization. On page 86, he denies having been a member of the alleged Trotskyite-Zinovievite bloc.

The Prosecutor in his final speech dwelt at length upon Smirnov's obdurate denials in a passage to which we shall pay particular attention in Chapter XXVI of this report. Smirnov, said Vyshinsky, had been the most persistent of the accused in his denials (ZK 153). This statement of Vyshinsky, taken together with further statements which clearly indicate that Smirnov confessed only under great pressure, and also with the highly questionable nature, hereinafter noted, of his own testimony against Trotsky and Sedov and of the other accused against him, justifies grave doubt, on the basis of the trial record alone, concerning the validity of his meager confession. And that doubt is not lessened by this further passage from the Prosecutor, which implies that Smirnov only became the "leader" of the "Trotskyite center" during the preliminary examination (or possibly in an unpublished section of the trial record):

> [Smirnov] pleaded guilty only to being the leader of the Trotskyite underground counter-revolutionary center. True, he said this in a somewhat jocular way. Turning to Ter-Vaganyan, Mrachkovsky, and Dreitzer, he said to them: "You want a leader? Well, take me." But you, accused Smirnov, were the leader. . . . (ZK 153–4.)

§ 44. It is impossible to avoid the suspicion that this uncooperative attitude of the accused Smirnov accounted for the failure of the Prosecutor to ask him the most obvious and necessary questions. In later sections of this report we shall have occasion to note certain instances of this failure. We cite here the following examples:

(1) Vyshinsky made no attempt to elicit from either Smirnov or Holtzman (also a refractory witness, although

apparently less so than Smirnov) any confirmation of Mrachkovsky's testimony to the effect that the letter sent by Smirnov through Holtzman

> informed Trotsky of the state of the Trotskyite organization and put before him the question of uniting with the Zinovievites. (ZK 42.)

(2) Vyshinsky did not, so far as the record shows, question Smirnov on the subject of the code which Holtzman testified Smirnov sent through him to Sedov, although certainly Smirnov, if he had sent such a code, would have been able to describe it, and his description would have added considerably to the weight of Holtzman's testimony.

(3) The Prosecutor and several of the accused insisted that Smirnov continued as an active director of the united center even after his arrest on January 1, 1933 (ZK 54, 86, 152); and the Prosecutor in his final speech stated that a code was discovered by means of which Smirnov communicated from prison with his companions outside. This code was not introduced in evidence, nor was Smirnov questioned about it. It was simply mentioned, and that only once, in the Prosecutor's summation.

Since Vyshinsky was at great pains to get the other defendants to confirm the conspiratorial rôle which Smirnov denied (ZK 38), it seems strange that he neglected to ask Smirnov himself questions which were clearly indicated by the testimony of the other accused, or by the statements of the Prosecutor himself. And his failure to do so casts further doubt upon the record in so far as concerns Smirnov's own alleged part in the conspiracy, and the rôle which he imputed to Trotsky and Sedov.

§ 45. If the Prosecutor appeared to handle Smirnov rather gingerly when it came to seeking confirmation of the testimony of other accused, he was very diligent in securing their testimony to the rôle attributed to Smirnov in the alleged conspiracy, as well as refutation of Smirnov's repeated denials of that rôle. And these witnesses accused Smirnov of a much more direct, active and important rôle than he would himself admit. We have already quoted Mrachkovsky's testimony to the alleged contents of the letter sent by Smirnov to Sedov through Holtzman. Mrachkovsky also alleged that he himself

> did everything with the knowledge of Smirnov, and that Smirnov knew the people with whom Mrachkovsky was preparing to commit terrorist acts. (ZK 43–4.)

Dreitzer testified that Smirnov had sent him to Sedov in 1931 to ascertain Trotsky's attitude on the formation of a bloc; also that Smirnov gave him direct instructions in 1932 to organize terrorist acts against Stalin and Voroshilov (ZK 51–2). Zinoviev affirmed that Smirnov was Trotsky's personal representative and even deputy in the U.S.S.R.; also that in the formation of the alleged united center the leading rôle on behalf of the Trotskyites was played by Smirnov, and that he displayed more activity than anyone else. (ZK 53, 73.) Kamenev

> fully confirms the leading part played by I.N. Smirnov in the Trotskyite part of the terrorist Trotskyite-Zinovievite center, . . . (ZK 66.)

He also stated that, knowing Smirnov had been abroad and established contact with Trotsky, the Zinovievites were convinced that the terrorist instructions conveyed to them by Smirnov and Mrachkovsky "were the exact instructions of Trotsky" (ZK 66).

From these and similar statements it becomes clear that the alleged active participation of Smirnov in forming the alleged terrorist center is crucial for the charge that it existed; and that his alleged rôle as Trotsky's representative is crucial for the charge that Trotsky participated in its formation and direction. This testimony would be more impressive if it were not so contradictory, as we have already pointed out (§ 35), as to make Smirnov's alleged activity in initiating the conspiracy appear fantastically absurd. It must also be noted that while it may be taken as direct evidence against Smirnov, it has no value as direct evidence against Trotsky or Sedov. Whether or not the other accused believed or assumed that Smirnov was speaking for Trotsky is wholly irrelevant to the question whether or not he actually did so; and the question whether or not Sedov was an authority for them (ZK 80) is wholly irrelevant to the question whether or not Sedov gave Smirnov instructions on terrorism or, if so, whether those instructions came from Trotsky. Smirnov steadily denied that Sedov's "opinion" on terrorism represented Trotsky's instructions. Therefore, even where the accused or witnesses (as Safonova—ZK 76) state that Smirnov informed them that Sedov's alleged instructions came from Trotsky, their testimony, being fourth-hand hearsay—what they say Smirnov said Sedov said Trotsky said—can not be considered worth anything in the face of Smirnov's denials.

§ 46. On the question of the alleged conversation about terrorism in 1931, Smirnov's was the only direct testimony produced against Sedov. It is, therefore, a matter of Smirnov's report of this conversation against Sedov's. While Sedov's testimony belongs in the category known as self-serving, there is strong presumptive evidence in favor of his version, even in the record of the trial itself. There is agreement between Smirnov and Sedov that the purpose of the exchange of addresses and password was the sending of information from Smirnov to Sedov (ZK 79; CR 8). There is nothing in the evidence which indicates any understanding between them that the information was to be conspiratorial. And only hearsay evidence uncorroborated by either Holtzman or Smirnov contradicts Sedov's testimony concerning the contents of the report he received from Smirnov through Holtzman. Sedov was actively interested in Trotsky's paper *(Bulletin of the Opposition)*, which dealt chiefly with Soviet affairs. According to both his testimony and that of Trotsky, it was becoming very hard to get information out of Russia (PC 38; CR 39). It is understandable, therefore, that he would take advantage of the opportunity to receive such information from Smirnov who, according to Sedov, although he had become an adversary, was not nearly so bitter as others. (CR 39.) It is more difficult to understand how Smirnov came to take the risk of such a connection. However, it does not tax credulity to assume that he was moved to do so by the fact that he had once been Trotsky's friend, and Sedov's (PC 89; CR 2–3), and a member of the Opposition, and still felt a certain sympathy with Trotsky and his point of view even though he had broken with both politically. This assumption is supported not only by Sedov's statement, just quoted, but also by the striking fact that Smirnov alone among the principal accused did not in his final plea brand Trotsky with the stigma of fascism or counter-revolution. "Why did I take the counter-revolutionary path?" said Mrachkovsky. "My connection with Trotsky—that is what brought me to this." "Thus we served fascism," said Kamenev of himself, Zinoviev and Trotsky. "My defective Bolshevism," said Zinoviev, "became transformed into anti-Bolshevism, and through Trotskyism I arrived at fascism." (ZK 165–171.) Smirnov, on the other hand, is reported in a passage which is in startling contrast to these statements:

> There is no other path for our country but the one it is now treading, and there is not, nor can there be, any other leadership than that which history has given us. Trotsky, who sends directions and instructions on ter-

rorism and *regards our state as a fascist state,* is an enemy; he is on the other side of the barricades; he must be fought. (ZK 171.) [Italics ours.]

Finally, since Smirnov as a "capitulator" was regarded by both Trotsky and Sedov as a political adversary (PC 75; CR 3; also Chapter VIII of this report), it seems unreasonable to suppose that Sedov, in his first conversation with him after his capitulation, would incontinently urge the need of a new and terrorist line and insist that Stalin must be killed.

We are therefore convinced that Sedov conveyed to Smirnov no "opinion" or instruction on the necessity of terrorism against Soviet leaders, either on his own behalf or Trotsky's.

§ 47. There remains the question of Trotsky's alleged communication with Smirnov through Yuri Gaven. The failure to summon this witness, upon which we have already commented (§ 17, 6), constituted in our opinion one of the worst flaws in the procedure of the Court. In the absence of Gaven's confirmation, Smirnov's admission that he received through Gaven Trotsky's instructions on terrorism remains unconfirmed by any direct evidence whatever. From Smirnov's testimony it appears that this communication consisted of a letter from Trotsky as well as "verbal conversation" with Gaven (ZK 42).

It must be noted that a written instrument quoted as evidence but not produced in court is subject to perversion by the person purporting to relate its contents. Such an account, given from memory, constitutes at best the narrator's interpretation of those contents, unverifiable by comparison with the instrument he purports to quote. Therefore the testimony of the person purporting to relate the contents of such an instrument is hearsay evidence as concerns those contents. Moreover, the use of such hearsay evidence to corroborate other testimony of the narrator, accompanied either by no explanation as to the instrument's absence or by the mere statement that it was lost or destroyed, warrants doubt not only of the interpretation put upon it but even of its ever having existed. Such a suspicion becomes doubly justified where, as in the present instance, the person who allegedly delivered the instrument is not summoned to corroborate the testimony to its existence.

From the Prosecutor's questions and Smirnov's answers concerning Trotsky's alleged communication through Gaven, it is not clear when Smirnov is giving the contents of the alleged letter and when he is relating Gaven's alleged "verbal conversation." We can only say, therefore, that as that testimony relates to the alleged letter it is hearsay, and subject, furthermore, to the suspicion indicated in the foregoing paragraph. As it relates to verbal instructions allegedly conveyed by Trotsky through Gaven it is double hearsay, being Smirnov's testimony to what Gaven said Trotsky said.

In view of the nature of Smirnov's testimony concerning this alleged communication, in view of the Prosecutor's failure to call the witness Yuri Gaven, and in view of his further failure to make any attempt to secure Trotsky's testimony, we consider that this testimony of the accused Smirnov as against Leon Trotsky is worthless.

§ 48. On the basis of all the evidence and all the above considerations, we conclude that in so far as it applied to Smirnov's confession of conspiratorial communication with Trotsky and Sedov, this statement of Vyshinsky in his summation was correct:

> Smirnov himself did not utter a single word of truth here . . . (ZK 134.)

11

The testimony of E.A. Dreitzer

§ 49. The second basis of the charge against Trotsky and Sedov in the August trial is the testimony of the accused Dreitzer. The record states (it is not clear whether this is Dreitzer's testimony or not) that

> Dreitzer was one of the most prominent Trotskyites. He had been the chief of Trotsky's bodyguard. Together with Trotsky he had organized the counter-revolutionary demonstration [see § 229] on November 7, 1927. When Trotsky was in exile in Alma-Ata Dreitzer organized the communications between Trotsky and the Moscow Trotskyite center. (ZK 51.)

However, no evidence was presented in support of these allegations. Dreitzer testified that in the autumn of 1931 he

> took advantage of a business trip to Berlin to establish contact with Trotsky at the instructions from I.N.

Smirnov. Smirnov's definite instructions were to ascertain Trotsky's attitude on the question of a *bloc* between the Trotskyites and the Zinovievites. In Berlin he twice met Sedov (Trotsky's son), in a café in Leipzigerstrasse. Sedov then told him that Trotsky's instruction would be sent on later. (ZK 51–2.)

He further testified that in October, 1934, his sister brought him from Warsaw a German cinema magazine which an agent of Sedov's had given her, in which he "had no difficulty in discovering" a letter written in invisible ink in Trotsky's own hand, instructing Dreitzer to carry out immediately terrorist acts against Stalin and Voroshilov.

Dreitzer at once passed the letter on to Mrachkovsky who, after reading it, burnt it for reasons of secrecy. (ZK 52.)

Although this letter, having allegedly been destroyed, could not be introduced in evidence, both Dreitzer and Mrachkovsky purportedly gave its contents, the former in part verbatim. (ZK 22, 43.) Mrachkovsky stated that he received the letter in Kazakhstan. (ZK 43.)

§ 50. Smirnov's only admission concerning Dreitzer was that he received him in his apartment as an active Trotskyite;

however he allegedly discussed with him, not terrorism but "the general situation in the country." (ZK 53.)

Therefore, Dreitzer's is the only direct testimony that Smirnov instructed him to see Sedov in Berlin and ascertain Trotsky's attitude on the formation of a bloc. Indeed, it is the only testimony on this point in the published record of the trial, except for the statement that "Mrachkovsky fully confirms Dreitzer's testimony."

§ 51. Leon Trotsky testified that Dreitzer was of the younger generation and was an officer in the Red Army; that when he, Trotsky, left the Kremlin after his expulsion from the Party, Dreitzer was among the army officers who organized a bodyguard for him; that Dreitzer had been in the Left Opposition, was expelled with it at the Fifteenth Party Congress, and had thereafter capitulated; and that he, Trotsky, had never communicated with him in any way since 1928. Trotsky testified that Dreitzer had never been close to him and that he had even forgotten his name until reminded of it by his wife. (PC 89–90.) He denied that Dreitzer had established contact with him in 1931, or that he had ever heard anything from Sedov about Dreitzer. He denied that he had sent Dreitzer the letter written in invisible ink which Dreitzer testified he received. (PC 224.)

§ 52. Leon Sedov testified that he had never seen or known Dreitzer, although he knew that in 1927, shortly before Trotsky's deportation, Dreitzer had been a member of Trotsky's bodyguard, and that Dreitzer had been in the Left Opposition from 1923 or 1924. He denied that any meeting had ever taken place between them either in 1931 or at any other time. He also denied having sent the letter in invisible ink which Dreitzer alleged he had received from him, and pointed out that Dreitzer had failed to give exact details concerning the place of transmission of this letter or the identity of Sedov's alleged agent. He also pointed out that Dreitzer would have had to develop the ink in order to discover the letter, and that elementary precaution would have dictated its being recopied in invisible ink before being sent on to Mrachkovsky, who was some 4,000 kilometers away,* in exile and therefore under the surveillance of the

---

* Sedov mistakenly says that Dreitzer stated he had received this letter from his sister at Warsaw. According to the record of the trial, Dreitzer's

Soviet police. But if the letter had been recopied, said Sedov, Mrachkovsky would not have been able to recognize Trotsky's handwriting, as he testified he did (ZK 43). Therefore, he argued, the letter was obviously a concoction, with the object of fabricating false proof against Trotsky and at the same time involving himself. (CR 25–6.)

§ 53. There is agreement between the trial record on the one hand and Trotsky and Sedov on the other, that Dreitzer had been a member of Trotsky's bodyguard, although Trotsky and Sedov do not state that Dreitzer was the chief of this bodyguard. Dreitzer's testimony to his alleged conversations with Sedov on Smirnov's instruction is not only not confirmed by Smirnov himself, but it is denied by Sedov. Dreitzer's testimony, corroborated by Mrachkovsky, that he received a letter from Trotsky in 1934, is denied by Trotsky, and by Sedov, through whose agent it was allegedly received.

§ 54. We have seen (§ 49) that according to Dreitzer the purpose of his alleged mission to Sedov in the autumn of 1931 was to ascertain Trotsky's attitude on the question of a bloc between the Trotskyites and Zinovievites; and that his is the only testimony to this alleged mission (§ 50). It is pertinent to consider this testimony in relation to that of other accused on the formation of the alleged bloc. We have already noted (§§ 34–6) the contradictions in this testimony, as they bear upon the credibility of the alleged conspiracy. We shall confine ourselves here to those aspects of it which bear upon the credibility of Dreitzer's confession.

According to both Zinoviev and Ter-Vaganyan, negotiations for the formation of a bloc were begun in 1931. Zinoviev stated that he conferred with Smirnov at that time concerning a union on the basis of terrorism, and that this was done on Trotsky's instructions (ZK 72). Ter-Vaganyan

---

sister brought him the letter *from* Warsaw. The record does not show where Dreitzer was.

stated that in the autumn of 1931 the Trotskyites began negotiations for union with the Zinovievites, "after Smirnov came back from Berlin," and that the terroristic stand was clear "because the instructions had already been brought" (ZK 110–11). And during the examination of Smirnov, according to the record,

> it appears . . . that the formation of the *bloc* was the result of direct negotiations . . . on the basis of the first instructions on terror received by Smirnov from Trotsky through Sedov in 1931. (ZK 83.)

If this testimony is true, then there does not appear to have been any reason for Smirnov's sending Dreitzer to Sedov in order to ascertain Trotsky's attitude toward the formation of a bloc.

On the other hand, Mrachkovsky is quoted in the indictment as having testified that Smirnov, in the middle of 1932,

> put before our leading trio the question of the necessity of uniting our organization with the *Zinoviev-Kamenev* and *Shatskin-Lominadze* groups . . . It was then decided to consult *L. Trotsky* on this question and to obtain his directions. . . . (ZK 21.)

During the trial Mrachkovsky stated that Smirnov raised this question in the second half of 1932, argued in favor of a bloc, and at that time sent a letter through Holtzman, putting the matter before Trotsky (ZK 41–2).

If Mrachkovsky's testimony (which according to the indictment was "fully confirmed" by Dreitzer himself—ZK 22) is to be accepted as true, then it seems highly unlikely that Smirnov would have sent Dreitzer in the autumn of 1931 to put before Trotsky a question which he did not put before his fellow "Trotskyites" until more than half a year later, and concerning which he then questioned Trotsky in a letter sent through Holtzman.

Thus, taken in connection with either of the two foregoing accounts, the alleged mission of Dreitzer appears meaningless and improbable from the record itself. Nor does his testimony gain in appearance of credibility from his having "fully confirmed" Mrachkovsky's testimony which, if his own story is to be believed, he must have known to be false. It stands, moreover, as a bare statement, unsubstantiated by the slightest detail concerning the means by which he got in touch with Sedov, or any information about their two alleged conversations beyond Sedov's assurance that "Trotsky's instruction would be sent on later." We note that Holtzman, who really did convey a message to Sedov from Smirnov, was able to state how he got in touch with him, and the password by which he identified himself. It is reasonable to assume that if Smirnov had also sent Dreitzer to Sedov, he would have given him the telephone number and the password with which he supplied Holtzman.

§ 55. Dreitzer's testimony concerning his alleged visit to Sedov is thus open to the gravest doubt on the basis of the trial record alone, without consideration of extrinsic evidence.

Its truth or falsehood obviously depends in the last analysis upon that of the charge against Smirnov, whose alleged agent he was. We have already stated (§ 46) our conclusion that Sedov never conveyed to Smirnov any "opinions" or instructions on terrorism either on his own behalf or on Trotsky's. Therefore, Smirnov could have projected no "Trotskyite-Zinovievite bloc" in pursuance of those instructions. Therefore, we find that Dreitzer's testimony concerning his alleged mission from Smirnov to Sedov in 1931 is false.

§ 56. Concerning Trotsky's alleged letter in invisible ink,

the Prosecutor failed to ask the most obvious and necessary questions. The indictment states that Dreitzer *handed* this letter to Mrachkovsky (ZK 22). From Dreitzer's testimony we learn that he received it in October, 1934, and "at once" *passed it on* to Mrachkovsky (ZK 52). But Mrachkovsky testified that he received it in December, 1934, while in Kazakhstan (ZK 43). Where did Dreitzer receive it? And if he *handed* it to Mrachkovsky "at once," then why did Mrachkovsky receive it only in December? If Dreitzer did not hand it to Mrachkovsky but sent it to him, then by what means? Sedov correctly argues that Dreitzer would have had to develop the letter in order to "discover it." Moreover, if he had not read it he could not have remembered its contents. Mrachkovsky, on the other hand, could not have recognized Trotsky's writing unless he had received the original letter. But to send such a letter several thousand miles, and to an exile, must surely have been extremely dangerous.

No witnesses were summoned to testify on this important matter. Nor did Vyshinsky summon Dreitzer's sister to tell what agent of Sedov's delivered the letter to her, how he got in touch with her, how Sedov knew she was in Warsaw, etc. We are thus asked to believe two hearsay versions of the alleged contents of an incriminating letter which appears to have been twice transmitted under the most doubtful conditions. We refer our readers to § 47 of this report, which applies to this letter equally with that allegedly received by Smirnov. We should be justified in assuming from the record of the trial alone that this alleged letter to Dreitzer never existed. But since Dreitzer was allegedly connected with the "terrorist line" through Smirnov (ZK 51–2), it follows that if the testimony connecting Smirnov with that line is false as we hold it to be (§§ 46, 48) there remains no basis for the assumption that Dreitzer was drawn into a terrorist conspiracy by Smirnov, and consequently none for a belief that he was drawn into a terrorist conspiracy at all. Thus the doubt inspired by the record itself concerning the existence of the letter containing terrorist instructions which he allegedly received from Trotsky, is converted into certainty that such a letter never existed.

§ 57. On the basis of all the evidence we find that Dreitzer never acted as a go-between for Smirnov and Sedov for the purposes of a terrorist conspiracy; and that he never received terrorist instructions from Trotsky through Sedov or anyone else.

12

The testimony of E.S. Holtzman

§ 58. The third basis of the charge against Leon Trotsky and Leon Sedov in the August trial is the confession of the accused E.S. Holtzman. We have already considered in Chapter X of this report Holtzman's testimony that he acted as an emissary from Smirnov to Sedov. On the basis of the conclusions stated in that chapter we find that Holtzman never acted as a liaison man between Smirnov and Sedov for the purposes of any terrorist conspiracy.

§ 59. Holtzman also testified that at Sedov's suggestion he arranged to meet him in Copenhagen during Trotsky's stay in that city in the autumn of 1932. According to Holtzman:

> Sedov said to me: "As you are going to the U.S.S.R., it would be a good thing if you came with me to Copenhagen where my father is. . . ." I agreed, but I told him that we could not go together for reasons of secrecy. I arranged with Sedov to be in Copenhagen within two

or three days, to put up at the Hotel Bristol and meet him there. I went to the hotel straight from the station and in the lounge met Sedov. About 10 A.M. we went to see Trotsky. (ZK 100.)

Trotsky, he said, gave him terrorist instructions (§ 36) and told him he was preparing a letter for Smirnov, but since Holtzman was leaving that day would not write it. Since Trotsky could not put his instruction in writing, said Holtzman,

> . . . I accepted it in verbal form and communicated the exact sense of it on my arrival in Moscow. (ZK 101.)

He did not state to whom he communicated the sense of it. But the passage just quoted follows a previous statement that Trotsky told him to deliver the alleged instructions to Smirnov and no one else. The Prosecutor did not ask Smirnov whether or not he received this message from Holtzman; and in his summation he himself misrepresented the record, apparently in order to discredit both Smirnov and Holtzman:

> Holtzman . . . said that he had received these instructions, but did not communicate them; and you think this can be believed. (ZK 158.)

During his conversation with Trotsky, Holtzman testified,

> very often Trotsky's son Sedov came in and out of the room. (ZK 100.)

And it was Sedov, according to Holtzman, who brought about the termination of the interview:

> At that moment Sedov came in and began hurrying us to finish the conversation. . . . (ZK 101.)

§ 60. Leon Trotsky testified that he was in Copenhagen from November 23 to December 2, 1932; that he went there from Turkey at the invitation of the Social Democratic Students, for the purpose of giving a lecture on the Russian Revolution (PC 29); that he was accompanied by his wife, his secretary, Jan Frankel, a French friend, P. Frank, a German friend, Oscar (full name in our possession); that an American couple, the Fields, accompanied his party on the ship from Turkey to Marseille; that in Copenhagen his party occupied a villa of five or six rooms and lived strictly incognito; that his friends organized a guard of five or six persons for both day and night, and this guard controlled all visits to him so that it would have been impossible for anyone who wished to see him simply to walk into his room. (PC 135–9.) He testified that he did not know whether or not he ever knew E.S. Holtzman, since there were several Holtzmans in the Bolshevik Party, but that he had been in communication with no one of that name since his exile (PC 91). Since, however, E.S. Holtzman met his son Sedov in Berlin in 1932 and gave him, as he, Trotsky, subsequently learned, some factual reports about the situation in the U.S.S.R. which were published in the *Bulletin*, this, he said, might be interpreted as an indirect communication (PC 592). He denied that he had seen anyone by the name of Holtzman during his stay in Copenhagen (PC 139). He identified twenty-seven people who were with him or visited him during that period and stated that his only Russian-speaking visitor was one Senin (Sobolevitzius), one of two brothers who later organized a split in the Trotskyist organization in Berlin (PC 137–40).

Trotsky denied that his son, Sedov, was in Copenhagen at any time during his stay there, but affirmed that his son's wife was there. His son, he said, was in Berlin at the time, and he was in daily contact with him by telephone. He declared that Sedov met him in Paris on December 6, 1932, having received a visa from the French government in consequence of a telegraphic request from Mrs. Trotsky to Herriot, the French Prime Minister. Trotsky testified that he then saw his son for the first time since Sedov's departure from Prinkipo for Berlin in February, 1931. (PC 140, 145, 593.)

Trotsky also stated that the villa occupied by his party was that of a dancer, and that its furnishings were so peculiar that anyone visiting him must have been struck by them; yet not one of the accused in the Moscow trial who allegedly visited him in Copenhagen mentioned his surroundings (PC 172). He further called attention to the failure of these witnesses to mention the false report of the death of one of the leaders of the alleged terrorist conspiracy, Zinoviev, which appeared in the press at that time (PC 147).

§ 61. Trotsky's testimony was fully corroborated by his secretary, Jan Frankel, who testified before the Preliminary Commission that he made the trip to Copenhagen with Trotsky and was constantly with him during his stay there, described the organization of the guard, and stated that no one could have seen Trotsky without his knowledge, since all decisions concerning the admission of visitors were made by Trotsky, Raymond Molinier and himself. He stated that Trotsky's address in Copenhagen, a villa on Dalgas Boulevard, was known only to a Mr. Boeggild, since deceased, a Danish Social Democrat who had charge of the arrangements for Trotsky's lecture; to the Chief of Police; and to Trotsky's close friends.

Frankel said that Trotsky and his wife occupied one bedroom on the upper floor of the villa, and their daughter-in-law, Jeanne Martin des Pallières, shared the other with Lucienne Tedeschi. The remaining room, which was very small, was used by Trotsky as a study. Some visitors, he said, saw Trotsky alone, but before they entered they were first identified and announced, and in order to reach Trotsky's study they were obliged to pass by the guard of five or six people on the ground floor. He said that Trotsky never left the house alone. One day, he testified, when it was thought that journalists had found out his address, Trotsky went to a little pension, accompanied by Raymond Molinier, Oscar, and Gérard Rosenthal. Frankel testified that he frequently talked by telephone to Sedov in Berlin during that period about Sedov's attempts to get to Copenhagen. (PC 158–165.)

§ 62. Leon Sedov denied that he invited Holtzman to go to Copenhagen and declared that he himself had never been in Copenhagen in his life (CR 11). He stated that the passport for foreigners with which he had been provided in Berlin was good only from August 31 to November 1, 1932; that after that date he could not have left Germany with a regular visa from the Danish authorities, without a renewal of his permit to reside in Germany; that he did not secure this renewal until December 3, 1932, the day after Trotsky's departure from Copenhagen; that on that same date he received a French visa, in consequence of a telegraphic request from his mother to the French Premier, Herriot; and that he went to Paris, where he met his parents. He stated that while his parents were in Copenhagen he was in daily communication with them by telephone from Berlin. (CR 12–13.) He presented his passport to the *Commission Rogatoire* which, after examining it,

> acknowledged that what he had just said was clearly apparent from the data contained in the passport. (CR 12.)

Sedov also stated that

> . . . there can no longer be any doubt whatever that the Hotel Bristol of Copenhagen was closed in 1917, and that no hotel of that name existed in Copenhagen in 1932. Some months after the trial there was talk of a mistake that had occurred and that the non-existent hotel had been confused with a pastry shop which apparently ex-

isted in Copenhagen in 1932. But it is obvious, in my opinion, that this attempt to correct the evident lie of Holtzman does not tally with his very clear statement that we met in the lobby of the hotel; pastry shops do not have lobbies. (CR 12.)

He further (CR 22) called attention to a passage in the record of the trial, also cited before the Preliminary Commission (PC 172), in which the defendant Olberg, whom he knew in Berlin and who was in a better position than other defendants to be informed concerning his comings and goings at that period, stated:

> Before my departure for the Soviet Union I intended to go to Copenhagen with Sedov to see Trotsky. Our trip did not materialize, but Suzanna, Sedov's wife, went there. . . . (ZK 87.)

Sedov called attention to the failure of the prosecution to make any attempt to clarify this irreconcilable contradiction between Olberg's testimony and that of Holtzman (CR 22).

§ 63. Three witnesses testified before the *Commission Rogatoire* concerning Sedov's alleged trip to Copenhagen and other matters connected with the charges against Trotsky and Sedov. Eugene Bauer,* a German physician living in Paris, testified that he belonged to the Trotskyite movement until 1934, when he "withdrew from it after a rather heated polemic" and joined the German Socialist Workers' Party. He stated that at the time of Trotsky's visit to Copenhagen he was on intimate terms with Sedov; and that he conversed with him daily in Berlin by telephone, from

---

* A pseudonym: being a political refugee the witness did not give his real name, which is in our possession.

the time of Trotsky's arrival in Copenhagen, concerning his own proposed trip to that city. Sedov having finally given up hope of going with him, Bauer said, he himself left for Copenhagen on December 1 with one Sobolevich (Sobolev-itzius, Senin; § 60), who was at that time a comrade but has since become an agent of the GPU. He arrived in Copenhagen, he said, at 6 A.M. on December 2, and left at 11 A.M. with Trotsky for Esbjerg. He left Esbjerg for Berlin on the morning of December 3, and on his arrival there telephoned Sedov. The witness showed the sub-commission his German passport, which bore two stamps of the Danish police, one dated December 2, 1932, and another dated December 3, 1932, but no German stamps.* (CR 44.)

In a written deposition certified by the Special Committee, Bauer states that Sedov saw him off from the station in Berlin on the evening of December 1, and that he telephoned Sedov in Berlin on the evening of December 3. He also states that Sedov was not in Esbjerg during his stay there. (PC Exh. 16, S II/8.)

§ 64. Alexandra Pfemfert (Alexandra Ramm, Trotsky's German translator—PC 95) testified that during the two or three years Sedov lived in Berlin he received his mail at the address of herself and her husband; that since his mail consisted chiefly of letters from his father, not a day passed without his coming to their home to get his letters or telephoning to find out whether there was any; that at the time of Trotsky's stay in Copenhagen Sedov came not only once but even twice a day. She testified that the influential lawyer Cohn, who has since died in Palestine, made vain efforts to secure a visa for Sedov (see also Trotsky's testimony—PC 138). She declared that she could state quite definitely that Sedov was able to leave Berlin for Paris only at the end of

---

* We are informed that as a general rule the German officials did not stamp passports at this border.

Trotsky's stay in Copenhagen. (CR 48–9.)

§ 65. Franz Pfemfert testified that he lived for many years in Berlin; that immediately after the war he belonged to the Communist Party, from which he was expelled in 1921 or 1922; that he then continued to adhere to the Spartacist movement, but belongs to no political movement at present. He fully corroborated his wife's testimony summarized above. (CR 50.)

§ 66. B.J. and Esther Field of New York testified before the New York sub-commission that they had been members of the Communist League of America, which was part of the International Left Opposition to which Leon Trotsky belonged; that they joined this organization in 1931 and were expelled in 1934; that they went to Prinkipo in August of 1932 to work with Leon Trotsky, and remained there until the middle of November, when they left on the same ship with Trotsky for Copenhagen; that they did not go from Marseille to Copenhagen with Trotsky, but travelled separately and arrived in Copenhagen on November 23; that in Copenhagen they went daily to work at Trotsky's house immediately after breakfast and remained there until eight or nine o'clock in the evening; that during the time they were in Trotsky's house they saw no visitor by the name of Holtzman; and that they were sure Trotsky had no Russian visitors. They stated that they knew Senin (Sobolevitzius) visited Trotsky, but that Senin was a member of the German Trotskyite organization, and not a Russian. They testified that they met Leon Sedov in Berlin in June or July of 1932 and saw him frequently during their two weeks' stay; that they saw Sedov's wife in Copenhagen but that Sedov himself was not there; that Trotsky, to their knowledge, often talked by telephone with Sedov in Berlin during that period. (NY 3–29, 37, 51–58, 71–72.)

Mr. and Mrs. Field also testified that they stayed at the Grand Hotel during their sojourn in Copenhagen and that there was a candy store in the same street as that hotel but not adjacent to it, since there were shops between the entrance of the hotel and that of the candy store. Mrs. Field stated that this candy store was called "Bristol." Mr. Field did not remember the name. (NY 8, 14–16, 54–5.) Mrs. Field was shown a copy of *Soviet Russia Today,* introduced before the Preliminary Commission (Exh. 16, II, Annex 3), in which appears what purports to be a photograph of the Grand Hotel and the *Konditori* Bristol in Copenhagen. The witness declared that the photograph appeared to her to have been tampered with, and did not properly represent the relation between the Grand Hotel and the Bristol Confectionery as she remembered it. She declared that the candy shop was farther from the hotel than it appeared to be in the photograph; also that there was a large sign over the Grand Hotel surmounted by a crown, and that this sign did not clearly show in the picture. She also called attention to a black spot on the photograph which she said covered up a café connected with the hotel. (NY 32–5.)

§ 67. The documentary evidence introduced before the Preliminary Commission and the *Commission Rogatoire* bearing on the testimony of those witnesses in the August trial who claimed to have seen Trotsky in Copenhagen, is very voluminous. Exclusive of numerous excerpts from the Danish press, Exhibit 16—on Copenhagen—alone of the Preliminary Commission contains 67 documents accepted in evidence. And there are documents in other exhibits which bear in whole or in part on this testimony. Therefore, we are able to cite only the most important items. The same method will be followed in making use of other documentary material in this case. The material itself will be published in a subsequent volume.

§ 68. The most important documents in our possession bearing on Holtzman's testimony are as follows:

(1) Two notebooks and one examination paper, bearing

stamps and signatures of professors, showing Sedov's presence at the *Technische Hochschule* in Berlin on November 25 and 27, 1932. Sedov testified that the examination took place on November 26, and that it was on the 27th that the paper was marked and the notation made of the grade given him (CR 14). These documents were shown by him to the *Commission Rogatoire* and were later introduced in evidence by Leon Trotsky. (PC 590; Exh. 16, S II/10, a, b, c.)

(2) Sedov's attendance-book, bearing on its cover the printed title *Belegbuch für Stud.*, *Technische Hochschule, Berlin*, and bearing on three separate pages the signature of Professor Hanner, with a stamp, November 29, 1932; also on the seventh page a stamp, November 25, 1932, and an illegible signature (CR Exh. 15).

(3) Photostats of the pages of the passport shown by Sedov to the *Commission Rogatoire*, having on page 7 a permit to remain in Germany *(Aufenthaltserlaubnis)* dated August 31, 1932, and good until December 1, 1932; and on page 10 a renewal dated December 3, 1932, and good until January 2, 1933; also, on page 11, a permit to leave and return to Germany, dated December 3, 1932, and good until December 17, 1932; also, on page 13, a French visa dated December 3, 1932, and good for five days; also, on the same page, a stamp of entry affixed at the French border, dated December 4, 1932. (PC Exh. 16, II/1, a.)

(4) A holograph letter from Leon Trotsky to Leon Sedov, written on two pages from a small notebook, and beginning:

> Dear Liovoussiatka, so it seems that we shall not succeed in meeting; between the arrival of the boat at Dunkerque and the departure of the boat from Marseille, there is just time to cross France. To wait for the next boat (a whole week!) will not, of course, be permitted us. . . .

The letter ends with the words:

> Mother embraces you (she is still in bed; it is seven
> o'clock in the morning), she will probably write to you
> today. (*Ibid.*, S II 9.)

Above the signature appears the date, 3/XII, 1932, and the
words, *kaiuta parokhoda* (cabin on board ship).

(5) A postcard (holograph) from Natalia Sedov-Trotsky
to her son, bearing the postmark "Esbjerg 3/12/32" and addressed to Frau F. Pfemfert at a Berlin address. (This post-
card corroborates the testimony of Mr. and Mrs. Pfemfert
that Sedov's mail was sent to their address—§§ 64, 65.) It
begins:

> My darling Levik: This morning papa sent you a brief
> note, written in haste, through Erwin.*

Mrs. Trotsky expresses her grief at having been unable to
see her son in Copenhagen, and ends:

> I would have so much liked to receive your letters.
> Where did you send them? . . . I want to continue hop-
> ing that a "miracle" will occur and that we shall see each
> other. (*Ibid.*, S II/13.)

(6) Six holograph letters by Leon Sedov to his mother
at Copenhagen. Five of these letters were shown by Sedov
to the *Commission Rogatoire* (CR 15), and the six letters
were later transmitted to the Commission by Leon Trotsky. A letter to the Commission from Natalia Sedov-Trotsky
states that some, if not all, of these letters were ultimately
delivered to her, if not by mail then through comrades, and

---

* The first name of "Eugene Bauer." (§ 63.)

if not at Copenhagen then in Prinkipo. The fact that the letters which she received were in her son's archives she explains with the statement that when she and her husband were expelled from France (PC 31–2) they left their archives in their son's care.

These letters are dated November 21, November 26 (three), November 28, and December 2, 1932 (PC Exh. 16 S II/11, a–f). The first begins.

> My dears! In about 36 hours you will find yourself but a few hours from Berlin; however, I cannot come to see you! The Germans have not yet given me permission for continued residence, without which I can neither have a Danish visa nor will I be able to return to Berlin.

One of the letters of November 26 contains the following passage:

> If you are able to extend your visa, I hope to come to you in ten to fourteen days, perhaps earlier.

(7) A copy of a telegram from Natalia Sedov-Trotsky to Premier Herriot, dated Copenhagen December 1, 1932, requesting him to authorize a visa for her son so that he may meet her on her way through France; also a copy of a telegram from the French Foreign Office to the French Consulate in Berlin, dated December 3, 1932, authorizing the visa (*Ibid.*, II/2, a, b).*

---

* Although the Foreign Office supplied these copies, they have refused to certify them (CR 13; also letters in our possession). However, since they have been widely published and the Foreign Office has never denied their authenticity, the Commission considers itself justified in accepting them in evidence.

(8) Depositions of people who were in contact with Sedov in Berlin during Trotsky's stay in Copenhagen. Among these is an affidavit (Prague) by Anna Grylewicz. Mrs. Grylewicz states that her husband, Anton Grylewicz, was the organizational leader of the Trotskyist group in Berlin, publisher of numerous pamphlets by Leon Trotsky and also of the *Bulletin of the Opposition*, on which Leon Sedov worked; that all correspondence relating to these matters was addressed to their home, which was also the office of the German group; that she and her husband were in daily contact with Sedov, either personally or by telephone; that during her husband's absence in Copenhagen, from November 22 to December 1, 1932, Sedov called her up daily and she talked with him about the mail that had been received, therefore she knows that Sedov was in Berlin during the entire period of her husband's absence; that several days after her husband's return from Copenhagen, Sedov left for Paris, where he stayed for about a week. (*Ibid.*, II/4.)

(9) Depositions of people who were with Trotsky during his stay in Copenhagen. Among these are the following:

(a) A statement by Raymond Molinier, editor, present political adversary of Leon Trotsky (PC 175, 190), certified by the Special Committee (§ 11, 6). Molinier says that he was charged with the arrangements for Trotsky's sojourn in Copenhagen, and that on his way there he passed through Berlin to consult Sedov. At that time Sedov informed him that he was unable to go to Copenhagen. Molinier states:

> I remember very well his refusal to go to Denmark illegally in view of his precarious situation in relation to the Prussian Social-Democratic authorities. . . .

Molinier says that he arrived in Copenhagen on November 19, 1932, and that he rented in his own name a furnished villa for Trotsky at 155 Dalgas Boulevard, belonging to an artist who was leaving Copenhagen for several months. He says that Trotsky was never alone in the house; that

> during his entire stay comrade Jan Frankel and I were responsible for his security. In agreement with him we arranged all matters concerning all visits he would have to make and those he should receive. We therefore knew exactly the comrades having interviews with him and the visits he had; there was no kind of visit from anyone named Holtzman or from anyone unknown to us.

Molinier mentions the press report of Zinoviev's death and says that several comrades asked Trotsky to give his opinion of Zinoviev. This he did in a brief talk

> . . . in which he recalled Zinoviev's services to the Russian Revolution, but dissociated himself quite definitely from Zinoviev's zigzags during the Revolution and during the oppositional struggle in Russia.

He states that he took Trotsky and his wife for some drives and that he accompanied Trotsky on a visit to Stauning, president of the Social Democratic Council, to discuss his application for an extension of his visa. He corroborates Frankel's statements concerning Trotsky's activities in Copenhagen, his brief visit to a pension near the city, and the telephone conversations to Sedov in Berlin. Mr. Molinier says that he flew from Copenhagen to Le Bourget after Trotsky's departure from Copenhagen, met him at Dunkerque and travelled with him to Marseille. He states that in Paris at the Gare du Nord they met Sedov, who also accompanied his parents to Marseille. (PC Exh. 16, I/19.)

(b) A deposition by Pierre Naville, journalist, of Paris, certified by the Special Committee, states that Naville was with Trotsky throughout his stay in Copenhagen, having met him at Esbjerg upon his arrival in Denmark, and that he returned with him to Dunkerque on the steamship "Bernsdorff." The testimony of this witness confirms that of Trotsky, Frankel and Molinier concerning Trotsky's life and activities in Copenhagen and the organization of his guard. He describes the house in detail, states that it belonged to a dancer, that it was full of knick-knacks and little pieces of furniture in frightful taste, and that no one would be able to forget the numerous photographs of the dancer on the walls of the rooms. The telephone, he says, was in the small vestibule of the villa, and over this telephone Trotsky and his wife had several conversations with Sedov in Berlin. He states that Bauer and Senin arrived on the morning of December 2, and that because the preparations for departure prevented a discussion Bauer accompanied Trotsky to Esbjerg. (*Ibid.*, 16, I/2.)

The statements in this deposition are confirmed by the following people who were also with Trotsky during that period: Denise Naville, Julien (full name in our possession), Lucienne Tedeschi, Feroci, Gérard Rosenthal. All of these people were identified by Leon Trotsky in his testimony before the Preliminary Commission (PC 137).

(c) A deposition by Oscar (also known as Otto; identified § 55) certified by the Special Committee, in which he states he made the trip from Istanbul to Denmark with Trotsky as one of his secretaries. Oscar's testimony corroborates that cited above. He says:

> Since I was almost constantly in Trotsky's house, I met every single visitor. Holtzman, Berman-Yurin and Fritz David were absolutely not among the visitors. . . . Sedov, Trotsky's son, was not in Copenhagen. . . . I personally knew Sedov very well . . . it is absolutely out of the question that Sedov could have been in Copenhagen without my knowing it. I met him only on the morn-

ing of December 6 in Paris at the Gare de Lyon, when
he entered Trotsky's compartment. Sedov travelled with
Trotsky to Marseille. (PC Exh. 16, I/3.)

(d) The wife of Leon Sedov, Jeanne Martin des Pallières, in
a deposition certified by the Special Committee, corroborates
the testimony quoted above concerning Sedov's failure to get
to Copenhagen, and her own presence there; also concerning
Trotsky's life in Copenhagen, his activities, and the organization of his guard, and concerning Mrs. Trotsky's telegram
to Herriot. She says that when she arrived in Copenhagen
she did not know the address of Trotsky and his wife, which
was being kept secret, and had a long wait before she found a
comrade who could conduct her to their house. She further
testifies that she talked with her husband a couple of times
from Copenhagen to Berlin. She states that at the end of
Trotsky's stay in Copenhagen she went to Paris, travelling
by way of Hamburg with Lucienne Tedeschi. In Paris her
husband joined her and they accompanied Leon Trotsky and
his wife to Marseille and from there to the Italian frontier.
(PC Exh. 16, I/18, a.) Her testimony that she went to Paris
through Hamburg is corroborated by a postcard, stamped
"Hamburg 3/12/32," addressed to Mme. Martin des Pallières,
in Paris, and signed "Jeanne" (Ibid., I/18, b).

(e) Jeanne des Pallières' testimony concerning her trip
to Paris from Copenhagen is corroborated by Lucienne Tedeschi in a deposition certified by the Special Committee.
This witness also states that she several times obtained the
telephone connection from Copenhagen to Sedov in Berlin
for Natalia Trotsky. (Ibid., I/13.)

(f) Anton Grylewicz (identified in 6 above), in an affidavit (Prague) states that he was with Trotsky in Copenhagen
from November 23 to December 1, 1932. He corroborates
the witnesses quoted above concerning the method of in-
troducing visitors to Trotsky, and states that during his stay

in Copenhagen no one who spoke Russian visited Trotsky. Concerning Sedov's absence he says:

> Trotsky's son, L. Sedov, was not in Copenhagen, a fact which I can confirm under oath. I was in the same house with Trotsky every day and I know that Trotsky as well as his wife and the wife of Sedov telephoned to Sedov every day. I myself twice took advantage of these conversations to speak with Sedov. My wife, who during my absence spoke directly or over the telephone with Sedov every day, communicated in many letters sent me at Copenhagen her conversations with him. (*Ibid.*, I/4.)

(g) Gérard Rosenthal, Trotsky's French lawyer (PC 137), in a deposition certified by the Special Committee, states that he accompanied Trotsky to Copenhagen and back to France. He corroborates the testimony quoted above concerning Trotsky's life in Copenhagen, his guard, etc. Rosenthal, however, differs from other witnesses in that he does not mention Trotsky's having used a small room on the second floor as a study. Instead he describes a bedroom where he says Trotsky remained most of the time. He corroborates the testimony given above concerning the absence of Sedov, whom he says he knew personally; also concerning the telegram sent to Herriot by Natalia Sedov-Trotsky. (*Ibid.*, I/9.)

(10) Certified photographs, and print of the architect's drawings, of the villa at 155 Dalgas Boulevard, Copenhagen-Frederiksberg; with a certification by the *Frederiksberg Kommunes Tekniske Forvaltning* that the plan correctly represents the villa as it was in 1932. This material confirms descriptions of the villa by various witnesses. (*Ibid.*, S I/20, 21.)

(11) An affidavit (Copenhagen) by Alfred Kruse, assistant to the Central Tax Control, a department of the Danish Ministry of Finance. Mr. Kruse states that he offers his testimony in order to show how difficult it was even for Communists

and persons intimately acquainted with Russian questions to get in touch with Trotsky during his stay in Copenhagen. He says that although during the early years of the war he had known intimately several members of the Bolshevik Party, especially Bukharin and Pyatakov, and had even twice travelled to Russia on secret missions for the Bolsheviks, his letter requesting an interview with Trotsky in Copenhagen remained unanswered; that he had great difficulty even in obtaining a ticket for Trotsky's lecture and was able to hear it only because he finally secured a press card. In consequence of these difficulties, Mr. Kruse concludes that it was quite impossible to see Trotsky in Copenhagen without obtaining permission from the people who surrounded him; therefore there must be many such people who are in a position to confirm or deny Holtzman's testimony that he saw Trotsky in Copenhagen. (*Ibid.*, S I/22.)

(12) Documents bearing upon the question of the Hotel Bristol:

(a) An affidavit (Copenhagen) by Alfred Kruse (identified above) stating that he was born in Copenhagen and grew up in that section of the city where the Hotel Bristol was situated; that the Bristol was well known to foreign tourists; that when the Russian Imperial ships visited Denmark, the officers met in the restaurant of the Hotel Bristol, which must therefore have been well known in Russian pre-revolutionary official circles and was probably included in tourists' handbooks; that the hotel was closed in 1917 and its premises transformed into offices. (*Ibid.*, S II, Annex 6.)

(b) A photograph of the old Hotel Bristol in Copenhagen, from *För og Nu*, 1917, p. 337, with the original caption, which states that the Bristol was built in 1901–2, and that after 15 years it has gone out of business, and the building has been sold to the Absalon Insurance Company, which will transform it into offices. (*Ibid.*, S II, Annex 5.)

(c) *Soviet Russia Today*, New York, March, 1937, having on page 7 what purports to be a radio-photograph of the *Konditori* Bristol and the Grand Hotel in Copenhagen. (*Ibid.*, II, Annex 3.) This is the photograph shown to Mrs. Field (§ 66).

(d) Two photographs of the *Konditori* Bristol and the Grand Hotel, transmitted to the Commission by A. Vikelsoe Jensen of Copenhagen, which show a newspaper kiosk and two shops between the confectionery and the hotel, where the photograph cited above shows black; also, over the entrance to the hotel, a horizontal electric sign, "Grand Hotel," and between two large windows an entrance to the café, which do not appear in the photograph from *Soviet Russia Today*. (*Ibid.*, S II, Annex 7, b, c.)

These two photographs corroborate the testimony of Mr. and Mrs. Field concerning the relation between the Grand Hotel and the Bristol Café or Confectionery. However, Jensen writes us that in 1932 the Confectionery was, as he remembers it, situated where the two shops are today.

(e) An affidavit (Copenhagen) by A. Vikelsoe Jensen, who states that he was a member of the Social Democratic Students' group which invited Trotsky to Copenhagen. Jensen refers to a ground-plan of the Bristol Confectionery and the Grand Hotel which appeared in *Arbeiderbladet* (organ of the Communist Party, Copenhagen) on January 29, 1937, and which, he says, entirely misrepresents the relation between the two. He states that the entrance to the Confectionery was not immediately beside the newspaper kiosk shown between that entrance and the entrance to the hotel, but farther to the right, so that in order to reach the Confectionery it was necessary to go through shops at the right which were to be seen from the street. The two enterprises, he says, were conducted entirely separately, although the proprietor of the Confectionery was the wife of the proprietor of the hotel. There was at that time a door connecting the lobby of the hotel with the service-rooms of the Confectionery; but it was chiefly used by the personnel of the hotel, and only rarely by guests. According to the Hotel Inspector, he says, a normal person could never confuse the two concerns, and therefore no "Hotel Bristol" could result from such a confusion. In 1936, he states, the Confectionery was moved one house to the right, making room for three shops. (*Ibid.*, S II, Annex 6.)

This affidavit appears to contradict Jensen's letter, quoted above. If the café in 1932 occupied the place where the two shops are today, then in order for shops to have been situated between the entrance to the hotel and that to the café, as stated by both Jensen and the Fields, they must have occupied a space in front of the café.

§ 69. In our opinion, Trotsky correctly argues (PC 522) that the failure of the Prosecutor to question Holtzman on what passport he used to travel to Copenhagen, and how he obtained it, discredits both the trial and the Prosecutor himself. Holtzman, as a Soviet official, abroad on official business (ZK 98), could hardly have used his own passport without explaining his trip to his superiors. Moreover, if he had done so, then Vyshinsky, who introduced in evidence Olberg's Honduran passport and Hrasche's Czech passport of 1919, would surely have introduced Holtzman's also, to show that he had really made the trip. If Holtzman used a false passport it was the Prosecutor's duty to ascertain under what name he travelled, and what nationality he assumed. For as Trotsky argues,

> Holtzman's testimony could be verified immediately if we knew what passport he used in journeying from Berlin to Copenhagen. Can one imagine a court procedure in which the Prosecutor, under such circumstances, does not question the defendant about his passport? (PC 522.)

We also note the failure of the Prosecutor to remark the striking contradiction between Olberg's testimony and Holtzman's concerning Sedov, a contradiction which could have escaped no Prosecutor in possession of his senses and at all interested in ascertaining the truth. As the record stands, one is almost forced to suspect that Holtzman, testifying the day after Olberg, placed Sedov in Copenhagen with the intent of indicating to the world that his testimony was false. Holtzman did not give Trotsky's address or tell how he and Sedov went there; he said nothing of Trotsky's surroundings or the people with him; and the Prosecutor asked him no questions. Nor did Vyshinsky ask Berman-Yurin and David, who both testified that they went to Copenhagen through Sedov, whether Sedov was there or not. Moreover, Vyshinsky did not ask Smirnov whether Holtzman delivered Trotsky's alleged "verbal instructions," and in contradiction of the record represented Holtzman as having denied that he did so. Thus even the record of the trial itself is far from convincing in this matter of Holtzman's trip to Copenhagen—to which only Holtzman testified.

§ 70. The fact that there was no Hotel Bristol in Copenhagen in 1932 is now a matter of common knowledge. It would obviously, therefore, have been impossible for Holtzman to meet Sedov in the lobby of a Hotel Bristol. Yet Holtzman clearly stated that he arranged to "put up" at the Hotel Bristol and to meet Sedov there; and that they met in the lounge.

The Commission has already stated (§ 9) that having vainly solicited the participation of the Soviet government in its inquiry, it is obliged to regard the records of the trials as embodying the case for the prosecution. The speculations which have been widely circulated in the Comintern press and other publications friendly to the Soviet régime, to the effect that although there was no Hotel Bristol in Copenhagen Holtzman may really have meant the Bristol Café or Confectionery, are mere speculations and must remain so in view of the fact that the Soviet government, by executing Holtzman, has made it forever impossible for him to explain his falsehood. However, since they have been so widely disseminated and, with documents purporting to answer them, have been placed before us, we consider them here, even though they are not, strictly speaking, germane to the case for the prosecution, being in the nature of semi-official apologia.

There are the following possible explanations: (1) Holtzman might have arranged to meet Sedov in some hotel which he mistakenly remembered as the Bristol. (2) He might have arranged to meet him in the Bristol Confectionery. But if the English version of the record is correct, he arranged to "put up" at the Hotel Bristol—and one does not arrange to "put up" in a confectionery. Moreover, he stated that he met Sedov in the lounge. A plan showing the alleged relation in 1932 between the Bristol Confectionery and the Grand Hotel, from *Rundschau* (organ of the C.I.) No. 6, February, 1937, was introduced before the Preliminary Commission (PC Exh. 16, II, Annex 1). In this plan, which *Rundschau* offers in support of the theory that Holtzman referred to the Bristol Confectionery, the Confectionery has no lobby. This places one, as Trotsky argues (PC 520) in the position of having to decide whether the meeting took place "in the vestibule without the 'Bristol' or in the 'Bristol' without the vestibule." (3) There is also the possibility that Holtzman confused the Grand Hotel with the Bristol Café. But such a mistake must have been bewildering to Sedov, who had never been in Copenhagen. Assuming he tried to meet Holtzman at a Hotel Bristol, he must have expressed surprise at finding him—one assumes after some difficulty—either in a "Bristol Confectionery" or a "Grand Hotel." Under such circumstances, as Trotsky correctly argues, Holtzman could have made such an error only *before* the meeting. *After* the meeting, the confusion would have been impressed upon his mind and he could not, in the trial, have spoken of a meeting in the Bristol Hotel. (4) *Rundschau's* theory is that of *identification*. It says that the "Café Bristol" has long been a meeting place for Danish and foreign Trotskyites, and draws from this the conclusion that to Trotskyites the name of the café must have been identical with that of the hotel. In the first place, the testimony we have quoted above indicates that the two establishments were clearly separate. In the second, it seems to us more probable that if the café were as well known to Trotskyists as *Rundschau* claims, they would not identify it with a separate establishment of another name. To illustrate, a great many foreigners are familiar with the famous Café de la Paix in Paris; but we doubt whether many of them know that it occupies the ground floor of the Grand Hotel and that the two even have the same address. One does not easily identify a well-known café with a hotel of a different name even if they happen to be contiguous. Their uses are too different. But the identification of hotel and café in this case is obviously necessary to support the theory that Holtzman met Sedov in the Bristol Café, without at the same time invalidating his testimony that they met in a lounge.

It seems unlikely that Holtzman, as a Soviet official abroad on official business (ZK 98), a Soviet official moreover, whose "Trotskyite allegiance was kept a particularly profound secret" if the Prosecutor is to be believed (ZK 158), would have arranged to meet the son of Leon Trotsky in a notorious Trotskyite rendezvous, especially after having refused to travel with him "for reasons of secrecy." It also seems unlikely that if the Café Bristol had been thus internationally known, it would have taken *Rundschau* five months to learn of its existence and its reputation.

§ 71. Thus the speculative rectification of Holtzman's falsehood is not convincing. But of one thing we may be sure: Holtzman could not have met Sedov either in the

Grand Hotel or the Bristol Confectionery unless Sedov was in Copenhagen. And the evidence proving that Sedov was not in Copenhagen during Trotsky's sojourn is conclusive. First, we have his own statement and that of Trotsky that he was not in Copenhagen. Second, we have the testimony of four witnesses who state that they spoke with him daily in Berlin. Third, there is the testimony of those persons who either spoke with him by telephone from Copenhagen to Berlin or heard others do so. Fourth, there are his note-books, exercise paper and attendance-book from the *Technische Hochschule* showing his attendance during that period. Fifth, there is his passport, which completely corroborates his testimony. Sixth, there are his letters to his mother, clearly showing that he was not with her. Seventh, there is Trotsky's letter of December 3 to Sedov, indicating by its contents that Sedov had not met his parents in Copenhagen. Eighth, there is Natalia Sedov-Trotsky's postcard, stamped Esbjerg, 3/12/32, indicating the same fact, and mentioning Trotsky's letter. Ninth, there are the statements of people who were constantly with Trotsky, who knew Sedov, and who testify that they did not see him in Copenhagen and that he was not there. Tenth, there is the statement of the accused Olberg that he and Sedov had planned to go to Copenhagen together, but "our trip did not materialize." And finally, there is Natalia Sedov-Trotsky's telegram to Herriot, and that of the French Foreign Office to the Consulate in Berlin authorizing a visa for Sedov.

Even if we assume that Trotsky could have managed to see Holtzman without the knowledge of the friends who constantly surrounded him, the fact remains that Holtzman could not have been conducted to Trotsky by Sedov. But Holtzman is very precise in his testimony on this point, and also mentions Sedov's frequent intrusions upon the conversation. He thus relegates the whole interview to the realm of the imaginary.

§ 72. We therefore hold the evidence to prove conclusively: (1) that Sedov was not in Copenhagen at the time of Trotsky's visit to that city; (2) that Holtzman did not meet Sedov and go with him to see Trotsky; (3) that Holtzman did not see Trotsky in Copenhagen.

13

The testimony of Valentine Olberg

§ 73. The fourth basis of the charge against Trotsky and Sedov in the August trial is the testimony of the accused Valentine Olberg, who stated that he was a member of the German
Trotskyite organization from 1927 or 1928; that his contact with
Sedov began in 1930 and was arranged by Anton Grylewicz;
that this contact was established by correspondence with Sedov,
who passed Trotsky's commissions on to Olberg. He testified
that he met Sedov in May, 1931, when Sedov arrived in Berlin,
and saw him frequently thereafter, either in a café on the Nürn-
bergerplatz or in Sedov's apartment. (ZK 86–7.) He is quoted
in the indictment as having testified during the preliminary
hearings that he began active Trotskyite work at the beginning
of 1930, that he was Trotsky's emissary in Germany, that he
maintained connections with the Soviet Union, using addresses
which he had from Sedov. (ZK 23.) Olberg stated that:

> The first time Sedov spoke to me about my journey
> was after Trotsky's message in connection with Trotsky's

being deprived of the citizenship of the U.S.S.R.* In this
message Trotsky developed the idea that it was necessary
to assassinate Stalin. This idea was expressed in the following words: "Stalin must be removed."

Sedov showed me the typewritten text of this message and said: "Well, now you see, it cannot be expressed in a clearer way. It is a diplomatic wording."
Sedov also said that it was necessary to send a number
of people to the Soviet Union; it was then that Sedov
proposed that I go to the U.S.S.R. He knew that I spoke
Russian and he was sure that I could gain a foothold
there. (ZK 87.)

He stated that not having definite citizenship he had difficulty about a passport, but was soon able to procure one in
the name of Freudigmann; that before leaving for Russia he
intended to go to Copenhagen with Sedov to meet Trotsky;
that their trip did not materialize but that Sedov's wife went,
and on her return brought a letter from Trotsky agreeing
to his trip and expressing the hope that he would succeed
in carrying out his mission (ZK 87); that he went to Russia
at the end of March, 1933, lived in Moscow for six weeks
and then went to Stalinabad, where he obtained a position
as teacher of history; but that

> as he had no documents regarding military service,
> he was obliged to return abroad and went to Prague.
> (ZK 88.)

The purpose of his visit, he testified,

> was to prepare and carry out the assassination of Com-
> rade Stalin. (ZK 88.)

---

* See §§ 17, 4a, and 177.

In Prague, Olberg said, he succeeded in procuring a Honduran passport (§ 17, 4a) through the aid of one Tukalevsky, "an agent of the fascist secret police," with whom his younger brother Paul was connected. This arrangement, he said, was sanctioned by Trotsky, and the money for the passport, 13,000 Czech kronen, was provided by Sedov. Before going to Russia again, Olberg testified, he visited Berlin, where, on Tukalevsky's advice, he saw one Slomovitz, whom he had known previously, and who told him that the German Trotskyists had come to an agreement with the fascists. (ZK 90.) (See §§ 194–201.)

In March, 1935, Olberg allegedly went again to Russia, but only on a tourist visa; therefore he had to return to Germany after a few days. Three months later, he testified, Sedov ordered him to make another attempt; and in July, 1935, he went again to Russia, remained in Minsk a short time and then went to Gorky, where

he soon obtained employment in the Gorky Pedagogical Institute, where he remained until his arrest. It was here, in Gorky, that plans were worked out for an attempt on the life of Comrade Stalin. (ZK 90–1.)

Even before his arrival in Gorky, he said, he learned from Sedov that there was an underground Trotskyite movement in the U.S.S.R., whose leaders were Smirnov and Mrachkovsky. He also knew about Bakayev. (ZK 92.)

§ 74. Leon Trotsky testified as follows concerning Olberg:

He wrote me from Berlin—it was in 1929, I believe, or the beginning of 1930—as many other young people from different countries, asking me information about the situation in Germany; and about the situation in Russia he also wrote. I answered the more or less serious letters I received. We had a correspondence over some months. All his letters are in my possession. I have copies of my answers also. During the sojourn of my son in Berlin—Leon Sedov—he came into relations with him and furnished me from time to time quotations from Russian books, Russian books from libraries, and some services. Then he wished to enter into collaboration with me as my Russian secretary. I needed a Russian secretary. I asked my friends in Berlin, Franz Pfemfert, the editor, and his wife, who is my translator in German, Alexandra Ramm, what was their opinion of the young man. They notified him to come and see them, and on that occasion, he made an absolutely negative impression. I have in my possession both letters. They describe him as a very doubtful young man, and maybe an agent of the GPU. (PC 94–5.)

Trotsky further testified that he never saw Olberg, and that all his relations with him were through political and theoretical correspondence (PC 95). Questioned about his communications with the Soviet Union he testified that his method was to write his opinions on post-cards and send them to trusts and known businesses; and that sometimes answers were received; that there were also three or four Russian comrades who helped to write post-cards to friends of the Opposition in Siberia, containing general news; that articles from his *Bulletin* were also copied and sent in this way; that this method was used because post-cards were not so severely controlled as letters by the Soviet censorship; that it sometimes succeeded up to 1931, after which the control became so effective that communication became almost impossible. Trotsky testified that he never said anything to his friends in Russia that he did not say in his *Bulletin;* but that these communications were conspiratorial in the sense that the Soviet censorship did not approve them, and confiscated them. (PC 128–33; 264–6.)

§ 75. Leon Sedov, questioned by the *Commission Rogatoire* concerning the origin and development of his relations with Olberg, said:

> In 1930, Olberg on his own initiative wrote Trotsky a letter, political in nature, from Berlin. As a result, from this date there was an exchange of correspondence between Olberg, Trotsky and myself. . . . Later, but still in 1930, Olberg asked Trotsky to employ him as secretary. Thereupon Trotsky wrote to Mr. and Mrs. Pfemfert asking them to secure information about Olberg. On April 1, 1930, these two comrades replied that taking all information into account, one must place no confidence in Olberg, because he might very well be an agent of the GPU. Naturally Trotsky took good care not to choose Olberg as his secretary. Later, when I arrived in Berlin from Istanbul at the end of February, 1931, I met Olberg, and since I had to make some purchases of books for my father, turned to him for these purchases. (CR 20.)

Sedov denied that his relations with Olberg were ever intimate, although for some time he did not believe the fears of the Pfemferts concerning him were well founded:

> I thought, rather, that we were dealing with a megalomaniac who was slightly psychopathic, and with whom there was no use having very close relations. (CR 21.)

He stated that he called on Olberg only for small so-called technical services, such as the purchase of books or the reading of proofs; that he never received him at his home, and was even careful not to give him his address; that the Pfemferts were his intermediaries in dealing with Olberg, and that Olberg wrote to him in their care. He pointed out that Olberg evidently did not know his wife's name, having mentioned her in the trial as Suzanna, whereas her name is Jeanne. He stated that since his wife did not return from Copenhagen direct to Berlin, but instead went to Paris, Olberg's statement that on her return she brought a letter from Trotsky was obviously a lie; that if Trotsky had wished to send Sedov a letter to Berlin, he would have given it to two friends who were going to Berlin directly; and that even if Trotsky had given such a letter to his wife, he, Sedov, would have received it in Paris and thus would have taken it to Berlin himself, "supposing always that such a letter ever existed." (CR 21–3.)

On Olberg's testimony that after Trotsky's "message" in connection with his being deprived of Soviet citizenship Sedov had shown him a stenogram of this "message," Sedov commented that it was extremely unlikely that he would have done so since this message, which was nothing else than Trotsky's protest addressed to the Central Executive Committee of the Soviet Union, had been published in the *Bulletin*, No. 27, March, 1932.

On the question of Olberg's relation to the Left Opposition, Sedov stated that

. . . Olberg, after having been refused admission into our movement, had joined a local group of the Wedding quarter in Berlin, composed—if I am not mistaken—of about fifty members, and known as the Landau group. In the autumn of 1930 this group was admitted collectively into our movement. Thus, as from this date, Olberg, although not admitted individually, belonged to our tendency. I hasten to add, however, that in April/May, 1931, the entire Landau group was expelled, and that when in February, 1932, Olberg applied personally for admission into our tendency, his application was turned down. (CR21.)

Sedov testified that after a police raid on his home, the exact
date of which he did not remember, he was obliged to go to
the office of the Chief of Police and undergo a long examination, in the course of which he was struck with the fact
that he was asked again and again about his relations with
Olberg; and that this fact contributed to his decision, towards
the middle of 1932, to have nothing more to do with Olberg.
He denied that he had had anything to do with the purchase
of Olberg's Honduran passport. (CR 21.) He called attention
to the implausibility of Olberg's statement about Smirnov,
Mrachkovsky and Bakayev (§ 73), saying that at that time
(July, 1935) he, Sedov, could not have helped knowing that
Smirnov had been in jail and Mrachkovsky in exile since
January, 1933, and that Bakayev had been arrested in De-
cember, 1934. (CR 24.)

§ 76. Eugene Bauer (identified § 63) testified that Olberg

adhered to our movement in 1930, when the movement
was organized in Germany.* At that time, like most of
our adherents, Olberg was a member of the German
Communist Party. In the beginning of 1931, the group to
which Olberg belonged left our movement, and therefore
Olberg was no longer with us after that period. At the
end of 1932 he asked to come back to us, and I remember perfectly having talked with him and having had
his request rejected. After that I heard nothing more of
him until the time of the Moscow trial. As I remained
in Berlin until July, 1933, I am in a position to exclude

---

* In 1927, the left wing opposition in the Communist Party of Germany
was led by Ruth Fischer and A. Maslow and though supporting the Opposition Bloc in the Communist Party of the Soviet Union adhered in
actuality to the Zinovievist section of that bloc. The Trotskyist Opposition was organized at a conference in Berlin in 1930 as a result of the
unification of the Minority Group of the Lenin League *(Leninbund)*
and the so-called "Wedding Opposition."

the possibility of Olberg's having had up to that time any connection with our movement, and I believe I can also exclude the possibility of Sedov's having had contact with him, because at the time of leaving Berlin, Sedov did not fail to indicate to me the persons, non-members of our movement, with whom he might have been in touch, and Olberg was not among them. If Olberg had been, I believe Sedov would have told me so. (CR 45.)

The witness declared that Sedov had not intervened with him to get Olberg's application for re-admission to the party accepted, as he believed Sedov would have done had he had relations with Olberg, since he had done so with regard to other comrades. He denied that there had ever been the slightest connection between the German Opposition and the Gestapo. (CR 45–6.)

§ 77. Alexandra Pfemfert (identified § 64) testified that Trotsky, in view of many services which she and her husband had rendered him, naturally turned to them for all possible information concerning a certain Olberg who had applied for the position of his secretary; that she had never seen Olberg up to that time but when she met him her impression of him was most unfavorable; that he put too many questions, lacked tact, and appeared to have a most disagreeable, hysterical temperament (CR 47–8); that

either because Olberg wrote to Sedov on postal cards, or because Sedov frequently asked me to read him Olberg's letters over the telephone, which I could read because they were written in Russian, it was possible for me to follow closely the correspondence between Sedov and Olberg, and I remember perfectly that many times Olberg asked Sedov to fix meeting places with him, owing to the fact that on Sedov's explicit demand we had never given Olberg Sedov's address; and it even happened that sometimes, when Sedov authorized me to do so, I informed Olberg by telephone at what time he could speak to Sedov by telephone at our house. That is why I do not remember his ever having tried to meet Sedov at our house; and certainly he must have understood that we wished to keep him at a distance. As for the contents of the letters and cards Olberg sent Sedov, I remember that it was a question of little matters such as the correction of proofs, etc. (CR 49.)

§ 78. Franz Pfemfert (identified § 65) stated that when Trotsky was exiled to Turkey he, Pfemfert, had placed his services, for purposes of information, etc., and his extensive archives at Trotsky's disposal; that Trotsky often turned to him for information about persons and events, and did so in the case of Olberg. Pfemfert corroborated his wife's testimony to their first meeting with Olberg, and added:

At that time, Olberg presented himself at our house, and I saw him for the first time. He told me that although he was employed in the *Inprecorr** office, he sympathized with Trotsky and would like to become his secretary. Naturally, he put me a pile of questions, especially on the subject of the treatment he would receive. . . . I then wrote Trotsky that even if Olberg was not an agent of the GPU he was not the man he needed, that I begged him not to allow him to cross the threshold of his house. My wife also wrote Trotsky to the same effect. . . . (CR 50–51.)

§ 79. The most important documentary evidence in our possession concerning the defendant Olberg is as follows:
(1) Ten holograph letters in Russian from Olberg to Trots-

---

* *International Press Correspondence.* Official publication of the C.I.

ky, dated January 10, 1930, to March 4, 1931, and six typewritten answers (copies) in Russian from Trotsky to Olberg,
dated January 30, 1930, to April 27, 1930 (PC Exh. 8, I/1–16).
Olberg's first letter begins:

> The impossibility of elucidating the views of the Op-
> position on certain important problems impels me to
> turn to you with these lines . . .

and goes on to weigh certain Oppositionist views as he un-
derstands them against the line of the official Communist
Party, which he neither accepts nor rejects entirely. He ends,
"With your aid I hope to elucidate the actual state of affairs."
(No. 1.) Trotsky answers in a letter which begins:

> In your letter you pose a number of questions of prin-
> ciple which should be answered with whole treatises. But
> the point is that the Opposition has already written not
> a little on these questions in the past. I am quite unin-
> formed as to what you have read of all that. It would be
> a good thing if you were to write me at least a little bit
> about yourself: Have you been long in the movement,
> where have you been in the last few years, what Oppo-
> sitional literature have you read?

This letter ends:

> Do you read the Russian *Bulletin of the Opposition*?
> There the answer is given to a number of the questions
> you have posed. In any case, for the sake of successful
> continuance of our correspondence I shall await from
> you information of rather autobiographical character.
> (No. 2.)

Olberg answers on January 28:

... I am a Latvian. Five years in the movement. Of these I spent the first three years in Latvia. Even then I could not accept Stalin's theory of the possibility of Socialism's victory in one country. Stalin's Chinese policy seemed to me even then profoundly erroneous. I did not believe in the existence of "Trotskyism." . . . In the summer of 1927 I came to Berlin and began to seek the literature of the Opposition and about the Opposition. Reading *Pravda* convinced me of the Opposition's correctness. I went to Maslow [see § 76 n.]. . . . The man who was then leader of the German Opposition pushed me away from it; . . .

I read what the German Opposition has published. (In its German platform there is not a little which is wrong.) I followed the movement from the sidelines.

I have obtained the *Bulletin* from comrades and am reading it. In so far as I am in agreement with the Opposition on fundamental questions I expect to work with it. . . .

N.B. I forgot to say about myself that the last two years I have engaged in journalism. I wrote, by the way, in the *Inprecorr.* (No. 3.)

The correspondence continues with discussion of political questions, chiefly having to do with the internal situation in the German Opposition; of problems connected with the distribution of Opposition literature; of Olberg's services to the Left Opposition. Trotsky suggests that Olberg's knowledge of Russian would be very useful to the Oppositionists in Berlin (No. 4). Olberg, in discussing the disagreements among the Oppositionist factions in Berlin, says: "Naturally, being a new man, I am not told everything . . ." (No. 7). He suggests that it might be feasible for one of the Germans to make a short trip to the Soviet Union in order to establish contacts (No. 9). Trotsky answers that this idea is quite correct, but

. . . for such an enterprise a comrade is needed with experience, careful, resourceful. It is not so simple to find the suitable person . . . meanwhile it is necessary to use all kinds of amateur means for the transmission of data and documents. If the "open letter"* reaches the right person in one copy, it will make its own way from there on. (No. 10.)

Olberg's letter of May 2, 1930 (No. 13) mentions in a post-script Trotsky's last letter to Olberg, dated April 27, 1930 (No. 12). Thereafter he makes no mention of letters received from Trotsky. His letters up to that date, after the first, invariably acknowledge letters from Trotsky.

(2) Sixteen holograph letters in Russian from Olberg to Leon Sedov, dated March 1, 1930, to February 23, 1931, and one copy of a typewritten letter in Russian from Sedov to Olberg, dated July 11, 1930. (PC Exh. 8, II/1–16.) These letters deal almost exclusively with such matters as the publication and distribution of Opposition literature, Olberg's services in this work, etc. Olberg suggests that a trip to the Soviet Union by one of the Germans or Frenchmen is essential to the distribution of the *Bulletin* in Russia (No. 2). He sends quotations from Kalinin, Stalin, Bukharin (No. 5). He expresses his willingness to write to the exiled comrades (Nos. 4, 6) (See § 74), informs Sedov that he has found it impossible to copy the whole of Trotsky's Open Letter (see 1, n.) on a postcard, and that his wife has copied it on two postcards which are being mailed at different times (No. 4). Sedov's letter to Olberg expresses his concern because he is not receiving mail, and asks him to check up on the Berlin addresses. He also reminds him of some quotations Olberg

---

* Open Letter to the Communist Party of the Soviet Union. *Bulletin of the Opposition*, No. 10, April, 1930; *The Militant* (New York), May 24, June 7 and 14, 1930. (See § 206.)

has promised to send him (No. 10).

(3) Documents concerning Olberg's personal characteristics, his Honduran passport, and his past:

(a) A letter in German from Franz Pfemfert to Leon Trotsky, dated April 1, 1930. Pfemfert says:

> ... Olberg made the most unfavorable impression it
> is possible to conceive. ... I had scarcely taken a seat in
> my workroom ... when he asked a few such tactlessly
> formulated questions that I had to answer with a few
> counter-questions: When did you come to Germany?
> (Answer: I have been living here for a long time.) What
> is your occupation? (Answer: I worked until January with
> the editorial staff of the *Inprecorr*.) I really already had
> enough. I was painfully impressed by the fact that a man
> who had just left the service (wholesale discharges for the
> purpose of rationalization) and therefore until now had
> been at least passively ... a Stalinist, was changing so
> quickly, and trying with all signs of a sensation-hungry
> journalist to explore confidential matters about T. and
> the Opposition in general.
>
> ... O. has no business there, because within twenty-
> four hours he would prove himself an unbearable burden
> to you; certainly later too. Because he would work up his
> visit into "volumes," if indeed he didn't work it up into
> reports to the GPU. (PC Exh. 8, III/1.)

(b) Alexandra Pfemfert (§ 77) in a holograph letter in Russian to Trotsky, dated April 2, 1930, says:

> ... But, Lev Davidovich, when we heard talk to the
> effect that Olberg should go to see you, we were sim-
> ply horrified. He is an intolerable fellow, tactless, dis-
> orderly, God forbid that you should have him in your
> house ... he will take to instructing not only you but

the Lord God himself, if he had a chance to meet Him.
. . . When he talks with a person he almost sits on his
nose, grasps his arms . . . in a word the most unsuitable
aid. . . . (*Ibid.*, III/2.)

(c) A letter from Franz Pfemfert to Trotsky, dated 5/4/30,
corroborates Sedov and Bauer on Olberg's connection with
the Opposition:

> . . . Concerning the Olberg episode. His shift to the
> Opposition is . . . as follows: He bought Opposition pam-
> phlets. There he found Grylewicz's address. The latter
> referred him to Wedding (where he appeared as already
> "legitimized"). Then to K.L. [Landau; see § 75], and thus
> he was able in a few days to appear suddenly at the Con-
> ference—as a "delegate" with a "recommendation from
> Prinkipo." This is something fearful. I asked L. [Landau]
> yesterday how he came to know O. and what ground he
> had for trusting him. Answer: I know nothing more about
> him than letter [*sic*] from Prink. and Wedding.
>
> Tomorrow he, O., can already present himself with
> twenty names and the day after gain access to the most
> internal things. (*Ibid.*, III/3.)

(d) A holograph answer to a questionnaire, and a supplement
thereto, written by Olberg's mother (name in our possession). The authenticity of these documents is attested in a
covering statement by Dr. Salomon Schwartz of Vanves,
France, which says:

> Through the Parisian co-workers of the New York
> Commission of Inquiry, I have placed before the Com-
> mission some letters from Mrs. B——, the former Mrs.
> Olberg, mother of Valentine and Paul Olberg. Mrs. Olberg
> wrote these letters in answer to my inquiries (through

her former husband, Paul Olberg, now living in Stockholm). For the authenticity of these letters I vouch in
every way. (*Ibid.*, S III/6, c.)

Olberg's mother states that her son first went to Russia in
1933, because he was about to be expelled from Germany as
an undesirable alien; that he used the passport of a friend
(name in the document), since he had only a Nansen passport with which he could go nowhere; that he received a Soviet visa through the Berlin Intourist; and that the money
for this visa was paid by a relative (name in the document)
to whom she bound herself to return it; that Olberg got a
position in Stalinabad Center, Asia, as a teacher of history
in the higher schools; that the bad climate, his wife's illness,
and his wish to legalize his status by obtaining a passport
in his own name, made him decide to leave Russia; that in
July, 1933, Olberg and his wife, on their way out of Russia,
stopped to see her in Kemern, Lithuania, where at a family
conference it was decided he should go to Prague and his
wife to her relatives, that in Prague Olberg should live with
his brother Paul, a student, for reasons of economy, and try
to get Soviet citizenship; that his application for Soviet citizenship was refused; that a lawyer in Prague whose name
she does not remember, but it was not Benda, as alleged in
the trial, undertook to get him Honduran citizenship for
which he did not have enough money to pay, and therefore
the same relative came to his assistance once more; that after difficulties about a Russian visa Olberg at last received
it, through the intercession of this relative with the Berlin
Intourist,

with pay for his expenses and a stay of two weeks in
Moscow. And so, for a second time Valentine Olberg
journeyed to the U.S.S.R. again through Intourist on a
visa paid for by [a relative].

She says that during this second trip he obtained a position in Gorky, and that she is sure he made no third trip to Russia, since she always heard from him weekly and had frequent letters from him and his wife from Gorky until January, 1936, after which date her letters to him were returned and she knew nothing more about him until she learned from the newspapers about the trial of August, 1936. She is sure that if he had left Russia after his second trip to that country she would have received letters from him from Europe or their correspondence would have been interrupted. (*Ibid.*, III/6, a, b.)

(4) The deposition of Jeanne Martin des Pallières corroborates her husband's testimony concerning the nature of his relations with Olberg. We have already cited (§ 68, 9, d, e) her testimony and that of Lucienne Tedeschi that she went from Copenhagen to Paris by way of Hamburg. Jeanne des Pallières states that she remained in Paris for several days after her husband had returned to Berlin. (PC Exh. 16, I/18.)

§ 80. There is agreement between the evidence in our possession and Olberg's testimony in the Moscow trial on the following points:

(1) Olberg corresponded with Sedov and met him personally after Sedov's arrival in Berlin in 1931.

(2) Olberg maintained connections with the Soviet Union in the sense that he undertook to write to exiled Oppositionists. (See § 79, 2.)

(3) Olberg went to Russia for the first time in 1933, on a passport which was not his own. He got a position teaching history in Stalinabad. He remained only a short time.

(4) Olberg went to Russia a second time on a Honduran passport.

(5) Olberg obtained employment in Gorky.

(6) Sedov did not go to Copenhagen at the time of Trotsky's visit to that city in 1932.

§ 81. On all other points there is complete disagreement.

The evidence introduced before this Commission shows that Olberg's contact with Trotsky and Sedov was not arranged by Anton Grylewicz, but initiated by Olberg himself in a letter to Trotsky. His own letters to Trotsky and Sedov indicate no intimate connection with either. His letters to Trotsky show that his testimony that he had been a member of the Berlin Trotskyist organization from 1927 or 1928 was completely false; on the other hand, the evidence shows that although he had been in Berlin "a long time" he was unknown at the beginning of 1930 not only to Trotsky himself but to the Trotskyists in Berlin. It shows that he never joined the Opposition as an individual and was officially connected with it only as a member of a group which was admitted collectively and then expelled. Sedov says he joined in the autumn of 1930. Pfemfert's letter (§ 79, 3, c) shows that at least as early as April, 1930, he appeared at a conference as a "delegate," and that Pfemfert feared he would soon gain full access to Opposition affairs. Sedov and Bauer agree concerning his expulsion from the Opposition with the Landau group, and his failure to obtain readmission as an individual. Olberg and his mother give quite different reasons for his first journey to Russia, and for his return; and Olberg's mother corroborates Sedov's testimony that Sedov had nothing whatever to do with procuring or paying for Olberg's Honduran passport. His mother places Olberg's employment in Gorky at the time of his second trip to Russia and discounts the possibility of a third trip. Bauer's testimony that Sedov did not intercede for Olberg to get him readmitted to the Opposition, and did not, upon leaving Berlin,* mention Olberg as one of the people with whom he had been in contact appears to corroborate Sedov's own testimony that he broke off relations with Olberg about the middle of 1932.

---

* Sedov's passport shows that the visa on which he entered France as a resident was dated March 23, 1933.

§ 82. Olberg's confession in the August trial was uncorroborated by any other evidence than the passport which proved that he entered the Soviet Union as a Honduran citizen. It is impugned in its vital points by his own letters, by the testimony of Trotsky and Sedov corroborated by the Pfemferts, Bauer, and Olberg's mother, and by other evidence cited above.

That Olberg was not "Trotsky's emissary in Germany" is evident from his own letters, and from the testimony of Sedov, the Pfemferts, and Bauer. His statement that Grylewicz arranged his contact with Trotsky and Sedov appears to have been invented in order to lend credibility to this alleged confidential relationship. Had he told the truth, which was that he approached Trotsky in January, 1930, as a stranger to both Trotsky and the Opposition, the claim of a confidential relation dating from that time would have appeared doubtful to say the least. But when he said that the contact was arranged by Grylewicz, he gave an appearance of truth to his testimony that he had belonged to the German Opposition from 1927 or 1928, and created the impression that he possessed the confidence of its organizational leader.

In his testimony Olberg said that he met Sedov in May, 1931. Since Sedov arrived in Berlin in February of that year, the date of their meeting, if Olberg correctly stated it, would appear to indicate that their correspondence had established no very close relationship between them. We note also that Olberg placed the securing of his first passport (in the name of Freudigmann) before Trotsky's trip to Copenhagen (November, 1932), whereas he gave the date of his departure for Russia as "the end of March, 1933." If this sequence is correct, it indicates no very great promptness on his part in attempting to carry out the alleged instructions to prepare an attempt on Stalin's life. We find his mother's explanation of his removal to Russia more credible than Olberg's; more especially since the record of the trial corroborates her testimony that he had no German citizenship. It is a matter of common knowledge that Communists were obliged to flee Germany after Hitler came to power; certainly a Communist without German citizenship would have found it difficult to remain.

While we are on this question of Olberg's passport, we may note that according to his mother,

> On my son's first journey to the U.S.S.R. he utilized Fr.'s passport only to pass the frontiers. During his further stay in the U.S.S.R. he lived under his own name, V.O. All the documents testifying to his irreplaceable need in the service were issued to him in his own name, V.O. (PC Exh. 8, S III/6, b.)

The documents to which she refers were testimonials which he obtained before his first return from Russia

> from the respective institutions of the indispensable nature of his work in the People's Commissariat of Education. . . . (*Ibid.*, S III/6, a.)

It appears from this that the Soviet authorities were aware during Olberg's first stay in Russia that he was there on a false passport; yet they allowed him to hold a position and even gave him testimonials, in his own name, to the value of his work. This indicates an inexplicable degree of lenience; it also indicates that not all the real facts about the Russian phase of Olberg's career were brought out in the trial, although it is difficult to believe that if the preliminary investigation was at all serious they were unknown to the Prosecutor.

The record states that on his second trip to Russia Olberg could not stay long because he had only a tourist visa. Yet the following colloquy indicates that his third trip, if he made one, was also made on a tourist visa:

VYSHINSKY: Did you obtain the Honduras passport after your second return?

OLBERG: The second time also I came on the Honduras passport.

VYSHINSKY: Did you come on a tourist visa?

OLBERG: Yes, but I had the Honduras passport.

VYSHINSKY: How were you able to get an extension of that passport the second time?

OLBERG: I managed that . . . (ZK 91.)

Since Olberg alleged that he made three trips to the Soviet Union, obviously his *third* trip would be his *second* return, if the word return here means his return to the U.S.S.R. If it refers to his second return to Germany, as it appears to, since he obviously did not procure the passport after his second and last return to Russia, then the period indicated by the Prosecutor must have been the period after Olberg's *first* trip to Russia on the Honduran passport. Olberg's use of the word "also" indicates that he refers to his second trip to Russia as a Honduran citizen, and so does Vyshinsky's question about how he got the passport extended a second time. The further exchange of question and answer clearly indicates that the second time he used the Honduran passport he had only a tourist visa. If Olberg's second trip was fruitless because he had only a tourist visa and had to return to Germany after a few days, then it is peculiar that the Prosecutor did not ask him how he arranged to remain in Russia after a third trip under precisely the same conditions.

As regards the letter to Sedov from Trotsky which, according to Olberg, Sedov's wife brought with her on her return from Copenhagen, one might assume that because of its alleged conspiratorial nature Trotsky entrusted it to her rather than to comrades returning direct to Berlin— although such caution would not have been at all in keeping with the general recklessness of Leon Trotsky's conduct as represented by those of the accused who allegedly saw him or received communications from him. However, in that case she would surely have turned it over to her husband in Paris, and he would himself have brought it to Berlin. In fact, the evidence shows that Trotsky did send his son a letter by one of the two German comrades who were returning to Berlin, precisely as Sedov argued he would have done. The letter is the one in our possession, which was quoted in the preceding chapter (§ 68, 4). In this letter Trotsky states that he is writing at 7 A.M. In her postcard to her son, post-marked with the same date, Natalia Sedov-Trotsky says:

> This morning papa sent you a little letter, written in haste, through Erwin. (§ 68, 5.)

Erwin is the first name of "Eugene Bauer" (§ 68, 5, n.). Bauer and other witnesses state that he accompanied Trotsky to Esbjerg, and Bauer states that he left Esbjerg on December 3, 1932, the date of Trotsky's letter and his wife's post-card. It is remarkable that Leon Sedov, who told the *Commission Rogatoire* about this letter from his father, stating that he had already transmitted it to the Commission (CR 12–13) failed to mention, when testifying later about Olberg, a fact so favorable to his own case as the transmission of this letter from Trotsky through Eugene Bauer.

The passage in Trotsky's Open Letter of 1932 in which, according to Olberg, Trotsky developed the idea that it was necessary to assassinate Stalin will be discussed in Chapter XXII of this report. Olberg's testimony on the alleged connection of the Trotskyists with the Gestapo will be discussed in Chapter XXIV. It suffices to state here that Olberg falsified the Open Letter, and that his testimony concerning the Gestapo is controverted by the evidence in our possession.

§ 83. Summing up, the evidence in our possession shows that Olberg lied on the following points: 1) his connection with the Left Opposition; 2) the way in which he established contact with Sedov and Trotsky; 3) the reason for his first return from Russia; 4) the circumstances under which he obtained his Honduran passport; 5) the meaning of Trotsky's Open Letter; 6) the alleged connection of the Trotskyists with the Gestapo.

These lies, on points vital to his testimony, sufficiently indicate that Olberg was anything but a credible witness. In the face of so much falsehood, it would put an extreme tax upon credulity to believe that he was in Russia as an emissary of Trotsky and Sedov for any purpose whatever. One might, of course, assume that he concealed his terrorist instructions from his mother, as indeed he probably would have done had he had such instructions. But his own discredited testimony and all the other evidence before us points to the opposite conclusion. His correspondence with Trotsky not only proves that Olberg lied about his connection with the Left Opposition; it also proves that Trotsky stopped writing to Olberg shortly after receiving adverse reports about him from the Pfemferts (§ 79, 1). Trotsky's letters to Olberg furnish no basis for an assumption that he would have engaged Olberg for confidential missions of any kind; nor is it reasonable to assume that he would have entrusted such missions to a man about whom he had received such emphatically unfavorable reports as are contained in the letters of the Pfemferts. It is also unreasonable to assume that Sedov would have entrusted any confidential mission to Olberg, in view of these reports and of the nature of his own relations with Olberg as indicated in Olberg's letters to him and described by himself, his wife and the Pfemferts. Much less, therefore, would it be reasonable to assume that either Trotsky or Sedov would have employed Olberg as agent in a terrorist conspiracy, assuming they had had any occasion to use such agents.

§ 84. We find, therefore, that Olberg's confession is worthless as proof of the charges against Leon Trotsky and Leon Sedov in the August trial. On the basis of this conclusion, and of the evidence cited above concerning Olberg's character, his relations with the Opposition, and in particular with Trotsky and Sedov, we find that Olberg never went to Russia with terrorist instructions from Trotsky and Sedov.

14

The testimony of K.B. Berman-Yurin and Fritz David

§ 85. The fifth and sixth bases of the charge against Trotsky and Sedov in the August trial are the confessions of K.B. Berman-Yurin and Fritz David (I.I. Kruglyansky). These two accused were closely connected in the trial, and no connection was established between them and the other accused. They were implicated in alleged terrorist acts only through their confessions that they went to Russia in pursuance of terrorist instructions from Trotsky himself. Therefore we consider them together.

§ 86. Berman-Yurin testified that he was "particularly trusted" by Trotsky (ZK 26); that he met Trotsky through Sedov, to whom Anton Grylewicz had introduced him in Berlin. Sedov, he said,

> systematically tried to persuade me, and convinced me, that the fight against the Communist Party was a fight against Stalin. (ZK 93.)

159

At the end of 1931, he testified, Sedov asked him whether he knew a trusted and reliable German who could be sent to Moscow on an important mission. He named Alfred Kundt, a "staunch Trotskyite." Kundt agreed to undertake the mission, and received two documents (whether from Sedov or Berman-Yurin is not clear) with instructions to establish personal contact with Smirnov in Moscow and hand them to him. One document, Berman-Yurin said, concerned Trotsky's latest position on questions referring to the international situation, mainly Germany. The second, which he read very carefully, stated that

> it was necessary to prepare to adopt resolute and extreme means of struggle, and that . . . resolute people sharing Trotsky's position had to be selected. Particular attention . . . was to be paid to the Trotskyites who were members of the C.P.S.U., but who were not compromised as Trotskyites in the ranks of the Party. The organization was to be built up on the principles of strictest secrecy, in small groups, not connected with each other, so that the discovery of one group might not lead to the discovery of the whole organization. (ZK 93–94.)

Kundt, he said, left for Moscow in January–February, 1932.

> A few days later it became known that he had been at the secret address, had handed over the documents, had received a reply as had been arranged, but had not met Smirnov as the latter was not in Moscow. (ZK 94.)

In November, 1932, Berman-Yurin said, Sedov for the first time spoke to him openly

> about the necessity of preparing to assassinate the leaders of the C.P.S.U. Evidently, Sedov noticed that I was

wavering and he said that Trotsky would be in Copenhagen shortly and asked me whether I would not like to go there and meet Trotsky. I, of course, expressed my agreement. (ZK 94.)

According to Berman-Yurin, he arrived in Copenhagen early in the morning, between the 25th and 28th of November, was

met at the station by Grylewicz and we went to see Trotsky. Grylewicz introduced me to Trotsky and left; I remained in the room alone with Trotsky. (ZK 94.)

Trotsky, he said, questioned him about his work in the past, and asked him why he had gone over to the position of Trotskyism, a question which he answered in great detail. Then Trotsky informed him that Stalin must be physically destroyed, and that people were needed who would agree to sacrifice themselves to this "historic task." This ended the first conversation. Trotsky left to go somewhere and Berman-Yurin waited in the apartment for his return. That evening they continued the conversation. He asked Trotsky how individual terrorism could be reconciled with Marxism, and Trotsky answered that problems could not be treated in a dogmatic way; that a situation had arisen in the Soviet Union which Marx could not have foreseen; and that in addition to Stalin, Kaganovich and Voroshilov must be assassinated. He also said that a defeatist attitude must be adopted in case of "intervention against the Soviet Union"; that the Trotskyites must join the army but would not defend the Soviet Union. During this conversation, he said, Trotsky nervously paced up and down the room.

After I had given my consent he said that I must get ready to go to Moscow, and as I would have contact with the Comintern I was to prepare the terroristic act taking advantage of this contact. . . . that the terroristic act should, if possible, be timed to take place at a plenum or at the congress of the Comintern, so that the shot at Stalin would ring out in a large assembly. This would have a tremendous repercussion far beyond the borders of the Soviet Union and would give rise to a mass movement all over the world. This would be an historical political event of world significance. Trotsky said that I should not have contact with any Trotskyites in Moscow, and that I should carry on the work independently. I replied that I did not know anybody in Moscow and it was difficult for me to see how I should act under these circumstances. I said that I had an acquaintance named Fritz David, and asked whether I might not get in touch with him. Trotsky replied that he would instruct Sedov to clear up this matter . . . (ZK 95–6.)

Berman-Yurin said that he went to Moscow in March, 1933, with instructions from Sedov to look up Fritz David; that he did so, and that they prepared the terroristic act together. They planned at first to carry it out at the Thirteenth Plenum of the Executive Committee of the Communist International, for which David was to procure Berman-Yurin a ticket of admission. David failed to get the ticket; whereupon they decided to postpone the act until the Congress of the Comintern.

The Congress was to have convened in September, 1934. I gave Fritz David a Browning pistol and bullets to hide. . . . (ZK 96.)

Once more David failed to get a ticket for Berman-Yurin. It was decided that he himself should do the shooting. But he was unable to do so because he was sitting in a box with many people. In December David allegedly informed Ber-man-Yurin that an emissary of Sedov had been to see him and demanded to know why the act had not been performed. Again in May, 1936, Berman-Yurin said, David informed him that an emissary of Sedov, a German, had visited him and accused them of being inactive, irresolute and cowardly, and had demanded that they take advantage of any oppor-tunity that might arise to assassinate Stalin. At the end of May Berman-Yurin was arrested and his terrorist activities were stopped. (ZK 96–7.)

§ 87. Fritz David testified that he established contact with Sedov in August, 1932; that in one of their conversations Sedov informed him that Trotsky "was to come to Europe and would like to see me"; that David travelled on a false passport (ZK 112). He did not tell how he learned Trotsky's address in Copenhagen or the date on which he arrived there. He described his alleged conversation with Trotsky in terms practically identical with those used by Berman-Yurin, except that

> Trotsky instructed me to behave in the U.S.S.R. in such a way as not to show any deviations from the gen-eral line of the Party, and when writing for the press to adhere strictly to the Party line, and under no circum-stances to reveal the threads after the terroristic act was committed. (ZK 113–14.)

David stated that he arrived in the Soviet Union in March, 1933, and met Berman-Yurin, who had sought him out on Sedov's instructions. He corroborated Ber-man-Yurin's testimony about their terrorist plans and their failures—except that the reason he gave for the first failure was that Stalin did not attend the Plenum—and about the two messengers who sought him out to accuse them of insufficient activity and order them to speed up their terroristic act. The Prosecutor, in summing up David's activity, said:

> ... you made preparations for an attempt on the life of Comrade Stalin, timing it for the Seventh Congress in 1935. (ZK 115.)

§ 88. Leon Trotsky testified that he had never heard the names of K.B. Berman-Yurin and Fritz David (I.I. Kruglyansky) before he saw them in the news-reports of the trial (PC 94); and that he did not see them during his stay in Copenhagen (PC 138).

§ 89. Leon Sedov testified that he never met Berman-Yurin and up to the time of the trial never knew he existed; and that all Berman-Yurin had said about meetings between them was completely false. After the trial he learned that Berman-Yurin, known in Berlin as Stauer, had belonged to the official Communist Party (CR 17). He said he had read articles by Fritz David in *Izvestia*, but denied that he had ever known David and declared that David's testimony about their alleged meetings was false (CR 18). He showed to the *Commission Rogatoire* the issue for October 11, 1936, of the *Deutsche Volkzeitung*, official Communist organ published in Prague, in which appeared on page 4 a communiqué announcing the expulsion from the Communist Party of Germany of a number of members for alleged relations with Trotskyists-Zinovievists. The first name on the list was that of Fritz David (Kruglyansky) of Berlin. The third name was that of Hans Stauer (Berman-Yurin) of Berlin. (CR 20.)

§ 90. Eugene Bauer testified that he never knew Berman-Yurin and never heard of him until after the trial, when he learned that Berman-Yurin belonged to the illegal Communist apparatus of Berlin, and had been employed at the Soviet Commercial delegation; that if Berman-Yurin had belonged to the Trotskyist movement he believed that he, Bauer, would

have known of it. He stated that he had known Fritz David
as a writer, but not personally; that it was common knowledge that David was an editor of the *Rote Fahne**

> and a bitter adversary of our movement in the sight and
> knowledge of everyone. (CR 43–4.)

§ 91. We have already quoted (§ 61) the testimony of
Trotsky's secretary, Jan Frankel, concerning the conditions
under which Trotsky lived in Copenhagen, the strict guard
which was organized by his friends for his protection, and
the impossibility of any visitor getting to see Trotsky without the knowledge of himself and Raymond Molinier, who
arranged all visits, and of the members of the guard. Mr.
Frankel stated that no one by the name of Berman-Yurin
or Fritz David had asked to see Trotsky during his visit to
Copenhagen, and that he, Frankel, had seen no such people.
(PC 165–6.)

§ 92. Both Esther and B.J. Field (identified § 66) denied
that anyone by the name of Berman-Yurin or Fritz David
visited Trotsky in Copenhagen. (NY 12, 56.)

§ 93. We have quoted above (§ 68, 9) from the documents
in our possession which bear on Trotsky's conditions of life
in Copenhagen, his activities and the visits he received. We
therefore quote here only a few further passages concerning these two defendants:

(a) Anton Grylewicz (identified § 68, 8), in an affidavit
(Prague) testifies that

> A day or two before Trotsky's lecture, my wife noti-
> fied me from Berlin that Sch———, an engineer employed
> by a large Berlin concern, was coming; and I met him

---

* Official organ of the Central Committee of the Communist Party of
Germany, formerly published daily in Berlin.

at the station. I would especially like to emphasize the fact that Sch—— first went to my hotel with me. The claim made by Berman-Yurin, whom I do not know, that I met him at the station, is a complete invention. (PC Exh. 16, I/4.)

The engineer Sch——, he says, was not brought into contact with Trotsky until a day or two after his arrival. At the present time Sch—— is under arrest in Austria.

(b) Pierre Naville (identified § 68, 9, b) states:

> If a Holtzman or a Berman-Yurin had been present at any time, I would have known or suspected it. (*Ibid.*, I/2.)

(c) Erich Kohn, former leader of the Hamburg Left Opposition, states in an affidavit (Oslo) that the development of his views has separated him widely from Trotskyism and the Trotskyist organization. He says that he was in Copenhagen from November 25 to December 4, 1932, and until Trotsky's departure was with him daily either in the same room or near by. He says:

> Since during this time I came in contact with all Trotsky's real visitors, I know that neither Holtzman, Berman-Yurin, nor Fritz David was among them. (*Ibid.*, I/6.)

§ 94. There is nothing in the record of the trial to show why either Trotsky or Sedov should have "particularly trusted" either Berman-Yurin or David. The record itself indicates that they were members of the official Communist Party (ZK 95, 113). Nothing appears in the record which explains why Sedov, if he wanted a reliable man to send to Russia on a terrorist mission, would have addressed himself to a Stalinist whom he had met only a short time before rather than to a member of his own group such as Anton Grylewicz, its organizational leader, who had allegedly originally introduced him to Berman-Yurin (ZK 93), or Eugene Bauer, who, according to his written deposition (PC Exh. 16, S II/12), was one of the leaders of the German section of the Trotskyists. For that matter, if Alfred Kundt, whom Berman-Yurin allegedly recommended to Sedov as a "staunch Trotskyite," had been a member of the Trotskyist group, one might think that Sedov himself, being a member of the same group, would have been able to get in touch with him without a Stalinist intermediary. Another question which the record does not answer is this: If Sedov sufficiently trusted Berman-Yurin at the end of 1931 to permit him to read a conspiratorial communication to Smirnov and to select an emissary to take the risk of delivering it, why did he dare to "speak openly" to him only a year later—November, 1932, to be exact—about the necessity of preparing to assassinate the leaders of the C.P.S.U.?

We also note that the record is most unsatisfactory concerning the alleged terrorist communications which Kundt is supposed to have taken to Smirnov. His instruction allegedly was to make contact with Smirnov and deliver these communications in person. However, Berman-Yurin stated that Kundt went to the secret address, handed over the documents and received a reply but did not meet Smirnov as the latter was not in Moscow. The Prosecutor did not ask Berman-Yurin from whom this reply was received if not from Smirnov, or whether Kundt ever delivered it to anyone; nor did he, although Smirnov was sitting before him, address any question to him about these alleged communications. (ZK 93–4). Concerning the value of Berman-Yurin's testimony to their contents we refer our readers to § 47 of this report.

Another pertinent question overlooked by the Prosecutor was the name used by David in his false passport; nor did

he produce the official Danish record (which, it must be assumed, he could easily have procured) of David's entrance
into Denmark on such a passport. Still another question
the Prosecutor did not ask Berman-Yurin was how Sedov's
emissary could have asked Fritz David in December, 1934,
why Stalin had not been killed at the Seventh Congress of
the Comintern. The Congress did not take place until 1935,
and Vyshinsky himself noted this fact.

According to Berman-Yurin, Sedov sent him to Copenhagen, there to meet Trotsky, precisely because Sedov, having spoken about the necessity for terrorism, noticed that
Berman-Yurin was wavering on the new "terrorist line." (ZK
94) Are we to assume that Sedov did not inform Trotsky of
the reason why he was sending Berman-Yurin to see him?
Surely, if we assume that Trotsky and Sedov were embarking on anything so dangerous as a terrorist campaign, we
must suppose that Sedov would have warned Trotsky of
Berman-Yurin's state of mind. It seems, therefore, absurd
to suppose that Trotsky would have instructed a "wavering"
Stalinist to make a terrorist attempt on Stalin involving not
the mere risk but the absolute certitude that it would cost
him his life. For according to the record Trotsky insisted that
Berman-Yurin and David should make an attempt on the life
of Stalin at an international assembly, such as a Plenum or
a Congress of the Comintern, so that it would "reverberate
throughout the world." Leaving aside the obviously absurd
implication that unless Stalin were killed in an international
assembly his assassination might pass unnoticed, it is a little
hard to believe that Trotsky would thus have demanded the
supreme sacrifice from two Stalinists whom he had never
seen before, one of whom was wavering in his acceptance
of the alleged terrorist line, and the other allegedly known
to Sedov himself only since August of 1932. Certainly the
record would not have suffered here if the Prosecutor had
undertaken to establish the exact motivation of these two

alleged Stalinist renegades. It would have gained considerably in the appearance of honesty if he had called their attention to their lack of agreement on a point as important as the reason for their failure to carry out their alleged plan to kill Stalin at the Thirteenth Plenum.

With regard to Berman-Yurin's alleged request that Trotsky allow him to get in touch with "an acquaintance named Fritz David" in Moscow, it seems exceedingly strange that Trotsky, assuming that he had revealed to Berman-Yurin information as confidential and as dangerous as the supposed terrorist instructions, would have withheld from him the comparatively unimportant information that he already knew about David, who either had visited him or would visit him in Copenhagen. According to David, Sedov told him that Trotsky wanted to see him. Therefore, one must assume that even if David had not already been there, Trotsky was expecting him. Yet there is nothing in the record to indicate that Trotsky mentioned David's visit to Berman-Yurin. Moreover, it may be noted that Berman-Yurin spoke as though Fritz David were already in Moscow, but the record states that both he and David went to Moscow in March, 1933. The Prosecutor did not question Berman-Yurin on this point. The record, therefore, does not show how Berman-Yurin knew that David was to be in Moscow.

We note, moreover, that Berman-Yurin's testimony clearly indicates that he spent an entire day in Trotsky's "apartment." We hold that this would have been absolutely impossible without the knowledge of Frankel, Molinier, the Fields, and the other people who surrounded Trotsky during his stay, and who deny that Berman-Yurin was among his visitors.

Before we leave this subject of Trotsky's alleged terrorist instructions to accused in the August trial who claimed to have seen him in Copenhagen, we remark the validity of Trotsky's comments upon the lack of details in their testimony which would have given that testimony an appearance of verisimilitude. None of them tells where or how Trotsky lived, how he went to see him, by what people he was surrounded; none mentions the peculiarity of the furnishings of the villa he occupied, of which there is ample evidence in the testimony before us; none mentions the press reports of the death of his alleged coconspirator Zinoviev, of which we also have ample evidence. On the other hand, such details as they do give are incorrect: Holtzman's references to Sedov's presence; his statement and that of Berman-Yurin that Trotsky paced the room during their conversations (the evidence of those witnesses who were with Trotsky shows that he received visitors in a very small room crowded with furniture, in which "pacing" would have been impossible). David furnished no details whatever concerning his own visit to Trotsky.

In view of all the considerations stated above, we hold the record of the trial to be completely worthless so far as concerns the connection of Berman-Yurin and David with Trotsky, Sedov and the alleged terrorist line. It is pertinent to note here the interesting fact that the three defendants, Olberg, David, and Berman-Yurin, although testifying that they received in November, 1932, Trotsky's instructions to proceed to Russia on terrorist missions, did not, according to their own testimony, arrive in Moscow until March, 1933. Why this long delay in carrying out missions so urgent and important? Olberg's mother states that her son went to Russia because Hitler's rise to power in Germany made it impossible for him to remain there. We know from the record of the trial and from the record of their expulsion, cited above, that both Berman-Yurin and Fritz David were members of the official German Communist Party. It seems reasonable, therefore, to assume that their departure for the Soviet Union was due to the same cause as that of Olberg, namely, the impossibility of safely remaining any longer within the borders of Nazi Germany.*

§ 95. On the basis of the record itself and of the evidence cited in this chapter and Chapter XII, we hold that neither Berman-Yurin nor David received terrorist instructions from Trotsky in Copenhagen, or saw Trotsky during his sojourn in that city.

---

* As we go to press we are in receipt of a deposition by Gunter Rei-mann, a German exile who was lately in New York. This deposition (PC Exh. 9, S 3), certified by the Secretary of the Commission, states that Reimann has never belonged to the Trotskyist movement; that he knew Berman-Yurin in Berlin; that Berman-Yurin was a Russian, former member of the C.P.S.U., and also an active member of the German Communist Party; that he returned to Russia in pursuance of an order from the Russian Party representative in Berlin, accompanied by a threat of expulsion from the Party in case of refusal; and that the reason for this order was the wish of the Soviet government to avoid embarrassment through the possible arrest of a Russian Communist doing anti-fascist work in Germany.

15

The testimony of N. and M. Lurye

§ 96. Two other defendants, Moissei Lurye and Nathan Lurye, who allegedly went from Germany to Russia for the purpose of committing terrorist acts, are not specifically mentioned in the verdict of the Zinoviev-Kamenev trial among those whose evidence is said to have convicted Trotsky and Sedov. However, since they are mentioned in the indictment (ZK 23) among the alleged agents who received directly from Trotsky and Sedov instructions to organize the assassination of Stalin, Voroshilov, Kaganovich and others, their testimony may properly be considered here.

§ 97. Nathan Lurye testified that he went to Moscow in April, 1932, on a special mission of the Trotskyite organization for the purpose of committing terrorist acts; that all his Trotskyite activities from 1927 onward had been directed toward sapping the power of the Soviet State; that the first person with whom he became intimate when he became a Trotskyite was Moissei Lurye, at the end of the summer of 1927. He stated that early in 1932 Moissei Lurye told him it was time to go to the U.S.S.R. and carry on terrorist work there; that he arrived in the U.S.S.R. with instructions to establish connections with the Trotskyites he had known in Germany and to carry on terrorist work together with them. In pursuance of these instructions, he established contact with Konstant and Lipschitz, members of a terrorist group to which a German engineer-architect, Franz Weitz, member of the German National Socialist Party, also belonged. Weitz, he said, had been sent to the U.S.S.R. by Himmler, at that time chief of the Hitler *Schutzstaffel* and subsequently chief of the Gestapo, for the purpose of committing terrorist acts. Lurye testified that from September, 1932, to the spring of 1933 his group was engaged in preparing an attempt on the life of Commissar Voroshilov; that they frequently went to Frunze Street armed with revolvers; that they saw Voroshilov's car going down Frunze Street but it was travelling too fast for them to fire. Therefore, they decided that that plan was useless and ceased watching Voroshilov's car. They next turned their attention to the acquisition of explosives for the purpose of bombing Voroshilov in some street. In July, 1933, N. Lurye testified, he was sent to Chelyabinsk to work in his profession of surgeon. While there he tried to meet both Kaganovich and Ordjonikidze, who visited that city, in order to commit terrorist acts against them. In this he failed. In January, 1936, he went to Leningrad on a scientific mission. Passing through Moscow he met Moissei Lurye, who instructed him to make an attempt on the life of Zhdanov. He intended to do this during the demonstration on the first of May, and armed himself with a Browning revolver, medium size. However, although he succeeded in getting into the demonstration in the Uritzky Square, he marched by Zhdanov too far away to be able to shoot him. (ZK 101–5.)

§ 98. Moissei Lurye testified that he went to Moscow on March 4, 1933, with terrorist instructions from Ruth

Fischer and Maslow which "were the instructions of Trotsky himself." He testified that he had been connected with Fischer since 1924, and since 1925 in opposition work in the Zinoviev faction; and that he had been connected with Maslow since 1927. On arriving in Moscow, he communicated his instructions to Zinoviev's former personal emissary in Berlin, A.V. Hertzberg, with whom he, Lurye, had been connected in Zinovievite work from November, 1927, until the end of 1931, and who "enjoyed the particular confidence of Zinoviev." In the beginning of August, 1934, he gave Zinoviev detailed information about these instructions and about the activities of Nathan Lurye's terrorist group. He had been connected, he said, with Nathan Lurye approximately from April, 1933, to January 2, 1936. He testified that he had instructed N. Lurye to make an attempt on Ordjonikidze's life when the latter visited the Chelyabinsk tractor works, and that he had also instructed him to make an attempt on the life of Zhdanov; also that he had been connected with the Fascist agent, Franz Weitz. (ZK 105–8.)

§ 99. Leon Trotsky testified that he had never known or had any relations with M. Lurye and N. Lurye and saw their names for the first time in the published reports of the first trial (PC 94). Ruth Fischer and Maslow, he said,

are former leaders of the German Communist Party, and were my bitter adversaries. Then they became Oppositionists, Zinovievists. They capitulated after Zinoviev, and in the time indicated in these depositions they were absolutely antagonistic to me. (PC 225.)

§ 100. Eugene Bauer testified:

I was acquainted, not personally but from having heard him speak, with M. Lurye. At that time he went

under the name of Alexander Emel.* The speech at which
I was present was in fact directed against the Trotskyist
movement, and Lurye has always been one of the extreme adversaries of that movement. (CR 45.)

§ 101. The most important documents in our possession
concerning these two accused are as follows:

(1) A deposition by Eugene Bauer, certified by the Special
Committee, in which Bauer states that he had never heard of
Nathan Lurye, and that Moissei Lurye, as Alexander Emel,
was occupied as a theoretician in the Communist Party of
Germany; that M. Lurye had belonged in 1927 to the Zinoviev opposition but thereafter became loyal to the official
party and from 1929 to 1931 played a certain rôle as theoretician, historian and propagandist; that he was one of the
leaders of the propaganda section of the Communist Party
of Germany, but that in the beginning of 1932 at the time
of a little zigzag of the Party he was removed as a scapegoat;
that he was not only not a Trotskyist but a specialist in the
fight against Trotskyism. (PC Exh. 16, S II/8.)

(2) Concerning the identity of Nathan Lurye and of Konstant and Lipschitz, mentioned by him, we have an affidavit (New York) by Dr. Maria Blume, resident in Germany
up to March, 1935, and now residing in New York City. In
a letter to the Commission Dr. Blume informs us that she
has never been a member of any political party; and that
she submitted her affidavit in the interest of truth, and not
from any motives of partisanship. In the affidavit she states
that she knew Dr. Nathan Lurye in Berlin and was very well
acquainted with his wife, Nekha Adunskaya, having been
born in the same town in Russian Poland and later attended
the same university in Germany; that Dr. Nathan Lurye, a

---

* In the record of the trial his name is listed as "Lurye, Moissei Ilyich
(Emel, Alexander)." (ZK 39,179,180.)

Polish Jew by birth, studied medicine in Germany, graduated from the University of Berlin in 1926 or 1927 and later obtained a position in one of the suburban Berlin hospitals; that he worked there until the year 1931–32 when "like all other foreigners residing in Germany he was deprived by governmental decree of the right to employment"; that he, therefore, applied for work in the Soviet Union and left for that country at the beginning of 1932; that at the end of that year his wife joined him, and from her Dr. Blume learned that Nathan Lurye was employed as a surgeon in the Kremlin Hospital, Moscow.

Dr. Blume further states that Esther Adunskaya, Nathan Lurye's sister-in-law, was married to a German worker by the name of Erich Konstant; that Esther and her husband, both of whom were Communists, left for the Soviet Union in 1925 or 1926, and their last address known to Dr. Blume was Gorodskaya 2/7, Apt. 89, Moscow. She states that Pavel Lipschitz was born in Russian Poland, attended the *Technische Hochschule* of Berlin and graduated as an engineer at the end of 1931; that like Nathan Lurye, he was deprived of the right to work in Germany; that he applied to the Soviet Embassy for work in the Soviet Union and went there in the beginning of 1932. She states that Nekha Adunskaya Lurye, Nathan Lurye, and Pavel Lipschitz were to her knowledge members of the Communist Party of Germany and did not display either privately or publicly any Oppositionist tendencies; that Pavel Lipschitz and the Adunsky family, being fellow-townsmen, maintained close relations. Dr. Blume concludes that out of her personal knowledge she is able to state that the relations of Nathan Lurye, Konstant and Lipschitz were primarily those of relatives and fellow-countrymen. (PC Exh. 9, 1.)

(3) A photostat of an article by Alexander Emel (Moissei Lurye) from page 3077 in No. 96 of the *International Press Correspondence (Inprecorr)*, November 15, 1932. In

this article Lurye states that the bourgeoisie needs a better propagandist against the Soviet Union than the Social Democracy which the workers no longer believe, and that Leon Trotsky at the moment fulfills this function for the bourgeoisie; that the letters from the Soviet Union which appear in the *Bulletin* are widely reproduced in government journals, especially in such countries as Italy, Poland, Hungary, and Papen Germany; and that Trotsky enjoys a very peculiar sympathy on the part of the police of Pilsudski's Poland, where his articles are made much of in the fascist press and the censor is always at his service. Such articles, he says, as "Trotskyism in the Light of Marxism," cannot appear in Poland. They are completely forbidden by the censor. Only one word remains on the whole page: "Confiscated." (*Ibid.*, 2.)

§ 102. We note that neither of the Luryes offered any direct evidence of his alleged connection with Trotsky. Moissei Lurye testified that the instructions which he received verbally from Fischer and Maslow actually came from Trotsky. One must assume that if he received such instructions he took the word of Fischer and Maslow on this point; in other words, his testimony was hearsay. Nathan Lurye was even more vague. He testified merely that his terrorist instructions came from "the Trotskyite organization." We note also that whereas Nathan Lurye stated that Moissei Lurye was the first person with whom he became intimate after he became a Trotskyite, and placed the beginning of their intimacy at the end of the summer of 1927, Moissei Lurye dated his connection with Nathan Lurye only from April, 1933. The testimony of M. Lurye follows in the record immediately after that of N. Lurye; yet no attempt of the Prosecutor to reconcile these conflicting statements is recorded.

We have quoted Bauer's testimony to the effect that M. Lurye belonged in 1927 to the Zinoviev opposition but thereafter became loyal to the official party and played a

certain rôle therein from 1929 to 1931. Lurye's testimony
indicates that he was engaged in Zinovievite work up until
the time of his departure for Russia (ZK 106). Since Zinoviev had capitulated in 1928 and had been readmitted to the
Party (§ 24) it may, of course, be quite logically assumed
that Lurye's theoretical, historical and propagandist work
for the official Communist Party of Germany, an example
of which we have quoted, was identical with Zinovievite
work. On the other hand, if either of the Luryes had been
engaged in Trotskyite work in Berlin it seems strange indeed
that Nathan Lurye remained unknown to the Trotskyists
and that Moissei Lurye was known to them only as an official Stalinist propagandist.

In the case of the Luryes, as in that of Berman-Yurin and
David, the Prosecutor made no attempt whatever to establish any motivation for their alleged terrorist undertakings.
Moreover, the nature of the preparations for terrorist attempts to which these two witnesses confessed are better
calculated to excite mirth than to command credence.

§ 103. In view of all these considerations, and the evidence
in our possession concerning these defendants, we find no
basis whatever for the attempt in the Zinoviev-Kamenev
trial to link Moissei Lurye and Nathan Lurye with Leon
Trotsky or the Trotskyist movement, or with an alleged
"terrorist line."

16

The 'parallel' or 'reserve center'

§ 104. The Definition of the Charge in the "Report of Court Proceedings in the case of the Anti-Soviet Trotskyite Center" begins as follows:

> The investigating authorities consider it established: 1) that on the instructions of L.D. Trotsky there was organized in 1933 a parallel center consisting of the following accused in the present case: Y.L. Pyatakov, K.B. Radek, G.Y. Sokolnikov, and L.P. Serebryakov, the object of which was to direct criminal, anti-Soviet, espionage, diversive and terrorist activities . . . (PR 18.)

On Page 5 of the indictment it is stated that the investigation of the case of the united Trotskyite-Zinovievite center established that in addition to the united center

> there existed a so-called reserve center, formed on the direct instructions of L.D. Trotsky, for the eventuality

of the criminal activities of the Trotskyite-Zinovievite *bloc* being exposed by the organs of the Soviet government. The convicted members of the united Trotskyite-Zinovievite center, *Zinoviev, Kamenev,* and others, testified that the reserve center consisted of *Y.L. Pyatakov, K.B. Radek, G.Y. Sokolnikov,* and *L.P. Serebryakov,* all known for their past Trotskyite activities.

The preliminary investigation of the present case *established that the so-called reserve center was actually a parallel Trotskyite center,* organized and operating under the direct instructions of *L.D. Trotsky,* now in emigration. [Our emphasis.]

According to the indictment, therefore, the reserve center and the parallel center, both allegedly formed on Trotsky's direct instructions, were identical.

§ 105. We have already pointed out (§ 33), in discussing the united center, that there is no direct evidence in the published record of the Zinoviev-Kamenev trial indicating the attitude of either Trotsky or Sedov toward the formation of that center or their rôle, if any, in its formation. This is equally true as concerns the reserve center. Indeed, the only one of the accused in that trial who mentioned that center was Kamenev (§ 32). Zinoviev mentioned Sokolnikov among the "so-called 'individuals'" who approached Kamenev and himself (ZK 72); Reingold stated categorically that Sokolnikov was a member of the alleged united Trotskyite-Zinovievite center (ZK 54–5); and Evdokimov placed Sokolnikov among those who attended a conference in Kamenev's apartment in the summer of 1934 at which it was decided to expedite the assassination of Kirov, but without stating in what capacity Sokolnikov was present (ZK 48). None of the accused mentioned Pyatakov in the published record; even the accused Kamenev, in telling who were the leaders selected for the reserve center, mentioned only Sokolnikov, Serebryakov, and Radek (ZK 67). Pyatakov's name is mentioned only once in this record: by Vyshinsky. In a statement after the examination of the accused at the evening session of August 21—the last session at which testimony was taken—Vyshinsky mentions Pyatakov among several people who have been referred to in the testimony of Kamenev, Zinoviev, and Reingold as being involved in their criminal activities (ZK 115–16).

§ 106. So much for the reserve center and its members in so far as they figure in the record of the August trial. Although the indictment in the January trial expressly stated (§ 104) that the investigation in the Zinoviev-Kamenev trial established that this reserve center was formed on the direct instructions of L.D. Trotsky, this statement is nowhere borne out in the published record of that trial. Indeed, the accused Kamenev said:

> Knowing that we might be discovered, we designated a small group to continue our terrorist activities. (ZK 67.)

Not only did he *not* say that this group was designated on Trotsky's instruction; but it must be noted that nowhere in the record of the August trial does Kamenev claim any direct communication whatever with either Trotsky or Sedov. The versions of the origin of this center which were brought out in the testimony of the second trial also failed to establish the charge that it was instigated and its members selected by Trotsky. We consider first the testimony on this point by those two members of the alleged center who claimed direct contact with Trotsky, namely: Pyatakov and Radek.

§ 107. Pyatakov testified that in a letter from Trotsky which he received through the accused Shestov at the end of November, 1931, the second point was the "necessity of uniting all anti-Stalin forces" in order "to use every means to remove Stalin and his immediate assistants" (PR 32). Like all the accused in both trials who had occasion to mention this phrase, "remove Stalin," Pyatakov interpreted it as implying violence. He testified that he devoted the interval between the end of November, 1931, and a trip to Berlin in the middle of 1932 "to restoring Trotskyite contacts and cadres," especially in the Ukraine through Loginov and Livshitz (the first a witness and the latter one of the accused in the second trial) (PR 33–36). This testimony is especially significant in that it places Pyatakov's activity not only before the formation of the reserve center but even before that of the main united center. On page 36 he testifies that he met with Sedov in Berlin in the middle of 1932, and began to

> relate to him what I then knew about the activities of the Trotskyite-Zinovievite organization which were beginning to develop

—a statement which places the activities of a Trotskyite-Zinovievite bloc before its date of organization as fixed in the indictment of the first trial and in much of the evidence in both trials, and also indicates that Pyatakov knew about the bloc and its activities even before he was informed about them. For on the very page he states that after his return to Moscow in the *autumn* of 1932, Kamenev

> . . . very clearly and distinctly informed me about the Trotskyite-Zinovievite center which had been formed. (PR 37.)

Since the Prosecutor, who was in a position to attempt to secure a clarification of these apparent contradictions, did not see fit to do so, and since the Commission is obviously not in a position to make that attempt, we simply note them and pass on to Pyatakov's further account of this interview with Kamenev which, he said,

> was very important from the point of view of forming the reserve center, what became later the parallel Trotskyite center. (PR 36.)

Kamenev, said Pyatakov,

> . . . mentioned the names of a number of people who belonged to the center and informed me that they had discussed the question of including in the center people who in general had been prominent Trotskyites in the past, such as myself—Pyatakov, Radek, Sokolnikov and Serebryakov, but they had come to the conclusion that this was inexpedient. As Kamenev said . . . it was desirable, in case the main center was exposed, to have a reserve Trotskyite-Zinovievite center. He had been authorized officially to ask me whether I would agree to join that center. . . . I gave Kamenev my consent to join the reserve center. (PR 37.)

§ 108. From this testimony of Pyatakov it appears, first, that the reserve center was at least in process of formation in the autumn of 1932, although the indictment places its organization in 1933; secondly, that it was being formed on the initiative of the main or united center; and, thirdly, that it was to be not a Trotskyite but a Trotskyite-Zinovievite center. But Pyatakov, on the very next page after this account, gives a second version. He states that in 1932 he had a conversation with Radek during which they discussed the

> very great predominance of Zinovievites in the main center, and whether we should not raise the question of making certain changes in the composition of the main center. (PR 38.)

They decided that this could not be done, as it would give rise to unnecessary disputes in the Trotskyite underground organization. Then

> The idea occurred to us that in addition to the main center . . . we ought to have our own Trotskyite parallel center which could serve as a reserve center in case the main center was exposed, and which at the same time would carry on practical work independently in accordance with Trotsky's directives and his lines. . . . Radek and I were disturbed by the thought that in the economic retreat after we had seized power the Zinovievite section of the *bloc* would go too far, and something had to be organized to counteract it. At all events, we then agreed to ask Trotsky's opinion about this. (PR 38.)

Here we have a version in which the idea of a reserve center was cooked up by Pyatakov and Radek as a conspiratorial measure against the Zinovievites. Pyatakov goes on to say that

> A little later (this was already in 1933), during one of my meetings with Radek, he informed me that he had received a reply from Trotsky, that Trotsky categorically urged the necessity of preserving complete unity as well as the *bloc* with the Zinovievites. . . . As for converting our center into a parallel center, he said that this would accelerate the gathering of forces and preparation of the necessary acts of terrorism and wrecking. (PR 38–9.)

Thus Pyatakov and Radek seem to have queried Trotsky about the formation of a parallel Trotskyite center, and Trotsky seems to have answered a query about the conversion of the "Trotskyite-Zinovievite reserve center" into a

Trotskyite parallel center. For Pyatakov again formulates this alleged communication from Trotsky as follows:

> In regard to converting the reserve center into a parallel center, he gave us his blessing. (PR 40.)

§ 109. The accused Radek "fully confirmed" this testimony of Pyatakov, and went into even greater detail about the reasons why he and Pyatakov thought it necessary, "while outwardly preserving the *bloc* to have our own organization to counterbalance it," and why "we tried to apply the idea of a reserve center in the form of a parallel center" (PR 40–41). He stated that it was he who wrote the letter asking Trotsky's opinion, and that he established communication through Vladimir Romm, who at that time was a Tass correspondent abroad. It is therefore pertinent to consult the testimony of the witness Vladimir Romm, who appears from the record of the trial to have served Radek and Trotsky not only in the capacity of liaison man but also in that of close confidant. Romm testified that in the autumn of 1932, when he was in Moscow, Radek told him that

> in pursuance of Trotsky's directives, a Trotskyite-Zinovievite *bloc* had been organized, but that he and Pyatakov had not joined that center. Radek went on to say that the idea had arisen of creating a reserve, or parallel center, on which the Trotskyites were to predominate, in order to have a reserve center in the event of the functioning center being discovered. (PR 139.)

Here we have a third version—a parallel center not exclusively but merely predominantly "Trotskyite." Since Radek seems to have had no secrets from his liaison man, we learn that the people whom Romm understood to be prospective members of this reserve or parallel center were Radek,

Pyatakov, Serebryakov and Sokolnikov—that is, except for Pyatakov they were precisely those people whom Kamenev mentioned in the first trial as having been selected for the reserve center by the main or united center, and they were precisely (including Pyatakov) the people allegedly mentioned to Pyatakov by Kamenev (§ 107) as "people who in general had been prominent Trotskyites in the past," and who had not been invited to serve on the main center because it was desirable "to have a reserve Trotskyite-Zinovievite center," in case the main center should be exposed.

After providing this significant information, which we shall discuss later, Romm went on to testify that it was clear to him that only *Pyatakov* and *Radek* were to write the letter which Radek had asked him to convey to Trotsky; that according to his understanding, this letter was to be a

> request for directives concerning the idea of creating a parallel center. . . . Evidently, whether to create or not to create, and of whom it was to consist. (PR 140.)

One of the arguments advanced by Radek, said Romm, was "that the Zinovievites predominated in the functioning center." Then comes the following colloquy:

> VYSHINSKY: Hence, they had decided to organize such a center and only wanted sanction, or did they ask for advice on the question, how to decide?
>
> ROMM: My impression was that they had decided the question in the affirmative, that is to say, that it was necessary to do it, and that the letter would be written in order to obtain sanction.
>
> VYSHINSKY: What was written in that letter, did you know?
>
> ROMM: Yes, because the letter was handed to me and then concealed in the cover of a German book before

my departure back to Geneva in the autumn of 1932.
(PR 140.)

Romm went on to state that at the end of July, 1933, he met
Trotsky in the Bois de Boulogne, and that the purpose for
which Trotsky met him was:

> As far as I could understand, in order verbally to con-
> firm the instructions contained in the letter I was taking
> to Moscow. He started the conversation with the ques-
> tion of creating the parallel center. . . . He agreed with
> the idea of the parallel center but only on the impera-
> tive condition that the *bloc* with the Zinovievites was
> preserved . . . (PR 141.)

From this version it appears that Pyatakov and Radek
asked Trotsky neither about the idea of forming an independent Trotskyite parallel center nor about converting the
reserve center into such a parallel center, but about the idea
of creating a parallel Trotskyite-Zinovievite center on which
the Trotskyites should predominate; and that Trotsky's reply sanctioned not the *conversion* of the reserve center into
a parallel center, but the *creation* of a parallel center "only
on the imperative condition that the *bloc* with the Zinovievites was preserved."

§ 110. A word here about dates: The only letter Romm
mentioned having received from Radek for Trotsky in 1932
he placed in September (PR 143). Since he had already testified that the letter inquiring about the creation of a parallel
center was handed to him in the autumn of 1932, we must
assume that it was this letter which he received in September.
We have already noted (§ 107) that Pyatakov would appear
from his own testimony to have known about the existence
and activities of the main center not only some months before
the date of its organization as given in the indictment in the

first trial but even before he himself had been informed about it. It now appears that Radek told Romm that a Trotskyite-Zinovievite center had been formed, criticized its predominantly Zinovievite membership, and in agreement with Pyatakov sent a letter to Trotsky asking his opinion about creating a parallel center—all a month or two before he himself learned that the main Trotskyite-Zinovievite center had been formed, and indeed even somewhat before he had himself "decided to return to the road of struggle." For although Radek testified (PR 87) that Trotsky wrote him in February, 1932, that negotiations for a bloc were under way, he definitely placed his own decision to "return to the road of struggle" at "approximately the end of September or of October, 1932," and his knowledge of the actual formation of the bloc at the end of October or beginning of November, 1932 (PR 87). At that time, he said, he had a talk with Mrachkovsky, and asked him, "Where and how do you intend to act?" Mrachkovsky inquired whether he had had a letter from Trotsky, and what he had decided. According to Radek:

> I replied: . . . I have decided to go with you. Then I asked him how they visualized the struggle, and what progress had been made in the matter of joining with the Zinovievites. . . . He replied quite definitely that the struggle had entered the terrorist phase and that in order to carry out these tactics they had now united with the Zinovievites and would set about the preparatory work. (PR 88.)

But the "preparatory work" of Radek and Pyatakov, if the record is to be believed, had already been done. With a wonderful prescience, they had perceived the danger lurking in the "predominantly Zinovievite" membership of the "functioning" united center, not only before either of them learned of its existence but even before it did exist, and hastened to ask for Trotsky's "directives" about the creation of a Trotskyite parallel center, or possibly a center on which the Trotskyites should predominate, in order to counteract the influence of the Zinovievites. This unity in wisdom and in action is all the more impressive in that it took place, if one is to believe Radek's testimony, some three months before they saw one another. In answer to a question from Vyshinsky, "Whom did you meet at that time . . ." he says:

> We agreed that we should meet as little as possible. . . . If it is a question of my meetings with my colleagues of the reserve center—Trotskyites—I saw Pyatakov in December, 1932, a second time at the end of 1933. . . . (PR 91–2.)

§ 111. It is interesting, in view of Radek's own confirmation and elaboration of Pyatakov's testimony about the parallel center, and his later confirmation of Romm's testimony (PR 145), to note that according to his own testimony he learned not only about the main center but also about the reserve center and its proposed personnel from Mrachkovsky:

> Later Mrachkovsky told me that since the struggle would be a very severe one and the sacrifices would be enormous, they would like to preserve certain cadres in the event of defeat, that is to say, in the event of arrest, and he said that "this is why we have not included you in the first center." He said this in reference to me, Pyatakov, and Serebryakov.
>
> VYSHINSKY: And did he speak to you about Sokolnikov?
>
> RADEK: He spoke to me about him later. At this juncture the talk was about Trotskyites. . . . (PR 88.)

This version, it will be noted, tallies with Kamenev's and with Pyatakov's first version of the formation and personnel of the reserve center; save that Kamenev did not mention Pyatakov, and Pyatakov placed Sokolnikov among those people whom Kamenev mentioned to him as having been prominent Trotskyites in the past (§§ 32, 105, 107). It also tallies with the versions given by the other two alleged members of the reserve or parallel center, which we shall now proceed to examine, pausing only long enough to note that Radek, as if to refute as completely as possible Romm's testimony (which he later confirmed) about his and Pyatakov's knowledge of the composition of the united center as early as September, 1932, answered as follows Vyshinsky's query whether Mrachkovsky told him anything about Bakayev and Reingold:

> When he later *outlined the scheme of organization of the bloc,* he named Dreitzer as the direct leader of the terrorist organization on our side, and Bakayev as the leader on the Zinovievites' side. (PR 89.) [Italics ours.]

And on page 91 he says that he learned from Dreitzer about the Zinovievites. This testimony of Radek stands in the record between Pyatakov's and Romm's. It contradicts Pyatakov's second version (confirmed by Radek) of the formation of the reserve or parallel center, and is contradicted by Romm's version. Yet Vyshinsky, when Romm had finished, said:

> Accused Radek, you have just heard Romm's explanations. It seems to me that Romm's statements tally with yours. (PR 145.)

§ 112. The other two members of the alleged parallel or reserve center, Serebryakov and Sokolnikov, explicitly denied having had direct communication with Trotsky (PR 42, 555). No attempt was made to impugn their testimony, and no evidence was introduced to show that they had had direct contact with either Trotsky or Sedov. According to Serebryakov, Mrachkovsky came to see him in the autumn of 1932 and told him that a Trotskyite-Zinovievite bloc had been formed, and who its members were; also that the center had decided to create a reserve center in the event of its being exposed (PR 168). It is curious in this connection that although Kamenev (§ 32), Pyatakov (§ 107), Romm (§ 109), and Radek (§ 111) included Serebryakov among the members originally designated for the reserve center, and though all of these witnesses except Kamenev explicitly fixed 1932 as the year in which that center was planned, Serebryakov himself testified that he was invited to join it only at the end of November, 1933, by Pyatakov, when the two of them met in Gagri (PR 41). From this it would appear that Mrachkovsky's purpose in informing Serebryakov a year earlier about the formation of the reserve center was merely that of indulging in a little conspiratorial gossip. However that may be, it should be noted that Serebryakov's version of the formation of the reserve center coincides with that of Kamenev, and with Pyatakov's first and Radek's second version. Serebryakov did not state that Trotsky had given instructions for the formation of this center. On the contrary he said that "the center had decided" to create it.

§ 113. The accused Sokolnikov, fourth member of this alleged parallel or reserve center, not only claimed no direct contact with either Trotsky or Sedov, but expressly differentiated between himself and the members "of Trotskyite origin." He said:

> . . . between the members of the center of Trotskyite origin there were closer, more intimate and more trustful relations than there were with me. . . . (PR 159.)

His attitude on this point is independently confirmed. Although Pyatakov included Sokolnikov among those whom

Kamenev mentioned to him as having been prominent Trotskyites in the past, Kamenev himself, in the first trial, set Sokolnikov apart from the "Trotskyites" in speaking of the projected reserve center (ZK 67). Zinoviev included him, with Smilga, among the so-called "individuals" who allegedly approached himself and Kamenev (ZK 72). Radek said of Sokolnikov that Mrachkovsky

> . . . spoke to me about him later. At this juncture the talk was about Trotskyites. (PR 88.)

On page 107 Radek explicitly states that Sokolnikov "was representing the Zinovievite organization"—a statement which, if accepted, invalidates the claim of the indictment that the reserve center was a parallel Trotskyite center, and also Pyatakov's second version, confirmed by Radek himself, of the formation of the parallel, or reserve, center.

Sokolnikov not only denied in his final plea that he was in communication with Trotsky (PR 555), but throughout his testimony he repeatedly stated that his knowledge of Trotsky's directives came through Pyatakov and Radek; and on page 159 he speaks of

> . . . a number of communications . . . made to me in the name of Trotsky, who not only guided the parallel center, but also gave instructions to those members of the center with whom he had close relations.

Sokolnikov was explicit about the formation of the alleged reserve center. He testified that he learned from Kamenev about the personnel and terrorist aims of the united center. Vyshinsky asked him:

> You accepted Kamenev's proposal regarding the organization of the reserve center and regarding its composi-

tion, or did you discuss its composition?

SOKOLNIKOV: Kamenev told me at the time—this was at the end of summer, 1932—that he would conduct negotiations on the formation of the reserve center. (PR 147.)

Thus, if we accept "the end of 1932," as stated in the indictment in the August trial, for the date of organization of the united center, it would appear that Sokolnikov learned from Kamenev about the plan for a reserve center even before the united center was formed. There follows a series of questions and answers which illustrates the juridical quality of the trial:

> VYSHINSKY: He would conduct negotiations? With whom—did he tell you?
>
> SOKOLNIKOV: No.
>
> VYSHINSKY: And you did not bother to ask who else would be in it?
>
> SOKOLNIKOV: He told me in general terms that he would speak with Tomsky [referred to in these trials only as a member of the Right; not of either center]. But he did not say with whom personally he was going to speak besides.
>
> VYSHINSKY: And what do you think, with whom could he have spoken?

Having thus consulted Sokolnikov's thoughts about the intentions of the dead Kamenev, the Prosecutor leads him into a flat contradiction of his previous testimony:

> SOKOLNIKOV: Regarding possible candidates for the center? Those were the same persons who were afterwards made members of the parallel center.
>
> VYSHINSKY: But which of these candidates did Kamenev specifically name to you in that conversation?

SOKOLNIKOV: I can not recall if he named all of them.
VYSHINSKY: But whom did he name?
SOKOLNIKOV: I recollect he named Pyatakov and Radek.
VYSHINSKY: And they afterwards joined the center?
SOKOLNIKOV: Yes. (PR 147–8.)

On pages 150 and 158, Sokolnikov again mentions Kamenev as a source of information; and on page 167, in denying that he was a member of the united center, he refers to his confrontation with Kamenev and quotes him as follows:

Kamenev stated that he had had conversations with me in the summer of 1932, that they did not want to put me on the united center because they thought it necessary to reserve me . . . so that I could be utilized in the event of the united center being exposed. . . . Kamenev said then that this was precisely why I did not go on the united center but was selected for the reserve center; and this corresponds with the facts.

Here we have again the Kamenev-Zinoviev version of the date of formation of the united center (§§ 34–8), and apparently also Kamenev's version (at second hand) of the date of projection of the reserve center. Vyshinsky thereupon quotes as follows from what purports to be the testimony of Kamenev, as set forth in Vol. VIII, p. 45, of the preliminary hearings:

In conversations with Zinoviev we became convinced that it was necessary to create a leading group of the Trotskyite-Zinovievite organization in the event of our being exposed. It was precisely in this connection that I conducted negotiations with Sokolnikov and obtained his full consent. (PR 168.)

No word here, either from Sokolnikov or Kamenev, about instructions from Trotsky. We have remarked that Kamenev made no claim to having had contact with Trotsky or Sedov. Here it appears that the idea of the reserve center occurred to himself and Zinoviev, who also claimed no direct contact with Trotsky or Sedov.

§ 114. Thus we have, from the four members of the alleged reserve center, who might reasonably be supposed to have known how it was formed, two distinct versions of the way in which the center came into being. In one of these it was established as a reserve "Trotskyite-Zinovievite" center, and its members selected, by the united center; in the other, the idea of a parallel Trotskyite center "occurred" to Pyatakov and Radek, who wrote to ask Trotsky's opinion about it. Vyshinsky made no effort to reconcile these mutually contradictory versions. In one it was formed in 1932; in the other it was projected in 1932 and a "conversion" was sanctioned by Trotsky in 1933. The witness Romm gave still another version (confirmed by Radek) in which Pyatakov and Radek asked Trotsky's advice, not about a parallel Trotskyite center, but about a reserve center on which the Trotskyites were to predominate, and received his approval of that plan. It should be borne in mind that according to Romm's testimony, his alleged conversation with Trotsky (§ 109) consisted of a verbal confirmation of the contents of the letter in which Trotsky was answering Radek's query about forming a parallel center. The Prosecutor gave no sign of being aware that Romm's version of this answer differed from that of Pyatakov, "fully confirmed" by Radek. Nor did he take any note of the fact that Pyatakov's version of it made it appear that Trotsky, having been asked one question, had answered another (§ 108). Let us assume, for the moment, that Pyatakov and Radek really asked Trotsky, not about the formation of a "parallel Trotskyite center," but about the conversion of the "Trotskyite-Zinovievite reserve center" into a parallel center; then a question arises which would certainly have been pertinent to the record: How did Pyatakov and Radek expect to be able to do this without offending the Zinovievites? Moreover, Pyatakov's account (confirmed by Radek) of this answer from Trotsky implies the obvious question: Did Trotsky, in "giving his blessing" to the conversion, advise Radek how it could be done while preserving that "complete unity as well as the *bloc* with the Zinovievites," the necessity of which he "categorically urged"?

§ 115. Another question arises, and that a basic one: What is meant by the "conversion" of the reserve Trotskyite-Zinovievite center into a parallel Trotskyite center? Does not the phrase imply changes in membership—that the Zinovievites on the center were to be dropped? But there is no indication that the membership of the center was ever changed. The indictment expressly states that the reserve center consisted of Pyatakov, Sokolnikov, Serebryakov, and Radek; and all versions of its initial membership bear out this statement, with these exceptions: Kamenev did not include Pyatakov (who according to the indictment and his own confession was a Trotskyite member); Sokolnikov did not include Serebryakov (a Trotskyite according to the indictment and his own confession); while Serebryakov stated that he joined the center in 1933, a year after he had been informed about it. Moreover, the witness Romm explicitly stated that he understood from Radek that the members of the parallel center were to be—Pyatakov, Sokolnikov, Serebryakov, and Radek! And it was those same four men who were tried in January, 1937, as members of the alleged Anti-Soviet Trotskyite Center which according to the indictment was identical with the reserve center. Nowhere in the record of either trial is it alleged that there were others.

Thus we find that the reserve center and the parallel center were identical in membership from the beginning. What, then, was "converted"? Possibly it was a matter of withdrawing from connections with the Zinovievites and taking orders only from Trotsky? But Sokolnikov, according to Radek, represented the Zinovievites. And Sokolnikov explicitly stated that Kamenev, in the beginning of 1934,

> informed me about the defeatist position taken by Trotsky. . . . Incidentally, one definite result of this conversation was that Kamenev warned me that someone might approach me with inquiries. (PR 148.)

On the same page Sokolnikov states that his work in the *parallel* center began only in the summer of 1935. Again, Pyatakov, in speaking of the efforts of the parallel center to convert itself into the main center in 1935, says:

> In a word, we endeavored to carry out the decision of the main center which in 1934 had been transmitted to all the four members of the reserve center: By Kamenev to me and Sokolnikov, and by Mrachkovsky to Radek and Serebryakov. (PR 54.)

§ 116. Obviously that explanation does not hold. We therefore pass from questions which should have occurred to the Prosecutor and the Court to questions which conceivably may have occurred to them, and certainly must occur to anyone who honestly tries to understand the prosecution's side of this case—which is the only side the records contain. Were there not possibly some political considerations involved in this matter of "conversion"? The consideration, for example, that the charges of treason, sabotage, and terrorism would be more effective politically against Leon Trotsky if he could be made to appear solely responsible; more especially since Zinoviev and Kamenev were dead and there were no prominent Zinovievites remaining to be discredited? But how to do this? Prominent "Trotskyites" were no longer numerous;

and three of these, Pyatakov, Serebryakov, and Radek, had already been implicated in the alleged crimes of the united center. Sokolnikov too. To try Pyatakov, Radek, Serebryakov and Sokolnikov as the Trotskyite-Zinovievite reserve center would be to preserve the connection with the main center indicated in the August trial, and to involve them in all the alleged crimes of that center—and Trotsky. To try them as a parallel Trotskyite center formed and acting on Trotsky's "direct instructions" would be to shift to Trotsky sole responsibility for their activities, and also possibly help to justify a great many activities of which the members of the united center appear to have died in ignorance—at least so far as the record of their trial shows. And the second date of formation—1933—would be useful in linking Trotsky, through Romm, with the formation of the center. This could not be done earlier, for Romm was stationed in Paris and Geneva, while Trotsky, until July 17, 1933, was in Turkey.

We are not stating that these considerations were behind the strange "conversion" of the Trotskyite-Zinovievite reserve center into a parallel Trotskyite center. Indeed, it seems to us that if they had been, it would have been in the interest of the prosecution to see to it that the testimony to that "conversion" at least made sense. We only remark that some such considerations would have supplied a motive for this conversion which was no conversion—a motive, that is, for the prosecution. Since an analysis of the testimony sufficiently establishes that no actual conversion took place, there could obviously have been none on the part of the accused themselves.

§ 117. In none of this conflicting testimony, we repeat, is there the slightest evidence, direct or indirect, that Trotsky either instigated the formation of the alleged reserve or parallel center, or selected its members. At most his alleged rôle consisted in approving what other people had either done or suggested doing. And the nature of the evidence brought out by the Prosecutor, which we have analyzed above, leaves not the shadow of a basis for belief that he did even that much.

§ 118. Another "conversion" which seems to have taken place chiefly if not exclusively in the pages of the record, is that of the parallel center into an operating center. Pyatakov first mentioned this:

> I met Sokolnikov much later, in the middle of 1935, when we spoke concretely about converting the reserve, or parallel, center into an operating center, since at that time the main center had been broken up and its members arrested and sentenced. Sokolnikov came to see me at the People's Commissariat of Heavy Industry and said that it was time to become active as a certain lull had set in after the arrests. (PR 39.)

Later he said:

> The characteristic feature of our criminal work in the period from the middle of 1935 to the end of 1935 and the beginning of 1936 was that this was a period when the "parallel center" endeavored to convert itself from a parallel center into the main center and to intensify its work in accordance with the directives we had received from Trotsky, since at that time we had a number of meetings here with Sokolnikov and Tomsky. . . . Just then the new phase began. (PR 54.)

Pyatakov's first version of this change would seem to indicate that up until the middle of 1935 the parallel center had not been operating—had really been a reserve center. This version was corroborated by the accused Sokolnikov, who stated that his work on the parallel center began in the summer of 1935, except for one commission in 1934 (PR

148). Later he spoke of meeting Pyatakov in 1935, "after the parallel center had commenced its activities" (PR 149). But in his final plea he said:

> And later, in 1935 . . . when the parallel center began to resume its work . . . (PR 552.)

It is impossible to tell what all this means: whether the parallel center became an operating center in 1935—which certainly would imply that it had not operated before—whether it converted itself into the main center, or whether it resumed activities which had been discontinued. Pyatakov's first statement, quoted above, is peculiar when juxtaposed with the following exchange of question and answer ("fully confirmed" by Radek) on the very next page:

> VYSHINSKY: Hence, we can take it that the "parallel center" has been operating since 1933?
> PYATAKOV: Yes.
> VYSHINSKY: It was a parallel center precisely because it operated simultaneously with the main center?
> PYATAKOV: Yes. (PR 40.)

Certainly there is nothing in the testimony of Pyatakov, Radek, or Serebryakov which indicates either that the parallel center was inactive until 1935 or that it ever suspended activities, to resume them in that year. All three confessed to continuous activity, Radek from the autumn of 1932, Serebryakov from the autumn of 1933, and Pyatakov even from the date of his alleged meeting with Sedov in 1931—a year before the alleged formation of the main center and two years before the date of formation of the reserve center as given in the indictment. Even Sokolnikov, although he spoke of the activities of the parallel center as having been "commenced" and "resumed" in 1935, testified to having had "connections" with terrorist groups before that date.

Just what was meant by the "conversion" of the parallel center into an "operating" center, or by the "commencement" or "resumption" of its activities, therefore, remains unclear; and the Prosecutor made no attempt to throw light on this question.

§ 119. What was meant by the intensification of activity which Pyatakov mentions in the second quotation above (§ 118) is implied in the quotation itself. Pyatakov went on to explain that in a conversation which he had with Sokolnikov "much attention was paid to the question of expanding the *bloc.* . . ." (PR 54). They decided, he said, that form must be given to their relations with the Rights, so as to organize the overthrow of the government in conjunction with them. Sokolnikov undertook to meet Tomsky, and did so, and he, Pyatakov, also had a conversation with Tomsky. In December Sokolnikov told him that "Tomsky had fully agreed to an organized joining of the *bloc.*" Whereupon Pyatakov told him of his own talk with Tomsky, in which the latter had said that

> he considered it absolutely necessary to organize terrorist and all other kinds of work, but that he would have to consult his comrades, Rykov and Bukharin. This he did later, and then gave me a reply in the name of all three. . . . Radek had connections with Bukharin. (PR 55.)

Although Sokolnikov in his testimony confined himself to telling what he allegedly knew about negotiations with the Rights conducted by Kamenev, in his final plea he stated that in 1935

> the Rights, as represented by Tomsky, who was empowered to do so by the whole central group of the Rights, gave their consent to joining the *bloc.* (PR 552.)

§ 120. If we turn to Radek's testimony concerning his "connections with Bukharin," we find that he did not mention any "negotiations" concerning the Rights' joining the bloc. He testified only to "conversations about terrorism." The first, he says, took place in June or July, 1934, after Bukharin came to work for *Izvestia*. At that time they conversed "as members of two centers which were in contact with each other" (PR 99). After the Kirov assassination, he said, two or perhaps three conversations took place at the end of December, 1934. They became convinced that "this murder had not produced the results the organizers had expected," and

> Already at that time we said to ourselves: either this act, the result of the tactics of individual terrorism, demands the cessation of terrorist actions or it demands that we go further and commit a terrorist act against a whole group. (PR 100.)

Thus Radek placed in December, 1934, the first discussions of "group terrorism," which plays an important rôle in the testimony concerning the activities of the alleged center in 1935. Before this he had testified, concerning this "new stage" (PR 76) or "new expanded tactic" (PR 77), that he and Pyatakov had discussed whether they could carry it out; and in answer to Vyshinsky's question, "Hence, in January, 1936, the question of expediency already rose among you?" he said:

> This was not in January, 1936, all this refers to January, 1935. (PR 76.)

Pyatakov, too, testified to discussions of this question with Sokolnikov, Radek and Serebryakov, and later with Tomsky, but without mentioning an exact date. He stated that

We discussed the question of carrying out Trotsky's directives to the effect that not scattered blows, but a concentrated terrorist blow was needed. (PR 71.)

But Pyatakov did not tell how or when they received these "directives" from Trotsky. Radek, however, made good the deficiency:

RADEK: I assert that not one of us is refuting the investigation material. It was testified that Trotsky's directive concerning a group terrorist act arrived in January, 1936.

VYSHINSKY: Trotsky's directives concerning terrorist acts, group terrorist acts, were received by you?

RADEK: They were. . . .

VYSHINSKY: Before that directive, were preparations for terrorist acts being made in our country?

RADEK: Before we received Trotsky's directives we took our own bearings. (PR 74.)

Even before this, Radek, in reply to the Prosecutor's question whether he had a conversation with Pyatakov about summoning Dreitzer, stated:

There was a talk in July, 1935. When we first gathered together after the murder of Kirov there arose the question that it was senseless killing single individuals. . . . Either abandon terrorism altogether, or start seriously organizing mass terrorist acts which would give rise to a situation bringing us nearer to power. (PR 72.)

And later he expatiated on the considerations which prompted the adoption of the idea of "group terrorism," without, however, linking up these considerations with any "directive" from Trotsky, and added:

I discussed this question in July, 1935, with Bukharin, with Pyatakov and Sokolnikov. (PR 101.)

Pyatakov, on the other hand, in speaking about their efforts to "ascertain the available forces," again explicitly stated:

I must say that all this was done in the course of carrying out the main directive of Trotsky, who demanded the execution of a group terrorist act. . . . (PR 73.)

Thus the record contains two separate and distinct versions of the phase of "group terrorism," in one of which the idea occurred to Radek and Bukharin in December, 1934, more than a year before Trotsky's "directive" was received, and was discussed between Radek and Pyatakov in January, 1935, exactly a year before this "directive" was received, and among Pyatakov, Radek, Sokolnikov and Bukharin in July, 1935, six months before the "directive" was received. In the other version, that of Pyatakov, the conversations about it and the efforts to "ascertain the available forces" all took place "in the course of carrying out Trotsky's directive"— which according to Radek, who allegedly received it, arrived only in January, 1936.

Naturally the question arises, What communications from Trotsky did Radek allegedly receive in January, 1936? If we turn to page 57 we find that he is explicit on this point— except that he neglects to tell how he received the letters and Vyshinsky neglects to ask him. Before quoting him, we must remark that Vyshinsky places Pyatakov's return from Berlin, after his alleged flight to Oslo, in 1936 (PR 77). Radek says:

I must say that there was no third letter in which it is alleged the conditions orally conveyed to Pyatakov were put in writing. Pyatakov is mistaken on this point.

After his return two letters arrived simultaneously, but these referred precisely to wrecking and to the situation in the international working-class movement. These letters were in reply to the enquiry I sent in the autumn of 1934, but evidently, while in transit, they were delayed in London and arrived late, in January. (PR 57.)

These are the only *letters* which Radek mentions having received in 1936; in the passage quoted above he speaks about a "directive." And certainly there is nothing here about "group terrorism." Moreover, we may note that if these alleged long-delayed letters were in answer to an enquiry from Radek to Trotsky in the autumn of 1934—he did not tell how he conveyed it—that enquiry, in order to concern "group terrorism," must have antedated Radek's own "first ideas" on this subject, which he definitely connected with his alleged conversations with Bukharin at the end of December, 1934. Vyshinsky, we note, never asked Radek how Trotsky's "directive" was received.

If one accept Pyatakov's version as true, then the alleged conversations about group terrorism must have taken place not in 1935 but in 1936, *after* the receipt of Trotsky's alleged directive. But this hypothesis is excluded by the evidence. Pyatakov said that he did not meet Radek after January, 1936 (PR 69–70). Radek said that his last talk with Pyatakov, Sokolnikov, and Serebryakov was that in which they discussed the "directives" Pyatakov had brought from Trotsky in January, 1936, and that he did not see any member of the bloc after March (PR 121, 132). Moreover, he stated that after the receipt of these directives he did nothing to undo what had been done, but took no further steps (PR 132). Pyatakov stated that after that time both he and Radek "pursued an ostrich-like policy—we hid our heads in the sand, but did nothing of importance" (PR 69). Serebryakov said that he did not see either Radek or Pyatakov after January, 1936

(PR 171); he mentioned no conversation with Sokolnikov. The last conversations with Radek and Pyatakov to which Sokolnikov testified allegedly took place in January, 1936 (PR 152); he mentioned no conversation with Serebryakov. According to all four of the accused, their January conversations concerned Trotsky's December "directives" to Pyatakov; therefore it is pertinent to mention that in no account of those alleged directives is there a word to be found about "group terrorism." Moreover, it must be remembered that Radek explicitly stated that the directive on group terrorism was received by him in January, 1936.

On the basis of the record itself, then, it is clear: (1) that Trotsky's alleged "directive" on group terrorism was received only in January, 1936, and that the accused Radek, who allegedly received it, made no mention of it in stating the contents of the two letters which he testified he received in that month, nor did he state how he received it; (2) that the members of the "center" did not meet after January, 1936; (3) that the alleged conversation about "group terrorism" therefore could not have taken place in July, 1936; (4) that all the alleged conversations on this subject, about whose dates the accused are explicit, took place in 1934 and 1935 if at all. Obviously, therefore, if a policy of "group terrorism" was adopted by this alleged center it was adopted independently of any "directives" from Leon Trotsky. In the opinion of this Commission, the nature of the evidence is not such as to inspire the belief that such conversations ever took place, that such a policy was ever adopted, or that such "directives" were ever received. Indeed, we consider that the shocking discrepancies which we have pointed out, when taken in conjunction with others either already discussed or hereinafter mentioned, entirely discredit the testimony given in the trials themselves in so far as it concerns the alleged complicity of Trotsky and Sedov in any anti-governmental activity which may have been taking place in the U.S.S.R.—and this quite apart from any evidence offered in rebuttal.

§ 121. In the case of the parallel center, as in that of the united center, account must be taken of the fact that most of the testimony is hearsay in so far as it concerns Trotsky and Sedov. The constant reiteration of references, occurring on almost every page, to Trotsky and Trotskyites, has the cumulative effect of concealing from all but the most cautious and analytic reader the quantity and quality of the evidence which, even in the prosecution's own case, purports to implicate Trotsky and Sedov.

We have already shown that of the four alleged members of the parallel center only two claimed direct contact with Trotsky, namely: Pyatakov and Radek. So far as the record shows, Pyatakov's contact with Trotsky consisted in one alleged letter from him in 1931 (PR 32), and one alleged interview with him in 1935 (PR 60–66); and that of Radek in six letters from him: February–March, 1932, August–September, 1933, April, 1934, December, 1935, and (two) January, 1936 (PR 56, 57).

Of the thirteen accused not members of the center, none claimed any direct contact with Trotsky. Of the five witnesses, one, Vladimir Romm, claimed to have met him at the end of July, 1933, in the Bois de Boulogne.

Thus three people among the seventeen accused and five witnesses testified to any direct contact with Leon Trotsky. Only one member of the center, Pyatakov, claimed direct contact with Sedov. He testified to two interviews with Sedov in the summer of 1931 and one in the summer of 1932. Of the other thirteen accused, one, Muralov, testified that he received three letters from Sedov (according to the accused Shestov, one of these was from Trotsky; but Muralov did not say so). (See § 163.) The accused Shestov testified to four meetings with Sedov in 1931. The witness Romm testified to five interviews with Sedov between the summer of 1931 and that of 1934. To sum up, three of the seventeen accused and five witnesses claimed contact with Trotsky; four claimed contact with Sedov; and five claimed contact with Trotsky or Sedov or both. Such of the others as claimed knowledge of Trotsky's "directives" got it, their own testimony reveals, at second or third or fourth hand, as the following summary shows:

(1) The accused Serebryakov claimed to have had his information from Mrachkovsky, Pyatakov, and Radek, and to have received instructions from Pyatakov through Livshitz. He implicated the accused Knyazev, Mdivani (neither witness nor accused) and several others. (PR 41, 168–174, 354.)

(2) The accused Sokolnikov claimed to have had information from Kamenev, Radek and Pyatakov. He implicated the accused Muralov, the witness Loginov, Tomsky and Bukharin and Uglanov (neither witnesses nor accused), and several others. (PR 147–168.)

(3) The witness Loginov testified that he had all his information and instructions from Pyatakov. He implicated the accused Rataichak, Hrasche, and others. (PR 178–192.)

(4) The accused Livshitz got Trotsky's "instructions" partly at fourth hand from Sedov through Pyatakov through Loginov, and partly at second and third hand through Pyatakov and Serebryakov. (PR 35, 118–19, 173, 174–5, 333–357.) He implicated the accused Knyazev, Turok, and others.

(5) The accused Boguslavsky testified that he got information on the center from Smirnov, and directives on wrecking work from Pyatakov and Muralov. (PR 192–201.) He implicated Shestov, Stroilov, Drobnis, and others.

(6) The accused Drobnis testified that he got information from Smirnov, instructions from Pyatakov, and certain information about other individuals from Shestov, though he did not claim that Shestov told him anything which came from Sedov or Trotsky. He implicated Muralov, Boguslavsky, Norkin, and Stroilov of the accused; also Rakovsky, Smilga and Safonova (a witness in the August trial). (PR 205–11.)

(7) The accused Stroilov's sole connection with Trotsky consisted in having read at some unspecified date Trotsky's "Life."* He was allegedly involved in conspiratorial work through a double blackmail practiced upon him, in reverse directions, in Germany and the Urals—in the latter by Shestov. (PR 247–257, and with respect to Shestov, also 238–9.)

(8) The accused Norkin allegedly received his information and instructions from Pyatakov and Rataichak. (PR 50–52, 279–292.)

(9) The German witness Stein implicated Shestov only (p. 293–98) among the accused, otherwise telling of sabotage on the part of German engineers.

(10) The accused Arnold testified mainly about his variegated career and various pseudonyms (PR 303–326), and also implicated Shestov (PR 326, 331) who in turn implicated Muralov (PR 330).

(11) The accused Knyazev implicated Livshitz (342–344); in other words his testimony is fourth-hand as far as alleged instructions from Trotsky and Sedov are concerned.

(12) The accused Turok allegedly had his instructions from Pyatakov, Livshitz, and Maryasin (neither an accused nor a witness). He implicated Knyazev. (PR 345–47, 362–70, 393–96.)

(13) The accused Rataichak allegedly had instructions from Pyatakov both directly and through Loginov. He implicated Hrasche, Pushin, and others. (PR 188, 408–33.)

(14) The accused Hrasche testified to having been a Czechoslovakian and later a German spy. He denied any connection with "Trotskyism" (§ 17, 1) and testified that he first learned during the trial about the existence of a "Trotskyite group."

---

* It is typical of the methods of the prosecution that Vyshinsky indulged in the following prejudicial question: "And you combined all this: member of the All-Russian Central Executive Committee and at the same time conspired with German agents, and read Trotsky?" (PR 250.)

(PR 430.) He implicated Rataichak, Norkin, and others.

(15) The accused Pushin implicated Rataichak and the witness Tamm. (PR 408–37.)

(16) The witness Tamm implicated Pushin only. (PR 440–41.)

(17) The witness Bukhartsev testified only regarding arrangements for the alleged flight of Pyatakov to Oslo. (PR 77–80.)

§ 122. This summary has an import. In the first place, it throws much light upon the procedure of the whole trial with respect to its aim to elicit the truth. In the second, it definitely establishes that the only testimony that has any standing with respect to the charges against Trotsky and Sedov is, in the first rank, that of Pyatakov and Romm, in the second rank, that of Radek and the totally unknown figure, Shestov, and in the third rank that of Muralov.

THE PYATAKOV-RADEK TRIAL: DEFINITIVE CHARGES AGAINST TROTSKY AND SEDOV

17

The testimony of Y.L. Pyatakov

§ 123. The first basis of the charge against Leon Trotsky and Leon Sedov in the Pyatakov-Radek trial is the testimony of the accused Pyatakov, who claimed to have had three interviews with Leon Sedov and one letter from and one interview with Leon Trotsky. We consider first his testimony concerning Sedov.

Pyatakov testified that in the summer of 1931, being in Berlin, he was told by I.N. Smirnov (Chapter X) that Leon Sedov had a special message to him from Trotsky and very much wished to see him. He met Sedov, he said, in a café known as "Am Zoo," where Sedov told him that

... Trotsky had not for a moment abandoned the idea of resuming the fight against Stalin's leadership, that there had been a temporary lull owing partly to Trotsky's repeated movements from one country to another, but that this struggle was now being resumed, ... Further, that there was being formed, or had already been formed—I cannot now recall—a Trotskyite center. It was a question of uniting all the forces capable of waging a fight against Stalin's leadership. The possibility was being sounded of restoring the united organization with the Zinovievites.*

Sedov also said that he knew for a fact that the Rights also in the persons of Tomsky, Bukharin and Rykov, had not laid down their arms, that they had only quieted down temporarily, and that the necessary connections should be established with them too. (PR 22–3.)

Pyatakov testified that he consented to take part in the struggle; whereupon Sedov outlined the "new methods of struggle," that is to say, "terrorism and wrecking." According to Pyatakov, Sedov further said that Trotsky drew attention to the fact that a struggle confined to one country would be absurd and that the international question could not possibly be evaded.

Some weeks later, he said, Smirnov told him that Sedov wished to see him again; they met in the same place, and Sedov instructed Pyatakov to place as many orders as possible with two German firms, Borsig and Demag, where

the additions to prices that would be made on the Soviet orders would pass wholly or in part into Trotsky's hands for his counter-revolutionary purposes. (PR 26–7.)

Pyatakov confessed that he afterwards placed "a fairly large number of orders" with those firms and paid them excessively at the expense of the Soviet government. (PR 27–8.)

In the summer of 1932, Pyatakov testified, he had a third meeting with Sedov in Berlin, and

began to relate to him what I knew about the activities

---

* See § 21 of this report.

of the Trotskyite-Zinovievite organization which were beginning to develop. (PR 36.)

But Sedov said he knew about that and wanted to hear what was being done in the provinces. So Pyatakov told him

. . . about the work of the Trotskyites in the Ukraine and in Western Siberia, about the contacts with Shestov, N.I. Muralov, and Boguslavsky who were in Western Siberia at that time. Sedov expressed extreme dissatisfaction, not his own, as he said, but Trotsky's dissatisfaction with the fact that things were moving very slowly, particularly in regard to terrorist activities. (PR 36.)

§ 124. Leon Sedov testified that he had had no interview with Pyatakov since 1927; that Pyatakov was one of the first to leave the Left Opposition, and that later he allied himself with the Radek tendency, which was the most vicious in attacking the Left Opposition. Sedov said:

. . . sometime in May, 1931 or 1932, I espied Pyatakov on *Unter den Linden*. As soon as he saw me, he turned his back on me, but not before I had had time to hurl at him an insulting epithet such as "traitor" or some similar word. (CR 28.)

Sedov pointed out that the story about his alleged meeting with Pyatakov in Berlin had been first related by Drobnis* during the Novosibirsk trial, and called attention to the fact that as related by Drobnis this meeting was not between Sedov and Pyatakov only, but included Smirnov. (The report of Drobnis's testimony about this alleged con-

---

* One of the accused in the January trial, who was a witness in the trial of the Kemerovo engineers at Novosibirsk in November, 1936.

versation appeared in *Pravda*, November 22, 1936. We have examined this report, and find it to be as Sedov represented it.) Sedov stated that when Leon Trotsky, then in Norway, learned of Drobnis's statement, he wrote to his lawyer, Puntervold,

> advising him that my mother recalled having received a letter from me in 1931 in which I recounted my chance meeting with Pyatakov in *Unter den Linden*, in the manner which I have explained above. My father's lawyer thereupon wrote to me asking what I had to say about the conference of three mentioned by Drobnis. I replied denying this fairy-tale, but as the lawyer had not made the slightest reference to the *Unter den Linden* incident, it was my father who first recalled it to my mind in a letter from Norway, dated December 2, 1936. It was thus only on December 11 that I wrote to my father's lawyer relating the incident to him. (CR 28–9.)

Sedov called the attention of the *Commission Rogatoire* to Pyatakov's allegation that, according to Sedov, there had been a lull in the struggle due to Trotsky's movements from one country to another (PR 22), and remarked that at that time Trotsky had not left Istanbul. As for the underhand dealings which he, Sedov, was supposed to have urged on Pyatakov in order that the Trotskyites might get a kickback on orders placed with Borsig and Demag, he denied that he had ever had any relations with those two firms or with any other German commercial or industrial firm. He further pointed out that when questioned about this matter Pyatakov was

> extremely careful not to give the slightest detail regarding the way these dealings were to be manipulated so as to produce revenue for us. (CR 30.)

He stated that

> If we had had such resources at our disposal, we would
> not have had to lead such a difficult administrative life as
> it is evident that we did lead both from a consideration
> of our accounts, which were made public on many occa-
> sions, and from the irregularity with which our *Bulletin*
> made its appearance. (CR 30.)

He reaffirmed that he had had only one interview with
Smirnov—that arranged at the time of their chance en-
counter in Berlin (Chapter X), and denied that Smirnov had
acted as an intermediary between himself and anyone else.
He remarked that Smirnov had never once during the first
trial spoken of having acted as a go-between in arranging
a meeting for Sedov with either Pyatakov or Shestov, and
stated his conviction that Smirnov's name had been used in
the Novosibirsk and second Moscow trials precisely because
he had already been condemned and executed. And of course,
he remarked, an intermediary was necessary, since Pyatakov
and Shestov could not have known Sedov's address. He noted
that Pyatakov, in speaking of their alleged meeting in 1932,
did not tell how he, Sedov, had brought about this meeting,
which he denied ever took place. (CR 30.)

§ 125. Sedov's testimony to the exchange of letters through
Puntervold about his meeting with Pyatakov is corroborated
by that of Trotsky, who said:

> . . . It was very difficult to prove a positive fact by a
> negative fact—that my son did not meet Pyatakov. I
> tried to use our internment—we could not communicate
> without the police, the Norwegian police, censorship. I
> wrote through the intermediary of the police to Punter-
> vold, my lawyer, to ask my son—my wife remembered
> that he met him on the street under such and such con-

ditions. Pyatakov turned his back to him. My son cried "Traitor!" Puntervold sent my son a question: "What was your meeting with Pyatakov?" Our son confirmed to Puntervold what I have stated. (PC 220.)

§ 126. Eugene Bauer stated that

It is perfectly true that our movement, from the administrative point of view, was always hard pressed. I remember perfectly having had to pay the editor of our *Bulletin* at the time of Trotsky's trip to Copenhagen the entire sum of my salary, because it was the only way to get out our publication. Sedov always did what he could to help us administratively, but the results of his activity in this attempt were always quite inadequate, and never did I hear it said that Sedov could obtain, by means of a percentage or otherwise, large subsidies from German firms, as Pyatakov said at the time of the second trial. (CR 45.)

§ 127. We have the following documents corroborating the testimony of Leon Sedov and Leon Trotsky concerning the nature of Leon Sedov's meeting with Pyatakov in Berlin:

(1) A holograph letter in German from Leon Trotsky to Michael Puntervold, dated November 26, 1936. In this letter Trotsky refers to the newspaper accounts of the testimony of the "witness" Drobnis in the Novosibirsk trial concerning an alleged conference of Pyatakov, Smirnov, and Sedov in Berlin, about which Pyatakov is supposed to have told Drobnis. He informs Puntervold that Mrs. Trotsky remembers having received in Kadikoy, Turkey, a letter from her son, who was studying in Berlin, in which he said that he had met "the redhead" (Pyatakov) on Unter den Linden; that he had looked him straight in the eye but that Pyatakov had turned away his face as if he did not recognize him. Trotsky states that it is very important that this version of his

son's meeting with Pyatakov has been put on paper before he and Mrs. Trotsky could possibly have received a single line about the Novosibirsk trial from their son. Puntervold will therefore be able, he says, to get a statement from his son about this meeting before he has written them about it or received anything from them. Then the two versions can be compared. (PC Exh. 19, III/4.)

(2) A letter from Michael Puntervold, Attorney, Oslo, November 30, 1936, to Leon Sedov, as follows:

> In the press-reports of the sabotage-trial of Novosibirsk there is a statement in the testimony of the engineer Drobnis to the effect that you had a conference in Berlin with Smirnov and Pyatakov. I would be very grateful to you if you would give me your statement on this as soon as possible, and as exactly as possible. (CR Exh. 13.)

(3) A holograph letter in French from Leon Trotsky to Leon Sedov, dated December 2, 1936. This letter chiefly concerns the theft of Trotsky's archives in Paris. It ends as follows:

> Mama has made a statement for Puntervold on your "meeting" with Pyatakov in Berlin (she remembers it better than I). You must give Puntervold your version in order that they may be compared. (CR Exh. 14.)

(4) Certified copies of two letters from Leon Sedov to Michael Puntervold, dated December 3 and 11, 1936. In the first of these letters Sedov denies the alleged meeting with Smirnov and Pyatakov. He says:

> I hold it also to be absolutely out of the question that Smirnov himself had any political relations with Pyatakov, for to hold any political conversation with Pyatakov certainly meant to be denounced by him to the GPU.

In this connection I may mention the role of K. Radek (who belongs in the same category with Pyatakov) in the shooting of Blumkin. Blumkin came to Radek and told him about his meeting with Trotsky in the year 1929 in Istanbul. Radek handed Blumkin over to the GPU, and Blumkin is known to have been shot. (PC Exh. 19, S III/5.)

Sedov also calls attention to the fact that the official Soviet press, in commenting on this testimony of Drobnis, remarked that the alleged conference "took place under the wing of the Gestapo," and points out that no Gestapo existed in the year 1931. (The Commission has verified this statement. See *Pravda*, November 23, 1936.)

In the letter of December 11, Sedov says that his father's letter of December 2 has reminded him of the following incident:

One time in Berlin—I can not remember precisely whether it was in 1931 or 1932 (I think it was on the first of May as I went along *Unter den Linden* on the way to see the demonstration in the *Lustgarten;* however it could have been another demonstration, not absolutely that of May 1)—I met Pyatakov face to face. As he saw me he turned his back on me, as though he had not recognized me. If I am not mistaken, I threw at him *sotto voce* some term of opprobrium. (PC Exh. 19, S III/6.)

§ 128. Concerning Pyatakov's testimony on his alleged meetings with Sedov, we note the following defects and false statements in the record of the trial:

(1) Pyatakov does not state how Trotsky discovered that he, Pyatakov, was ready for that "re-entry into the Trotskyite counter-revolution" which he dates from his first meeting with Sedov. At the time of that alleged meeting Pyatakov,

a "capitulator" holding a high government position, was allegedly in Berlin as the head of a large group of Soviet officials, on official business (PR 21–4). It therefore seems unlikely that Trotsky would have instructed either Sedov or Smirnov (assuming he was in touch with him) to confide the "new line" to Pyatakov, without having first made very sure of his attitude. Yet from Pyatakov's testimony it appears that Smirnov told him about this "new line" at their very first meeting in Berlin, and informed him that Sedov had a special message for him from Trotsky. It also appears that Sedov, at their first meeting, unhesitatingly revealed the whole alleged terrorist line to this "capitulator" in high office, and even hinted at treasonable relations with foreign powers (PR 23). A little more light on Pyatakov's conversion to the policy of terrorism and wrecking would have made these apparent indiscretions of Smirnov and Sedov more convincing. And a credible motivation for this conversion would have made Pyatakov's ready acceptance of terrorism and wrecking more convincing. According to Pyatakov, by 1931 he had developed

> definite differences with the leadership of the Party on the grounds of the complete removal of Trotsky from the leadership and his banishment abroad, and because Kamenev and Zinoviev were not being given any leading Party and government work. (PR 26.)

Such grounds would be credible as motivation for opposition to the leadership; they are hardly credible as motivation for entering a treasonable conspiracy which might—and presumably did—cost Pyatakov his life.

(2) Pyatakov's statement that Sedov in 1931 attributed the "temporary lull" in the fight against Stalin's leadership to "Trotsky's repeated movements from one country to another" is a patent falsehood, since it is a matter of common

knowledge that Trotsky resided uninterruptedly in Turkey from the date of his exile from the Soviet Union to that of his trip to Copenhagen in November, 1932. Sedov, in 1931, could not have been unaware that his father had not left Turkey since his exile began.

(3) We have already pointed out (§ 107) that Pyatakov could not have informed Sedov in the summer of 1932 about the activities of the Trotskyite-Zinovievite organization if he, Pyatakov, learned of its formation from Kamenev only after his return from Berlin in the autumn of 1932.

(4) If Pyatakov actually placed "a fairly large number of orders" with Borsig and Demag at prices higher than the Soviet government was paying other foreign firms, nothing could have been easier for the Prosecutor than to substantiate his testimony on this point by presenting to the Court the records of those orders and orders to other firms, for purposes of comparison. He did not do so, and his failure to document this testimony throws grave doubt on the truth of Pyatakov's statement. Moreover, it was obviously in order for the Prosecutor to ask Pyatakov how he managed these operations in such a way as to conceal them from his chief, Ordjonikidze, and his other associates in the Commissariat of Heavy Industry. Surely Pyatakov could not have been the only person in the Commissariat who saw those orders. If they were passed by his associates and his superior, then it would appear that he had confederates. Neither the Prosecutor nor the Court showed the slightest interest in this important implication of Pyatakov's testimony.

§ 129. Reference to the testimony of Smirnov in the first trial (Chapter X) bears out Sedov's statement that Smirnov mentioned no such meetings with Pyatakov and Shestov in Berlin as Pyatakov and Shestov allude to. Smirnov admitted only one conversation with Sedov. Therefore the testimony of Pyatakov and Shestov is the sole basis in the record of either trial for belief that Smirnov acted as liaison man between themselves and Sedov. Nothing in Pyatakov's testimony bears out the testimony of Drobnis in the Novosibirsk trial concerning a meeting of Pyatakov, Smirnov and Sedov. However, Pyatakov testified that he remembered a conversation with Sedov and Shestov on the enlistment of non-"Trotskyites" in wrecking work (PR 162). This testimony follows in the record a statement of Shestov that he had conversations on the same subject with Smirnov, Sedov, and Pyatakov, but that he conversed with them not together but separately (PR 160). Thus Pyatakov's is the only direct evidence offered of his alleged meetings with Sedov. In view of the questionable nature of this evidence, and in view of the striking contradictions and falsehoods in Pyatakov's testimony already noted in Chapter XVI, and others which will be discussed later, we hold his testimony concerning Sedov to be unworthy of credence on the basis of the record of the trial alone.

As for the letters cited above concerning Sedov's meeting with Pyatakov on *Unter den Linden,* their value as evidence of the exact nature of that meeting is somewhat impaired by Sedov's failure to recall it in his first letter to Puntervold. It may be argued that although Trotsky, in the letter to his son which was introduced in evidence, said nothing of the nature of this "meeting," he might have sent another letter which was not introduced, in which he described the meeting in detail as his wife remembered it, in order that his son's version might tally with hers. However, we note that in his letter to Puntervold, Trotsky appears quite certain that his son will bear out his wife's version of this meeting; and that the letter to his son about it is dated December 2, whereas the letter to Puntervold is dated November 30. Had he written to Sedov describing the meeting in detail in order that his son might corroborate that version, it seems reasonable to suppose that he would have done so at least on the same date as his letter to Puntervold, if not before. But had Sedov received such a letter from his father before December 3, the date of his first letter to Puntervold, then surely he would have described the meeting in the letter of December 3. And if he had received such a letter immediately after his letter to Puntervold, then surely he would not have waited until December 11 to "remember" the incident. Moreover, if he and Trotsky had "framed" this meeting, Sedov would certainly not have mentioned to Puntervold that he had been reminded of it by a letter from his father and even added, as he did, a postscript to his letter of the 11th, saying, "I have already written to my father about this on December 7." It must also be noted that Trotsky was at that period living under close surveillance by the Norwegian police, a fact which both he and Sedov mentioned in their testimony. Moreover, Trotsky in his letter to Puntervold remarks that he will obtain from his police guard a receipt stating the day and hour when the letter is turned over to them. It would be absurd to assume that Trotsky would have attempted to arrange a frame-up with his son at a time when his correspondence was under censorship by the police of a government as inimical to him as was the Norwegian government from the time of the August trial until his deportation.

In view of these considerations, we hold that this exchange of letters has, in contradistinction to the record of the trial, every appearance of honesty; and that it constitutes important refutation of Pyatakov's testimony concerning his alleged meetings with Sedov; refutation which, we repeat, is hardly necessary in view of the nature of Pyatakov's testimony not only on this particular point but in general.

We have noted (§ 128, 4) the failure of the Prosecutor to document Pyatakov's statement concerning orders to Borsig and Demag and to ask him how he concealed the graft from his superior and his associates. Sedov's denial that the Trotskyists received money from such sources is corroborated by Eugene Bauer. It might reasonably be assumed that

Sedov would deny such connections or such transactions; and even that Bauer would do so, since although he is no longer a member of the Trotskyite organization, such an admission would nevertheless bring him into discredit. The argument that Bauer may not have known about Sedov's receipt of such funds is worth little if one accept the contention of the prosecution that Trotsky's followers abroad were aware of his counter-revolutionary designs. In any case if large funds had been available for Trotskyite propaganda they would necessarily have been aware of it. Another and equally important question, however, is, Whom did Borsig and Demag represent in these transactions and whom did they think Sedov represented? We can hardly assume that they would undertake to turn over large sums to Sedov merely as a personal favor or that they would undertake as a private enterprise the unpromising task of helping a couple of revolutionary émigrés to overthrow the Soviet régime. Nor can we assume that the transactions took place "under the wings of the Gestapo," since in 1931 the wings of the Gestapo had not fledged, nor was there any certainty that they would ever do so. It seems absurd to assume that German capitalists would have banked on Hitler, with or without the help of the Trotskyites, to overturn the Stalin régime in Russia before he had even succeeded in overturning the republican régime in Germany. And it seems equally absurd to suppose that Sedov and Trotsky would have done so. Moreover, such an assumption implies the question, How is it that both Sedov and Bauer, if the Trotskyites were in such excellent relations with Hitler, were both obliged to leave Germany after he came to power? There remains the possibility that Borsig and Demag were turning over large sums to Sedov in order to enable him to assist the government of the German Republic to undermine the Soviet régime. It was clearly the duty of the Prosecutor to clear up this question by querying Pyatakov concerning the basis of

Sedov's alleged collusion with the firm of Borsig and Demag. For it can hardly be assumed that Pyatakov acted blindly in a matter as dangerous as these alleged diversions of Soviet funds to Sedov and Trotsky. He must, therefore, have been in a position to clear up all the questions implied in his testimony to such diversions.

This Commission does not presume to determine whether or not Pyatakov did actually overpay the firms of Borsig and Demag, or, if so, for what purposes. Nor is this question germane to our inquiry, which concerns only the guilt or innocence of Leon Trotsky and Leon Sedov. It does, however, concern us that Vyshinsky, through his failure to document Pyatakov's testimony on this alleged diversion of funds, and his further failure to ask him the most obvious and necessary questions about it, left the record extremely vague not only as concerns the alleged benefit accruing to Trotsky and Sedov but even as concerns the diversion itself. As the record stands, we have only Pyatakov's uncorroborated testimony to the alleged transactions with Borsig and Demag, and to Sedov's connection with them.

§ 130. We have already stated (§ 129) our conclusion that Pyatakov's testimony is unworthy of credence on the basis of the trial record, and our further conclusion that Sedov's account of the nature of his meeting with Pyatakov is important as refutation of Pyatakov's account of meetings of a conspiratorial nature between them. We note, moreover, that since Pyatakov testified that Smirnov first revealed to him the alleged terrorist line, and put him in touch with Sedov, his testimony can not be true if Smirnov's testimony that Sedov proposed terrorism to him is false. We have already stated (§ 46) our conclusion that Sedov conveyed to Smirnov no "opinion" or instructions on terrorism. On the basis of that conclusion, and the considerations stated above, we hold that Pyatakov's testimony to his alleged conversations with Sedov in Berlin is sheer fabrication. Therefore, we hold that

Pyatakov's testimony concerning excessive payments to the firms of Borsig and Demag, in so far as it concerns Trotsky and Sedov, is also false.

§ 131. Concerning his alleged contacts with Trotsky, Pyatakov testified that at the time of his second meeting with Sedov in 1931, he requested Sedov to get him "supplementary explanations" from Trotsky on the "question of wrecking activities," and that Sedov told him he had already written to Trotsky and was awaiting a reply. In December, 1931, he said, the accused Shestov, on his return from Berlin, came to see him in his office in the Supreme Council of National Economy, and handed him a letter. (PR 29.) Shestov, questioned on this point, admitted that he went to see Pyatakov and handed him a letter which was one of two that he had received from Sedov in Berlin, secreted in a pair of shoes, after his, Shestov's, return from a trip to England. He insisted that he had handed this letter to Pyatakov not in December but in the middle of November. (PR 29–32.) Pyatakov admitted that it might have been in the middle of November. According to his account of this letter, which was not introduced in evidence, Trotsky wrote about three "fundamental tasks." The first was "to use every means to remove Stalin and his immediate assistants"; and "of course," said Pyatakov, "'every means' was to be understood above all as violent means." The second was to unite all anti-Stalin forces for this struggle. The third was to counteract all the measures of the Soviet government and the Party, especially in the economic field. (PR 32.) Vyshinsky asked Pyatakov, "What did you do with this letter or in connection with this letter?" and Pyatakov proceeded to tell what he allegedly did *in connection with* the letter, disregarding the question about what he did *with* it. (See § 47.)

§ 132. Since the truth or falsehood of Pyatakov's testimony about the receipt of these "supplementary explanations" depends upon that of his testimony concerning a second conversation with Sedov, and since we have already stated (§ 130) our conclusion that no conversations took place between them, we therefore hold that this alleged letter from Trotsky is apocryphal; and this quite apart from consideration of the testimony of Trotsky or Sedov or the accused Shestov who allegedly delivered it and whose testimony concerning his own alleged connections with Sedov we consider in Chapter XX.

§ 133. Between Pyatakov's testimony to this alleged letter from Trotsky and that to his next direct contact with him, he testified to a great many activities. We have already considered part of this testimony in Chapter XVI. We shall consider other parts of it in later chapters of this report. As regards his testimony to particular acts of sabotage and instructions to others to commit sabotage, we do not presume to state whether or not it is true. However, we repeat that the nature of his testimony in general is not such as to inspire confidence. We are, however, concerned with his testimony, and that of the other accused and witnesses, only in so far as it bears upon the charges against Leon Trotsky and Leon Sedov. Much of Pyatakov's testimony concerns "instructions" allegedly conveyed to him by Radek, who supposedly had them from Trotsky, and is therefore hearsay evidence. We do not consider that part of his testimony here, since we are interested only in his testimony directly involving Leon Trotsky.

Pyatakov testified that at the end of 1935, following the alleged receipt by Radek of a long letter of instructions from Trotsky, it was decided that Pyatakov should take advantage of a forthcoming business trip abroad in order to see Trotsky, since both he and Radek were "very much disquieted" by the contents of this letter (PR 56, 58). Radek, he said, suggested that in Berlin he should apply to Bukhartsev, who "had connections with Trotsky," to help him arrange this meeting. He arrived in Berlin on December 10, and

That same day or the next, I met Bukhartsev, who, taking advantage of a moment when nobody was about, told me that he had heard of my arrival a few days before, had informed Trotsky of it, and was awaiting news from Trotsky on the matter. The next day Trotsky sent a messenger, with whom Bukhartsev brought me together in the Tiergarten, in one of the lanes, literally for a couple of minutes. He showed me a brief note from Trotsky which contained a few words: "Y.L., the bearer of this note can be fully trusted." The word "fully" was underlined, from which I gathered that the person Trotsky had sent was an agent of his. (PR 58.)

Pyatakov said that according to this messenger, whose name was either "Heinrich" or "Gustav," Trotsky "strongly insisted" on having a talk with him, this insistence, as it later transpired, being due to the last letter Radek had sent Trotsky. (The last letter to Trotsky mentioned by Radek was allegedly sent in May, 1934; the last letter Romm testified he conveyed from Radek to Trotsky through Sedov was also allegedly sent in May, 1934—PR 107, 143. Radek mentioned an "enquiry" which he allegedly sent Trotsky in the autumn of 1934, by unspecified means.) "Heinrich" or "Gustav" asked Pyatakov whether he was prepared to travel by airplane, and Pyatakov agreed although, he said, he knew he was taking a great risk "of discovery, exposure, and anything you like." Whereupon the messenger arranged to meet him the next morning at the Tempelhof Airport. The next morning Pyatakov, according to his testimony, went directly to the entrance of the airdrome, where "Heinrich-Gustav" was waiting with a German passport which had been prepared for him. "Heinrich-Gustav"

. . . saw to all the customs formalities himself, so that all I had to do was to sign my name.

We got into an airplane and set off. We did not stop
anywhere, and at approximately 3 P.M. we landed at the
airdrome in Oslo. There an automobile awaited us. We
got in and drove off. We drove for about 30 minutes
and came to a country suburb. We got out and entered
a small house that was not badly furnished, and there
I saw Trotsky, whom I had not seen since 1928. It was
here that my conversation with Trotsky took place. (PR
59–60.)

Pyatakov's alleged conversation with Trotsky will be considered in Chapter XXIV of this report. Suffice it to state
here that he related it with a memory for detail which is
conspicuously lacking in his account of more concrete and
mundane matters. If he really "signed his name" on the false
passport, it would have been easy for the Prosecutor to verify
his testimony by securing from the Norwegian government
the record of his entry. But it seems unlikely that a Soviet
Commissar would have travelled on a German passport issued in his own name, since to do so must have involved a
certainty rather than a mere risk of exposure. If he travelled
under an assumed name, it would have been equally easy for
the Prosecutor to verify his testimony simply by ascertaining the name and asking the Norwegian government for the
record of entry of a person bearing it. Pyatakov was not explicit on this point, and Vyshinsky asked no questions. We
do learn, however, from Pyatakov's answer to a somewhat
belated question of the Prosecutor, that he gave his photograph for the passport, although he did not say when or to
whom (PR 79). He did not state whether he saw anyone else
in the small house in the country suburb, although he did
say that no one else was present at the interview, which "was
arranged very secretly by both of us" and lasted about two
hours (PR 60). He did not even state how long he remained
in Norway or how he returned to Berlin; we are obliged,

indeed, to turn to the testimony of the witness Bukhartsev in order to learn that he returned at all.

§ 134. This witness, who stated that he was "the special correspondent" of *Izvestia* and at the same time a member of the Trotskyite organization, testified that

> At the beginning of December, 1935, I learned that Pyatakov was coming to Berlin. A few days later a certain Gustav Stirner rang me up on the telephone. I had been put in touch with him by Radek. . . . He was Trotsky's man. . . . When Gustav Stirner telephoned me I told him that Pyatakov was expected to arrive within a few days. He said that this was very interesting and that he would try and inform Trotsky of this, and that probably Trotsky would want to see him. (PR 78.)

A few days later, said Bukhartsev, Stirner telephoned again that Trotsky very much wanted to see Pyatakov. Stirner, he said, told him that he had connections in Berlin and would make the arrangements. Bukhartsev "imagined" these connections were with German government officials. Stirner said "that a special airplane would take Pyatakov to Oslo and back." Bukhartsev testified that Stirner did not live in Berlin, but had given him as his address Oslo, General Post Office, *poste restante*. Bukhartsev did not see him after that. He did, however, see Pyatakov, who told him that "he had been and seen." Pyatakov confirmed this statement. (PR 79–80.)

Thus we may gather that Pyatakov returned from Oslo and even that he returned in the same special airplane that took him there. We do not, however, learn anything about the identity of Gustav Stirner, who allegedly procured the plane, for Vyshinsky did not see fit to question Radek, who had allegedly put Bukhartsev in touch with this "agent" of Trotsky. We do learn that Trotsky's prompt meeting with Pyatakov depended upon the fortunate chance that this

"agent" happened to be in Berlin and to telephone Bukhartsev a few days after the latter had learned that Pyatakov was
coming. Otherwise Pyatakov would presumably have had
to wait until after he had seen Bukhartsev and the latter at
his request had written to Stirner, *poste restante*, General
Post Office, Oslo, and Stirner had consulted Trotsky. As it
was, he was able to make his alleged flight "in the first half
of December."

§ 135. Pyatakov testified on January 23 concerning his
alleged flight. At the evening session of January 27, the
Prosecutor returned to the subject. In reply to his questions
Pyatakov reaffirmed that he had landed at an airdrome near
Oslo and said that he was too excited by the unusual nature
of the journey to note whether there were any difficulties
about the landing or the admission of the plane to the airdrome. Asked whether he had heard of a place called Kjeller, or
Kjellere, he replied in the negative. Vyshinsky then declared
that he had requested the People's Commissariat of Foreign
Affairs to make an inquiry, since he "wanted to verify Pyatakov's evidence from this side too"; and he asked to have the
following official communication put into the record:

> "The consular Department of the People's Commis-
> sariat of Foreign Affairs hereby informs the Procurator
> of the U.S.S.R. that according to information received
> by the Embassy of the U.S.S.R. in Norway the Kjellere
> Airdrome near Oslo receives all the year round, in accor-
> dance with international regulations, airplanes of other
> countries, and that the arrival and departure of airplanes
> is possible also in winter months." (PR 443.)

§ 136. Leon Trotsky testified that he met Pyatakov for
the first time during the Civil War; that Pyatakov had been
a member of the Left Opposition from 1923 to the end of
1927 and capitulated in February, 1928, and that he was the

first Trotskyist to capitulate publicly (PC 116–17). He stated that the last time he saw Pyatakov was in 1927. He denied that he had seen Pyatakov in or near Oslo in December, 1935, or at any other place, or that he had seen him since 1927 or had any communication with him, either directly or through some intermediary. He denied that he had ever heard the name of Bukhartsev before the trial (PC 210–11). He also denied knowing anyone by the name of Gustav Stirner (PC 560).

Trotsky stated that from June, 1935, until his internment in 1936 he and his wife lived at Weksal, a village near the small town of Hoenefoss, Norway, about two hours from Oslo by railroad or automobile over a hilly and difficult road. They made their home with the family of Konrad Knudsen, a prominent member of the Norwegian Workers' Party and a deputy to the Norwegian Parliament. On the ground floor of the house there were five rooms, three of which were occupied by the Knudsen family—Konrad Knudsen, his wife Hilda, his daughter Hjordis, and his son Borgar. The cook, a Norwegian woman, also lived in the house. Two rooms on the ground floor were occupied by Trotsky and his wife. For a time Trotsky's secretary, Jan Frankel, also lived in the house. Then he left and was replaced by Erwin Wolf, who lived in the house of a neighbor. His workroom, Trotsky said, adjoined the dining room, which was used by both families; and visitors who came to see him were obliged to pass first through a vestibule out of which opened both the kitchen and the dining room, and then through the dining room. He testified that the Knudsen family, although not sharing his political views, were very friendly to himself and his wife, and concerned for his safety; that they arranged all communications for him and saw every one of his visitors. According to Trotsky, visits to him were arranged as follows: Everyone who wished to see him was told to visit the bookshop of Hjordis Knudsen in Hoenefoss, which was in the same house as the office of the labor paper edited by Konrad Knudsen. There, visitors were told at what time Mr. Knudsen would be able to take them to Weksal in his automobile. During his stay with the Knudsens, Trotsky said, he received in all not more than twelve or fifteen visitors, and there were no Russians among them (PC 206–11). He said that in that period he went to Oslo with the Knudsens three or four times, for a day; that he never made any trip alone and indeed could not possibly have done so because

> . . . if I am on the street and recognized by the people I am absolutely helpless. I am surrounded by people, and especially in Norway—I don't speak Norwegian—I must have some Norwegian people who can defend me. (PC 209.)

Trotsky stated that the only time in December, 1935, when he was out of the Knudsen house was a brief period from the 20th to the 22nd, which he spent in a mountain cabin belonging to Knudsen, about an hour from Weksal but not in the direction of Oslo, accompanied by his wife, his secretary Erwin Wolf, Borgar Knudsen, and the Knudsen's cook (PC 211–15). He took this trip, he said, in an unsuccessful effort to improve his health, which was very bad during that month (PC 222).

Trotsky read into the record two statements which he had given to the world press during the January trial (and which were widely published), putting to the Moscow Court specific questions to be transmitted to the accused Pyatakov. The first of these, issued on January 24, the day after Pyatakov's testimony concerning his alleged flight, begins:

> If Pyatakov had traveled under his own name, all the Norwegian press would have carried this information. Consequently he must have traveled under another

name. All Soviet functionaries abroad are in constant telephonic and telegraphic communication with their embassies, commercial missions, and do not find themselves beyond the watch of the GPU for a single hour. How could Pyatakov have achieved this trip without the knowledge of the Soviet representatives either in Germany or Norway? (PC 215.)

Then follow precise questions concerning Trotsky's appearance and surroundings. On January 27 Trotsky gave to the press a list of thirteen questions. Both these lists, he said, were based on the press-reports of Pyatakov's testimony (PC 220). Certain questions concerning dates, hours, arrangements for the trip, and means of transportation are answered in the official record of the trial (§§ 133, 134), evening session of January 23, the day before Trotsky's first list of questions was given to the press. The other questions were not put to Pyatakov by the Prosecutor. Among them are the following:

Did Pyatakov have a Norwegian visa? Did he pass the night in Oslo; if so, in what hotel? How did he succeed in disappearing from the eyes of Soviet officials in Berlin and Oslo? How did he explain his disappearance on his return to Russia? Whom did Pyatakov meet in Trotsky's house? Did he see Trotsky's wife? On what precise date did Pyatakov fly from Berlin to Oslo? What name did he use on his German passport?

Trotsky also introduced evidence to show that according to the official in charge of the Kjeller airdrome in Oslo, no foreign plane landed there during the month of December, 1935. Counsel for the Preliminary Commission brought up the question whether Pyatakov's alleged flight might not have been arranged by German fascists in collusion with Norwegian fascists who were able to prevent the director of the airport from reporting the landing, and asked whether it would not be in the interest of the director, in such a case, to deny that the plane had landed. Trotsky argued that

> The director of the airdrome affirmed that there is a military patrol day and night, for customs reasons. Now, is it a lie or is it true? If he is a fascist, the Government is Socialist in Norway. There are different parties. Their papers sent their representatives to the airdrome . . . the fact is that the airplane must have remained from twelve to fifteen hours and there might have been other people at the airdrome. (PC 404–5.)

Questioned further whether if such an airplane did land, the Norwegian Government might want to deny it for diplomatic reasons, he said:

> I believe the Norwegian Government would be glad to denounce me immediately, because they interned me for four months, if not longer, only for the benefit of the Soviet Government. And if they had no reason to conceal it, it would be the best justification for their civil measures against me, because the Government is severely attacked by its own parties. . . . If the Government could use any evidence in my sojourn which would implicate me in counter-revolutionary propaganda, it would be glad to present all the proofs. It is also the reason why the director of the airdrome who gave the deposition, when my Norwegian lawyer asked him for a formal deposition for the Commission, said: "I have said it already. I cannot give you that without authorization of the higher authorities. They prohibit me from giving it." (PC 405.)

§ 137. The inquiry concerning the truth or falsehood of Pyatakov's testimony to this alleged flight falls into three parts: First, were Trotsky's conditions of life in Norway such that it would have been possible for him to arrange a meeting with Pyatakov which would be unknown to the people around him? Second, was he at any time during the month of December, 1935, ever in a position to receive a secret visit, or did he receive any Russian visitor with the knowledge of the people who were closest to him? Third, did Pyatakov, in the first half of December, 1935, fly to Norway, land at the airdrome near Oslo, proceed by automobile to a country suburb one half-hour from the airport, and there see Trotsky?

§ 138. Concerning Trotsky's mode of life and his political preoccupations during his sojourn in Norway, the New York Sub-Commission took the testimony of four witnesses. A.J. Muste of New York City testified that for a brief time, as a member of the Workers' Party of the United States, which was formed through a merger of the American Workers' Party to which he belonged and the Trotskyist Communist League of America, he had belonged to the Trotskyist organization; that the Workers' Party of the United States ceased to exist when the majority of its members voted for its dissolution and the entrance of its members into the Socialist Party; that he himself ceased connection entirely with the movement immediately after the trip to Europe in 1936 during which he saw Trotsky; and that he still holds a position which makes it impossible for him to belong to the Trotskyite organization (NY 44–7). He stated that he visited Trotsky at Hoenefoss near Oslo from June 28 to July 5, 1936; that he made the trip from Oslo to Hoenefoss by bus, leaving Oslo at about ten o'clock in the morning and arriving in Hoenefoss about noon. In Hoenefoss he was met by Mr. Knudsen, who took him in an automobile to Trotsky's house. This ride, he said, took about fifteen minutes, and the direction was away from Oslo rather than toward it. Altogether, he said, the distance from Oslo to the house where Trotsky lived was about two hours and a half. His description of the house corroborates Trotsky's. He stated that he and Mrs. Muste, who accompanied him, took their meals with the Trotskys and the Knudsens; that since the house was the home of the Knudsen family, its members were constantly present; that in order to reach Trotsky's study it was necessary to pass through the Knudsen dining room, where there was usually someone of the family present. He said he could not see how it would be possible for anyone to enter the house and hold any conversation here unknown to others than Trotsky and his wife, since the rooms opened into one another and the doors were ordinary sliding doors with big openings in between. (NY 38–50.)

§ 139. Three other witnesses, Harold Isaacs, Max Sterling, and Viola Robinson, of New York, testified that they had visitedTrotsky at Weksal. Their testimony concerning the distance from Oslo to Weksal, the way in which they were conducted to Trotsky's house, and the conditions under which he lived, corroborates that of Trotsky and Muste. (NY 115–19, 134–47.)

§ 140. The most important documents in our possession bearing upon Pyatakov's alleged flight to Oslo are as follows:

(1) An affidavit (Oslo) by Konrad Knudsen, signed also by his wife Hilda Knudsen and their daughter Hjordis Knudsen, stating that Trotsky and his wife were guests in the Knudsen home from June 18, 1935, to August 27, 1936, and that during this whole period, with the exception of a couple of brief interruptions for treatment at a hospital in Oslo, Trotsky resided with them, occupying with his wife a workroom and a bedroom whereas the dining room was shared by the members of both families; that they were thoroughly aware of all his visitors during this period; that no visitor could enter the house without the knowledge of the members of the household, and that Trotsky introduced them to all his visitors; that telephone calls were always received by the host or a member of his family and never by

Trotsky or his wife; that the few times Trotsky was away from the house he left in Knudsen's car and in Knudsen's company; that it is therefore excluded in the opinion of the deponents that Trotsky could have met other people than those with whom they became acquainted; that his visitors were Czechoslovaks, German emigrants, Englishmen, Frenchmen and Americans, and that there were no Russians among them; that Trotsky received no visitors during the month of December, 1935; that he spent two days of that month at their hut in the woods, and that this hut was not generally known and no one would have been able to find him there. (PC Exh. 19, I/1.)

(2) An affidavit (Charleroi, Belgium) by Trotsky's former secretary, Erwin Wolf, stating that he went to Weksal near Hoenefoss on November 15, 1935, to act as Trotsky's secretary and watch over his personal safety, and remained there until July 24, 1936. Wolf states that his workroom, which was at the same time the dining room of the Knudsen family, was immediately next to Trotsky's, and shut off from it by a thin sliding door which could not be locked. He says that it was an unbreakable rule of long standing never to leave Trotsky alone, since there was constant danger of an attempt on his life by white guards, fascists, or agents of the GPU. For this same reason no strange person was ever allowed to see Trotsky without first coming in contact with Wolf himself or with some member of the Knudsen family; nor was anyone ever admitted whose identity had not previously been ascertained. The rooms were so arranged that no one could enter Trotsky's workroom without first passing through a vestibule which could be watched by the Knudsen family from the kitchen, and through Wolf's workroom. He says:

In my statements to the *Manchester Guardian* of January 25, 1937, and the *Daily Herald* of January 29,

1937, I have already made it clear that Trotsky received no visit from a foreigner in the month of December, 1935, and that a secret visit to Trotsky was out of the question, since not only I myself but also the members of the Knudsen family knew every step of Trotsky's. It is quite possible that a few Norwegians who visited the Knudsen family eventually spoke also with Trotsky, but those cases would have to do with acquaintances of the Knudsen family.

Wolf names four visitors who saw Trotsky in November: Walter Held (PC Exh. 19, I/3), Fred Zeller from Paris, and two Canadians, Kenneth Johnston and Professor B. (Earle Birney, PC Exh. 19, I/5). He says further:

> I am above all in a position to state and to swear that Pyatakov's alleged visit to Trotsky is a pure invention, for the latter was in fact under my constant guardianship in December, 1935. In this month I left Trotsky only twice: at noon on the 19th of December I went to Oslo. . . . I was home by nine or ten o'clock in the evening of the same day. The second time I left Trotsky, if I am not mistaken, on the 26th of December, at nine in the morning and returned at ten o'clock in the evening. I was skiing in the neighborhood. But both during my first and my second absence, Trotsky was together with the members of the Knudsen family, with whom he took his meals. . . . I must emphasize that both times I left Weksal not at the suggestion of Trotsky or his wife, but on my own initiative, and that Trotsky knew only the evening before that I would not be there on the following day.

Trotsky's health, says Wolf, was bad during that month, and therefore Mr. and Mrs. Knudsen insisted that he go, over the

Christmas holidays, to Knudsen's hut. The initiative in this matter was taken by the Knudsen family, and it was they who, after a long resistance on Trotsky's part, obtained his consent and fixed the date for the trip. Trotsky left Weksal in an automobile driven by Knudsen on Friday, December 20, 1935, at about noon. With him were his wife, Knudsen's son Borgar, the cook Astrid, and Wolf. They drove first to Hoenefoss and then to the foot of the mountain Ringkollen. There a sleigh was rented, since Trotsky was too weak to make the climb on foot in the deep snow, and an auto could not make the trip up the mountain. Wolf describes in detail their stay at the hut. Among other things he says:

> The next morning Borgar and I spent in chopping wood, making a fire and preparing breakfast, which was taken between half-past ten and eleven. After everything was in order again we went, Borgar and I, on skis to the nearby lake Oiangen which was frozen over and covered with 60–70 centimeters of snow. There we could see that not the slightest sign of an airplane was evident. . . . Since Pyatakov said in Moscow that he made the trip to Trotsky in an auto, it is clear therefore that on this ground alone there is not even a shadow of a possibility that his alleged visit could have taken place in the Knudsen hut, to which not even the most modern tank could have broken through—thick woods, steep cliffs and so on. (PC Exh. 19 S I/8.)

(3) An affidavit (Oslo) by Borgar Knudsen states that he was with the Trotskys from December 20 to 22, 1935, when they and Erwin Wolf stayed at the Knudsen cottage; that a great deal of snow fell during those days so that it was impossible to leave the cottage without skis, and that since Trotsky had no skis he was not outside the cottage; that Trotsky received no visitors during those days and that no

one could have visited him without his, Borgar Knudsen's knowledge. (*Ibid.*, II/7.)

(4) An automobile map of South Norway (by K.G. Gleditsch; published by H. Aschehoug & Co.), sent to the Commission by Konrad Knudsen, on which he has marked the route from the Kjeller airdrome near Oslo to Hoenefoss and Weksal; with a covering letter from Mr. Knudsen stating that the distance from Kjeller through Oslo to Hoenefoss and Weksal is at least eighty-six kilometers or sixty English miles, and cannot possibly be covered by automobile in less than two hours. Mr. Knudsen says that the roads in Norway have hills and sharp swings, and that the speed limit is 60 kilometers or 42 English miles an hour. (*Ibid.*, S II/8, a, b.)

(5) *a.* A letter to Leon Trotsky from Andreas Stoeylen, lawyer, dated Oslo, March 16, 1937, stating that he is enclosing the following documents: (1) copy of a letter of February 10 to Director Gullichsen, Kjeller airport; (2) a letter of February 14, 1937, from Gullichsen to Stoeylen; (3) *Arbeiderbladet* No. 24, Friday, January 29, 1937; (4) a letter of February 27, 1937, from Gullichsen to Stoeylen. (*Ibid.*, II/3.)

b. A certified notarized English translation of (1) above. Mr. Stoeylen requests on Trotsky's behalf that Director Gullichsen provide him with four copies of a written statement confirming the fact that no airplane landed at Kjeller in December, 1935, as per Gullichsen's statement in Arbeiderbladet of January 29, 1937. (*Ibid.*, II/4, a.)

c. Original and certified, notarized English translation of (2) above, as follows:

Sir: In reply to your letter of 10th inst. I beg to state that my statement published in *Arbeiderbladet* is correct, as no foreign aeroplane landed here in December, 1935. However, before I make the four declarations for which you have asked me I find I must confer with superior authorities. I have not been able to see the proper person hitherto, I am sorry to say, and as I am leaving for England this evening I cannot get the question settled before I return on Monday the 22nd inst. I will then take up the matter again.

Yours truly
(Signed) Gullichsen (Ibid., II/4, b.)

d. Original and certified, notarized English translation of an article in (3) above, entitled "Pyatakov's Strange Voyage to Kjeller." The article reports an interview in which Director Gullichsen confirmed the fact that no foreign airplane landed at Kjeller Aviation Ground in December, 1935. Director Gullichsen, it says, before giving this information examined the customs register which is kept daily; and he added that it was out of the question that any airplane could land at Kjeller without being observed. He stated that the last foreign airplane to land at Kjeller before December, 1935, was a British plane coming from Copenhagen and piloted by the British aviator, Mr. Robertson, which landed on September 19, 1935; and that the first foreign airplane to land at Kjeller after December, 1935, arrived on the first of May, 1936. (Ibid., II/5.)

e. Original and certified, notarized English translation of (4) above, as follows:

Sir: In reply to your letter of 10th inst. and referring to my letter of 14th inst., I beg to state that I find that I cannot send you the four declarations for which you asked me.

I can only refer you to the interview published in Arbeiderbladet on the 29th/1 a.c.

Yours truly
(Signed) Gullichsen (Ibid., II/4, c.)

(6) Extracts from the Norwegian press concerning Pyatakov's testimony about his flight. Among these is a telegram

from Konrad Knudsen to Prosecutor Vyshinsky, which appeared in *Arbeiderbladet* (Oslo) on January 29, 1937. Knudsen informs Vyshinsky that it has been officially verified on that day that in December, 1935, no foreign or private plane landed at the airport near Oslo; also that as Trotsky's host he confirms that no conversation could have taken place in Norway between Trotsky and Pyatakov. (*Ibid.*, II/1.)

There is also an article from *Aftenposten* (Oslo), January 25, 1937, entitled "Pyatakov's Conference with Trotsky at Oslo Quite Improbable." It states that both the Kjeller and Gressholmen airports have denied that any civil airplane landed there during December, 1935; that all Russian citizens entering the country must have visas and are placed under careful observation; that in case Pyatakov had a foreign passport there is no reason why he should not have been there, but the chief of the Central Office of Passports, Mr. Konstad, has declared that he considers it quite improbable. Trotsky's host, Konrad Knudsen, it states, has declared that it is absolutely impossible that Trotsky could have received Pyatakov at that time. (PC Exh. 21.)

An article from *Tidens Tegn*, March 11, 1937, by Konrad Knudsen, discusses the theory advanced by that paper that Pyatakov landed on lake Oiangen while Trotsky was at the Knudsen cabin near there. Knudsen points out that the date of Pyatakov's alleged flight (between December 10 and December 15) does not tally with the dates of Trotsky's stay at the cabin. Moreover, Pyatakov said he drove half an hour and arrived at a suburb of villas, whereas

> Oiangen is situated in the middle of a thick forest. At that time there was one meter of snow on Oiangen; I am not an expert on flying, but this much I know, that it would be impossible to land an airplane without skis, and no airplane which came from Berlin would have skis. . . .
> An automobile was waiting, said Pyatakov. It is, howev-

er, an absolute impossibility for an automobile to reach
Oiangen in snow one meter deep. The roads are not open
in the winter. When in addition we know that the cabin
is near Oiangen—about ten minutes' walk—how can it
then be explained that he drove half an hour before he
reached the place? . . . Pyatakov did not remember much
in court, but if he had landed on Oiangen in one meter
of snow and had had to get through the snowdrifts in
an automobile, he would have remembered that. . . . (PC
Exh. 19, IV/6.)

§ 141. This Commission is obliged to note, first of all, the
fact that Vyshinsky had in his hands, even before the accused
were sentenced, Knudsen's telegram informing him of the official denials that any foreign or private plane landed at Kjeller
in December, 1935, and stating that Trotsky did not receive
Pyatakov during that month. Since Pyatakov's life and the
lives of the sixteen other accused presumably hung upon the
truth or falsity of his testimony, Vyshinsky's failure to confront him with this authoritative telegram in court constitutes,
in our opinion, criminal negligence. Indeed it provides strong
justification for the widespread suspicion that the whole trial
was a frame-up at which the Prosecutor himself connived.

We note also that Trotsky's two lists of questions, which,
as he pointed out in his final argument (PC 559), were highly
pertinent to Pyatakov's testimony concerning his alleged
flight, must have been known to the Prosecutor well before
the trial ended. A prosecutor interested in establishing the
truth would surely have put such questions to Pyatakov
without waiting for Trotsky to suggest them, since they were
clearly indicated by Pyatakov's testimony. However, since
he did not do so, a decent regard for the truth would have
forced him to confront Pyatakov with these questions after
Trotsky had suggested them, especially since Pyatakov had
implicated Trotsky, and the prosecution had offered Trots-

ky no opportunity to present his case. Trotsky's questions concerning Pyatakov's German passport were especially important (see § 133). And we know that the Prosecutor was not consistently indifferent on the subject of passports. He introduced in evidence during the August trial the Honduran passport of the accused Olberg; he produced for identification during the January trial the Czech passport of the accused Hrasche. He was not even entirely indifferent to the facts concerning Pyatakov's German passport, for he not only asked Pyatakov whether he gave his photograph, but was also curious to know where Stirner obtained the passport (PR 79). Therefore his failure to ask the all-important question as to the name in which it was issued must be regarded not as an oversight but as a deliberate and discreditable evasion.

His introduction of the statement about the Kjeller airdrome (§ 135) did not compensate for this cynical disregard for the facts, although one must assume that he considered that it would set all doubts at rest. The article in *Aftenposten* (§ 140, 6) appeared on January 25. Vyshinsky introduced this statement on January 27, saying that he "wanted to verify Pyatakov's evidence from this side too." We are unable to regard a statement that an airport receives airplanes of other countries the year round and that arrivals and departures are possible in winter months, as verification of testimony to the effect that a given foreign plane landed at that port in a given month; more especially in face of a denial by the officer in charge that such a plane landed.

This statement introduced by Vyshinsky is in our opinion useful for only one reason: it indicates that the Prosecutor expected the Court and the public to assume that Pyatakov's plane landed at the Kjeller airdrome. And indeed if it landed at an airdrome near Oslo it must have landed at Kjeller, since the ports of Gressholmen and Bogstad receive hydroplanes whereas Tempelhoferfeld, from which Pyatakov allegedly took off, is a field for land planes.

But if Pyatakov landed at Kjeller then he could hardly have seen Trotsky at Weksal, if one accept his own testimony that the drive to Trotsky's house took only half an hour. There is incontrovertible evidence that the distance from Kjeller to Weksal can not be covered by automobile in less than two hours. The map in our possession shows that the route from Kjeller to Hoenefoss leads through Oslo and that Mr. Knudsen has correctly represented the distance. In order to meet Pyatakov in a "country suburb" one half hour from the airport, Trotsky would have had to leave the Knudsen house and go to some other house in a "country suburb" near Kjeller. But we have his own testimony and that of his secretary and the Knudsen family, that he was not out of the Knudsen house during the first half of December. We also have the testimony of Trotsky's correspondence, which is not unimportant in this connection. Pyatakov testified that he arrived in Berlin on December 10 and saw Bukhartsev on that day or the next. On the day after he met Bukhartsev he allegedly met Trotsky's messenger, and on the following day made his trip to Oslo. That would place his flight on the 12th or 13th of December. At the request of the Chairman of the Preliminary Commission (PC 222) Trotsky submitted his correspondence for those two dates to our permanent representative in Mexico, Otto Ruehle. We are informed that on December 12, 1935, Trotsky wrote two letters, one in German to the Norwegian politician, Olaf Scheflo, and a long letter in French to the editorial board of the Parisian paper, *Révolution*. The letter to Scheflo begins:

> I am very sorry that the state of my health as well as that of my wife makes it difficult for us to travel to Oslo in these days. . . .

On December 13 Trotsky wrote two letters in French, one to the Politburo of the Bolshevik-Leninist organization in

France, the other a long letter to Biline, a member of that organization. Assuming that he was able to elude the Knudsens and his secretary on one of those days in order to have a secret meeting with Pyatakov at a place thirty minutes from Kjeller, he must necessarily have devoted a considerable part of the day to the trip. It seems hardly likely, therefore, that he would have found time in addition to write long letters, if indeed he had been able to find the inclination on the day of an interview so unusual. We may add that it seems to us impossible that he could have made the necessary preparations, which would certainly have involved ordering an automobile by some means unknown to the people around him, or that he could have been absent from the house for at least six hours—four hours to go and return and two hours for the interview—without their having known it.

The theory that Pyatakov landed at some place other than an airdrome is hardly worth entertaining. He twice states that he landed at an airdrome—the first time "in," the second time "near" Oslo (PR 60, 443). This is sufficiently explicit, and it must be assumed that Pyatakov was able to recognize an airdrome when he saw one. As for the theory that he landed on Oiangen while Trotsky was at Knudsen's cabin near that lake, it does not, as Knudsen pointed out in the article quoted above, fit with his testimony in time, topography, distance covered, or means of transportation used. Therefore we should be obliged to reject it even if we did not have the testimony of witnesses who were with Trotsky at that time and who state that he did not receive Pyatakov at the Knudsen cabin.

There remains the possibility that the officials at Kjeller connived with Trotsky's alleged agents in concealing the fact of Pyatakov's landing. This theory presupposes a willingness of all people connected with the airport—customs officials, mechanics, and so on, to maintain silence about the landing of the plane and the servicing that must have been necessary before it took off again. Judging by the statement of Director Gullichsen that no foreign plane landed at Kjeller between September 19, 1935, and May, 1936, it is an unusual occurrence for a foreign plane to land at that airport in the winter months; and it is much more difficult to conceal an unusual incident than a common one. We therefore regard this theory as farfetched. But even if we assume that such a thing did happen, the fact remains that Pyatakov would not have been able to drive to Weksal in half an hour, and that Trotsky could not have met him elsewhere without the knowledge of the Knudsens and Erwin Wolf. And if we assume that Pyatakov was simply mistaken about the length of the drive to Weksal—such a slip of memory is not impossible—there remains the testimony of the witnesses we have quoted, who state that Trotsky's living conditions precluded the probability of his being able to receive visitors unknown to the Knudsen family; and that of the Knudsens and Wolf that he received no visitors during December, 1935.

§ 142. We hold that the evidence concerning Pyatakov's alleged flight in the record of the trial is open to the gravest doubt; that the Prosecutor's silence, and that of the Court, in the face of published testimony impugning that evidence during the trial, warrants a suspicion of frame-up; that the doubt which the record inspires is converted by the evidence offered in rebuttal into certainty that no such flight took place. We therefore find that Pyatakov did not see Trotsky in December, 1935, and did not receive from him instructions of any kind; and that the disproof of Pyatakov's testimony on this crucial point renders his whole confession worthless.

18

The testimony of Karl Radek

§ 143. The second basis of the charge against Leon Trotsky and Leon Sedov in the trial of January, 1937, is the testimony of the accused Radek. We have already noted (§ 121) that Radek claimed to have received six letters from Trotsky. Radek twice stated (PR 41, 543) that he burned these letters.

Radek answered in detail the Prosecutor's "Tell us briefly of your past Trotskyite activities." He stated that he had joined the Trotskyite opposition during the Party struggle in 1923 and belonged to it and to its leadership until the time of his exile in January, 1928; that in exile he adhered to the Trotskyite position until the time of his declaration to the Central Committee of the C.P.S.U. in July, 1929 (see Chapter VIII), which was dictated by the conviction that Trotsky's position with regard to the impossibility of building socialism in one country was false, that the accusation of Thermidorianism made against the Central Committee by the Opposition was unfounded, and that the Five-Year Plan was a program for a great step forward. None the less, he said, he returned to the Party with certain tacit reservations:

> . . . I was convinced that in the future the development of the Five-Year Plan would either lead to the voluntary expansion of internal Party democracy, by the voluntary action of the Party leadership, or would be the cause of a split in the Party. (PR 82.)

He said that after his return to the Party he maintained his relations with his former Trotskyite associates, who, at the time when the struggle for the Five-Year Plan had become acute, began to flood him with information of the most pessimistic nature, "which most fatally affected my opinion of the situation in the country." Here, he said, there

> were those transgressions which would have justified my being brought to trial even if I had not belonged to the *bloc*. . . . For example, if you were to ask me about my responsibility for the murder of Sergei Mironovich Kirov, I must say that this responsibility began not from the moment I joined the leadership of the *bloc*, but from that moment in 1930 when a man with whom I had close relations—Safarov—came to me looking black in the face and tried to convince me that the country was on the verge of ruin, and I did not report this . . . If I had told the Party about Safarov's frame of mind, the Party would have got at the group of the former leaders of the Leningrad Young Communist League who later become the leaders of the assassination of Kirov. And so I declare that my responsibility dates not only from the time I joined the *bloc*, but that the roots of this crime lie in the Trotskyite views with which I returned . . . and in the relations I had retained with the Trotskyite-Zinovievite cadres. (PR 83–4.)

This passage, we may note, is remarkable not only as an example of that identification of criticism of Party policy with criminal activity which characterizes the utterances of both the accused and the Prosecutor throughout both trials, but also because it appears to contradict the claim made in the indictment and the evidence in the August trial, that the leaders of the Kirov assassination were the "Trotskyite-Zinovievite Center" and in particular the defendant Bakayev. Radek went on to state that in 1930–31 he

> believed that the economic offensive was being conducted on too wide a front, that the material forces available (number of tractors, etc.) would not permit of universal collectivization, and that if this general offensive were not slowed down this would, as we defined it by a catch-phrase, "end like the march on Warsaw," ... I thought it was necessary to hold back the offensive and to mass resources on definite sectors of the economic front. ... I was scared by the difficulties and thus became a mouthpiece of the forces hostile to the proletariat. (PR 84–5.)

He testified that he first learned that preparations were being made for a united Trotskyite-Zinovievite center in a letter from Trotsky, which he received in February–March, 1932. The Prosecutor asked him two very pertinent questions: Did Trotsky know that Radek had returned to the Party; and

> Why did he venture to write a letter containing fairly intimate political information to a Trotskyite who had returned to the Party? (PR 85.)

Radek answered the first question in the affirmative, and the second as follows:

. . . the Trotskyite leaders who maintained relations with me and who were at that time in communication with Trotsky, knew that I was in favor of holding back the offensive. (PR 85.)

He further testified that the "Trotskyite leaders" were afraid to speak to him openly about their activities because

. . . since the split with Trotsky in 1929 was connected with a great straining of personal relations between me and Trotsky, who regarded me as responsible, or one of those most responsible for the split of the Trotskyites, they feared to address me themselves and considered that this could be overcome only by relations between Trotsky and myself. And to all appearances they informed Trotsky, and, knowing my frame of mind, requested him to take the first step so as to make it easier for them to approach me. (PR 86.)

§ 144. The colloquy in which this passage appears is quoted in § 17, 1, of this report. Since this testimony of Radek purports to explain why Trotsky wrote him about the alleged conspiracy, it has an important bearing upon the credibility of his testimony to Trotsky's alleged letter. Vyshinsky, from his questions, appears to have been interested in interpreting Radek's testimony rather than in securing an explicit statement or in verifying his vague explanations. It would have been pertinent to ask him how he realized that "something was brewing" merely from seeing two people turn a corner. Instead, Vyshinsky says:

In a word, you already at that period noticed that they were engaged in some underground preparatory work?

And Radek, after answering that he "noticed that something was thickening, that sentiments were leading somewhere," proceeds to explain why "they did not speak openly." Vyshinsky did not ask how they could have known his frame of mind if they had not dared approach him. Nor did he ask any of the other accused whether or not he knew that Trotsky had been informed that "they sensed" that Radek was "in a depressed frame of mind"—not even Pyatakov, who had allegedly been in touch with Trotsky, Sedov, and Smirnov, and whose alleged conspiratorial activity began a whole year before the formation of the main center. Instead he re-formulated Radek's vague statement in terms equally vague, and ended this fantastic exchange of question and answer with the astounding comment:

> Now it is clear why your correspondence with Trotsky arose.

Evidently, if one wishes, one may take Vyshinsky's word for it. But nothing in the colloquy makes it clear in the slightest degree.

The unsolicited letter from Trotsky, which we are to assume resulted from Trotsky's learning in some unspecified way that Radek "was in favor of holding back the offensive," was hardly characterized by discretion, if one accept Radek's interpretation:

> At the end of the letter Trotsky wrote approximately as follows: "You must bear in mind the experience of the preceding period and realize that for you there can be no returning to the past, that the struggle has entered a new phase and that the new feature in this phase is that either we shall be destroyed together with the Soviet Union, or we must raise the question of removing the leadership." The word terrorism was not used, but when I read the words "removing the leadership," it became clear to me what Trotsky had in mind. (PR 87.)

And again on page 92 Radek answers "Of course" to Vyshin-sky's

. . . of the necessity of removing; consequently you understood that terrorism was meant?

Thus Trotsky, in February–March, 1932, is alleged to have sent to a "capitulator" who had returned to the Party, with whom his own personal relations had been greatly strained, and with whom he is not alleged to have had any previous communication since the "split" in his faction which caused the strain, a letter which made it clear to that "capitulator" that Trotsky had in mind terrorism against the leadership of the Soviet Union, and in which he definitely stated that a bloc was being formed between the Trotskyites and the Zinovievites. We have already remarked on the recklessness of Trotsky's conduct as represented in the records of these trials. This testimony of Radek offers a striking example.

§ 145. Radek testified that he received this first letter from Trotsky through Vladimir Romm (§§ 109–11, 114; Chap. XIX), an old friend of his whom he had known since 1922 and who, although never active in the Trotskyite opposition, "adhered to us on the Chinese question" (PR 93). He testified to five letters allegedly received from Trotsky after this first one: a letter in September, 1933, one in April, 1934, one in December, 1935, and two in January, 1936. He also mentioned a "directive" on group terrorism, allegedly received in January, 1936 (§ 120), but did not say how he received it or in what form. He stated that the letter of September, 1933, was received through Vladimir Romm (PR 545). He did not tell how the other four were received and Vyshinsky did not ask him. Romm testified that he delivered to Radek two letters from Trotsky: one in the spring of 1932, and another in August, 1933. (We note that Radek and Romm differ on the month in which this letter was received.) (PR 138, 142.)

Radek's testimony on the contents of the letter allegedly received from Trotsky in August–September, 1933, consisted in confirming the conflicting accounts given by the accused Pyatakov and the witness Romm (§§ 108–11), and a remark in his last plea that he was dumbfounded because Trotsky in this letter allegedly spoke of wrecking work as something taken for granted (PR 545). His testimony on the contents of the alleged letters of April, 1934, and December, 1935, is discussed in Chapter XXIV of this report. That on the contents of the two letters allegedly received in January, 1936, has already been noted (§ 120). We turn now to his testimony on the letters he allegedly sent Trotsky.

The first of these neither Pyatakov, whose testimony concerning it he confirms and supplements, nor Radek himself dates exactly. It is from the witness Vladimir Romm (confirmed by Radek) that we learn it was sent in September, 1932 (§§ 108–11, 114, for discussion of this letter and its contents). The second letter he mentioned having sent Trotsky, both he and Romm placed in May, 1934 (PR 107, 142–3). Its contents are discussed in Chapter XXIV. He mentioned, as we have noted (§ 120), an "enquiry" sent to Trotsky in the autumn of 1934, but did not state in what form it was sent, by what means, or what it was about. Romm stated that he received from Radek a letter for Trotsky in September, 1933 (PR 142, 143), but did not state its contents; and Radek, beyond a general confirmation of Romm's testimony, did not testify concerning this alleged letter. Nor did Vyshinsky question him about it.

§ 146. The accused Pyatakov twice mentioned a letter which, he implied, Trotsky had received from Radek just before Pyatakov's alleged flight to Oslo in the first half of December, 1935 (PR 59–60). Testifying on his alleged conversation with Trotsky, he said:

Trotsky had already received Radek's letter and he was particularly excited. (PR 60.)

Since the last letter Radek mentioned having sent Trotsky was that allegedly sent through Romm in May, 1934, one can hardly assume that Trotsky was still "particularly excited" about that letter; for Romm's testimony indicates that it was delivered to Sedov in May, 1934, and it can hardly be assumed, therefore, that it was "delayed in transit." Nor does it seem likely that Pyatakov would use the words "already received" of a letter delivered some eighteen months before the alleged interview. However, Radek did not see fit to mention this alleged letter, and the Prosecutor did not see fit to query him about it. Therefore, since Pyatakov's is the only testimony which mentions it, and since we have already held that Pyatakov did not see Trotsky and that his whole confession is worthless, it follows that his testimony about this letter is worthless.

§ 147. Leon Trotsky testified that he had known Karl Radek since 1909 or 1910; that he had no political relations with him before 1917; that Radek belonged not to the Russian but to the German Party;* that Radek in 1917 went with Lenin through Germany to Stockholm, where he remained as literary representative of the Russian Bolsheviks (PC 100); that he arrived in Russia after the October Insurrection, in 1917 (PC 593), and immediately joined the Bolshevik Party; and that he was active as a journalist. (PC 101.) He also said that Radek was active for a time in the Commissariat of Foreign Affairs, but the diplomats complained that it was impossible to say anything in his presence, because the next day it was known all over the city; therefore "We removed him immediately." He became a member of the Central Committee, and in that capacity had the right to attend the sessions

---

* Radek began his political career in the Social-Democratic movement of Galicia (1901). From 1904 to 1908 he worked in the Polish Social-Democratic Party. His connection with the German movement dated from 1908. See App. II.

of the Politburo (the most important executive organ of the Central Committee—PC 351). Lenin, Trotsky said,

> ... organized our meetings of the Politburo somewhat secretly to avoid Radek, because we did, as you understand, discuss very delicate matters in the Politburo. His reputation in these matters is absolutely established. (PC 101.)

Trotsky stated that from 1923 to 1926 Radek hesitated between the so-called Trotskyites and the German Right Opposition, but remained in good personal relations with him. During that time he wrote a well-known article, "Leon Trotsky, Organizer of the Victory," which appeared in *Pravda* of March 14, 1923. (PC Exh. 10. Excerpts from this highly laudatory article were read into the record of the Preliminary Commission, pp. 102–3.) In 1926, Trotsky said, Radek became a member of the bloc between the Trotskyites and Zinovievites (§§ 21, 24), was expelled with the Left Opposition at the Fifteenth Congress, was exiled to Siberia, and capitulated in 1929 (PC 105; PR 82). He stated that he had had no communication, either direct or indirect, with Radek since his own exile from the Soviet Union; that he had received no letters from him, and had sent him no letters through an intermediary (PC 116).

In his final argument, Trotsky said:

> Radek's outstanding characteristics . . . are impulsiveness, instability, undependability, a predisposition toward falling into panic at the first sign of danger, and exhibiting extreme loquacity when all is well. These qualities make him a journalistic Figaro of first-rate skill, an invaluable guide for foreign correspondents and tourists, but utterly unsuited for the rôle of conspirator. Among informed persons it is simply unthinkable to speak of

Radek as an inspirer of terrorist attempts or the organizer of an international conspiracy. (PC 523.)

He also quoted Lenin's remark with reference to Radek's "Lenin yields space to gain time," uttered during the controversy over Brest-Litovsk at the Seventh Party Congress:

> I return to what Comrade Radek said, and take this opportunity to emphasize that he has *accidentally* succeeded in uttering a serious thought;[*]

and Stalin's remark in 1924, at the Party Conference called shortly before Lenin's death:

> Most men's heads control their tongues; Radek's tongue controls his head.

"Who will believe," asks Trotsky,

> that I placed at the head of a grandiose plot an individual whose tongue controls his head and who is in consequence capable of expressing serious ideas only "by accident"? (PC 524.)

He also cites the progression of Radek's public "calumnies against the Opposition," culminating in "The Zinovievite-Trotskyite Fascist Gang and Its Hetman Trotsky" (PC Exh. 11) in August, 1936, and says:

---

[*] In checking this quotation we find that it appears as Trotsky gave it in Lenin's Collected Works, State Publishers, 1925 (Vol. XV, pp. 131–2). In the Third Russian edition of Lenin's Collected Works, published in 1935, the name of Riazanov has been substituted for that of Radek (Vol, XXII, p. 331). The editors neither explain the change nor even state that in earlier editions Radek's name figured in place of Riazanov's.

This, in its turn, was nothing else but a prelude to Radek's court testimony in January, 1937. Each succeeding step developed from the preceding one. This is precisely why no one would have believed Radek had he figured in the trial only as a witness for the prosecution. For his testimony against me to carry any weight, it was necessary to transform Radek into a defendant, suspending above him the Damocles sword of the death penalty. (PC 533.)

§ 148. We have already cited (§ 26) material introduced by Trotsky which fully corroborates Radek's statement about the straining of personal relations between himself and Trotsky. According to Trotsky, this had to do not merely with Radek's capitulation, but also with his denunciation of Blumkin (§ 26). From the time of this denunciation, said Trotsky, Radek was the most odious of all people to the Left Opposition, "because he was not only a capitulator but a traitor" (PC 108). There is nothing in all this evidence, or in Radek's testimony, to inspire a belief that Trotsky would have resumed relations with Radek; much less that he would have urged terrorism upon Radek in a letter written before Radek had approached him, and even before Trotsky's alleged co-conspirators had sounded Radek out. And Radek's statement that the roots of his alleged crime lay in the "Trotskyite views" which he did not wholly abandon and the "Trotskyite contacts" which he had continued to maintain, is weakened by his own statement in his final plea, that he joined the "Trotskyite organization" not because of Trotsky's "petty theories" or because he recognized his authority, but only because

there was no other group upon which I could rely in those political aims which I had set myself. (PR 542.)

Radek never stated what the aims were that he had set himself. Certainly to be in favor of "holding back the offensive" in order to avoid disaster does not sound like a criminal aim; nor does it sound like a convincing preparation for acceptance of the aim of removing the leadership through terrorism— an aim, be it noted, allegedly set by Trotsky, not by Radek. In our opinion, therefore, neither Radek's testimony as to his motivation in joining the alleged conspiracy, nor his testimony that it was an unsolicited letter from Trotsky which informed him of it and urged him to join, is convincing. It becomes incredible when one considers Trotsky's own testimony and the materials he has submitted in its support. We now turn to the factual aspect of Radek's testimony to his alleged communication with Trotsky.

§ 149. We have already remarked that Radek does not state by what means he received Trotsky's alleged letters of April, 1934, December, 1935, and January, 1936 (four in all). We may add that if in Soviet law the conditions and circumstances in which a piece of material evidence was obtained must be legally set down (Strogovich-Vyshinsky, p. 47) then certainly one might expect that when a court accepts the testimony of an accused or a witness concerning material evidence which according to that testimony no longer even exists, it would at least demand that the prosecutor be careful to ascertain the conditions and circumstances under which the accused or witness learned about or came by the absent evidence—more especially when the testimony concerning it is as contradictory as in this case (see § 47).

The truth or falsehood of Radek's testimony to the existence of five of the nine letters which allegedly passed between himself and Trotsky, among them Trotsky's alleged letter which induced Radek to enter the conspiracy, depends upon the testimony of Vladimir Romm. If Romm was a reliable witness, then there would be good reason to assume that Trotsky did get in touch with Radek in February, 1932, by means of a letter sent through Romm, and that Romm did thereafter convey one more letter from Trotsky to Radek and three letters from Radek to Trotsky; although since the letters were not introduced in evidence, all testimony to their contents would still be hearsay evidence, and open to doubt (§ 47). If, on the other hand, Romm is found not to have been a credible witness, then his untrustworthiness impugns the testimony of Radek.

§ 150. Before we pass to the testimony of the witness Romm, we may remark that while in general it is of course impossible for the Commission to inquire into the truth or falsity of evidence concerning letters and "directives" received by unspecified means, we are able to gauge the quality of Radek's testimony concerning Trotsky's alleged letter of December, 1935. For according to both Radek and Pyatakov, it was their alarm over Trotsky's dealings with foreign powers, of which this letter informed them, which caused them to decide that Pyatakov must endeavor to see Trotsky (PR 56, 58, 119–21). Radek was especially explicit and loquacious on this subject, setting forth in detail the considerations which the alleged letter inspired, and which convinced them that one of them must see Trotsky. If Pyatakov had not been sent abroad on business, said Radek, he himself would have taken advantage of an invitation to lecture in Oslo, in order to see Trotsky, so important was it that one of them should talk over the situation with him (PR 119).

We have already stated (§ 142) our conclusion that the testimony of Pyatakov concerning his alleged flight to Oslo and his alleged interview with Trotsky is false. It follows that the testimony of the accused Radek concerning this alleged journey and interview is also false. And if this testimony is false, then there is not the slightest reason to believe Radek's testimony (or Pyatakov's) concerning the alleged letter which caused the two of them to decide that Pyatakov must make the journey.

19

The testimony of Vladimir Romm

§ 151. The third basis of the charge against Leon Trotsky and Leon Sedov in the Pyatakov-Radek trial is the testimony of the witness Vladimir Romm. This testimony is important not only because that of Radek rests upon it, as we have said, but also because Romm was the only one of the seventeen accused and five witnesses, with the exception of Pyatakov, who claimed to have received instructions from Trotsky in person.

Romm testified that he had known Radek since 1922, and had been connected with him in 1926–27 in "joint Trotskyite anti-Party work"—thus confessing to a more active Trotskyite past than Radek ascribed to him. Romm said that he was a Trotskyite from the latter part of 1926 up to the time when he "temporarily left them about 1927," and that he returned in 1931 after a conversation with Radek in which Radek told him that he must be prepared, if necessary, to take advantage of his position as a foreign correspondent, and to serve as a liaison man. Romm stated that he was

Tass correspondent in Paris and Geneva. In the summer of 1931, he testified, he was put in touch with Sedov by Putna. In reply to Sedov's question whether he was ready to serve as liaison man with Radek, he consented, he said, and gave Sedov his addresses in Paris and Geneva. Romm did not say how Sedov ascertained that it was safe to ask such a service, which obviously must have involved great risk. We can not assume that Radek had posted him, since this alleged interview took place half a year before Radek allegedly received Trotsky's first letter. (PR 136–8.)

A few days before his departure for Geneva, said Romm, while he was in Paris, he received a letter posted in that city, addressed to him at the Tass office, and containing a short note from Sedov asking him to deliver to Radek an enclosed letter. He stated that he handed this letter to Radek when the latter visited Geneva in the spring of 1932 (PR 138), and in the subsequent conversation learned that the letter was from Trotsky, and

> that it contained instructions about uniting with the Zinovievites, about adopting terrorist methods of struggle against the leaders of the C.P.S.U., in the first place against Stalin and Voroshilov. (PR 139.)

Romm testified that in the autumn of 1932 he went to Moscow on official business, saw Radek and had the conversation with him which we have already discussed (§ 109). Passing through Berlin on his way to Geneva he posted a book containing the letter he had received from Radek (§§ 109–10) to an address which Sedov had given him: *poste restante* at one of the Berlin post offices. The post office, he said, was Französische Strasse, but he did not remember the box-number. The next time he met Sedov was in July, 1933, a few days after his arrival from Geneva, when Sedov telephoned him and arranged to meet him in a café on the

Boulevard Montparnasse. Sedov, he said, told him that he wanted to arrange for him to meet Trotsky. A few days later, Sedov telephoned him and arranged to meet him in the same café. From there they went to the Bois de Boulogne, where he met Trotsky. This meeting, he said, took place at the end of July, 1933. In addition to those "instructions" which we have already quoted (§ 109), Trotsky in this conversation, if Romm is to be believed, divulged to his liaison man some highly confidential and dangerous views about the need of terrorism, wrecking, diversion and defeatism.

At the end of the conversation, said Romm, Trotsky gave him Novikov-Priboi's novel "*Tsushima,*" and told him that a letter to Radek was concealed in the cover. Romm took this book with him to Moscow and handed it to Radek upon his arrival there in August, 1933 (§ 109). Upon his return from his vacation at the end of September, 1933, Radek gave him a letter to Trotsky, concealed in the cover of a German book, which he handed to Sedov in Paris in November. He said he met Sedov again in April, 1934, and Sedov, on learning that he was soon going to Moscow, asked him to bring back from Radek a detailed report on the situation. He delivered this message, and in May, 1934, Radek handed him a letter concealed in an Anglo-Russian technical dictionary, which he said contained a detailed report from the active center as well as the parallel center about the development of political and diversive work. This book Romm handed to Sedov in Paris. (PR 141–3.)

Summing up, Romm said that in the spring of 1932 he handed Radek a letter from Trotsky in Geneva; he received a letter from Radek in September, 1932; he received a letter from Trotsky in July, 1933; he received a letter from Radek in September, 1933, and one in May, 1934. Thereafter, he testified, he was sent to America as a correspondent of *Izvestia* and carried no more messages. (PR 143–4.)

§ 152. Radek, asked whether he confirmed Romm's testimony, stated that he did so except on one point. In Trotsky's first letter, he said, the names of Stalin and Voroshilov were not mentioned, although the letter spoke about terrorism. (PR 145.)

§ 153. We note that Romm invests the struggle of the Left Opposition from 1923 to 1927 against the majority with the invidious character of "anti-Party work"; in other words, his phrase implies that the open and legal oppositional struggle of that period within the Party was criminal in nature. Moreover, Radek's statement that Romm was not an active Oppositionist is borne out by Romm's apparent ignorance of the nature of this struggle. Speaking of Radek, Romm said: "I was connected with him in joint Trotskyite anti-Party work." And when Vyshinsky asked him, "What sort of work was that?" he could only repeat the phrase, "Trotskyite anti-Party work" (PR 136). Yet in spite of this apparent ignorance, we learn that his sentiments, after his conversation with Radek "in the autumn of 1930 and spring of 1931," "influenced by the difficulties of socialist construction, once again flowed into the old Trotskyite channel" (PR 137). This explanation of his motive for risking his head appeared to be sufficient for the Prosecutor and the Court, but it is hardly sufficient for the person who knows that "the old Trotskyite channel" had nothing whatever to do with terrorism, wrecking, and defeatism, or even for the reader of the trial record who remembers Pyatakov's testimony that Sedov outlined to him in the summer of 1931 (*after* Romm's alleged recidivism) the "new methods of struggle: . . . the forcible overthrow of the Stalin leadership by methods of terrorism and wrecking." (PR 23.)

Thus nothing in Romm's testimony indicates why he should have undertaken to further a terrorist conspiracy, and nothing in that of Romm or Radek indicates the slightest reason why Trotsky should have trusted him, not only with letters but with all the secrets of the alleged conspiracy; why, to use Trotsky's own words, he should have bared my innermost thoughts to a young man who did not even share my "defeatist" position. And all this on the basis of the fact that, in 1927, Romm supposedly agreed with Radek "on the Chinese question." (PC 546.)

§ 154. Leon Trotsky stated that he did not know Vladimir Romm; that he had never heard his name before the trial; that he reads the newspaper *Izvestia* only occasionally by chance, and never the foreign correspondence, and that although he reads *Pravda* regularly he never even reads the foreign correspondence in that paper; that he never met anyone by the name of Vladimir Romm in Paris; and that he never gave any letter to Vladimir Romm for the purpose of having it conveyed to Radek; that he never received any letter through Vladimir Romm from Radek and that the testimony of both Romm and Radek to that effect was absolutely false. (PC 183–5.)

Trotsky testified that he left Turkey for France in the steamship "Bulgaria" on July 17, 1933, accompanied by his wife, his collaborator Jean van Heijenoort, two Americans, Max Shachtman and Sara Weber, and a German, Adolphe (pseudonym; real name in our possession). (PC 174.) The cause of his removal to France, he said, was a change of policy after the election of May, 1932, when a Radical government, headed by Daladier, came into office. The matter of a visa had been broached to the French government by Trotsky's French translator in France, Parijanine. The government granted the visa on condition that Trotsky reside in Corsica, but his friend, Henri Molinier, an engineer, saw the higher officials and succeeded in persuading them to allow him to live for a certain time not in Corsica but in France itself. Molinier succeeded in getting permission for Trotsky to reside in one of the Southern Departments. Later the officials consented to allow him to remain in France. (PC 176–7, 181.)

Trotsky stated that he and his wife travelled under his

wife's name, Sedov, on passports for foreigners issued by the Turkish government (originals submitted to Otto Ruehle; photostats certified by him in our possession), and that their baggage was in charge of Max Shachtman and marked with his initials (PC 176, 196, 198). The ship arrived in the harbor of Marseille on July 24, 1933. He and his wife, however, did not go to Marseille but left the ship outside the harbor in a motorboat, in pursuance of arrangements made with the steamship company by Leon Sedov and Raymond Molinier (identified § 68, 9, a). This precaution was taken in order to conceal their movements. His son, who was in the motorboat, came aboard and handed a letter of instruction to van Heijenoort. Then Trotsky and his wife left the ship in the motorboat, in which, besides themselves and their son, were Molinier, two sailors, and an agent of the *Sûreté Générale* (name since changed to *Sûreté Nationale*). They landed at the small town of Cassis. The rest of his party proceeded to Marseille, where Shachtman remained to store the heavy baggage while van Heijenoort proceeded as far as Lyon with the small baggage, in order to give the journalists the impression that he was going to Paris. Sara Weber and Adolphe went to Paris from Marseille. This arrangement, Trotsky said, was unexpected by his party, who had supposed that they would all go together in the motorboat. (PC 176, 194.)

Upon arriving at Cassis, Trotsky testified, they found two automobiles awaiting them, in one of which were Raymond Leprince, not his political follower, and another Frenchman, Laste (full name in our possession), at that time his political follower but since his adversary. In the two cars Trotsky, his wife and son, Molinier, Leprince, and Laste started across Southern France toward Royan. Since Trotsky was suffering from lumbago and the movement of the car caused him great pain, they stopped overnight in a hotel in the small town of Tonneins. They arrived in St. Palais, near Royan, on the 25th at two or three o'clock in the afternoon at a villa, "Les Embruns," which had been rented for them on July 18 in the name of Henri Molinier. Soon after their arrival a fire, caused by the sparks from a locomotive, broke out near their villa, burning the shrubbery around the house and a small summer house in the garden. Since a great many people gathered around the house, Trotsky went out and sat during the fire in the automobile, which was in the road. The incident, he said, was reported in the local press, but his name was not mentioned since he had not been recognized. Some months later, after he had been discovered at Barbizon, this incident of the fire, he testified, was reported in the Paris press. Trotsky said that he remained in St. Palais until October 9, 1933, in ill health and spending about half the time in bed and the rest in the house or walking in the garden, in the company of friends who visited him. Living with him were his wife, his secretary van Heijenoort, Sara Weber, Vera Lanis, the wife of Raymond Molinier, who was in the villa when they arrived, and until the end of July, Ségal, a business associate of Molinier, who was also there when they arrived; also, for more than a month, Laste, who had accompanied them to St. Palais. A young French comrade, Beaussier, also came to Royan and remained for more than a month, but not in the house. (PC 174–180.) (Trotsky here omits Adolphe—PC Exh. 18, VII/9.)

Trotsky further stated that the French police had the record of all his movements, since it had been arranged that he keep them informed by telephone; and that they were even informed by telephone of his overnight stay at Tonneins (PC 181). He had tried, he said, to obtain this record, but Henri Molinier, to whom he had written about it, replied that the officials refused to provide it as a matter of general policy, and specifically because Trotsky's case was against the Soviet government (PC 190).

Trotsky also testified that because of his illness a doctor, a friend of his, was summoned to Royan from another country, since because of their incognito they feared to call in a local physician (PC 189). He stated that on October 9 he went, with his wife, Henri Molinier, and a young Frenchman named Meichler, to Bagnères-de-Bigorre, in the Pyrenees, where their daughter-in-law, Jeanne des Pallières, joined them. They stayed three weeks, and in the beginning of November went to Barbizon, near Paris, where they remained until April or May of 1934, when the local authorities, who were not aware of his identity, discovered through a slight accident that he was there. Being angry because they had been kept in ignorance, they provoked a scandal. A campaign was begun against him in the reactionary press and taken up by *l'Humanité*, official organ of the French Communist Party, which accused him of being in France to help the Radical Socialist Party, then in control of the government, to organize an invasion of Russia. Thereafter he was obliged to become nomadic for a time, since he was hunted by the fascist press. He finally settled near the village of Domène, near Grenoble, in the Département de l'Isère, where he remained until he left for Norway. (PC 180–3.)

During his stay at St. Palais, Trotsky said, he received in all some fifty visitors. (PC 180.)

§ 155. Leon Sedov testified that he had never known Romm, and learned of his existence only at the time of the trial, since he rarely read *Izvestia*, preferring *Pravda*. He said:

> Regarding Romm's statements, I begin by emphasizing the implausibility of its having been Putna, military attaché of the Soviet Embassy in Berlin (and whom I did not know personally) who had the idea of sending an official journalist to me in order that he might get in touch with the enemies of the Stalinist régime. In any case there is not a word of truth in the story of my entering into contact with Romm; after which it is worth

emphasizing that according to Romm I appear to have begun by allowing nine months to pass without doing a thing, and without profiting by his good services, and that after these nine months I could find nothing better to do than to send him by mail a letter from my father of the highest importance, which obviously one would not send by mail if one wished to send it—above all, not addressed to the Tass agency at the risk of its being opened by some substitute of the person for whom it was intended. (CR 34.)

Sedov testified that during the latter part of July, 1933, he was not in Paris; that having learned that his father was to arrive in France, he left Paris on July 14 with two friends to find a place where his father could stay in accordance with the agreement made with the French authorities. They went first to Noirmoutier, and afterwards to the island of Oléron, then to Royan, where they stopped at the Hotel de l'Univers. On the 18th they signed a lease for the villa "Les Embruns," at St. Palais-sur-Mer, owned by a M. Pillet. On the 19th they left for Marseille, where they arrived on the 20th, having slept at Toulouse. On the 21st they were in Marseille, where a third friend joined them. Sedov testified that since l'Humanité had appealed to the Marseille dock-workers to make hostile demonstrations against Trotsky, and since there was also danger of demonstrations by White Russians, they arranged for the ship to stop outside Marseille off Cassis-sur-mer, and to have Trotsky disembark in a motor launch. The owner of the launch, alarmed because they did not look like tourists, tried at the last minute to refuse to go, and it was only with some difficulty that they persuaded him. Sedov's testimony concerning the trip from Cassis to St. Palais, their arrival there and the fire that broke out, corroborates that of Trotsky. He testified that from this date until October 9, 1933, Trotsky never left Royan and could not have done so had he wished because on his arrival at Royan he was ill with a lumbago so painful that in August it was necessary to summon a physician.

Sedov denied the meetings he was alleged to have had in November, 1933, and in April and May, 1934, with Vladimir Romm, and said that if he had really met Romm in April and May, 1934, it was unlikely that they would have failed to discuss his father's having been forced to leave Barbizon just at that time, and the campaign against him in the press, nothing of which Romm mentioned in his testimony. (CR 37–9.)

§ 156. Max Shachtman, journalist, of New York, testified before the New York Sub-Commission that he is very close politically to Leon Trotsky; that he first met him in 1930 in Prinkipo; that at that time Shachtman was a member of the Communist League of America, a Trotskyite organization. He stated that he met Trotsky for the second time in Prinkipo in 1933; that he accompanied him on his trip from Prinkipo to France on the S.S. "Bulgaria," which left Prinkipo about July 19 and arrived in Marseille on July 24. With Trotsky, besides himself, were Mrs. Trotsky, Sara Weber, Jean van Heijenoort, and the German émigré, Adolphe. He stated that the party travelled as "Max Shachtman and suite" in order to maintain Trotsky's incognito as long as possible. Trotsky, he said, travelled under the name Leon Sedov. The night before the ship arrived at Marseille the commandant of the ship informed Shachtman that he had received a wire from the Minister of the Interior directing him to stop the ship a short way out of Marseille. There a motor launch provided with an official flag would approach the ship, and Trotsky and anyone of his suite would disembark in this motor launch. Trotsky, said Shachtman, was not certain what the arrangements would be. In the motor launch when it came alongside, he said, were Leon Sedov, Raymond Molinier, and a man in uniform. According to

Shachtman, it was Molinier who came on board. Trotsky and his wife were rushed into the motor launch. The rest of the party proceeded to Marseille, where Shachtman remained for a few days to store the private belongings and library of Mr. and Mrs. Trotsky. The boxes, he stated, had all been marked with his initials by the Turkish authorities. He then went to Basle, and from Basle to Paris, arriving there on August 1. A day or two after his arrival he saw Leon Sedov, who told him what route his father had followed from Paris to Royan. He stated that he turned over the storage receipts for Trotsky's belongings to Henri Molinier in Paris.

Asked about Trotsky's health during this voyage, Shachtman testified that after they left Piraeus, in Greece, it took a turn for the worse, and he was confined to bed, unable to move. Mrs. Trotsky asked Shachtman to find out whether there was any way of getting medical assistance. He found that there was no regular doctor on board. Miss Weber had a mechanical device on the principle of an electric pad, with chemicals and a rubber bag, and this was applied to Trotsky's back in an attempt to relieve him. When Trotsky left the boat, it was with a considerable physical effort, said Shachtman, that he held himself erect.

Shachtman testified that his friends in Paris told him that it was inadvisable for Trotsky to have many visitors, in order that his stay at Royan might be as quiet as possible, and therefore counselled him against going to Royan before a couple of weeks. Since his return ticket to the United States was expiring and his affairs in America demanded his return, he left Paris without going to Royan. Before he left, he wrote a letter to Trotsky expressing his regret that he was unable to see him again (photostat in our possession). (NY 82–102.)

§ 157. Sara Weber, of Orange, N.J., testified before the New York Sub-Commission that she worked for Leon Trotsky from

June, 1933, to February, 1934, as his Russian-English stenographer and translator; that she made the trip from Prinkipo to France in 1933 with Mr. and Mrs. Trotsky on the "S.S. Bulgaria" which left Prinkipo on July 19 or 20 and arrived in Marseille on July 24. Her testimony concerning Trotsky's leaving the ship in the harbor of Marseille corroborates that of Trotsky, Sedov and Shachtman. She testified that she went from Marseille to Paris with Adolphe, and remained there three or four days with Leon Sedov's wife. On July 30 or 31 she left for Royan with Leon Sedov who had just arrived in Paris and was there for only one day.

Miss Weber's testimony concerning Trotsky's health on the voyage corroborates that of Trotsky and Shachtman. At Royan, she said, his health became continually worse, and it was necessary to call in a foreign physician. She remained at Royan from the time of her arrival until the end of Trotsky's stay there, during which time Trotsky remained continuously at the villa. She was with him again in Barbizon from November 3 until February 7, when she left for Paris. (N.Y. 73–81.) Miss Weber stated that she saw all of Trotsky's visitors at Royan during the time she was there, and mentioned a number of them by name. She stated that Trotsky's correspondence did not come direct to Royan but was brought from Paris by courier. (NY 103–6.)

§ 158. Davis Herron of New York testified before the New York Sub-Commission that he is a writer without political affiliation; that he visited Leon Trotsky for the first time in Prinkipo in August, 1932, after a trip to Russia as a member of a delegation of the National Students' League, an organization Stalinist in sympathy to which he belonged in 1931–32; that he visited Trotsky again at Royan in September, 1933, this visit having been arranged by Naville (identified § 68, 9, b), whose address Herron had from B.J. Field. Herron testified that he left Paris on the evening of September 11, and that the trip to Royan took one night; that he found Trotsky in bad health and spoke about it with his doctor, who was not French and whose name Herron did not know; that the doctor told him Trotsky had a nervous fever which came from overexertion, and expressed indignation because the French authorities would not allow him to go near Paris to a sanitarium for medical care. (NY 120–6.)

§ 159. Among the many documents in our possession bearing on the testimony of Vladimir Romm to the effect that he met Leon Trotsky in the Bois de Boulogne in the latter half of July, 1933, the most important are as follows:

(1) Six letters (certified copies) and two telegrams bearing on the attempt to secure permission for Trotsky to reside in France. The first of these is a letter from Trotsky to his French translator, Maurice Parijanine, dated April 30, 1933, expressing surprise at the receipt of a telegram from him, and doubt whether the French government will grant him a visa (PC Exh. 18, I/1). Another letter to Parijanine, dated June 7, 1933, states that he is enclosing an article intended for the French press, and remarks that

> in case the reaction in France continues to affirm that Trotsky is an agent and an ally of German imperialism, my article will be a sufficiently convincing refutation of this idiocy in so far as it needs to be refuted. In following the French press, I have become convinced that it does not understand the real plans of Hitler; but a fortunate chance has enabled me to hit upon a very important document which unmasks him. (PC Exh. 18, I/3.)

A letter from Trotsky to Deputy Henri Guernut, dated Prinkipo, May 31, 1933, thanks him for having interceded in his behalf with the French authorities. A letter dated June 29, 1933, from C. Chautemps, then Minister of the Interior, to Deputy Guernut, reads as follows:

You have called my attention to M. Leon Trotsky, famous Russian exile, who for reasons of health asks authorization to sojourn in France and then to make his
residence in Corsica. I have the honor to inform you that
the order of expulsion which concerned this foreigner
has now been withdrawn, and the interested party will
obtain without difficulty whenever he shall demand it,
a visa for France. (*Ibid.*, I/5.)

A telegram from Henri Molinier to Trotsky, bearing the
Buyuk-Ada-Istanbul stamp, and the date 7/7/33, and addressed to "Sedov," reads as follows:

Provisional sojourn south definite sojourn Corsica
stop continue inquiries. (*Ibid.*, I/6.)

A letter of the same date from Trotsky to Henri Molinier
discusses the alternative of a temporary sojourn in the South
of France or a direct removal to Corsica, and says:

If you think that we could settle comfortably in some
corner of the South, isolated enough to prevent the possibility of Stalinist scandals (or White Russian), that the
temporary sojourn might assuredly transform itself into
a permanent one, and that in consequence we could send
the heavy baggage (books and archives) to the Continent,
it would naturally be the most favorable solution, but it
appears to me quite problematical and if I mention it, it
is that the "analysis" may be complete. (*Ibid.*, S I/7.)

(2) A deposition by Henri Molinier, certified by the Special Committee, states that he was Trotsky's representative
in dealing with publishers and the press of France; that in
1933 he undertook, in agreement with Trotsky, all arrangements concerning the latter's sojourn in France; that he went

at once to the *Sûreté Générale* and was received by M. Cado, who sought to prescribe and regulate the conditions of Trotsky's residence. Cado suggested Corsica. Molinier protested that Trotsky had a regular visa and should have the right to live where he pleased. After an argument,

> M. Cado then abandoned his diplomatic attitude and declared peremptorily that the *Sûreté* was above all responsible for public order, that it believed the presence of Trotsky might disturb this order, and consequently demanded that Trotsky should reside only in such places as it approved. . . . Paris, the Seine, Seine-et-Oise, were forbidden, as also any working-class city; also the Riviera, because of the many White Russians. . . . Only the rural departments and cities of minor importance remained. The center of France was recommended.
>
> After several days, I returned to suggest Royan as the first place of residence. M. Cado called my attention to the fact that Royan was very near the island of Oléron where there was a colony of Communist children, that he considered Royan to be the center of a too-important settlement, and so forth. I had to put up a fight and make it clear that the villa in question was far from the center and isolated, in order to obtain the wished for permission to settle at "Les Embruns."
>
> It was arranged with M. Cado that the best way to avoid incidents was to organize a rigorous incognito. M. Cado declared that except for the director of the *Sûreté Générale,* he would keep the place of residence secret from everyone, functionaries and journalists, and that he would inform only the prefect of the department. . . .

Molinier states that he transmitted the necessary information about these conversations to those friends of Trotsky who were to meet him in Marseille, in order that they might inform Trotsky. He also insisted on being informed by them from day to day of the conditions of Trotsky's journey, installation, and sojourn in order that he should be the first to know about any difficulty. He had an understanding with Cado that in case the latter should learn of any occurrence out of the ordinary he would inform Molinier immediately. He several times called the attention of Sedov and of Trotsky's entourage to the inconvenience of visits to Royan, fearing that they might spoil the incognito. He states that he was thus called upon at this period to keep a daily and very careful watch over the activities of Trotsky and his friends, and can therefore

affirm in the most categorical fashion that Trotsky, as soon as he disembarked at Marseille, went at once by road to Royan and that he did not leave that city until the 9th of October as described below.

The statement of Vladimir Romm in the second Moscow trial to the effect that he met Trotsky in the Bois de Boulogne in July, 1933, is an absolute lie. Any movement of Trotsky from place to place at that time would have been known to me; all the more since the health of Trotsky during that period would not have permitted him to make without preparation such a journey, which would in fact have required an absence of several days, the use of an automobile, the mobilization of two or three friends to protect Trotsky, etc.—all of which could not have been done without my knowledge.

Molinier states that he accompanied Mr. and Mrs. Trotsky and Meichler to Bagnères-de-Bigorre, having first obtained permission from Cado and arranged that the party should travel as a family under the name Meichler; that he was with the Trotskys until October 14, when he was obliged to return to Paris. On his arrival he asked Jeanne Martin des Pallières to join the Trotskys, which she did several days later. On October 30 or 31 Trotsky, his wife, Jeanne Martin and Meichler took a train for Paris. Molinier met them with his car at Les Aubrais-Orléans and took them to Barbizon (Seine-et-Marne), where he had rented a secluded villa for them, having previously obtained authorization for Trotsky to reside in Seine-et-Marne. He took the passports of Mr. and Mrs. Trotsky to the office of the director of the Sûreté, where visas were affixed.

Molinier states that he is attaching to his deposition various documents (among these is the receipt for the rent of the villa "Les Embruns"). (*Ibid.*, VII/5.)

(3) Documents bearing on the location and leasing of the villa "Les Embruns" at St. Palais, near Royan. Among these are five postcards and one envelope addressed to Mme. Leprince and one postcard to M. and Mme. Vallart, at Rosny-sous-Bois, Seine, by Raymond Leprince from various points of the itinerary followed by himself, Leon Sedov, and Raymond Molinier, and postmarked as follows: Les Sables d'Olonne (Vendée), 16/VII/33; Royan (Charente-Inférieure), 18/VII/33; Agen (Lot-et-Garonne), 19/VII/33; Toulouse-Gare (Haute Garonne), 20/VII/33; Marseille-Gare (Bouches-du-Rhone) 21 and 24/VII/33; Marseille, 22 (the rest illegible). (*Ibid.*, II/5.) Also a statement by R. Roger, proprietor of the Hotel de l'Univers at St. Palais, dated March 26, 1937, and authenticated by the mayor of that town, that on the nights of July 16, 17 and 18, 1933, Messrs. Leprince, Molinier and Sildikov *(sic)* lodged in his hotel (*Ibid.*, II/2). Also a receipt for 4,500 francs in payment of rent for the villa "Les Embruns," made out in the name of Molinier, dated July 18, 1933, and bearing the signature "Blancan" and the stamp of the "Agence Blancan, Ventes et Locations, St. Palais." There is a statement by Mme. F. Renauleaud, 36 boulevard Thiers, Royan, and her daughter, L. Renauleaud, niece of the owner of the villa "Les Embruns," M. Pillet, who had authorized her to rent it for him in 1933. This statement, authenticated

by the Commissioner of Police at Royan, affirms that the villa was rented on July 18, 1933, to M. Molinier, who presented himself in the company of a blond young man with a foreign accent. (*Ibid.*, V/3.)

(4) Documents concerning Trotsky's arrival at Cassis and his trip to Royan. The first of these is a deposition by Natalia Sedov-Trotsky, dated March 1, 1937, and presented to the Preliminary Commission in Coyoacan (PC 198). Mrs. Trotsky states that a provisional sojourn in the South of France was authorized for herself and her husband by the French government; and that they left it to their friends in France to select their place of residence. They did not learn until their arrival in France that they were to live at Royan. Their baggage, including their library, went with them, in Shachtman's name, and his initials are still on the trunks (verified by the Preliminary Commission, PC 198). On board ship, she testifies, Trotsky became ill with a painful lumbago. By the time they arrived his condition had improved somewhat. Her testimony concerning their landing at Cassis and their trip across France corroborates that of Trotsky and Sedov. She names the three friends who accompanied her son. Upon their arrival at Royan, she says, they found awaiting them Vera Lanis and Ségal.

Mrs. Trotsky describes the fire which broke out soon after their arrival and states that she and her husband awaited the end of it in the automobile, which a neighbor had removed into the road. Trotsky's health, she says, became worse after this incident; therefore, at the beginning of September a friend, Dr. H., came from abroad to treat him. By the end of September he had produced an improvement in Trotsky's condition and advised him to go to the mountains for a rest. They went to Bagnères, where they remained until October 30, when they left for Barbizon. It was only in the middle of December that Trotsky was finally able to visit friends in Paris, where he spent a day. (*Ibid.*, VII/ 1.)

Among these depositions are statements by Raymond Molinier (identified § 68, 9, a), J. Laste and Raymond Leprince (both identified § 151), certified by the Special Committee. Molinier and Leprince testify that they accompanied Leon Sedov in his search for a villa for Leon Trotsky and that having finally rented the villa "Les Embruns" they proceeded to Marseille to meet Trotsky. Laste states that he arrived in Marseille on July 21 where he met three other comrades. All of these witnesses describe their trip to Cassis and the renting of the motor launch for the purpose of meeting Trotsky's ship. They describe in detail the trip from Cassis to Royan, including the overnight stop at a little village near Marmande, and the arrival at St. Palais. All mention the fire which broke out shortly after their arrival, and Laste describes it in detail:

It was the afternoon of July 25 towards four o'clock. The little train had just passed spitting smoke and flames in the midst of fields baked by the sun. I perceived a thick smoke and flames some 300 meters from the villa which seemed to be coming in our direction. I had hardly had time to inform Trotsky when the shrubbery in the garden began to burn. The suitcases, the automobile which was in the garden, were removed to the road with the aid of neighbors. At the end of an hour quiet was restored, thanks to the inhabitants of the surrounding houses, who had put out the fire with the aid of branches. The villa was intact but all the shrubs on the side toward St. Palais were reduced to cinders. . . .

Laste describes in detail the arrangement of the villa and the measures that were taken to assure Trotsky's safety. He states:

The staff of the villa numbered four or five persons in addition to Trotsky and his wife. His son left the villa towards the beginning, to return several weeks later. Two comrades who had made the trip from Marseille to St. Palais left us for good. On the other hand, the comrades who came from Prinkipo and from whom we had parted at Marseille (a Frenchman, a German, and an American of Russian origin) rejoined us. . . . (*Ibid.*, VII/8.)

Laste states that he remained at the villa for a month and that during that time Trotsky very rarely left the house. Raymond Molinier says:

> It is absolutely false that Trotsky left Royan at any time from his arrival to the 9th of October, 1933. How could he have done so? It would have been necessary for some one to drive him to Paris, and only my brother and myself had automobiles; moreover, such a voyage could not have passed unnoticed, since it would have necessitated at least three days absence, given Trotsky's precarious state of health. (*Ibid.*, VII/6.)

Leprince states that during the time he remained at Royan, that is, from the latter part of July to the first part of August, he saw Trotsky daily. He testifies that he, Leprince, returned to Paris with Sedov and Ségal. (*Ibid.*, VII/7.)

An article from the *Petit-Marseillais* of July 25, 1933, dated Cassis, July 24, and entitled "Trotsky's Second Kidnapping," describes the attempts of Trotsky's friends to rent a motorboat at Cassis in order to meet the "Bulgaria," and the reluctance of the boatman. It tells of Trotsky's arrival in Cassis at nine o'clock in the morning and the immediate departure of his party in two automobiles. (*Ibid.*, III/1.)

An affidavit (Charleroi, Belgium, PC Exh. 18, VII/9) by Adolphe, who accompanied Trotsky as one of his secretaries, corroborates the testimony already cited concerning the condition of Trotsky's health, and the arrival at Marseille.

A statement submitted to the Preliminary Commission by Jean van Heijenoort also corroborates this testimony, and states that when the ship was stopped Leon Sedov came aboard, gave van Heijenoort a letter, and then disembarked with his father and mother.

> According to the indications in the letter left by Leon Sedov, the residence in France was to be entirely secret, and in order to throw off journalists and intruders it was agreed as follows: At Marseille I would leave the other friends who had made the trip with us from Turkey to France; I would set out for Lyon with the baggage, and at Lyon if the journalists had been lost I would go to Royan.

Van Heijenoort states that he left for Lyon with the baggage on the afternoon of July 24, that he spent the night at Lyon and proceeded to Royan the next day.

> On arriving on the morning of July 26 I immediately reencountered Trotsky. I did not leave the villa at St. Palais before the first days of September for a short trip to Paris. During all this period, Trotsky never discontinued living at the villa. He did not leave it except for short automobile trips of an hour or two at the most during the month of August. (*Ibid.*, VII/2.)

(5) Documents concerning the fire at the villa "Les Embruns." Among these is a statement by the chief of the St. Palais fire department, M. Soulard, and the corporal, Hervé André, authenticated by the mayor of St. Palais. These witnesses declare that on July 25, 1933, a fire broke out around three o'clock in the afternoon near the villa "Les Embruns" and threatened the villa; that it was extinguished around four-thirty; that at the time of this fire they noted the ar-

rival by automobile of a gentleman who had come to live in the villa. They learned later that this gentleman was Trotsky. (*Ibid.*, V/1.)

Mme. Renauleaud and her daughter (quoted above, No. 3) say that at the fire on July 25 they saw M. Molinier, who had just arrived with several people. In the automobile they saw an elderly gentleman whom M. Molinier declared to be his ailing father. The blond young man who accompanied M. Molinier on the day that the villa was rented was also present on this day. (*Ibid.*, V/3.)

There is also a copy of a letter, dated 31 July, 1933, from A. Nougarède, director of the tramway company at Royan, to MM. Diot May Gibault et Cie, rue de Chateaudun 17, Paris. This copy is certified by M. Nougarède, whose signature is authenticated by the Royan Police Commissioner. The letter states that a fire took place on July 25 on the property of M. Pillet, and that investigation by the Royan police has indicated the responsibility of the tramway company. It requests that MM. Diot May Gibault & Company cover the loss. (*Ibid.*, V/2.)

A clipping from the *Journal* (Paris), April 25, 1934, contains an article dated Royan, April 24, telling the story of the fire at "Les Embruns." It mentions one of the new occupants of the villa who insisted upon remaining in the automobile, and whom M. Molinier declared to be his ailing father. The article says that this person was none other than Trotsky. It states that the occupants of "Les Embruns" lived surrounded by great mystery and remained until early in October. (*Ibid.*, V/4.) The date of the fire is given as July 18. We have a deposition, dated March 26, 1937, authenticated by the Police Commissioner at Royan and signed by Albert Bardon, honorary notary and correspondent, and editor of the Royan paper *La France*. Bardon states that early in April, 1934, he published in his paper an article concerning Trotsky's sojourn at St. Palais which was reproduced in the

Journal of April 25, and that this article contained an important error in date.

In fact it placed the arrival of Trotsky at St. Palais on July 18, 1933, whereas he arrived in reality on July 25, 1933. This error arose from a confusion between the date on which the villa was rented and the date of the tenant's arrival. On the other hand, the date of arrival coincided with that of the fire. (*Ibid.*, V/5.)

(6) Depositions by two people who were at the villa "Les Embruns" when Trotsky arrived; certified by the Special Committee. The first of these is by Vera Lanis, wife of Raymond Molinier, who is at present Trotsky's political adversary (PC 188). Vera Lanis states that she was entrusted with the preparation of Trotsky's dwelling, "Les Embruns," at Royan; that she left Paris around the 22nd or 23rd of July, and that she put the villa in order, being helped on the last day by Ségal; that she was present at the fire which took place on the day of Trotsky's arrival, and that friends and neighbors, in extinguishing the fire, turned the kitchen upside down; that she remained continuously in the villa, helping with the housework, until the end of August; and that

I saw Trotsky several times every day and it is simply a fable to say that he left Royan, where he arrived on the 25th of July, during the month of July or August. I can state that he remained constantly in the house quite indisposed and that he almost never went out. If Trotsky had absented himself, I, who did the cooking and served at the table three times a day, would certainly have been aware of it. (*Ibid.*, IV/3.)

Maurice Ségal states that he arrived at the villa on July 24, 1933, and assisted Mme. Lanis in putting it in order;

that Trotsky arrived the next day around noon with his wife and several other people; that he, Ségal, remained several days at the villa, occupying a room on the ground floor with Leprince, and that he saw Trotsky daily; that he returned to Paris with Leprince and Sedov; that they had two mishaps en route, and that because of the resultant delay and uncertainty Sedov finished the trip by motor-bus. (*Ibid.*, IV/4.)

(7) Depositions of people who arrived at St. Palais after July 31, 1933. Adolphe, who states that he arrived in Royan from Paris on August 1 or 2, 1933, lists as follows the visitors received during this period:

> Jakob Schwab, for four or five consecutive days. According to a remark made in one of my private letters in this period it was around the 16th to the 19th of August; de Kadt of the Dutch O.S.P.; a deputation of the Dutch R.S.A.P. with H. Sneevliet. . . . Smith and Jennie Lee of the English I.L.P. the 29th of August; and P.J. Schmidt of the Dutch O.S.P., if I am not mistaken. From the L.C.I. came E. Bauer, Witte, L. Lesoil, G. Vereecken, R. and H. Molinier; a tall Belgian comrade; W. Nelz, Walter Held; members of the French Communist League; J. Laste and Y. Craipeau, who also mounted guard; Beaussier, Gourbil of St. Palais-sur-mer, who came once with two other friends from the vicinity, one from Oléron and another, and who brought another time a sympathetic railway worker from Royan. From the German section there was Schmidt of Danzig, who for a certain time helped as secretary and as a member of the guard. A doctor came from [a foreign country] to give Trotsky medical treatment. From time to time the barber, Comrade Lhuillier, came from Paris to cut Trotsky's hair and beard. . . . I also saw a chauffeur in the company of R. Molinier and a worker engaged at the time as a dishwasher in a Royan

hotel. From Paris came a deputation of Jewish comrades; also Feroci. Writers: Malraux; also Parijanine. Also the German, Erde. I do not remember other persons but there were surely more. I forgot Sternberg of the S.A.P. (*Ibid.*, VII/9.)

An affidavit (St. Moritz) by the doctor* who was summoned to treat Trotsky at Royan, states that he was at Royan from September 4 to September 17 or 18, 1933. It corroborates the testimony quoted above concerning the state of Trotsky's health during his stay at "Les Embruns." (*Ibid.*, VIII/17.)

Pierre Naville, in a statement certified by the Special Committee, testifies that he visited Trotsky at Royan on September 9 or 10, 1933. Naville says that during July and August he was living in Paris and did not leave that city, and that he received during that period several letters from Trotsky. He gives extracts from these letters, dated July 31, August 17, 25 and 21. (*Ibid.*, VIII/5.)

J. Gourbil of St. Palais-sur-mer, in a statement authenticated by the mayor of that city, says that several times he visited Trotsky at "Les Embruns," and that

> Anyone who saw the system of defense organized in July and August, 1933, at St. Palais, to protect the life of Trotsky, and who hears him accused of having conversed at that period on a bench in the Bois de Boulogne with an envoy of Radek, has the right to say that the peak of police inventiveness coincides with that of the ridiculous and the absurd. (*Ibid.*, VIII/14.)

An affidavit (Amsterdam) by J. de Kadt of Haarlem, Holland, states that as a secretary of the Independent Social-

---

* Since this physician lives in a semi-fascist country, we do not give his name or his nationality.

ist Party of Holland (OSP) he visited Leon Trotsky in the summer of 1933:

> As it was quite impossible at that time to meet L.D. Trotsky in Paris, I had to travel to Royan where I arrived on August 24 and stayed in Trotsky's house in the neighborhood of Royan till August 25.
>
> As on August 27 and 28 there was an international conference of independent socialist parties and groups at Paris, it would have been of great importance to Trotsky to attend this conference in order to state himself his doctrines there and have the opportunity to meet some of the socialist leaders who were assembled there. It was, however, impossible for him to leave Royan. . . . (*Ibid.,* S VIII/28.)

De Kadt states that he is not a Trotskyist and has never at any time adhered to any of the so-called Trotskyist organizations; that at this moment he is not a member of any party or political group; that he is an independent socialist writer and editor of the independent socialist magazine, *De Nieuwe Kern.*

An affidavit (Amsterdam) by H. Sneevliet of Amsterdam, Chairman of the Dutch Revolutionary Socialist Workers Party (R.S.A.P.) and member of the Dutch Parliament since 1933, states that he visited Trotsky at Royan, France, August 18–22, 1933. Mr. Sneevliet's deposition will be quoted in Chapter XXIV of this report. (*Ibid.,* S VIII/26.)

Charles Andrew Smith of 81 Arcadian Gardens, London, England, Doctor of Philosophy at the University of Durham, states in an affidavit (London) that at the conclusion of a conference held under the auspices of the International Bureau of Revolutionary Socialist Unity in Paris on August 27 and 28, 1933, a suggestion was made that one of the national leaders of the Independent Labour Party of Great Britain should meet Leon Trotsky, then resident in the South of France, to discuss with him the international political situation; that the three national leaders of the Independent Labour Party at this conference were James Maxton, Archibald Fenner Brockway, and John Paton; that

> It was explained to us in Paris that the said Leon Trotsky could not possibly come up to Paris to meet the said James Maxton, Archibald Fenner Brockway, and John Paton and others, as he would very gladly have done, not only because of the long journey involved in travelling from the South of France to Paris, but also on account of repeated threats against his life and of incitement in the fascist press of France to his assassination.

Smith says it was decided that he as a member of the National Administrative Council should visit Leon Trotsky. He left Paris on Monday night, August 28, 1933, and travelled overnight to Royan.

> On arriving at the place of residence of Leon Trotsky at the place aforesaid, I found the same closely guarded and the said Leon Trotsky was constantly attended by armed followers who were obviously living in real apprehension of attack. . . .

He says that he had an interview of several hours with Trotsky on August 29, 1933, and that he returned to Paris that night. He concludes:

> The whole circumstances of my visit to the said Leon Trotsky lead me to believe that at that time circumstances were such that it would seem to be highly improbable that during that month the said Leon Trotsky could have spent any time in Paris. . . . (*Ibid.*, VIII/18.)

An affidavit (London) by John Paton of Welwyn Garden City, Stratfordshire, England, states that he was general secretary of the Independent Labour Party from 1927 to 1933; that he was in Paris on August 27 and 28, 1933, at a conference held under the auspices of the International Bureau for Revolutionary Socialist Unity, that he expected to see Leon Trotsky in Paris during this visit, but learned that it was impossible for Trotsky to leave the South of France; that he consequently visited Trotsky at Royan on August 29, 1933, with P.J. Schmidt, of the Independent Socialist Party of Holland. He says:

> I had been informed that it would be necessary for me to undertake the long and troublesome journey to Royan aforesaid if I was to see the said Leon Trotsky, as I was informed that he never left his place of residence. All this information confirmed what I had already been told by J. de Kadt of the Independent Socialist Party of Holland whom I met in Paris and who had previously visited the said Leon Trotsky. I interviewed the said Leon Trotsky at Royan aforesaid on the 29th day of August, 1933. The said Leon Trotsky then remarked that he had to exercise great care in maintaining privacy and restricting his movements so that no excuse should be offered for seeking to turn him out of France. (*Ibid.*, VIII/19.)

An affidavit (Amsterdam) by P.J. Schmidt of Amsterdam states that he travelled to Royan to see Trotsky in the company of John Paton, then general secretary of the I.L.P. Mr. Schmidt places the date of this visit to Trotsky on August 30 to 31, 1933.* (*Ibid.*, S VIII/27.)

---

* This date seems more probable than that of August 29, given by Mr. Paton, since if Mr. Paton and Mr. Schmidt had visited Trotsky on August 29 their visit would have coincided with that of Mr. Smith, who does not mention them and is not mentioned by them.

An affidavit (London) by James Maxton of London, member of the British House of Commons, corroborates the statement of Charles Andrew Smith to the effect that Maxton was obliged to return to England from the conference in Paris without visiting Leon Trotsky because Maxton was unable to spare the time to make the necessary trip to the South of France. (*Ibid.*, VIII/20.)

(8) Five letters written by Trotsky to people in Paris at the end of July, 1933, of which two are dated July 30 and three July 31. Among these is the letter of July 31 addressed to Pierre Naville (see 7 above). (*Ibid.*, VI/2–6.)

(9) Various documents illustrating Trotsky's political preoccupations during his stay at Royan. The more important of these documents will be cited in later sections of this report.

§ 160. The testimony of the witness Vladimir Romm begins, as we have noted, with a lie—his identification of the Opposition of 1926–7 with "anti-Party work." We have noted his apparent ignorance of the nature of Opposition activity; the want of any credible motivation for his having undertaken the dangerous tasks attributed to him in connection with the alleged conspiracy; his failure to state—and Vyshinsky's failure to ask him—how Sedov learned that he was ready to risk his life by undertaking those tasks. Moreover the doubt inspired by Radek's testimony concerning the contents of Trotsky's initial letter (§ 144) naturally extends to the testimony of Romm that he delivered it, and to his own account of its contents. It seems to us incredible that Sedov would have sent such a letter as Radek and Romm described to the address of the Soviet news agency in Paris, where it might easily have been opened by someone else than Romm and thus have brought about the exposure of the alleged conspiracy. It also seems incredible—indeed preposterous—that Trotsky, upon arriving in France, would have hastened more than half-way across that country merely to confirm to a strange liaison man the contents of a letter he was sending to Radek. And Romm's testimony about this conversation and the events that led up to it is open to serious doubt in view of the fantastic contradictions which we have pointed out in the testimony concerning the formation of the parallel center (Chapter XVI).

Romm's testimony, therefore, is not convincing. Yet the Prosecutor's sole attempt to secure corroboration of this testimony consisted in securing its confirmation by Radek, whose own testimony had contradicted in advance its most important points. Assuming that Romm told the truth, more convincing corroboration was available. This Commission, as we have already stated, holds that one of the outstanding defects in the procedure of the January trial was the failure of the prosecution to produce the French police record of Trotsky's movements at this period, which it could presumably easily have obtained from the friendly government of France. We have quoted Trotsky's statement that he attempted to obtain this record. Six separate attempts to secure it have been made on our own behalf, two of them by high French officials. The answer to each request was that the record is in the keeping of the director of the *Sûreté Nationale,* and for reasons of state cannot be given out. The *Comité pour l'Enquête sur le Procès de Moscou* has also vainly attempted to obtain possession of this record. Since the French government is on friendly terms and in *quasi* alliance with the Soviet government, it is reasonable to assume that if this record of Trotsky's movements bore out the testimony of Vladimir Romm, the French government would not hesitate to reveal it; and that its refusal indicates unwillingness to embarrass a government with which it is in friendship and virtual alliance. Therefore we hold that the refusal of the French government to make this record public constitutes strong presumptive evidence that it does not bear out the testimony of Vladimir Romm.

The positive evidence that Romm testified falsely is impressive both in its mass and its cohesion. All parts of it—the testimony of witnesses, letters, telegrams, excerpts from the press, etc.—fit together into a record of Trotsky's first months in France which establishes conclusively: (1) that Trotsky arrived in France on July 24, 1933; (2) that he disembarked from the "Bulgaria" by motorboat and landed at Cassis, from which place he proceeded direct to St. Palais, spending one night en route; (3) that he remained at St. Palais without interruption until October 9, 1933.

We hold that all this evidence proves conclusively that Leon Trotsky did not meet Vladimir Romm in the Bois de Boulogne either in the latter half of July, 1933, as stated by Romm, or at any time between July 24 and October 31, 1933. We hold that this evidence proves also that Leon Sedov was absent from Paris during the latter half of July, 1933, and did not return to that city before the very end of July or the first part of August (Miss Weber says on July 30 or 31; Shachtman and Leprince say early August); and that he could not, therefore, have had with Romm both of the interviews to which Romm testified. But if Romm's testimony about the first interview was false, there is no reason to believe his testimony about the second. Moreover, even if we assume that Sedov returned to Paris in time to see Vladimir Romm at the end of July, it is clear from all the evidence in our possession that he could not have gone with Romm to the Bois de Boulogne to see Trotsky, as Romm stated, since Trotsky did not leave St. Palais between the date of his arrival there, July 25, 1933, and October 9, 1933.

§ 161. We therefore hold that Romm's testimony concerning his alleged meeting with Trotsky at the end of July, 1933, is false. And since his evidence on this crucial point is false, it follows that all his testimony concerning his alleged activities as a liaison man between Sedov and Trotsky on the one hand and Radek on the other is not worthy of credence. And since the testimony of Radek to conspiracy with Leon Trotsky rests primarily upon that of Romm and secondarily upon that of Pyatakov, which we have also held disproved, we hold Radek's testimony to be also false. We therefore hold that none of the letters allegedly exchanged between Trotsky and Radek, whether through Vladimir Romm or by unspecified means, ever existed, and that all testimony to the contents of these alleged letters is sheer fabrication.

20

The testimony of A.A. Shestov

§ 162. The fourth basis of the charge against Leon Trotsky and Leon Sedov in the Pyatakov-Radek trial is the testimony of the accused Shestov. Shestov stated that his criminal activities began at the end of 1923, when as a student of the Workers Faculty of the Moscow Mining Academy he was an active advocate of the Trotskyite platform; that at the end of 1924 he "deceived the Party for the first time" by declaring at a Party meeting that he had abandoned Trotskyism; and that at the end of 1925 he "again began to fight the Party actively." (PR 233.)

Here again we note the identification of political opposition with criminal activity.

At about the end of February, 1931, Shestov said, he was sent from Novosibirsk, where he was working, to Moscow on official business. At that time he was a member of the board of the Eastern and Siberian Coal Trust. Hearing that a group of directors, headed by Pyatakov, was to be sent to Berlin, he obtained permission to go, and was in Berlin at the beginning or in the middle of May. He asked Pyatakov, he said, whether his statement published in the press had been the result of a real renunciation of Trotskyism, or was a forced step. Pyatakov asked him whether he had read the latest literature on sale in Berlin (nature not specified), and advised him to get in touch with I.N. Smirnov. He did so, he said, and Smirnov told him that

> the situation in the Soviet Union has sharply changed, and I must understand that an open struggle was impossible. The task of the Trotskyites now was to win the Party's confidence and then to renew the attack with doubled and trebled force. (PR 234.)

Smirnov, he said, advised him to discuss with Sedov "the new and latest course." He allegedly saw Sedov at the Nikolai restaurant, where Sedov, in response to his question, What were the specific tasks which Trotsky "placed before us Trotskyites,"

> . . . said that his father held that the only correct way, a difficult one but a sure one, was forcibly to remove Stalin and the leaders of the government by means of terrorism. Then I remarked that this was partly true because we had really got into a blind alley. Therefore it was necessary either to disarm or to map out a new path of struggle. (PR 234.)

Thereupon, he said, Sedov, seeing that Shestov was being influenced by his words, advised him to get in touch with the firm of Fröhlich-Klüpfel-Dehlmann, which was assisting, under a contract, in sinking mines in the Kuzbas (Kuznetsk Basin), saying that this firm was of help in sending mail to the Soviet Union; and if this firm did them a favor, they should reciprocate by furnishing it with certain information. In answer to Shestov's protest, "You are simply proposing that I become a spy," Sedov, he said, told him not to be squeamish; that if he accepted terrorism and undermining activity in industry, he, Sedov, could not see why he should fail to accept this also. Shestov said he told Sedov he would consult Smirnov and then give him "a reply one way or another." At the end of the interview, said Shestov, they went to Berlin and entered the Baltimore restaurant, where Sedov introduced him to a Mr. Schwartzmann, a man dressed as a waiter, and told Shestov that when he wanted to get in touch with him Schwartzmann would convey the message. (PR 234–5.)

Turning back to pp. 160–162 of the record, we find that Sedov, apparently in this same conversation—at all events in a conversation in May, 1931—appears to have informed Shestov of the line on undermining Soviet industry through wrecking and diversion and told him it was necessary to enlist "non-Trotskyite wreckers" for this purpose. Thus it appears that Sedov, whom according to Shestov's testimony at this point he had never met before this conversation (on page 31 he testifies that he met Sedov in January, 1931, some five months before Shestov's arrival in Berlin and one month before Sedov's arrival), confided the "new line" on terrorism to Shestov at their very first meeting, appeared to take for granted his acceptance of sabotage, and even proposed that he "become a spy." Such indiscretion seems daring, not to say foolhardy, when we remember that Shestov, according to his own testimony, was a Soviet functionary, and at that very moment was in Berlin on an official mission. One would think Sedov must have suffered considerable anxiety until he learned whether this hesitant Soviet functionary would consent to "become a spy" or decide that it was his duty to denounce the whole conspiracy to the GPU. Shestov, however, seems to have settled that matter in his own mind even before he talked with Smirnov. In the beginning of June, he said,

. . . after I had assimilated all that I had heard from Smirnov and Sedov, I arrived at the conclusion that it was too late to retreat. Smirnov and the others knew me as a convinced Trotskyite, the more so that personal association with Smirnov, Sedov and Pyatakov made us more intimate and I decided that I would be at the side of my leaders. (PR 235.)

About the middle of July, said Shestov, he met Smirnov, who asked him bluntly, "How is your mood?" He replied that he had no personal mood but did as Trotsky taught them— stood at attention and waited for orders. Smirnov then, he said, told him that a definite decision had been made "to get into power by organizing assassinations, by acts of violence against Stalin, his Political Bureau and his government; whereupon Shestov "agreed wholeheartedly to carry on this work." He informed Smirnov of Sedov's instruction to get in touch with the firm of Fröhlich-Klüpfel-Dehlmann, saying, "In that case I shall be a spy and diversionist." Smirnov, he alleged, told him to "stop slinging big words like 'spy' and 'diversionist' about," and defended the enlistment of German diversionists in the mobilization of counter-revolutionary forces. After this conversation, said Shestov, he consented to establish connections with the German firm. (PR 235–6.) Vyshinsky asked him:

> VYSHINSKY: What year was that?
> SHESTOV: That was about the middle of June, 1931.
> VYSHINSKY: Did both meetings take place in 1931?
> SHESTOV: Yes, in the spring.
> VYSHINSKY: Did you stay in Berlin after that?
> SHESTOV: I remained abroad until the beginning of November; I went to London. (PR 236.)

Thus Shestov places his conversation with Smirnov "about

the middle of July," "about the middle of June," and "in the spring." He testified that he had two more conversations with Sedov, in one of which he told him of his conversations with Smirnov and Pyatakov, and during the other received a pair of shoes containing letters for Pyatakov and Muralov (§ 131). In November, said Shestov, he left for the Kuznetzk Basin, but before his departure he met the director of Fröhlich-Klüpfel-Dehlmann, and made a deal by which that firm would undertake to maintain communications with the Trotskyite organizations in the Soviet Union and to organize wrecking and diversion together with the Trotskyites, in return for which services the latter would supply the firm with secret information and aid its representatives in diversionist work (PR 238). Shestov later testified that he left for England in the middle of November, 1931, after this alleged conversation, and that on his return trip he was in Berlin for about three weeks; that he met Sedov twice at the end of October and after that he left for the U.S.S.R. (PR 241.) On page 31 he testifies that on his return from England he went to Schwartzmann and told him he must see Sedov; that he met Sedov in the Baltimore restaurant and received the shoes with the letters. According to Shestov, a letter was secreted in each shoe; one letter marked "P" for Pyatakov; the other "M" for Muralov. He stated that he delivered the letter marked "P" to Pyatakov in the middle of November, 1931, in Moscow, having arrived there on November 7 (PR 30); and that upon his arrival in Novosibirsk he got in touch with Muralov and delivered the other letter to him. (PR 31, 241–2.) He placed his arrival in Novosibirsk between November 20 and 30. But Muralov testified that he received this letter in 1932. (PR 217.)

§ 162. Leon Trotsky testified that he never knew A.A. Shestov and that he first saw his name in the reports of the trial (PC 126).

§ 163. Leon Sedov testified that he had never known or

met Shestov. He remarked that Shestov had been a witness in the Novosibirsk trial and that at that time while declaring that he had received terrorist directives from Pyatakov in 1931 he made no mention of Sedov. As authority for this statement, Sedov referred to the official report of the trial in *Pravda*, November 22, 1936, and also to an article in *Pravda*, December 24, 1936, signed by Roginsky, assistant prosecutor of the U.S.S.R. Sedov declared that this omission justified the conclusion that the allegations of Shestov in the trial of January, 1937, were a concoction invented after the Novosibirsk trial. (CR 30–1.)

Sedov denied that he was ever acquainted with the firm of Fröhlich-Klüpfel-Dehlmann, or that anything in Shestov's testimony concerning him was true (CR 31). He further called attention to Shestov's statement that he met Sedov in Berlin in January, 1931, and stated that at this date he was in Istanbul, as could be proved by his passport, and that he arrived in Berlin only on February 25, 1931. He also pointed out the contradiction between this statement of Shestov and his statement that he arrived in Germany in the month of May and at about the same time met Sedov; also the contradiction between Shestov's statements that he went to Moscow early in November, 1931, and was in Novosibirsk by November 20–30, and his statement that he went to England in the middle of November, 1931. (CR 32.)

§ 164. We have already stated above (§ 130) our opinion that the testimony of Pyatakov concerning his alleged contacts with Sedov is fabrication. Therefore, we hold his corroboration of Shestov's testimony implicating Leon Sedov to be worthless. Moreover, according to Shestov, he conversed with Pyatakov and Sedov separately. His is therefore the only direct testimony to his alleged meetings with Sedov; and as Sedov pointed out and the above résumé confirms, that testimony contains extraordinary contradictions concerning the dates of his meetings with

Sedov and of his own movements—contradictions which appeared to disturb neither the Prosecutor nor the Court. We have, furthermore, verified Sedov's statements concerning Shestov's testimony in the Novosibirsk trial. In what purports to be an official verbatim report of that trial (evening session, November 20) published in *Pravda* November 22, 1936, Shestov said:

> When I was in Berlin I received a direct directive from Pyatakov to carry on undermining terrorist work in the Kuzbas. He knew that I was a worker in the Kuzbas, and he said that I should rigidly coordinate my activity with the representative of the Trotskyite organization here in Siberia, Muralov.

In the January trial, on the other hand, Shestov said:

> . . . I received exact instructions from Sedov, from Pyatakov, and Smirnov that my activities must be exclusively under the control of Muralov. . . . (PR 222.)

This statement is nowhere borne out in the reports of Shestov's testimony in the Novosibirsk trial as they appeared in *Pravda*. There is no mention of either Sedov or Smirnov in that testimony, or in the quotations from Shestov in the indictment or the reference to him in Prosecutor Roginsky's summation. Nor are they mentioned in the verdict. On November 22, a mention of the alleged meeting of Pyatakov, Smirnov and Sedov (§ 124) is interpolated in the purported record of Drobnis's testimony; Shestov is not included. As reported, Shestov's testimony implicated only Pyatakov and Muralov. His alleged connection with Sedov and Smirnov is first mentioned three days after the verdict, in Roginsky's article (November 24), to which Sedov referred. But Roginsky, curiously, illustrated this alleged connection with the passage from Shestov quoted above, in which he mentioned only Pyatakov and Muralov. Thus Shestov's alleged connection with Sedov and Smirnov appears to have been an afterthought on the part of the Prosecutor.

Shestov's testimony concerning the supposed deal with Fröhlich-Klüpfel-Dehlmann is as questionable as that of Pyatakov about his dealings with Borsig and Demag. On whose behalf and for what purpose was this firm collecting secret information and conducting wrecking and diversive activities in the Soviet Union? That a foreign business firm might offer a Soviet functionary a *quid pro quo* to get contracts renewed (PR 239) or to secure preference over competing firms—this is understandable. But this is a very different matter from engaging in sabotage which, if discovered, would necessarily discredit that firm and result in its exclusion from the Soviet Union. For this sort of thing it must, one would think, have some political motive. What was it? Hardly the mere fact that the director of the firm was "Sedov's friend" (PR 238). No business concern would be likely to engage in "diversive and criminal activities" on the basis of its director's personal friendships, at great risk to its standing and its business. Did this firm believe that the "Trotskyites" would soon be in power and would thereupon award it large contracts? Shestov himself says the Trotskyites "had no support whatever among the workers and peasants" (PR 162); and surely if this firm "had their people . . . in the Kuznetsk Basin" (PR 238) they must have been in a position to know this. Were they acting on behalf of the German government? At that time Germany was still a democracy in good relations with the Soviet government, and the Bruening government was in power. Was Bruening conspiring with the "Trotskyites" to displace Stalin? With what motives? All these questions were pertinent to the testimony of Shestov. The Prosecutor asked none of them.

The record is extremely contradictory concerning the letter which Shestov was supposed to have carried to Muralov in one of a pair of shoes. We have already noted those contradictions which concern the dates on which Shestov received and delivered this letter. More important, however, is the contradiction between Shestov and Muralov concerning the nature of this alleged communication. Muralov states that the letter was from Sedov and says:

> I knew him very well, often met him in Trotsky's apartment, and I knew everything about him, including his physical defect—a fact which Shestov confirmed, so I made sure that this letter was not a forgery. I recognized the handwriting. (PR 217.)

Before we proceed to Shestov's version, we note Sedov's testimony that in his youth, when Muralov knew him, it is true he squinted with one eye, but that at the time when Shestov allegedly met him in Berlin he had been completely cured of his defect. (CR 33.) If this is true, Shestov, we think, can hardly have "confirmed" a physical defect which Sedov no longer possessed.

As Shestov described the communication which he delivered to Muralov, it consisted of two letters, one from Trotsky and the other "a letter from the Foreign Bureau which I personally deciphered." Shestov testified that Muralov requested him to decipher this letter, saying that its arithmetic made his eyes hurt, and "then gave me the letter and the code." He did not say how Muralov and Sedov—who had not previously been in communication, if one is to believe Muralov's testimony—had arranged this code; nor did the Prosecutor ask either him or Muralov. Nor did Shestov state in whose hand this long letter was written, or whether it was typewritten. (PR 242–3.) Vyshinsky asked no questions, although the contradiction between Shestov and Muralov was sufficiently important to warrant disbelief that the letter ever existed.

As we have noted, Shestov's testimony is open to serious doubt on the basis of the record alone. And this doubt is increased by a comparison of his confession as witness in the Novosibirsk trial and his confession as accused in the January trial.

We have already noted that Pyatakov's corroboration of Shestov's testimony is worthless. Like Pyatakov, Shestov claimed that it was Smirnov who put him in touch with Sedov. We have held (§ 46) that Smirnov received no "opinion" or instructions about terrorism from Sedov in 1931 (the prosecution did not charge Smirnov with having discussed wrecking and diversion with Sedov). Therefore, Smirnov can not have introduced Shestov to Sedov for purposes of a terrorist conspiracy, or informed Shestov of an agreement reached with Sedov about terrorism and wrecking. Moreover, we have already pointed out (§ 132) that if Pyatakov did not meet Sedov there is no ground for believing that he received a letter from Trotsky as a result of such meetings— a letter which, as described by Pyatakov, alluded to them in the words, "I am very glad that you have followed my requests" (PR 32). But since Shestov testified that he delivered this letter, then obviously if no such letter was sent, Shestov knowingly lied. And if he lied about this letter there remains not the slightest basis for crediting either his testimony or Muralov's concerning the letter which he allegedly received from Sedov for Muralov at the same time.

§ 165. In view of all these considerations we hold the testimony of the defendant Shestov concerning his alleged meetings with Sedov and his alleged services as go-between for Sedov and Muralov to be worthless.

21

The testimony of N.I. Muralov

§ 166. The fifth basis of the charge against Leon Trotsky and Leon Sedov in the January trial is the testimony of the accused Muralov. Muralov dated his "fall" back to 1923, when he signed the Declaration of the Forty-Six.* He remained in the Trotskyite organization, he said, until he was expelled from the Party and exiled to Western Siberia. Thereafter he continued to adhere to the Opposition platform submitted to the Fifteenth Congress. He answered in the affirmative Vyshinsky's question:

> And you continued to adhere to this up to the most recent time, and, remaining on these political positions, you waged the struggle? (PR 231.)

---

* Submitted on October 15, 1923, to the C.C. of the C.P.S.U. by forty-six Communist leaders, including Pyatakov, Preobrazhensky, Sosnovsky, Byeloborodov, Sapronov, Muralov, Antonov-Ovseyenko, Kossior, Sere-bryakov, Raphael, etc. It supported, substantially, the views on workers' democracy advanced by Trotsky in the dispute then current.

Thus the Opposition platform, which criticized the internal and foreign policy of the majority, is made to appear a basis for alleged criminal activity. (See §§ 181, 230 concerning this platform.)

Muralov stated that for eight months he denied "any part in underground work," and explained that this was due to political motives, to resentment of his arrest, and to his attachment to Trotsky, which "began when he was People's Commissar and I was commander of the Moscow Military Area" (PR 232). At last,

> . . . I said to myself, almost after eight months, that I must submit to the interests of the state for which I had fought for twenty-three years, for which I had fought actively in three revolutions, when my life hung by a thread dozens of times. (PR 233.)

Muralov stated that when he was in Moscow he learned from Smirnov that he had been abroad and seen Sedov (Chapter X). Smirnov, he said, told him "about Trotsky's new line about resorting to terrorism. . . ." On his arrival in Novosibirsk, he said,

> . . . I arranged to meet Sumetsky and Boguslavsky and told them what Ivan Nikitich Smirnov had proposed, which I accepted as proper. (PR 216.)

He did not tell why he accepted terrorism as proper, and Vyshinsky did not ask him. He stated that "in the next year" he again saw Smirnov in Moscow and learned from him

> . . . that there was something new, namely the program of economic terrorism. . . . Whose line is it? I asked. He said it was also Trotsky's. (PR 217.)

Muralov also testified that he saw Pyatakov in Moscow in 1934 and 1935; that in 1934 Pyatakov told him about the agreement with the Rights and about the composition of the reserve center (PR 218); and that in 1935, after the assassination of Kirov, they discussed group terror (PR 224–7). He did not say that Pyatakov told him anything which came from Sedov or Trotsky.

Muralov testified that he received three letters from Sedov; that allegedly received through Shestov (§ 164); another through Seidman, a Trotskyite engineer, in 1932; and a final one in 1933. The one received through Seidman, he said, was really meant not for him but for Smirnov, and

> . . . instructed us to accelerate terrorist acts against Stalin, Voroshilov, Kaganovich and Kirov. (PR 218.)

That received in 1933, he said, informed him that "the old man is pleased with our activities" (PR 218).

Muralov stated that his communication with Sedov was maintained through Shestov. The letter of 1933, he said, was brought by a German specialist whom Shestov had commissioned. All his correspondence with Sedov, he said, was sent through Shestov. (PR 227.) Vyshinsky asked Shestov:

> How did you establish connections with the German specialists working in the Kuzbas, what addresses did you use, why did they carry out your commissions? (PR 228.)

Shestov, in answering, did not state what addresses he used, and the Prosecutor did not press him for an answer on this important point. Nor did he ask either Shestov or Muralov what became of these alleged letters.

§ 167. Leon Trotsky testified that

> Muralov was a member of the Central Control Commission, one of the heroes of the Civil War, and commander-

in-chief of the Moscow Military District, my friend and my companion in hunting. We were in the best relations with him. He is not a political man. He is a soldier, a revolutionary soldier, and very honest, an exceptionally honest man. He abandoned the Opposition without any declaration, a written declaration. But he abandoned politics. He became a "spetz" [specialist] just as Pyatakov, and stayed in Siberia. He is an agronomist by profession. (PC 124.)

He stated that in 1931 and 1932 he had tried many times to communicate with Muralov, Rakovsky, and others, but was obliged to abandon the attempt because the control became very severe. Beginning with 1930, he testified, the GPU began to accuse people in relations with him of espionage, so that to communicate with him became very dangerous. Since 1931 or 1932, he said, he had not received any letter from Muralov or sent him any (PC 124). Questioned by his counsel on his statement that Muralov was an honest man, and asked whether he was honest in his confession concerning Sedov's letter, he said:

> His deposition is false, but I am absolutely sure that it was the false deposition of a simple soldier, to whom they stated after the assassination of all the others: "You are a friend of Trotsky. Now, you understand you cannot have Trotsky here. He is in exile." They were threatening him: "Stalin is the chief of the state. We have Japan from one side, and Germany from the other. The activity of Trotsky is dangerous. Trotsky completely recognizes Zinoviev and Kamenev. You must confess. You will be shot." He, as a soldier, confessed. (PC 341.)

Asked by counsel for the Commission whether he excluded the desire of the defendants unselfishly to serve the Party as a motive for confession, he answered:

... I can admit it for Muralov ... the psychosis of war is now the most important factor in the hands of the bureaucracy. Everything is explained by the war danger. People like Muralov and others read only the Soviet papers. They don't know foreign languages. For years they read that I am abroad, acting against the Soviet Union, that I am in alliance with Lord Beaverbrook and Winston Churchill. Every one of them says, "It is false, but it is possible that everything is true." He is not in connection with me and he is ... shaken in his confidence. That is from one side. From the other: "Stalin is the chief of the country. If we fight against Germany and Japan, we will fight under the leadership of Stalin. You are a friend of Trotsky, but you can't invite him to come here. In the situation his activities are prejudicial to the defense of the Soviet Union."

At the time he merely hesitates. He hesitated for one, two, three months. He hesitated for eight months. They showed him one deposition, one confession after another. Then this man broke down. He satisfied them in every way. (PC 395–6.)

Asked whether he thought Muralov believed the charges against him, Trotsky said:

I cannot admit that he accepted the accusation as it is, because he took upon himself the same false accusation. But my oppositionist activity, my critique against the ruling caste—it is possible that it seemed to him prejudicial to the defense of the Soviet Union. (PC 396.)

§ 168. Leon Sedov testified that Muralov was an old Bolshevik who remained his father's friend until the latter's exile; Sedov declared that Muralov was the only one of their former friends involved in either trial who—although he

renounced political activity—had not made a public declaration renouncing their movement; that he had not seen
Muralov since the end of 1927, and after the end of 1928 had
had no correspondence with him. He denied that he had sent
to Muralov any of the three letters which Muralov stated
he had received from him, or that he had ever known the
engineer Seidman who, Muralov said, had delivered the second letter. (CR 32–3.)

§ 169. We have already discussed (§ 164) the contradictions
concerning the first of these alleged letters—contradictions
which render its existence incredible on the basis of the record alone. As for the second, it seems odd that Sedov should
have sent to Muralov, in Western Siberia, a letter meant for
Smirnov, who would appear from the record of both trials to
have been in Moscow in the year 1932, except for a possible
sojourn abroad which is alluded to in the testimony of the
accused Ter-Vaganyan (ZK 109–10). Muralov's testimony to
the contents of the third letter is something of a curiosity,
as the only instance in either trial record where Trotsky is
represented as being in the slightest degree satisfied with
the activities of the alleged conspirators, who were supposedly risking their reputations and their lives in carrying
out his orders.

We have quoted (§§ 167, 168) Trotsky's statement, corroborated by Sedov, that Muralov abandoned the Opposition,
and politics, without making any written declaration. During
the trial Muralov, in answer to a question from Vyshinsky,
confirmed that he had continued "up until the most recent
time" to adhere to the Opposition platform of 1927, and
"remaining on these political positions . . . waged the struggle" (PR 231). In the first place, as we shall have occasion
to note in later chapters, the Opposition platform of 1927
provided no basis whatever for the alleged criminal activities which Muralov, prompted by Vyshinsky, based upon it.
In the second place, if Muralov continued to adhere to this

platform—and the ruling faction may easily have suspected that he did so, since he had not formally "capitulated"— then he must have been under constant surveillance by the Soviet police, like other exiled Oppositionists (§ 30). Therefore the conspiratorial activity to which he confessed would appear, for this reason alone, to have been improbable, and even impossible.

§ 170. Muralov's testimony that Smirnov informed him of "Trotsky's new line about resorting to terrorism" and about the new line on wrecking is obviously false if Smirnov himself got no such "line." We have already stated (§ 48) our conclusion that Smirnov confessed falsely. Therefore we hold this testimony of Muralov to be false. Muralov's testimony to the first and third of his alleged letters from Sedov depends upon that of the accused Shestov. We have already (§ 165) held the testimony of Shestov implicating Leon Sedov to be worthless. We hold, therefore, that the testimony of Muralov to these letters is also worthless. It follows, naturally, that his testimony to the second letter is worthless. In so far as his testimony to his alleged conversations with Pyatakov may be construed as involving Trotsky and Sedov, we hold, on the basis of our conclusions concerning the confession of Pyatakov (§§ 130, 142) that this testimony is also false. Moreover, in our opinion, the passage which we have quoted from Muralov (§ 166) concerning the motive for his confession lends plausibility to Leon Trotsky's interpretation of that confession.

§ 171. This finishes our consideration of the definitive charges against Trotsky and Sedov in the Moscow trials of August, 1936, and January, 1937. Before proceeding to discuss the credibility of these charges in general, we return to the subject of letters quoted as evidence but not produced in court. In addition to what we have stated (§ 47) about the value of such evidence, we note once more the remarkable indifference of both Prosecutor and Court concerning the means by which several of the letters cited in the trials as evidence against Trotsky and Sedov were received, and what became of them thereafter. The Commission might assume that *one* such letter had been destroyed. It can not assume that all have been, or accept as credible the mere unsupported testimony of various witnesses to their contents; especially in view of the contradictions contained in that testimony, and also in view of the fact that one of these alleged letters (that "concealed in the double wall of Holtzman's suitcase") was a published document whose contents were falsified by the Prosecutor himself (§ 177).

Part 4

The credibility of the charges

22

The charge of terrorism

§ 172. According to the Definition of the Charge in the August trial, the only purpose of the alleged Trotskyite-Zinovievite bloc was the assassination of the leaders of the Communist Party and the Soviet Union (ZK 37). In the January trial, terrorism was one of the charges against the alleged parallel center (PR 18). The principal accused in both trials confessed to knowledge of Trotsky's alleged terrorist instructions and of the existence of various terrorist groups. Following is a partial list of these "terrorist groups":

1. *Zinoviev-Kamenev trial:* The Shatskin-Lominadze group; the Gayevsky group; the Esterman group; the Nikolayev-Kotolynov group (or the Rumyantsev-Kotolynov group—Leningrad); the Yakovlev group (Moscow or Leningrad).

2. *Pyatakov-Radek trial:* The Zaks-Gladneyev group (Zinoviev's group—Moscow); the Mdivani group (Transcaucasia); the Prigozhin group (Leningrad); the Friedland group; the Byeloborodov group (Rostov-on-Don); the Dityateva group (Tula); the Yurlin group (Urals); the Zeidel group;

the Ukraine group; the Kashkin-Nikolayev group (Tomsk); the Khodoroze group (Western Siberia); the Cherepukhin group (Western Siberia).

A number of individual terrorists were also named by the various accused and witnesses. The Prosecutor made no attempt to establish the exact membership of the groups mentioned.

§ 173. It is evident even from this incomplete list of alleged terrorist groups that the alleged conspiracy ramified wide-ly—into Caucasia, Transcaucasia, the Ukraine, Siberia—and involved a large number of people. It is therefore astonishing, assuming that the evidence represents the truth, that it was discovered only after five years (according to several accused it began in 1931), and that during those five years, in spite of "intense activity," it resulted, according to the records them-selves, in precisely one assassination: that of Commissar S.M. Kirov, on December 1, 1934. One is forced to assume, and the records go far to bear out the assumption, that the "intense activity" imputed to the alleged terrorists was chiefly in the line of conversation. Indeed the records contain so much conversation about conversations on terrorism that they are likely to conceal from any but the most careful scrutiny the extreme disproportion between the extent and duration of the alleged terrorist activity, and its concrete result.

More particularly is this true because various "prepara-tions for attempts" are confessed to and are duly character-ized by the Prosecutor as "dastardly crimes." Few details of these alleged attempts are given, and such as are given indicate such feebleness in planning and such want of reso-lution on the part of the executants as to inspire skepticism rather than conviction. Certainly there is nothing about them in the slightest degree in keeping with the records of certain principal accused, such as Smirnov, leader of the famous Fifth Army during the Civil War and conqueror of Kolchak; Muralov, a leader of the October Revolution in Moscow and former Commander of the Moscow Military

area; Mrachkovsky, one of the heroes of the Civil War in the
Urals and former head of the Urals Military District; Drobnis, a soldier of the Civil War, twice condemned to death by
the Whites and once shot by them and left for dead. These
men had records of courage, resolution, and action in the
service of the Communist revolution and the Soviet state.
It is hardly credible that if they had decided to overthrow
the Soviet government through terrorism they would have
gone about it in such dilatory and amateurish ways as the
alleged preparations for terrorist attempts indicate they used,
or that they would have selected such questionable agents as
the accused Arnold, for example, whose fantastic testimony
concerning his biography takes up many pages of the record
of the January trial, and who testified that through his reluctance to sacrifice his own life he twice failed to kill Soviet leaders—Ordjonikidze, Molotov, Eiche, and others—in
automobile wrecks. (PR 328–9.)

We have already remarked Vyshinsky's failure to establish
any credible motivation on the part of people who confessed
to plans for terrorist attempts which must certainly have cost
them their lives. It is one of the outstanding features of both
records. According to these records, the principal accused, and
the alleged director of their activities, Leon Trotsky, hoped
to attain power through the conspiracy. Their agents could
hardly hope for anything but death. The Prosecutor grants
them no revolutionary motive. The records, therefore, would
have been more convincing had he attempted to establish
what their motives were.

§ 174. The records would also have been more convincing
had the Prosecutor taken the trouble to secure corroboration
of the testimony concerning the one murder which allegedly
resulted from the alleged terrorist conspiracy.

Zinoviev, Kamenev, Bakayev, and others confessed that
the assassination of Kirov was ordered by the united center
on direct instructions from Trotsky (e.g., Kamenev, ZK 31–2).

As Trotsky pointed out before the Preliminary Commission (PC 484), the Soviet Government had witnesses available who must have been able to corroborate this testimony, if it was true. For on January 23, 1935, the head of the Leningrad GPU and eleven other GPU agents were secretly tried, convicted, and sentenced to from two to ten years at hard labor, on the ground that they "possessed information concerning the preparations for the attempt on S.M. Kirov . . . and failed to take the necessary measures." Why were these men not summoned to tell what they knew about this alleged work of the united Trotskyite-Zinovievite terrorist center? Why were Medved and his associates never even mentioned in either the August or the January trial? We must assume that their guilty knowledge was established at their own trial, for the verdict stated that they "took no measures for the timely exposure and prevention" of the plot "although they had every possibility of so doing." Why, then, did that evidence not lead immediately to the exposure of the Trotskyite-Zinovievite center? One must assume either that the evidence brought out in their trial involved no such center, or that for some inexplicable reason the "intense terroristic activity" of the Trotskyites-Zinovievites was allowed to proceed with impunity for some eighteen months after the Soviet government had knowledge of it—in other words, that the régime placed itself open, in case of a further assassination, to precisely the same criminal charge upon which it had convicted Medved and his associates.

§ 175. The principal accused in both trials testified that they adopted terrorism as a means of coming into power. The testimony of the alleged instigator of the conspiracy by which this end was to be accomplished was neither taken nor asked for. The attitude, past and present, of Leon Trotsky toward individual terrorism as a means to power is highly relevant to the credibility of this charge, on which he was twice convicted without a hearing.

Trotsky's position is stated in the following passages, among others, from his testimony and his final argument before the Preliminary Commission:

> . . . If we were to be for terror, if we were to be of the opinion that by individual terror we could help the working class in its movement forward, I would proclaim it and appeal to the best elements of the working class to resort to individual terror. Say what is, what is necessary; that is the first rule of my thoughts and my actions. If I say I am against terror it is not because I am afraid of Stalin's police or any other police; it is only because I am a Marxist, for mass action and not individual terror. (PC 272–3.)
>
> . . . On the part of an opposition, terror presupposes the concentration of all forces upon preparing acts of terror, with the foreknowledge that every one of such acts, whether successful or unsuccessful, will evoke in reply the destruction of scores of its best men. An opposition could by no means permit itself such an instant squandering of its forces. It is precisely for this, and for no other reason, that the Comintern does not resort to terroristic attempts in the countries of fascist dictatorships. The Opposition is as little inclined to the policy of suicide as the Comintern. (PC 488–9.)

Trotsky stated that he began his active opposition to individual terrorism with an article published in London in 1902, when "the question of terrorism became very important in the Russian revolutionary movement" (PC 16). On the origin of this issue he testified:

> We had two great parties, the "Narodnaya Volya," "Will of the People" Party, and the Social Revolutionaries, which based their tactics upon individual terror. All Marxists in Russia began in the historic fight against in-

dividual terror. It was not a mystical or religious principle with the Marxists. It was a question of organizing the soul against the monster, of organizing the masses and educating them. Because the terrorist fight was a very glorious page in our revolutionary history, with great sacrifices of the best youth of our people, the Marxists made a terrible fight, ideological fight, against the ideology of terrorism, in order to turn the best elements of the youth to the workers. In this fight between Marxism and terrorism it is the action of the masses versus individual terror, the school which differentiated the strategy of individual terror, and the organized movement. It penetrated our psychology and our literature for decades. (PC 45.)

§ 176. We cite below typical passages from Trotsky's published writings at various points in his career:

Terrorist work, in its very essence, demands such a concentration of energy upon the "supreme moment," such an over-estimation of personal heroism, and lastly, such an hermetically concealed conspiracy as . . . excluded completely any agitational and organizational activity among the masses. . . . Struggling against terrorism, the Marxian intelligentsia defended their right or their duty not to withdraw from the working class districts for the sake of tunnelling mines underneath the Grand Ducal and Tsarist palaces. ("The Collapse of Terror and of Its Party," published in *Przeglad Socyal-demokratczny*, May, 1909. "Collected Works," Moscow and Leningrad: Gosizdat, 1926. Vol. IV, pp. 347–8.)

Whether or not the terrorist act, even if "successful," throws the ruling circles into turmoil, depends on the concrete political circumstances. In any case such turmoil can only be of short duration; the capitalist state is not founded upon ministers and cannot be destroyed with them. The classes it serves will always find new men, the mechanism remains whole and continues its work.

But the turmoil which the terrorist act introduces into the ranks of the toiling masses themselves is far more profound. If it is enough to arm oneself with a revolver to reach the goal, what need is there for the strivings of the class struggle? . . . ("Terrorism," published in *Der Kampf*, 1911. "Collected Works," Vol. IV, p. 366.)

In "The Kirov Assassination" Trotsky quoted the above passages from *Der Kampf*, and said:

To this article which counterposed to terrorist adventurism the method of preparing the proletariat for the socialist revolution, I can add nothing today, twenty-three years later. But if Marxists categorically condemned individual terrorism . . . even when the shots were directed against the agents of the Tsarist government and of capitalist exploitation, they will even more relentlessly condemn and reject the criminal adventurism of terrorist acts directed against the bureaucratic representatives of the first workers' state in history. . . . ("The Kirov Assassination," p. 16–17, December 30, 1934. New York: Pioneer Publishers, February, 1935.)

§ 177. In the August trial the Prosecutor cited only one of Trotsky's writings as substantiating the charge of Terrorism: Trotsky's Open Letter to the Central Executive Committee of the U.S.S.R. mentioned and its contents falsified by the accused Olberg (§§ 73, 83). We quote from Vyshinsky's summation:

. . . in March, 1932, in a fit of counter-revolutionary fury, Trotsky burst out in an open letter with an appeal to "put Stalin out of the way" . . . (ZK 127.)

The Prosecutor here repeated the falsification of the accused Olberg. The text of Trotsky's Open Letter to the C.E.C. of the U.S.S.R. was published in 1932 in many languages and countries. In this letter, which was published in the United States in *The Militant* (New York) of April 2, 1932, Trotsky called for the removal of Stalin in accordance with Lenin's last advice. We quote the relevant passage:

> Stalin has brought you to an impasse. You cannot come out on the road without liquidating Stalinism. You must trust to the working class, give the proletarian vanguard the possibility through free criticism from top to bottom to review the whole Soviet system and pitilessly cleanse it of the accumulated rubbish. It is time, finally, to fulfill the last urgent advice of Lenin, to remove Stalin.

We see no honest way to interpret this passage as calling for the assassination of Stalin, or to identify the free criticism for which it calls with individual terrorism. Indeed, the "last urgent advice of Lenin" might with quite as much justice be so interpreted. We quote from his so-called testament:

> Postscript: Stalin is too rude, and this fault, entirely supportable in relations among us Communists, becomes insupportable in the office of General Secretary. Therefore I propose to the comrades to find a way to remove Stalin from that position and appoint another man who in all respects differs from Stalin only in superiority. . . . ("The Real Situation in Russia," pp. 322–3. Edited by Max Eastman. New York: Harcourt, Brace and Company.)

We are not aware that the Soviet government has ever discovered anything terroristic about this passage from Lenin. That Stalin himself puts quite a different construction upon it is clear in the following quotation from a speech of his before the C.C. and the C.C.C. of the C.P.S.U.:

> It is said that in the "testament" in question Lenin suggested to the Party Congress that it should deliberate on the question of replacing Stalin and appointing another comrade in his place as General Secretary of the Party. This is perfectly true. . . . (*International Press Correspondence*, November 17, 1927.)

Since Lenin's advice to "remove Stalin" has never been interpreted to imply terrorism, and since Trotsky's repetition of that advice was not so interpreted for four years after the publication of his Open Letter, the reason for Olberg's reference to it becomes clear. Sedov's alleged implication that the words "remove Stalin" were a "diplomatic wording" for a call to assassinate him appeared to provide authority for the Prosecutor's falsification of this document. We have already held (§ 108) that Olberg's confession is worthless. Moreover, in our opinion it would be absurd to assume that Trotsky would suggest Stalin's assassination to the Stalinist Executive Committee of the Soviet Union, in a "diplomatic wording" or otherwise.

§ 178. Summing up in the January trial, Vyshinsky again mentioned "that letter of 1932 in which Trotsky issued his treacherous and shameful call, 'Remove Stalin.'" In addition he cited

> . . . a later document, the Trotskyite *Bulletin of the Opposition* No. 36–37, of October, 1933, in which we find a number of direct references to terrorism as a method of fighting the Soviet Government. . . . Trotsky speaks quite frankly about terrorism as a method which already in those years was put on the agenda of the practical activities of the Trotskyites.

In that programmatic article there is a section in which the question is asked: "Can the bureaucracy be removed by peaceful methods?" Trotsky and the Trotskyites regard our Soviet apparatus as a bureaucratic apparatus. In this chapter it is stated:

"Take the important question of how to proceed to reorganize the Soviet state." . . . An opponent of terrorism, an opponent of violence, should have said: Yes, peaceful means are possible on the basis, say, of the constitution.

But what do the Trotskyites say? They say:

"It would be childish to think that the Stalin bureaucracy can be removed by means of a Party or Soviet Congress. Normal, constitutional means are no longer available for the removal of the ruling clique." (This is what they slanderously call our government.)

"They can be compelled to hand over power to the proletarian vanguard" (they speak of themselves as a vanguard and evidently have in mind a "vanguard" like these gentlemen who engaged in murder, diversion and espionage) "only by force." (PR 507–8.)

We find that these quotations occur in the original text. However, Vyshinsky omitted those passages which show what Trotsky meant by "force," and which completely invalidate Vyshinsky's interpretation. For example:

We must set down, first of all, as an immutable axiom, that this task can be achieved only by a revolutionary *party*. The fundamental historic task is to create a revolutionary party in the U.S.S.R. from among the healthy elements in the old Party and from among the youth. . . . Through what ways could it assume power? As early as 1927 Stalin said, addressing the Opposition, "*The present ruling group can be eliminated only through civil war."* This challenge, Bonapartist in spirit, was addressed not to the Left Opposition but—to the Party. Having concentrated all the power in its hands, the bureaucracy proclaimed openly that it would not permit the proletariat to raise its head any longer. The subsequent course of events has added great weight to this challenge. After the experiences of the last few years, it would be childish to suppose that the Stalinist bureaucracy can be removed by means of a party or Soviet Congress.

In reality the last congress of the Bolshevik Party took place at the beginning of 1923, the 12th Party Congress. All subsequent congresses were bureaucratic parades. Today even such congresses have been discarded. No normal "constitutional" ways remain to remove the ruling clique. The bureaucracy can be compelled to yield power into the hands of the *proletarian vanguard only by force.*

All the hacks will immediately howl in chorus: The "Trotskyites," like Kautsky, are preaching an armed insurrection against the dictatorship of the proletariat. But let us pass on. The question of seizing power will arise as a practical question for the new party only when it shall have consolidated around itself the majority of the working class. . . .

Quite clearly Trotsky in this passage is calling not for individual terrorism but for revolutionary mass action. And equally clearly the Prosecutor, in his partial quotations and his comments upon them, deliberately identifies revolutionary mass action with individual terrorism. The distinction is obvious and historical.

§ 179. One may assume that if Trotsky anywhere at any time had come out for individual terror, the Prosecutor would have quoted him honestly. This he could not do because the fact is that all of Trotsky's writings on the problem reject individual terror and justify only revolutionary mass action. We therefore find that apart from the evidence in our possession which disproves the testimony connecting Leon Trotsky with the alleged terrorist conspiracy, the charge of individual terrorism is not only not proved but incredible.

23

The charge of sabotage

§ 180. The charge of sabotage is defined as follows in the official record of the second Moscow trial:

> 4) that, for the purpose of undermining the economic strength and defense capacity of the U.S.S.R., this center organized and carried out a number of wrecking and diversive acts at certain enterprises and on the railways, which caused loss of human life and the destruction of valuable state property. (PR 18.)

In his closing argument, Vyshinsky traced this alleged sabotage back to the struggle, in 1926, of the Left Opposition bloc of Trotsky, Zinoviev and Kamenev, against the Stalinist majority of the Party:

> The Trotskyite-Zinovievite *bloc* of 1926 was a *bloc* which turned the edge of its struggle against the cause of socialism in our country and for capitalism. Under

cover of false and sometimes outwardly seeming "Left" phrases about "super-industrialization" and so forth, the Trotskyite-Zinovievite gang in 1926–27 put forward proposals which, if adopted, would have undermined and broken the alliance between the workers and peasants, would have undermined the foundation of the Soviet state. They put forward such proposals as increasing the pressure on the peasantry, as ensuring "primitive socialist accumulation" by ruining and robbing the peasantry; they advanced a number of demands which if conceded would have broken the bond between town and country and thereby would have made real industrialization utterly impossible. Strictly speaking, these proposals and demands were on a line with the present acts of diversion and wrecking. Strictly speaking, there is only a difference in form between the wrecking and diversive acts of 1926–27 and those of the present time. . . . These proposals advanced by the then Opposition were merely a special form of the struggle against the Soviet state corresponding to the historical situation at that time. Ten years have elapsed and we see that they have taken to the path of wrecking, the path of destructive work, but in much sharper forms, corresponding to the new conditions, to the conditions of the fierce class struggle against the remnants of the capitalist elements. (PR 471.)

§ 181. The program of the "New Opposition" is available, at least in the United States, to anyone who wishes to compare the text with the Prosecutor's interpretation of it. It was published in 1928 by Harcourt, Brace and Company (New York), in a book edited by Max Eastman, under the title, "The Real Situation in Russia." This program discussed the industrial, agricultural, social and political, international and military situation of the U.S.S.R. at that time, under such headings as: The Situation of the Working Class and the Trade-Unions; The Agrarian Question and the Socialist Construction; State Industry and the Building of Socialism; The Soviets; The National Question, etc. It sharply criticized the policies of the majority and submitted certain "practical proposals." The section under this title in the chapter, "The Agrarian Question," begins as follows:

> *In the class struggle now going on in the country, the Party must stand, not in words but in deeds, at the head of the farm hands, the poor peasants, and the basic mass of the middle peasants, and organize them against the exploitative aspirations of the Kulak. . . .*
>
> Agricultural credits must cease to be for the most part a privilege of the well-off circles of the village. We must put an end to the present situation, which permits the savings of the poor, insignificant enough already, to be spent, not for their intended purpose, but in the service of the well-off and middle groups.
>
> The growth of private proprietorship in the country must be offset by a more rapid development of collective farming. It is necessary systematically and from year to year to subsidize the efforts of the poor peasants to organize in collectives. ("The Real Situation in Russia," pp. 67–8.)

This appears to us more like a proposal for equalization of condition among the peasantry than a proposal to rob them. We note, with reference to the Prosecutor's statement that the proposals of the Opposition would have "undermined and broken the alliance between the workers and peasants," that the Opposition program makes that same criticism of the results of the majority's policies:

> The "scissors," representing the disparity of agricultural and industrial prices, have drawn still farther apart

during the last year and a half. The peasant received for his product not more than one and a quarter times the pre-war price, and he paid for industrial products not less than two and two-tenths times as much as before the war. This overpayment by the peasants, constituting in the past year a sum of about a billion rubles, not only increases the conflict between agriculture and industry, but greatly sharpens the class-differentiation in the country. (*Ibid.*, p. 29.)

Without presuming to pass judgment upon the relative merit of Soviet policy and the Opposition's program at that period, the Commission finds that the Prosecutor, in representing this program as part of a struggle against the Soviet state which ended logically in the sabotage charged against the accused in the January trial, identified political opposition with criminal activity, and the majority of the Communist Party with the Soviet state. That the Stalinist majority itself did not regard this platform as criminal in 1926 and 1927 is evident in the fact that although it expelled the Opposition from the Party, it did not bring criminal charges against the leaders, but on the contrary later reinstated in the Party those who "capitulated," and even employed some of them, such as Radek, Pyatakov, and Smirnov, in responsible posts.

§ 182. In his testimony, Leon Trotsky stated as follows his attitude toward the economic development of the U.S.S.R.:

> . . . I defend the Soviet economy against the capitalist critics and the Social Democratic reformist circles, and I criticize the bureaucratic methods of the leadership. (PC 248.)

With reference to the industrialization of the Soviet Union, he said:

During the period from 1922 until 1929 I fought for the necessity of an accelerated industrialization. I wrote in the beginning of 1925 a book in which I tried to prove that by planning and direction of industry it was possible to have a yearly coefficient of industrialization up to twenty. I was denounced at that time as a fantastic man, a super-industrializer. It was the official name for the Trotskyists at that time: super-industrializers. . . .

The march of events showed that I was too cautious in my appreciation of the possibility of planned economy, not too courageous. It was my fight between 1922 and 1925, and also the fight for the five-year plan. It begins with the year 1923, when the Left Opposition began to fight for the necessity of using the five-year plan.

GOLDMAN: And Stalin at that time called you a super-industrialist?

TROTSKY: Yes.

GOLDMAN: He was opposed to the rapid industrialization of the country?

TROTSKY: Permit me to say that in 1927, when I was chairman of the commission at Dnieprostroy for a hydroelectric station, a power station, I insisted in a session of the Central Committee on the necessity of building up this station. Stalin answered, and it is published: "For us to build up the Dnieprostroy station is the same as for a peasant to buy a gramophone instead of a cow. . . ."

The Five-Year Plan had a long pre-history. It was elaborated, I believe—the beginning of the elaboration was 1926 or even 1925. The first plan was not announced publicly, but presented only to the Politburo. It was a plan in which the first year had a coefficient of nine, the second eight or seven, the last year only four—a declining line of growth. That was the beginning of a terrible fight. I named this plan "The Sabotage of Industry," not in the criminal sense as here charged, but in the sense that it was an absolutely cowardly conception of the possibilities created by the October Revolution. The second plan, elaborated in 1926, had a general coefficient of nine for all the five years. The Commissioners can find that in the book, "The Real Situation in Russia," in our platform. That was the second plan. At that time I fought for the possibility, and I tried to prove the possibility of having a coefficient of twenty—until twenty. . . . After our criticism, the first plan was rejected by the Politburo. The second, with the coefficient of nine, was confirmed by the Politburo. . . . The results of the first year showed that we were right. Then they changed the plan. . . .

During the second year the bureaucracy proposed to accomplish the Five-Year Plan in four years. In the *Bulletin* I protested vehemently. All impractical men—it is very characteristic of impractical men that before they began they did not see the possibilities, but when the possibilities were realized against themselves they were very frightened by the possibilities and then saw no limit. They began, under the whip of the bureaucracy, to raise the coefficients without paying any attention to the living conditions of the workers. They built up factories but no houses for the workers. It was necessary now to have a coefficient of 30 per cent and 35 per cent.

GOLDMAN: What was there to the contention that it was necessary to make haste in order to defend—prepare the Soviet Union against a possible attack?

TROTSKY: I wrote, and it was published and translated in several languages, that this hasty bureaucratic industrialization signified the inevitable accumulation of inner contradictions in industry itself. In the capitalist system, the necessary proportions are reached by competition between different capitalists, capitalist industries and enterprises. But in a planned economy it is necessary to foresee all the necessary proportions. It is not possible to foresee by abstractions. It is necessary to foresee, correct and perfect the plan by the opinion of the people, by the experience of the people, by the degree of satisfaction of its needs, by the proportion between the different industries, the different factories, and even the different sections of the same factories. Nobody built up Socialist economy before us. It is the first experience and the greatest in history. And then I warned more cautiously: "It is not possible to run away with yourselves. You will land in a crisis." . . .

GOLDMAN: Can you give us an idea, very generally, of the successes of the industrialization in the Soviet Union?

TROTSKY: The successes are very important, and I affirmed it every time. They are due to the abolition of private property and to the possibilities inherent in a planned economy. But they are—I cannot say exactly— but I will say two or three times less than they could be under a régime of Soviet democracy. (PC 245–9.)

Questioned concerning his attitude on collectivization, Trotsky replied:

It was parallel to my attitude toward industrialization, with a certain delay. Our fight for collectivization began a year or eighteen months later than our fight for industrialization. Our fight against the hasty collectivization also a year later than our fight against the hasty industrialization. In the Five-Year Plan adopted by the Politburo, not in the second version but in the third version with the high coefficient for industry—it was adopted that at the end of the Five-Year Plan the Soviet Union would have 20 to 22 per cent of the peasants in collective farms. But in the third year it was more than 60 per cent—in the third year of the plan. It was decided that all peasants must be collectivized during the first plan.

We protested that this was not possible: "You do not have the necessary agricultural machinery—tractors, and so on; and, what is more important, the necessary level of culture in the country, no roads, no cultivated technicians, and so forth."

. . . I never denied the successes of collectivization. On the contrary, I defended the collectivization against the bourgeois critics and the reformist critics. But at the same time I tried to defend the collectivization against the Soviet bureaucracy. This complete collectivization during five years did not give the economic, the necessary economic results, but it gave—I don't know the figures, but it is hundreds, thousands and millions of exterminated peasants. (PC 250–1.)

In answer to a question by Counsel for the Commission whether in his opinion sabotage of the Five-Year Plan by the Opposition would have been a practical measure for discrediting and overthrowing the Stalinist bureaucracy, Trotsky replied:

No. From my Marxian point of view every progress is based upon the development of the productive forces of mankind, and of the nation in that case. Now, the overthrow of the bureaucracy by the people is possible only on a higher political and cultural level of the people. It is necessary to raise the people, and not push them into the depths. By the disorganization of economy, we could create only the basis for social reaction. How can we hope then to vanquish the bureaucracy? (PC 388.)

In his final argument, Trotsky said:

The task of the prosecution is extremely complicated by the additional fact that from February, 1930, onwards,

I exposed in the press, systematically and persistently . . . the self-same vices of bureaucratized economy which are now being charged against a fantastic "Trotskyist organization. . . ." (PC 505.)

. . . I am ready to demonstrate with a collection of my articles in my hand that for seven years, on the basis of the official Soviet press reports, I untiringly warned against the ruinous consequences of skipping the period of laboratory preparation, of putting incomplete plants into operation, of supplanting technical training and correct organization by frantic and senseless reprisals, and, not infrequently, fantastic premiums. All the economic "crimes" referred to at the last trial were analyzed by me countless times—beginning in February, 1930, and ending in my latest book, "The Revolution Betrayed. . . ." (PC 507.)

The system of Stalin and his police and prosecution agents is quite simple. For major accidents in plants, and especially for train wrecks, usually several employes were shot, often those who shortly before had been decorated for achieving high tempos. The result has been universal distrust and discontent. The last trial was intended to personify in Trotsky the causes for the accidents and disasters. . . . For the GPU, it is no great labor to place before their victims the alternative: Either be shot immediately, or preserve a shadow of hope on the condition that you agree to appear in court in the guise of "Trotskyists," conscious saboteurs of industry and transportation. . . . (PC 508.)

§ 183. Trotsky's writings on Soviet economy are very numerous and readily available. We find them consistent with his testimony. For example, he sharply criticizes "bureaucratic methods" in an article which appeared in the *Bulletin of the Opposition*, No. 9, February–March, 1930. We quote:

Industry is racing towards a crisis, above all because of the monstrous bureaucratic methods of collating the plan. A five-year plan can be drafted, preserving the necessary proportions and guarantees, only on the condition of a free discussion of the tempos and the terms set, with the participation in the discussion of all the interested forces in industry, the working class, all its organizations, and above all the Party itself; with the free verification of the entire experience of Soviet economy in the recent period, including the monstrous mistakes of the leadership. . . . ("The New Course in the Economy of the U.S.S.R.: Economic Adventurism and its Dangers.")

His statement that he at once defends the Soviet economy and criticizes the bureaucratic methods of the leadership, is borne out by the following quotation:

The bitter character of the present campaign against "Trotskyists" has inspired the Russian emigrant press to new prophecies of the coming downfall of the Soviet power. . . .

As a matter of fact, there is not the slightest foundation for this talk of the approaching long awaited "end." The development of the productive forces of the Soviet Union is the most colossal phenomenon of contemporary history. The gigantic advantage of a planned leadership has been demonstrated with a force which nothing can ever refute. The near-sightedness and zig-zagging of the Stalin bureaucracy only the more clearly emphasizes the power of the methods themselves. Only the maniacs of the restoration can imagine that the toiling masses of Russia want to turn back to the conditions of backward Russian capitalism.

But it is no less an error to imagine that the economic successes in strengthening the new industrial régime have also automatically reinforced the political position of Stalin and his faction. . . . A people who have achieved a mighty revolution may temporarily, in difficult circumstances, hand over the guidance of their destinies to a bureaucracy. But they are not able to renounce politics for long. It would be blindness not to see that the very strengthening of the economic situation of the country sets the toiling masses in more and more hostile opposition to the omnipotence of a bureaucracy. The workers, not without justification, attribute to themselves the achieved successes, and follow the bureaucracy with more and more critical eyes. . . .

The campaign against "Trotskyism" now developing signalizes the twilight of the omnipotence of the Stalin bureaucracy. But therewith it foretells, not the fall of the Bolshevik power, but on the contrary, a new rise of the Soviet régime—not only its industry, but its politics and culture. . . . ("Is Stalin Weakening or the Soviets?" by Leon Trotsky, *The Political Quarterly*, London, July–September, 1932, pp. 320–2; also *New York Times*, May 8, 1932.)

Again, in the following passage, he criticizes the leadership and stresses the need for democratic control:

The rôle of the Soviet bureaucracy remains a dual one. Its own interests constrain it to safeguard the new economic machine created by the October Revolution against the enemies at home and abroad. . . . In this work, the world proletariat supports the Soviet bureaucracy without closing their eyes to its national conservatism, its appropriative instincts and its spirit of caste privilege. But it is precisely these traits which are increasingly paralyzing its progressive work. . . . An equilibrium between the various branches of production and, above all, a correct balance between national accumulation and consumption can be achieved only with the active participation of the entire toiling population in the elaboration of the plans, the necessary freedom to criticize the plans, and the opportunity of fixing the responsibility and of recalling the bureaucracy from top to bottom. . . . The partial crises converge towards the general crisis, which is creeping onward and which expresses itself in the fact that despite the titanic expenditure of energy by the masses and the great technological successes, the economic achievements keep lagging far behind, and the overwhelming majority of the population continues to lead a poverty-stricken existence. Thus, *the singular position of the bureaucracy*, which is the result of definite social causes, *leads to an increasingly more profound and irreconcilable contradiction with the fundamental needs of Soviet economy and culture.* Under these conditions, the dictatorship of the bureaucracy, although it remains a distorted expression of the dictatorship of the proletariat, translates itself into a primitive social crisis. The Stalinist faction is compelled ever-anew to destroy "completely" the "remnants" of old and new oppositions, to resort to ever more violent methods and to place in circulation amalgams which become more and more envenomed. . . . ("The Kirov Assassination," p. 12, Dec. 1934. New York: Pioneer Publishers, February, 1935.)

In the pamphlet, "Soviet Economy in Danger," we find the following criticism of the tempo of collectivization:

The headlong race after breaking records in collectivization, without taking any account of the economic and cultural potentialities of the rural economy, has led in actuality to ruinous consequences. It has destroyed the stimuli of the small commodity producer long before it was able to supplant them by other and much higher economic stimuli. The administrative pressure, which exhausts itself quickly in industry, turns out to be absolutely powerless in the sphere of rural economy. (p. 23. October, 1932. New York: Pioneer Publishers, February, 1933.)

Reviewing the history of collectivization in "The Revolution Betrayed," Trotsky wrote as follows:

... The real possibilities of collectivization are determined, not by the depths of the impasse in the villages and not by the administrative energy of the government, but primarily by the existing productive resources—that is, the ability of the industries to furnish large scale agriculture with the requisite machinery. These material conditions were lacking. The collective farms were set up with an equipment suitable only for small scale farming. In these conditions an exaggeratedly swift collectivization took the character of an economic adventure. . . . Collectivization appeared to the peasant primarily in the form of an expropriation of all his belongings. They collectivized not only horses, cows, sheep, pigs, but even new-born chickens. They "dekulakized," as one foreign observer wrote, "down to the felt shoes which they dragged from the feet of little children." As a result, there was an epidemic selling of cattle for a song by the peasants or a slaughter of cattle for meat and hides. . . . The destruction of people—by hunger, cold, epidemics and measures of repression—is unfortunately less accurately tabulated than the slaughter of stock, but it also mounts up to millions. The blame for these sacrifices lies not upon collectivization, but upon the blind, violent gambling methods with which it was carried through. (pp. 38–40. 1936. New York: Doubleday, Doran and Co., 1937.)

§ 183. In weighing Trotsky's testimony and his writings on Soviet economy against the allegations of the Prosecutor, we find (1) that Vyshinsky misrepresented the 1927 program of the Opposition; (2) that he identified criticism of the economic policies of the régime with sabotage of Soviet economy; (3) that Trotsky defended industrialization and collectivization even while he criticized the methods by which they were carried out; (4) that his criticisms of the economic policies of the régime during the period of the alleged conspiracy reveal an eagerness to prevent disaster which, if the charges against him were true, would be explicable on no other theory than that of camouflage, advanced by the Prosecutor himself (PR 509). Since, however, these criticisms develop in a consistent line both before and during the alleged conspiracy, and since, moreover, they are consistent with his theoretical position throughout his career, whereas the allegations of sabotage, wrecking, and diversion are not, we hold the theory of camouflage to be untenable.

§ 184. Trotsky's contention that these allegations constitute an attempt to cover up the mistakes of the régime is supported by evidence in our possession. The engineer Ivar Windfeld-Hansen, the "Wienfeld" mentioned in the January trial as a Danish Trotskyist (PR 431) by the accused Hrasche, self-confessed spy for the German intelligence service, has submitted a long deposition (PC Exh. 34, 1) concerning his professional connection with the chemical fertilizer industry in the Soviet Union and his relations with various officials, among them people formerly in the chemical industry who were either accused or mentioned as wreckers or "Trotskyites," such as Hrasche, Rataichak, Yushkewich, and the Danish engineer Kjerulf-Nielsen. He has submitted also a voluminous documentation of his statements. These documents are contemporary in date with Windfeld-Hansen's employment in Russia (May, 1932–July, 1934) or earlier. It cannot be charged, therefore, that they represent *ex post facto* reflections on the situation. They include his correspondence with the defendant Hrasche, his letters to other officials connected with the chemical industry, his reports to Soviet officials on matters pertaining to conditions in that industry, his journal during his second stay in Russia, and articles from the Soviet technical journals *Tekhnika* and *Za Industrializatsiu*. From this material three facts emerge:

(1) Windfeld-Hansen was extremely critical of the processes in use in the chemical fertilizer industry, and the methods of planning, construction, and research. He tried to persuade the officials to adopt foreign methods which he considered more efficient; and also, in making their plans, to take more into account the nature of Soviet raw materials, geographic conditions, and problems of transportation.

(2) Windfeld-Hansen, in spite of his differences with certain officials, was sympathetic to the Soviet Union and eager to help in building up its fertilizer industry. He repeatedly warned the officials, and even the GPU, that the methods in use in this industry would lead to disaster.

(3) His criticisms provoked a struggle in the chemical fertilizer industry over the processes in use, the consequences of bad planning, extravagance, etc. This struggle was reflected in critical articles in the Soviet technical papers.

§ 185. According to the accused Hrasche, "Wienfeld" (Windfeld-Hansen) was

> enlisted in Berlin by Davidson, the former vice-president of the All-Union Committee on Chemical Industries, and as was said in a letter which I afterward found by chance, Davidson wrote to Norkin [another accused] that this man was close to us in his views. (PR 431.)

Hrasche later testified that he found this letter "belonging to my predecessor," in his desk when he returned from his vacation in the middle of 1932. The accused Norkin there-upon declared that

> . . . as far as I know, Davidson never had any connection with Trotskyism. (PR 435.)

§ 186. Windfeld-Hansen declares that he was employed at the beginning of May, 1932, at the Soviet trade repre-sentation in Berlin, by Davidson, whose name was not told him. A few days earlier he had presented himself at that office and offered his services as an engineer. He had dealt with the trade representation for several days, when one day there appeared in the office a man who allegedly held a high position in the Soviet chemical trust, who looked at his references and made all arrangements for his employ-ment. Among these references was a letter of recommen-dation from the Soviet Ambassador to Denmark, Kobetzky, who had lived in Denmark before the Revolution and was a friend of Windfeld-Hansen's father.

Windfeld-Hansen states that he arrived in Moscow about May 12, 1932, and soon after his arrival was appointed as consulting engineer in the state planning office for the chemical industry, known as Giprokhim; that he remained in this position until the end of his first stay in Russia, Feb-ruary 1, 1933; that he returned to it in the beginning of August, 1933, and remained for a normal working year of eleven months.

He states also that he was never a member of any po-litical party; that having lost his position as a result of the world crisis he looked toward the U.S.S.R. as a place where an experienced engineer might hope to find scope for his ability and experience, and that this hope influenced his po-litical sympathies, although he knew little of communism or Marxist theory. Beginning in May, 1931, he says, after his return from Germany where he had been employed by the Dorr Company, he frequently delivered lectures of an economic-political character in which he dealt with the possible future economic development of the U.S.S.R. (The manuscript of one of these lectures is among the material submitted by him to the Commission, PC Exh. 34, 2.) He states that at that time he knew nothing of the controversy between Stalin and Trotsky, or of the existence of a Trotskyist organization (Left Opposition).

Windfeld-Hansen's deposition is divided into two parts. The first is a memorandum on the technical development of the Soviet phosphate fertilizer industry during and after his employment in Moscow; the second is a statement in the form of an interview with a German journalist (an émigré; name in our possession) concerning his activities in Soviet Russia, his relations with and impressions of Soviet officials, etc. The memorandum begins:

> Immediately after I had been employed in Giprokhim engineer Vogt showed me the drawings of the plants then under construction, namely: (1) the precipitate plant in Voskressensk, (2) a test plant in Tshernoretshe for production of ammonium phosphate, and (3) a test plant at the same place for production of ammonium sulphate from gypsum. I explained to him on the spot why these two test plants could never work (see memorandum to Kobetzky, of August 7, 1932). He did not seem to be very impressed by these statements, nor did he try to defend the faults which had been committed. He only declared that NIU [Scientific Institute for Fertilizers, in Moscow] had the responsibility for the research work and the processes constituting the base of the project work. To the memorandum to Kobetzky I may only add that I specially asked Vogt how they could have made such a blunder as to construct a big evaporation plant for ammonium sulphate solution exclusively of wrought iron,

every technician knowing that this material is rapidly corroded by this solution. He could not give any explanation, but finally he remarked that it was after all only a test plant to serve for a limited time. I pointed out that a laboratory corrosion test would have proved in some days that wrought iron was impossible even for a test plant. I stated these facts in two or three memoranda, which I handed over to him two or three days later, saying that I was sorry to be compelled to do so, but that otherwise I should perhaps be implicated in the responsibility. The 13th of June, 1932 (one month after my arrival), I submitted to him a calculation demonstrating that the precipitate process consumed not less than 30 per cent more sulphuric acid than double superphosphate, having in view the same grade of Central Russian phosphate rock. His attitude on this occasion will be seen from my memorandum to Kobetzky.

Windfeld-Hansen states that after some delay he was put to work temporarily in the laboratories of NIU in order

to show them in the laboratory how to produce a workable gypsum by the phosphoric acid process. I also took up the very difficult question of the high iron oxide content in the Russian phosphate rocks. I was very astonished when I discovered that apparently they had not considered this important question.

After a few weeks Professor Volfkovich* appeared and reproached him with having started his work without submitting any plan to the NIU; also because they remained without reports which they had expected a foreign engineer would

---

* Director of the Technological Section of the NIU, teacher in the Military Academy in Moscow.—W-H.

be able to produce within a short time. Windfeld-Hansen says that Volfkovich was evidently trying to pick a quarrel with him because of his criticisms; that he told Volfkovich that a "plan" was of course incompatible with the nature of most research work; that he had first of all to demonstrate the elements of phosphoric acid working practice to the NIU chemists, and that he would give reports as soon as he had some results; however, if Volfkovich was discontented with his work, he would not disturb him any more. Thereupon, he says, he returned to Giprokhim, where he remained until Volfkovich himself requested him to return to NIU, having been compelled to do so by the chemists there. During the rest of his first sojourn in Moscow, he says,

> I tried from time to time to take up some of the most urgent problems in the laboratories and test plants of NIU but without real results, because they lacked all necessary means for carrying out proper research and failed to give the necessary support.

He states that when Ambassador Kobetzky visited Moscow in August, 1932,

> I explained to him how bad the state of affairs was in the phosphate fertilizer branch and that a thoroughgoing reorganization would be necessary if a general breakdown was to be avoided at some future time. He asked me to write a memorandum on the whole situation, and I gave it to him the following day.

This memorandum, which explains the problems involved in utilizing the low-grade impure phosphates of Central Russia and the methods by which the Soviet fertilizer industry was attempting to solve them, has been submitted to the Commission by Windfeld-Hansen in a certified English translation. Because of its technical nature and its important bearing upon the testimony of the accused Rataichak in the January trial, we append it to this report (Appendix III). It shows that Windfeld-Hansen, three months after his arrival in the Soviet Union, informed the Soviet Ambassador to Denmark that the processes which Soviet engineers were attempting to use in the chemical fertilizer industry were not adapted to the raw materials to be treated, and that in consequence the plants projected or under construction would prove impracticable. We call special attention to his remarks about the plant at Voskressensk, which the accused Rataichak confessed having sabotaged in 1934 (PR 410–12); also to his statement that the men who were responsible for the experimental work and planning in the fertilizer industry, of which he is extremely critical, were the engineer Vogt and Professor Volfkovich. This memorandum, Windfeld-Hansen says, produced no results until late in the autumn, when a conference was held with the engineer Wolfsohn* as chairman, at which Britzke,† Volfkovich, and some of the leading chemists in the NIU were present and answered his complaints in long speeches "trying to explain all their faults and failures during the last years." Wolfsohn, he says,

> was very eager to conciliate with me the people of NIU and asked me warmly to collaborate with the leaders of NIU who had already admitted that they had falsely

---

* Chemical engineer of long standing, of German-Baltic origin, leader of the phosphate section in Glavkhimprom (Central Administration of the Chemical Industry), a division of the People's Commissariat for Heavy Industry in which Pyatakov was Assistant Commissar. Wolfsohn was arrested in 1933 for unknown reasons, and has not since been heard of.—W-H.

† Professor, academician, Director of the Scientific Institute for Fertilizers (NIU).—W-H.

understood many of their tasks. I declared that I was ready to do so but I maintained all my standpoints in the technical questions. The session was finished without a clear decision. Nothing was changed during the rest of my sojourn.

In the summer of 1932, he says, the engineer Küster, formerly employed by the Dorr Company and employed in 1932 by Giprokhim in Leningrad, came to Moscow. Windfeld-Hansen arranged that his experience should also be utilized by Giprokhim in Moscow. He took Küster to the experimental plants of the NIU, and by request of Giprokhim Küster wrote a memorandum stating that all the equipment in those plants was rather unfitted for the tasks in view.

When Volfkovich heard of this he became very agitated and reproached me for taking outsiders to the plants without his knowledge.

Windfeld-Hansen says that although engineer Vogt several times announced that they would make a trip to Voskressensk together he systematically avoided permitting him to visit the plant. However, he often sought Windfeld-Hansen's advice concerning matters connected with it. Although the latter made certain suggestions, he states that from the beginning of his connection with Giprokhim he considered this plant a hopeless failure that could never be remedied.

Windfeld-Hansen says that the Danish engineer, Kjerulf-Nielsen (also mentioned as a Trotskyist by Hrasche—PR 431), a member of the Russian Communist Party who was working in the analine industry in Moscow, interested himself in the struggle and tried to get the officials to heed Windfeld-Hansen's criticisms. His efforts also were without results. Windfeld-Hansen left Moscow in February, 1933, and went to Copenhagen, where he remained for five months, negotiating

with Giprokhim about the conditions of his re-employment.
During his absence there was a violent discussion in the
Russian technical papers, *Tekhnika* and *Za Industrializatsiu*,
beginning with a long article signed "Gagorin," in *Tekhnika*
(February 27, 1933),

> in which the whole work of NIU was severely criticized
> and mainly based on my memoranda. In the same issue
> appeared an article by me on the subject: double super-
> phosphate versus precipitate. I later on learned that the
> name Gagorin was a collective pseudonym for five chem-
> ists from the technical opposition in NIU.

Later a decision was reached by the Central Economic Board
on the question of the chemical industry, which Glavkhimprom* had submitted to the board. This decision, which was
not unanimous because several members had walked out
of the meeting in protest against the procedure, Windfeld-
Hansen calls "scandalous."

> Although it was at first stated that all the important
> points to which I drew attention were to be carried out
> without delay and that the new foreign methods should be
> utilized, the decision on the other hand made reproaches
> against the opposition in NIU on the ground of their
> "uncritical attitude" towards and their blind submission
> to foreign methods. Those people—the opposition—are
> characterized as being of low qualification in contrast to
> the "high quality leaders of NIU."

In August, 1933, Windfeld-Hansen resumed his work in
Giprokhim. In the autumn he began research work in the
laboratories of NIU. During this work he kept a journal which

* See footnote p. 344.

he has transmitted to the Commission. In the spring of 1934 he finished his experiments, with the following results:

> I succeeded in working out a process for mine-run phosphate rock which had previously been calcinated in a rotary furnace at about 1100 degrees C. By this process only 10–20% of the iron oxide went into solution, the strength of the acid was about 20% P_2O_5 and the gypsum was obtained chemically pure. This latter feature should make it possible to regenerate nearly all the sulphuric acid used for the process by means of the well-known Bayer process invented in Germany during the war and still employed by I.G. Farbenindustrie in one large plant, I think at Leverkusen. The pyrites in Western Europe and America . . . are in general too cheap to make this Bayer process economical. But in Russia there can be no doubt that it would afford great advantages as the pyrites mostly had to be transported by rails from Ural to the other parts of Russia. I did not succeed in convincing the NIU professors and Dobrovolski* on this point and their interest seemed to be drawn towards the flotation possibilities. They had carried this work out themselves, but I did not need any flotation. As far as I know they never considered the cost price of the pyrite in their calculations, or that the railways were always heavily overloaded.

Windfeld-Hansen states that in the spring of 1934 Kjerulf-Nielsen urged him to renew his complaints about the general situation,

> which seemed to us to be completely hopeless. The initial running of the Voskressensk plant had been started in

---

* Director of Giprokhim. Old worker. Formerly active in the Chemical Workers' section of the Profintern. Friend of Hrasche.—W-H.

the spring and a brigade of chemists from NIU was sent to Voskressensk to assist in the operation of the plant. . . . The plant yielded nearly no production at all. Breakdowns happened incessantly in all parts of the plant. Now of course I knew from my experience in other countries that this is quite normal during the initial running of such a chemical plant and this period of troubles can last for several months. But I felt more and more uneasy in view of the fact that no lines were still laid down for the whole future development, as will be seen from the newspapers quoted below. It seemed to me absolutely necessary to alarm authorities independent from the Commissariat of Heavy Industry. Kjerulf-Nielsen proposed to me to inform the GPU in order to avoid any responsibility for myself. I therefore at his request wrote a letter to him, which he immediately and personally brought to the headquarters of the GPU. In this letter I repeated the information which I had formerly given to Kobetzky and stated in very strong expressions that the large plants about to be constructed or projected in Ural were in great danger of being completely muddled and destroyed in the same way as the plant of Voskressensk which I considered as lost. We never heard anything from the GPU and no signs of attention from the GPU could be observed.

Later in the spring Windfeld-Hansen and Kjerulf-Nielsen visited Jurewich, head of the chemical section of the Central Control Commission, and Windfeld-Hansen recorded the conversation in his journal:

> . . . I mentioned no personality and made no complaints of anybody. However, to his question whether NIU solved their tasks I answered: that in general they did not solve their tasks. I oriented him on the pitiable

situation at Voskressensk but added that the misfortune was not very great as the process was not workable! . . . (PC Exh. 34, 4.)

§ 187. Windfeld-Hansen's contract was not renewed, and he left Russia in July, 1934. Immediately after his departure there was a discussion in the technical press on "the most fundamental questions of raw material base, transportation possibilities, and production program, even of the plants already existing." Windfeld-Hansen has sent us four copies of *Tekhnika* and one of *Za Industrializatsiu*. The first of these (*Tekhnika*, Oct. 9, 1933) antedates this discussion. It contains an article by Windfeld-Hansen himself on new foreign methods for the production of phosphoric acid. It criticizes the NIU for not having taken account of the first Dorr process (Appendix III). An appended editorial note urges the great need of taking into consideration the latest results of foreign experience in this field.

An article by A. Chavin in *Za Industrializatsiu* of July 6, 1934, attacks the Glavkhimprom because of the excessive expense and the delays in construction of the fertilizer plant at Aktjubinsk, and states that there is no guarantee that the equipment will resist phosphoric acid. It points out that the equipment at Voskressensk was very seriously damaged by phosphoric acid, and that the same thing may happen at Aktjubinsk. The author states his opinion that Glavkhimprom is not qualified to do the work as it should be done.

An article by the engineer I. Mirkin (chemist in the NIU) in *Tekhnika* of July 15, 1934, discusses the future of the Voskressensk plant. Mirkin points out that raw material rich in oxides of iron and aluminum is not suitable for the production of phosphate fertilizers, and that the precipitate, a sulphuric acid derivative, is the most expensive of fertilizers; therefore, bad quality and high cost definitely eliminate that type of raw material. He says that nevertheless the

Voskressensk plant insists, on Britzke's advice, on using this raw material, thus producing the lowest possible quality of fertilizer at the highest possible cost of production. An editorial note published with this article recalls that the most competent experts on phosphate fertilizers, among them Windfeld-Hansen, declared two years earlier that usable fertilizers could not be produced from non-concentrated (only washed or screened, not flotated) Jegorewski phosphate rock (the local raw material at Voskressensk). Later research work, it says, as well as the initial running of the Voskressensk plant, has proved that they were right.

An article in *Tekhnika* of July 21, 1934, is signed by the engineer S. Perelman, a chemist of the NIU who, according to Windfeld-Hansen, was jockeyed out of his position by Volfkovich because of his criticism of the methods in use. The article reports a conference of experts in the phosphate industry, and points out the sharp divergence of opinion among members of the Fertilizer Institute on the questions of raw materials and methods. An extremely critical article in *Tekhnika* of August 6, 1934, is signed A. Yakovlev. (One Yakovlev testified in the trial of August, 1936, that he had been commissioned by Kamenev to organize a terrorist group in the Academy of Sciences (ZK 70–1). We do not know whether this writer is the same Yakovlev.) This article quotes the engineer Levensohn concerning a special conference on raw materials in the office of the head of Glavkhimprom, Rataichak. The article states:

> It is exceedingly characteristic that except Academician Britzke, Professor Volfkovich and Engineer Vogt—people who are directly involved in the present not amusing state of affairs—all the experts participating in the conference decidedly expressed themselves against the use of non-concentrated phosphorites in the initial running of the Voskressensk plant. The chief engineer in

Glavkhimprom, Professor Yushkevich,* the chief of the planning section in Glavkhimprom, Ritzling, the leader of the phosphate section in Glavkhimprom, Engineer Levensohn, and Engineer Gosberg of Glavkhimprom, thereupon insisted that the Voskressensk plant should work with apatite concentrates. The reasons of these comrades are sufficiently clear. . . . Against this unanimous and authoritative opinion of a majority of experts of the phosphate industry, the voices of only three people are raised, *the least objective in this matter.*

The article also contains the following passage about the accused Rataichak:

> While discussing the question of what to do now with the Voskressensk plant, Comrade Rataichak flung altogether just reproaches at the management of NIU and the phosphates section of Giprokhim, the substance of which might be reduced to the one phrase, "What was the matter with you then?"

§ 188. Returning now to the deposition of Windfeld-Hansen, "Such," he says,

> was the state of affairs after I had left Russia as far as I have obtained information. That the solution of the questions should be that Pyatakov, Rataichak and Hrasche should dishonor themselves with completely inexplicable confessions, sentenced to death and shot, and further, Yushkewich and some of the leading engineers in the nitrogen branch (as it appears from the official trial report: Pushin, Golovanov, Tamm, whom I did not know)

---

* Mentioned by the accused Rataichak as one of his associates in wrecking and diversion (PR 418, 420).

should be arrested and put under similar accusations—
this solution I never would have dreamed of.

Questioned concerning the personality of the accused
Hrasche, Windfeld-Hansen refers to his interview in *Politiken* (Copenhagen). This interview, which appeared on
Jan. 29, 1937, was read into the record of the Preliminary
Commission. In it Windfeld-Hansen states that during his
stay in Russia Hrasche was head of the foreign bureau of
the Russian nitrogen industry. In this capacity, he was in
charge of arrangements concerning the living and working
conditions of foreign engineers and technicians in that industry. His own conditions of work, he states, were arranged
in Hrasche's office. Since Hrasche occupied a poor room in
the building of the nitrogen trust, where Windfeld-Hansen
also lived during his first stay in Russia, he came to know
him well and to esteem him highly. Windfeld-Hansen states
that in his controversies with the Russian specialists, he was
often supported by Hrasche or his staff; that Hrasche often
visited him, and met his Danish friends. (PC 232–34.)

In his deposition Windfeld-Hansen mentions among these
friends Kjerulf-Nielsen and Sigvard Lund, author of the
novel "Bread and Steel."* Windfeld-Hansen says that both
Lund and Kjerulf-Nielsen were and are today completely
loyal members of the Communist Party, and that Hrasche's
statement that they were Trotskyites was a deliberate falsification. He says that he often spoke with Hrasche about
politics, and that Hrasche intelligently defended the official
policy of the Party. Hrasche's own description of himself as
a professional spy without political convictions, is wholly ir-

---

* Also mentioned as a Trotskyist by Hrasche (PR 431). In an interview
with *Politiken*, January 28, 1937, Mr. Lund said, "I am neither an engineer nor a Trotskyist, neither was I ever employed in any Russian
factory." He stated that he had never heard Hrasche's name.

reconcilable, says Windfeld-Hansen, with his impression of the man and his high political standards.

Asked what, in his opinion, were the real reasons for the removal and criminal prosecution of Hrasche, Rataichak and Yushkevich, he answered:

> Scapegoats had to be found for the catastrophic development in the chemical industry. There is no indication that acts of sabotage were involved. My documents submitted and mentioned above will give you a better clue as to where the really guilty people are to be found. I cannot believe that my friend Hrasche could have committed acts of sabotage or espionage. I knew him too well for that.
>
> QUESTION: Rataichak is charged in particular with sabotage in the starting up of the Voskressensk plant. [PR 410–12.] Your material indicates that you undertook a special study of this plant as early as 1932. Do you consider it possible or probable that Rataichak could have committed sabotage as indicated in the record of the trial?
>
> ANSWER: No. The local raw material (Jegorewski phosphorite) was so poor and the technical procedure employed so uneconomical that the whole combination in all its fundamentals was a mistake. Furthermore, such a complete mess was made of all details in connection with the designing, purchase of equipment, and actual construction of the precipitation plant, that sabotage on the part of Rataichak or any other administrative officer was wholly superfluous, indeed, one can even say impossible.
>
> QUESTION: With whom, in your opinion, does the responsibility rest for the technical errors embodied in the Voskressensk combine?
>
> ANSWER: The documents I have submitted partly show

this. As time went on more and more people made themselves co-responsible inasmuch as they participated in the planning or later in the starting up of the plant. In addition, all the administrative and supervising agencies made themselves co-responsible inasmuch as they remained refractory to all complaints. Finally, the highest technical and scientific council of the Soviet Union made itself co-responsible inasmuch as in the year 1933 it backed up the methods and practices of the Fertilizer Institute (NIU) in Moscow after they had been subjected to severe criticism by technicians in the technical press (see the copies submitted of the periodical *Tekhnika*). The leading administrators in the Commissariat, Pyatakov and Rataichak, could feel themselves reassured and relieved of the burden of responsibility in view of such a stand by this supreme technical authority.

§ 189. The testimony of Windfeld-Hansen and the documents he has submitted convince this Commission that the testimony of the accused Hrasche that Windfeld-Hansen was a "Trotskyite" saboteur is false. Moreover, this material reflects a struggle in the chemical industry from which, it appears, the officials named by Windfeld-Hansen and other critics as responsible for the "catastrophic development" of that industry emerged victorious. We note that whereas Britzke, Vogt, Volfkovich, were not involved or mentioned as wreckers or "Trotskyites," at least five men who had opposed them—Rataichak, Hrasche, Yushkevich, Windfeld-Hansen, Kjerulf-Nielsen—are so involved or mentioned; and of these five, two were accused, convicted, and executed. We hold that Windfeld-Hansen's testimony and his documents provide strong justification for the assumption that he is correct in charging that these men were victimized as scapegoats.

§ 190. On an alleged specific act of sabotage, an explosion in the Tsentralnaya mine at Kemerovo in September, 1936, for which the accused Drobnis confessed responsibility at the Novosibirsk trial of November, 1936, and again in the Moscow trial of January, 1937 (PR 212–15), we have the opinion of a delegation of the French National Federation of Miners, of the *Confédération Générale du Travail*, who were in Russia at the time. Its members were: Vigne, national secretary, Kléber-Legay, associate secretary, Sinot, secretary of the Carmaux Miners, Planque, miners' delegate to Vermelles (Pas de Calais), and Quinet, Communist deputy. Drobnis stated that the explosion was brought about by damaging the ventilation system and allowing gas to accumulate in the pits (PR 212). The opinion of the French trade-unionists (Quinet excluded) on this testimony appeared in the French paper, *Syndicats*, of February 25, 1937, in the form of a letter from Kléber-Legay to Magdeleine Paz. Kléber-Legay wrote:

> . . . We did not believe and never will believe the accusations, we told Smerling [the interpreter]. And this is why:
>
> They (the responsible trade unionists) told us that there was a most severe service of inspection for the security of the mines. This functioned in the following manner: (1) an engineer designated by the people's commissar; (2) local and inter-local presidents of workers' unions, designated by the workers themselves; (3) delegates of the pits, of sections of the mines, designated by the workers themselves. These delegates, it appears, have full power. They can stop either a mine or a section of a mine, or even a whole field, if they consider that there is danger or threat of danger.
>
> We are unable to understand how with such an apparatus of inspection for the security of the mines it would be possible for engineers to operate in all secrecy in the preparation for such crimes, above all over a period of years.

As a miner, knowing perfectly the difficulties of a mine, having worked at it more than thirty years during twelve of which I was delegate for workers' security in one of the most gaseous mines of France, I defy any technician, however competent, to organize the systematic placing of a mine in an explosive state without the inspectors, even if they were complete idiots, perceiving it within an hour. If the service of inspection for the security of the mines at Kemerovo did not perceive this thing, it is either incompetent or non-existent. If it exists, it is even more culpable than the other accused, and since it is the mode in Moscow to shoot, its members should be the first to be shot. If it did not exist, then we were lied to about the protection of the workers' safety. . . .

But even if the service of inspection did not exist, I still say that it is impossible for a mine to be placed in an explosive state without anyone noticing it. There is the management, the supervision, the thousands of workers in these mines who would have seen and announced it. Is one to admit that all, even though they knew their lives to be in danger, would have maintained silence for the sole purpose of establishing with greater certitude the proof of the culpability of the accused, while at any moment they might all have perished if the thing existed?

No; technically, all are agreed, it is not possible to keep a mine in a permanently explosive state by the accumulation of fire-damp. The least-informed person on mining affairs would say as we do: No one could ever make us believe in such a possibility.

§ 191. To the testimony and documents of Windfeld-Hansen and the letter of Kléber-Legay we add the testimony of an engineer who has worked many years in the Soviet Union and who has informed us frankly and fully concerning conditions in Russian industry as he had occasion to observe them. He requests that his name be withheld, on the ground that its disclosure in connection with his criticisms might cause reprisals against his friends in the U.S.S.R. The Commission is able to vouch for his high standing, his integrity, and his good-will toward the people and the economy of the U.S.S.R. We regret the necessity of asking the public to take our word for the reliability of his testimony, but in the circumstances we can not do otherwise; and we offer it with full recognition of the reservations which this mode of procedure may put upon its acceptance. We may remark, however, that a similar procedure was adopted concerning the testimony of certain witnesses in the unofficial Reichstag Fire trial, which was organized with the cooperation of the official Communist Party of Germany, and was generally understood and accepted.

With regard to damages to industrial equipment in the U.S.S.R., this engineer testified as follows before the New York Sub-Commission:

> First, of course, even in America, there is a lot of damage that happens in plants. Machines break down and defects in a design will come up which require it to be changed. It was exactly the same in the Russian plants. . . . We had, first, machines break down due to carelessness in handling and overloading. We had a few cases, owing to poor material and poor design, where we had to do reconstructing. We had one or two minor cases where apparently there was direct sabotage, but not very serious, apparently done by somebody not very important. Some workman saw his chance, dissatisfied probably for some reason—saw his chance to do something. That was very rare; probably it did not happen any oftener than in American plants.
>
> . . . there was very much more breakdown and failure of equipment than there was in America.

GOLDMAN: What would you say is responsible for this larger percentage?

WITNESS: Poor materials, poor workmanship in construction, and in some cases, designs were poor. . . . They really went and carried the idea of mechanization too far for the character of the plant. When you are over-mechanized, if you have too much machinery in a plant, especially with inexperienced people, you will have a larger percentage of breakdowns and a larger percentage of repair-costs.

. . . There were continuous minor breakdowns, mostly at the beginning, and due to poor material and workmanship, and later on, due to the habit which they have of forcing production too fast, inexperienced men, machinery that has not been properly tuned up to put it rapidly into operation. And even after they get started, after the machinery is tuned up, by overloading. That is characteristic of plants all over the Soviet Union and the cause of very much trouble, very many breakdowns. It is the idea of the Udarniki, the theory of the Stakhanovite movement to force . . . speed-up movements. It is characteristic of all their industry to force everything too fast, speed it up too much, and that caused many breakdowns. (NY 155–7.)

Concerning the service of inspection in Soviet mines and plants, this witness testified that there always are workers' committees of inspection; that whereas these committees used to be appointed by the trade unions independent of the administration, they are now under the Central Control Commission and that whereas the former Workers and Peasants Inspection represented the workers, the inspection service of the Commission of Soviet Control represents also the government and the trusts. This change, he testifies, has placed the service of inspection in the hands of the bureaucracy. He states that the committees of inspection sent out by the Central Control Commission are often incompetent and that they often "simply whitewash the administration." (NY 178–82.)

He testified that there are abnormal delays in the construction and operation of Soviet plants, but that such delays as he has personal knowledge of were due not to sabotage but to confusion, incompetence, and the attempt to do more than was possible in the condition of Russian industry. There was a shortage of raw materials, construction materials, electric power, labor. There were delays in transportation, but his own experience convinced him that these were due entirely to inefficiency and the overloading of the railways. He declared that such "speed-up" campaigns as the "Udarniki," "Sabatnik," and "Stakhanovite" movements had had a bad effect on Russian industry, because they resulted in destruction of equipment through haste and bad workmanship. The Stakhanovite movement tended to disorganize plants because the necessary coordination of operations was sacrificed to the necessity of keeping the Stakhanovites supplied with work, so that they could maintain their records. Such workers earned as much as fifty rubles a day as against five for the average worker; and the special privileges granted them, such as apartments to themselves, tickets to sanitariums, etc., made the spread even greater. Besides, the Stakhanovite worker was granted honors, had his picture in the papers, etc. "The temptation to do poor work was inevitable." And the ordinary workers became discontented and resentful. (NY 184–93.)

They can't do or say a thing. They lay it all on the Party. Of course, most of this Stakhanovite movement has also made it very disagreeable for the administrators in the plant. They have given these Stakhanovites every advantage. If they don't, they may be reported as sabotaging the Stakhanovite movement and being opposed to it. Sometimes it is quite serious. They lose their jobs, are demoted, lose their standing. Also, the ordinary director, the technical director, the average manager, gets considerably less than the Stakhanovite worker. This causes their resentment. (NY 193.)

Asked whether he thought this dissatisfaction might have found expression in sabotage, he said:

It may be, but I didn't see any evidence of it. I saw an increase in breakdowns, in the poor quality of the work, but I don't think it was actually premeditated sabotage. It was just that they were losing their morale, their interest. (NY 194.)

He stated that throughout his stay in Russia he was continually in controversy with the officials of the trusts over these methods. He said:

But the people in charge, the clique that surrounds Stalin in Moscow, I don't see how they can help seeing these things, see how it damages things in building up. I am not the only engineer there who has seen these things and pointed them out to them. When I left I had a pile of reports on just this one subject of organization. But they had almost no effect. (NY 186–7.)

This witness also testified to one incident from his personal experience which has particular interest in relation to the testimony of Windfeld-Hansen. He tells of three Soviet engineers who had supported the correct contention of a foreign specialist that the designs for a certain plant were unworkable and should be revised before construction was begun. They were arrested and charged with being Trotskyite saboteurs. The contract of the foreign specialist was not renewed. (NY 165–8.)

Asked whether the general inefficiency in industry was such as to make sabotage superfluous in bringing about the conditions that are complained of, this witness said:

> You might put it this way: It was the general condition of inefficiency which made it easy to accuse a person of sabotage, to try to hold a man responsible for it when really it was just due to conditions over which he had no control.
>
> FINERTY: It was also easier for a person responsible for the inefficiency, so far as any person could be responsible, to blame it on sabotage than acknowledge his inefficiency?
>
> WITNESS: Yes, that is the key, I think, to the whole situation. (NY 211–2.)

§ 192. This Commission does not presume to judge whether or not those men who were actually tried in January, 1937, were guilty of sabotage. It can and does, however, state after careful study of the record that the fabric of the trial was so rotten as to render impossible a conclusion by any honest person concerning their guilt or innocence, or the nature of their crimes, if any. Preceding chapters of this report have sufficiently demonstrated this fact. We add here only a few considerations which relate to this specific charge.

We begin these considerations by quoting from Trotsky's final argument. After stating that the chronic diseases of Soviet industry were presented in the trial as the fruits of a malicious conspiracy led by Pyatakov, he says:

> However, it remains perfectly incomprehensible what, while all this went on, was the rôle of the state organs of industry and finance, and of the accounting authori-

ties, not to speak of the Party, which has its nuclei in all institutions and enterprises. If one believes the indictment, the leadership of economy was not in the hands of the "genial, infallible leader," but in the hands of an isolated man, already nine years in banishment and exile. (PC 504.)

We find this argument amply warranted by the confessions. We refer our readers to the testimony on sabotage of Pyatakov, alleged leader in sabotage under Trotsky's instructions. Pyatakov testifies to subversive administrative activities so various and extensive that it is impossible to see how they could have been carried on without the connivance of a great many officials and engineers, and even of government and Party functionaries. And Pyatakov's is by no means the only such testimony in this record.

Moreover, sabotage carried on all over the Soviet Union, in mines, factories, on the railways, must necessarily have required at least the passive cooperation of a great many workers (see, e.g., the opinion of the French trade unionists—§ 190). Yet the accused repeatedly stated that they had no support among the workers. Again, the motivation of the accused is uniformly unconvincing. The accused Knyazev, for example, testifies that his "waverings" were caused largely by his conviction that "it was impossible to improve the work of the railways by the methods that were then being employed" (PR 360). He thereupon admits that he knew that the railways were working badly because of Trotskyite wreckers, and then goes on to state that he believed the Trotskyites "were right in their struggle against the Party and that they could solve these problems in another way." The obvious absurdity of abetting saboteurs because he thought they would be able to solve the problems which troubled him—and which he knew to be of their making— was ignored by the Prosecutor; but it can hardly be ignored by the person who is looking for a motivation that at least makes sense.

The record, therefore, inspires grave doubt of the charge of sabotage. Since, according to the testimony, the sabotage was instigated by and carried on under the instructions of Leon Trotsky, the disproof of the evidence linking Trotsky with the alleged conspiracy impugns the testimony concerning acts of sabotage. On the other hand, the testimony of Windfeld-Hansen and our anonymous witness corroborates Trotsky's contention that the delays, disproportions, extravagance, etc., which the accused confessed were due to sabotage, are the chronic diseases of Soviet industry; that they are due to haste, overreaching, inefficiency, etc.; and that the expiation of these shortcomings by scapegoats is a usual method of whitewashing the régime.

§ 193. In view of all these considerations, and of the evidence cited, we find that the charge of conspiracy to sabotage Soviet economy, especially as it concerns Leon Trotsky and Leon Sedov, stands not only not proved but not credible.

24

The charge of agreements with foreign powers

§ 194. In the Zinoviev-Kamenev trial, the Definition of the Charge says nothing of agreements with foreign powers. However, the accused Olberg, M. Lurye, and N. Lurye, are quoted in the indictment as having confessed that they were connected with agents of German fascism. The Luryes confessed that they belonged to a terrorist group organized by one Franz Weitz, whom they described as an agent of Himmler, head of the Nazi Gestapo after its organization some time later (ZK 27–9, 75, 102–3, 107–8). The accused Olberg is quoted in the indictment as having testified in the preliminary examination that he was connected with the Gestapo and discussed with one of its officials

my first journey to Moscow and my plans concerning the preparation of the terrorist act. (ZK 25.)

He is also quoted as saying that this connection

was the line of the Trotskyites in conformity with the instructions of Leon Trotsky given through Sedov. (ZK 25.)

He testified that his Honduran passport was obtained with the help of Tukalevsky, an agent of the fascist police (§§ 73, 75, 76, 82), with whom his brother Paul was connected; and that Sedov sanctioned the arrangement and provided the money to pay for the passport. (ZK 89.) He also testified that after his return from his first trip to the Soviet Union he

> visited Slomovitz in Berlin, and she told me the following: During my absence the Trotskyite cadres dwindled to a small group, and they were now confronted by the dilemma: either to dissolve or to come to an agreement with the German fascists. The basis for the agreement was the preparation and carrying out of acts of terrorism against the leaders of the C.P.S.U. and the Soviet Government. Trotsky had sanctioned the agreement between the Berlin Trotskyites and the Gestapo, and the Trotskyites were in fact left free. (ZK 90.)

The Prosecutor made no attempt to identify Slomovitz.

Both Berman-Yurin and David testified that in their alleged conversations with Trotsky in Copenhagen he stated that in case of intervention against the Soviet Union the Trotskyites must adopt a defeatist attitude (ZK 95, 113). Dreitzer is quoted in the indictment as having testified that in 1934 he received a letter from Trotsky stating that one of the tasks before the Trotskyites was

> in the event of war to take advantage of every setback and confusion to capture the leadership. (ZK 22.)

The accused Mrachkovsky, to whom Dreitzer alleged that he had passed on this letter, testified that Trotsky had stated in it the necessity of adopting a defeatist attitude in case of war (ZK 43).

§ 195. Leon Sedov denied having had any connection whatever with the procuring of Olberg's Honduran passport (CR 21, 23). He declared that he had never known the Slomovitz of whom Olberg had spoken, and never heard of such a person before the trial (CR 24).

§ 196. Eugene Bauer denied that anybody by the name of Slomovitz had belonged to the German Trotskyist movement. (PC Exh. 16, S II/8.) Concerning the alleged connection with the Gestapo, Bauer testified before the *Commission Rogatoire*:

> It is not only abominable that they have ever been capable of speaking of a connection between the Trotskyist movement and the Gestapo, but I can bear witness, having belonged to this movement until October, 1934, that never did such connections exist. I have seen in the Reports of the Court Proceedings five or six persons supposed to have played the rôle of intermediary between the Trotskyists and the Gestapo. Not one of these persons ever belonged to the Trotskyist movement while I belonged to it. And to my knowledge, never did an agent of the Gestapo succeed in slipping into our ranks. Finally, I must emphasize the fact that the Gestapo has in no way spared us in the persecution it has carried on against all the anti-Communist movements in Germany, which is another absolute proof that this is a slander (CR 45–6.)

§ 197. In his testimony concerning Slomovitz, Olberg says, "I had known her previously." (ZK 90.) We quote from the deposition of Olberg's mother:

> I know nothing at all about the existence of such a person, but I am inclined to think that this is an invented

personality. The fact is, that in 1930, 1931, 1932, with a few breaks, I often visited my son in Berlin. In his house I met many of his friends and acquaintances and never heard the name Slomovitz. But when my son was yet a child, and lived with me in Riga, I had a client whose name was Slomovitz. She was an old woman who never left Riga, and had nothing whatever to do with politics. I often sent Valentine to her to collect money. For this reason I think that he mentioned the first name that came into his head, happening to recall the old lady. (PC Exh. 8, S III/6, a.)

§ 198. Among the documents in our possession are two handbills issued by the International German Communists, the Trotskyist organization in Danzig, and two issues of its illegal publication, *Spartakus*, one dated the end of September, the other the beginning of October, 1936. One handbill deals with the dissolution of the Social Democratic Party of Danzig by the fascist police, and states among other things that this party brought about its own destruction by feeding its followers on illusions and holding them back from the fight against fascism. The other accuses the Polish and German fascist régimes of sending the Spanish fascists arms with which to shoot down Spanish workers. The first *Spartakus* deals with the Zinoviev-Kamenev trial; it quotes the illegal paper of the Danzig Communist Party to the effect that

"The connection with the Gestapo does not surprise us. The Trotskyist group in Danzig have long been a center of stool-pigeons and provocateurs of the Danzig Gestapo."

To this charge *Spartakus* replies that shortly before the Zinoviev-Kamenev trial the official Communist Party in Danzig offered a united front to the Trotskyist organization.

The second number of *Spartakus* deals with the alleged betrayal of the Spanish revolution by France, Soviet Russia, and the Caballero régime; with the situation in Danzig, stressing again the need of a united workers' party to fight fascism; with the Nuremberg party-congress of the National Socialist Party, stating that Hitler offers himself as a super-Wrangel for the imperialist crusade against the Soviet Union.

In the same exhibit are issues of *Der Danziger Vorposten*, organ of the Danzig National Socialists (Nazis), of December 9, 1936, and January 8 and 12, 1937. They contain accounts of the arrests and trial of members of the Spartakus (Trotskyist) organization. We quote the headlines:

THE END OF THE DANZIG "SPARTAKUSBUND." Sixty communists arrested. Collaboration with Trotsky established. Comprehensive propaganda material confiscated. (December 9, 1936.)

THE "SPARTAKUSBUND" OF THE TrotskyiteS. The Jew Dr. Franz Jakubowski as organizer of the secret organization, the slanderous handbill campaign and incitement to strikes. (January 8, 1937.)

THE JUDGMENT AGAINST THE TrotskyiteS. Long prison-terms for the functionaries. The result of yesterday's session. (January 12, 1937.)

LONG PRISON TERMS FOR THE SPARTACISTS. The Jew Dr. Jacubowski sentenced to three and a quarter years in jail. Combined sentences thirteen years. (January 12, 1937.) (Com. Exh. 1.)

§ 199. We have also among our documents the text of a sound-film made by Trotsky for Left Opposition propaganda during his sojourn in Copenhagen—that is, during the period when he is alleged to have given defeatist instructions to the accused David and Berman-Yurin. In this film Trotsky sharply criticizes the policies of the Communist Party in the Soviet Union. The industrial conquests, he says, are important, and the cultural plane of the masses has visibly risen in the fifteen years of the Revolution. Therefore, party democracy should have been greatly expanded, but thanks to the bureaucracy the exact opposite has taken place. He also condemns the Communist policy in Germany, its identification of social democracy with fascism, its rejection of a united front, and the consequent refusal to create soviets, since soviets are possible only as the organizations of a united front of different workers' parties and organizations. He then says:

> We of the Left Opposition remain loyally devoted to the Soviet Union and the Comintern, with another loyalty, another devotion, than the official bureaucratic majority. (PC Exh. 16, III/2.)

The Commission has had the opportunity to compare this film with the text submitted to us. In the film there are a few minor omissions, and one significant interpolation. Toward the end, Trotsky injected these words, which do not appear in the typescript:

> The Soviet Union is our fatherland! We will defend it to the end.

We shall later cite further evidence submitted by Trotsky and other witnesses to prove that he has steadily advocated the defense of the Soviet Union. We cite this sound-film here because of its direct bearing upon the testimony of two accused in the Zinoviev-Kamenev trial that they received defeatist instructions from him in Copenhagen.

§ 200. We note that Dreitzer and Mrachkovsky, both of whom allegedly read the letter from Trotsky which they quote, give two different versions of his instructions concerning the attitude to be adopted in case of war—a fact which illustrates the dubious evidential value of testimony to the contents of written instruments not produced in court (§ 47). We have already found, moreover, on the basis of the record and of the evidence offered in rebuttal, that this alleged letter never existed. We have also found that Berman-Yurin and David did not see Trotsky in Copenhagen. Therefore, he can not have told them that a defeatist attitude must be adopted in case the Soviet Union became involved in war. Moreover, the probability of such instructions is disproved, in our opinion, by the sound-film quoted above, and also by the evidence on Trotsky's attitude toward defense of the U.S.S.R., quoted in succeeding sections of this chapter.

The falsity of Olberg's testimony has been demonstrated by his own letters and by the other documents and testimony of witnesses cited in Chapter XIII of this report. In view of this fact, we hold his mother's explanation of his mention of Slomovitz to be plausible. We note also that his mother's testimony contradicts Olberg's on the reason why Paul Olberg, alleged fascist agent, went to Russia. Olberg states that he advised Paul

> to go to the Soviet Union so that he could help me to gain a foothold. . . . He is an engineer, and it was much easier for him to obtain employment. He had genuine documents. At any rate not such fictitious papers as I had. (ZK 91.)

According to his mother, it was she who conceived the idea of giving Paul Olberg a trip to Russia as a pleasant surprise after his graduation as a chemical engineer in 1934 from the Technological Institute in Prague. She applied to the Riga Intourist for a visa, without informing Paul, and when it was granted sent for her son, outfitted him, paid Intourist for his visa and a two weeks' stay in the Soviet Union and

> sent him off to the Soviet Union with the following plan in mind: Should he be able to place himself, good. If he failed, he would come back. (PC Exh. 8, S III/6 a.)

Her son, she states, obtained a position in Gorky, and was well satisfied with his work. He applied for Soviet citizenship, which he apparently received just before his arrest.

Thus the evidence in our possession contradicts on every point the allegations concerning the connection of Trotsky and his followers with the Gestapo. We also attach weight to the fact that among the depositions accepted in evidence are those of the following Trotskyists or former Trotskyists who are refugees from Hitler's Germany: Leon Sedov, Adolphe, Eugene Bauer, K. Erde, Walter Held, Erich Kohn, Anton Grylewicz, Schneeweiss, Anna Grylewicz, Georg Jungclas, Oscar and Bruno (full names in our possession). We have rejected the depositions of two other Trotskyist refugees because they were not properly authenticated. If the German Trotskyists made a deal with the Gestapo whereby they "were in fact left free" after Hitler came into power, then why did they share the general fate of official Communists and other opponents of the Hitler régime? Again why were they arrested and placed on trial in Danzig? The literature of both the Trotskyists and the Hitlerites in Danzig (§ 198) shows the characteristic relation between a revolutionary opposition and the Hitler régime.

§ 201. The allegations in the August trial linking the Trotskyists outside Russia with German fascism warrant the following observations: If one assume that Trotsky was acting in agreement with the Gestapo, then his followers outside Soviet Russia either knew about it, or they did not. If they knew about it, then the question must arise, Why, in the various splits which have taken place in the Trotskyist organization (of which there is ample evidence in the material before the Commission), did not some disgruntled Trotskyist reveal the plot? If they did not know about it, then Trotsky must have been betraying his own followers, and the current campaign on the part of the official Communist Party, its press and its sympathizers against the Trotskyists as "agents of fascism" is wholly unjustified. We find, on the basis of the evidence cited in this and previous chapters, that there is no reason whatever to believe that Trotsky or his followers ever had any connection with agents of German fascism, as alleged by Olberg and the Luryes, or that Trotsky ever advocated defeatism as testified by Mrachkovsky, David, and Berman-Yurin. Therefore, in our opinion, the current campaign against Trotsky and his followers as fascist agents is unjustified by any evidence whatever.

§ 202. In the January trial, the Definition of the Charge states:

> 1) that, on the instructions of L.D. Trotsky, there was organized in 1933 a parallel center consisting of the following accused in the present case: Y.L. Pyatakov, K.B. Radek, G.Y. Sokolnikov, and L.P. Serebryakov, the object of which was to direct criminal, anti-Soviet, espionage, diversive and terrorist activities for the purpose of undermining the military power of the U.S.S.R., accelerating an armed attack on the U.S.S.R., assisting foreign aggressors to seize territory of the U.S.S.R. and to dismember it and of overthrowing the Soviet Power and restoring capitalism and the rule of the bourgeoisie in the Soviet Union.

> 2) that, on the instructions of the aforesaid L.D. Trotsky, this center, through the accused Sokolnikov and Radek, entered into communication with representatives of certain foreign states for the purpose of organizing

a joint struggle against the Soviet Union, in connection with which the Trotskyite center undertook, in the event of its coming into power, to grant these states a number of political and economic privileges and territorial concessions.

3) that, moreover, this center through its own members and other members of the criminal Trotskyite organization, systematically engaged in espionage on behalf of these states, supplying foreign intelligence services with secret information of the utmost importance.

The accused Radek, in his final plea, made the following statement which went unchallenged by the Prosecutor:

> ... But the trial is bicentric, and it has another important significance. It has revealed the smithy of war, and has shown that the Trotskyite organization became an agency of the forces which are fomenting a new world war.
>
> What proofs are there in support of this fact? In support of this fact there is the evidence of two people—the testimony of myself, who received the directives and the letters from Trotsky (which, unfortunately, I burned), and the testimony of Pyatakov, who spoke to Trotsky. All the testimony of the other accused rests on our testimony. (PR 543.)

This last statement is borne out by the trial record.

§ 203. The accused Radek testified that he received two letters from Trotsky, one in April, 1934, and another in December, 1935, in which he discussed the question of agreements with foreign powers. In the April letter, according to Radek,

> ... Trotsky stated that he had established contacts with a certain Far Eastern state and a certain Central European

state, and that he had openly told semi-official circles of these states that the *bloc* stood for a bargain with them and was prepared to make considerable concessions both of an economic and territorial character. (PR 106.)

Radek testified that he and Pyatakov decided that they could not go beyond "endorsing the mandate for negotiations" since they themselves could only negotiate with third-rate people, did not know just what Trotsky had said, and moreover considered it unwise to conduct negotiations under the eyes of the People's Commissariat of Internal Affairs. Therefore, he sent a letter to Trotsky through Romm in May, 1934. In this letter, he said, he told Trotsky that the bloc approved the fact that he was seeking contact with foreign powers and that he personally considered that it could only compromise itself by establishing such contact directly. Moreover, he warned Trotsky, he said,

that it was one thing to take the stand that war would create the conditions under which the *bloc* would come to power, and another thing to try to bring about this war. (PR 108.)

Trotsky's letter of December, 1935, according to Radek, discussed two "so-called variants—coming to power in time of peace and coming to power in time of war" (PR 56). The first variant, Radek testified, Trotsky considered impracticable.

Consequently the practicable plan remained that of coming to power as a result of a defeat. And this . . . signified for him that while up to that time Trotsky abroad and we here in Moscow had spoken of an economic retreat within the framework of the Soviet state, a radical change was indicated in this letter. (PR 113.)

The main points of the letter, he said, were (1) the maintenance of the stand of 1934 that defeat was inevitable; (2) "that now the problem of restoring capitalism was openly set before us. . . . As an inevitable result of the defeat of the U.S.S.R., of the social consequences of this defeat; and of an agreement on the basis of this defeat"; (3) the condition of replacing the Soviet power by a Bonapartist government, which meant fascism without its own finance capital and serving foreign finance capital; (4) the partition of the country, including the surrender of the Ukraine to Germany and the Maritime Province and the Amur region to Japan; the payment of indemnities in the form of supplies of food, raw materials, and fats, extending over a long period of years, and the guarantee to the victorious countries of a certain participation in Soviet imports; (5) Japan to be supplied with Sakhalin oil and to be guaranteed oil in event of a war with the U.S.A., and no obstacles to be placed in the way of the conquest of China by Japanese imperialism; (6) no obstacles to be placed in the way of the expansion of German fascism. (PR 115–16.)

§ 204. In his account of his alleged conversation with Trotsky near Oslo in 1935, Pyatakov said:

> He told me that he had come to an absolutely definite agreement with the Fascist German government and with the Japanese government that they would adopt a favorable attitude in the event of the Trotskyite-Zinovievite *bloc* coming to power. . . . He then told me that he had conducted rather lengthy negotiations with the Vice-Chairman of the German National-Socialist Party—Hess. (PR 63–4.)

He then proceeded to list the conditions on which German support was to be had, as Trotsky allegedly stated them. These were, a general favorable attitude toward German interests and the German government on questions of international policy; the cession of certain territories to Germany, German exploitation of certain natural resources of the Soviet Union; coordination of "the destructive forces of the Trotskyist organizations" with forces from without acting under the guidance of German fascism in case of war; and within the country a "very serious retreat" in the direction of capitalism. (PR 64, 65.)

§ 205. Such, in brief, were the alleged directives of Trotsky concerning agreements with foreign powers, and the consequences which those agreements would have upon the territorial integrity and the economy of the Soviet Union. According to Radek, Trotsky stressed the necessity of "spreading and intensifying wrecking and diversive activities," pointing out that the recognition of the bloc by Germany and Japan would be only a "scrap of paper" unless the bloc were strong, and that its strength would be measured by the extent of its subversive activities. He stated that the diversive actions of the Trotskyites were to be agreed upon with the general staffs of the two countries (PR 116). Radek testified that the new feature of these directives was that "defeat was linked up with foreign instructions" (PR 119); that the direct arrangements with foreign general staffs had not existed before. He went at length into the reasons why this letter was disturbing to the leaders of the bloc. In 1934, he said, they had regarded defeat as inevitable; now the Soviet power had grown so strong that to follow a defeatist course would be to thwart a possible victory. (PR 124.)

A significant feature of Radek's testimony on Trotsky's alleged letter of 1935 is his statement that Trotsky

> realized that the master of the situation, with whose aid the *bloc* could come to power, would be fascism—on the one hand German fascism and on the other the military fascism of another Far Eastern country. . . . we were confronted with the prospect of having to accept everything,

but if we remained alive and in power, then owing to the victory of these two countries, and as a result of their plunder and profit a conflict would arise between them and the others, and this would lead to our new development, our "revanche." But this was a prospect from the realm of fiction. (PR 114–5.)

Radek stated also that he believed Trotsky's new program would break up the bloc, since all of its leaders could not be depended upon to support a policy of partition of the U.S.S.R. He and Pyatakov, he said, decided that this formula had become untenable; that they could not take responsibility for it, and, therefore, they decided to call a conference. (PR 120–1.) He says:

> Pyatakov went to see Trotsky; I don't know why Pyatakov did not speak about this here, for it was perhaps the most vital point in his conversation with Trotsky—when Trotsky said that a conference meant exposure or a split. (PR 121.)

Thus it appears that Trotsky, too, believed that the alleged policy would break up the bloc. Radek said that after Pyatakov's return the center decided to hold the conference anyhow, and agreed upon a number of persons whom they would invite, and that this was his last talk with Pyatakov, Serebryakov and Sokolnikov. (PR 121.) In his final speech he gave a confused account of the reasons why this conference never took place. In the terrorist organization, he said, there were people of various kinds, and people connected with foreign intelligence services, but he did not know this at the time. He had to admit, he said, the possibility that

> someone was prowling around us. And the moment we allowed this secret to escape from the control of these

four people, from that moment we should be absolutely powerless to control the situation. (PR 547.)

He intimated that he was suspicious of Dreitzer, and said:

> . . . But when Dreitzer failed to appear in January and, after having received my summons to the conference, came to Moscow and did not come to see me—he was in Moscow in 1935 and did not come to see me—it became clear that Trotsky, on the basis of the correspondence I had had with him, and perceiving Pyatakov's resistance and our misgivings about the defeatist line, was creating some other devilish business in addition to the parallel center. I conclude this from the fact that Dreitzer avoided us in 1935. (PR 547–8.)

Radek himself testified that it was in January, 1936, after Pyatakov's return from Berlin, that they decided to call the conference, and agreed upon a number of persons to be invited (PR 121). Therefore, if Dreitzer failed to see Radek in 1935, his failure can obviously have had nothing to do with the proposed conference. And since Radek dated his and Pyatakov's misgivings from the receipt of Trotsky's alleged "December directives" of 1935, he could hardly have concluded, from Dreitzer's failure to appear in 1935, that Trotsky was "creating some devilish business" inspired by those misgivings. Radek went on to say that Pyatakov told him Trotsky had said during their alleged conversation in Oslo that "cadres of people were being formed who had not been corrupted by the Stalin leadership." When he read about Olberg, he said, it became clear to him that

> Trotsky was organizing agents who had passed through the school of German fascism. And I found the direct reply to this when the question of the conference arose.

It was clear to me that if Dreitzer learnt that we were putting the question of Trotsky's directives on such a footing that it might again lead to a split, as was the case in 1929, then before we succeeded in doing so we should be put out of the way ourselves. (PR 548.)

Thus it would appear that Radek realized, after reading about Olberg during the trial of August, 1936, that Trotsky was using German fascist agents; and therefore he became afraid in January, 1936, that Dreitzer might put the parallel center out of the way if it "put Trotsky's directives on such a footing that it might lead to a split." He went on to state that he therefore could not tell people about the conference, and that

when we did tell them, the arrests had begun and it was impossible to get them together. (PR 548.)

§ 206. At least one alleged fact emerges clearly from what purports to be Radek's explanation of the "backstage aspect of this conference": the conference never took place. Vyshinsky in his final speech commented upon Radek's failure to convene the conference, and asked rhetorically:

What would they have discussed at this conference? The restoration of capitalism? The dismemberment of the U.S.S.R.? The partitioning of the territory of the U.S.S.R.? Territorial concessions? Selling our territory to the Japanese and German annexationists? Espionage and wrecking? They concealed these points of their program, its main points. But we know that hidden things shall be brought to light. And this shameful program of the anti-Soviet Trotskyite *bloc* was also brought to light. (PR 493.)

To prove that this program really existed, he quoted No. 10 of the *Bulletin of the Opposition* of April, 1930, which he said "contains what in essence is the same thing." (PR 494.)

We have examined the article from which Vyshinsky quotes, and we find:

(1) This article by Trotsky is an Open Letter to the members of the Communist Party of the Soviet Union. We note that it is the same letter about which Trotsky wrote in his correspondence with the accused Olberg, mentioning its introduction into the Soviet Union (§ 79, 1). If the alleged program set forth in this article was really treasonable, it seems strange that Trotsky should have announced it publicly in his *Bulletin of the Opposition* rather than in a secret letter to his alleged co-conspirators. It seems even more strange that he should have announced it in an Open Letter to the ruling party of the Soviet Union. But strangest of all is the fact that it took the Soviet government six years to discover the treasonable nature of this document.

(2) The Prosecutor, as in other cases already cited, falsified the contents of this Open Letter by omitting pertinent passages. The Letter begins with the words:

> Dear Comrades: The present letter is impelled by a feeling of greatest alarm over the future of the Soviet Union, and the destiny of the proletarian dictatorship. The policy of the present leadership, that is, the narrow group of Stalin, is driving the country at full speed towards the most dangerous crises and convulsions.

Even Vyshinsky's quotations from this Open Letter indicate that it was a criticism of government policy, and not a program for dismemberment of the Soviet Union, the restoration of capitalism, etc. We give his quotations:

> ". . . All the same, retreat is inevitable. It must be carried out as soon as possible. . . .
> ". . . Put a stop to 'mass' collectivization. . . .

". . . Put a stop to the hurdle race of industrialization. Revise the question of tempo in the light of experience. . . .

". . . Abandon the 'ideals' of self-contained economy. Draw up a new variant of a plan providing for the widest possible intercourse with the world market. . . .

". . . Carry out the necessary retreat, and then strategical rearmament. . . .

". . . It will be impossible to emerge from the present contradictions without crises and struggle. . . ." (PR 494.)

And here are the passages from which Vyshinsky lifted his quotations. The slight, but sometimes significant, differences in the wording of the passages he actually quoted are due to the fact that we have had these passages retranslated directly from Trotsky's original Russian:

The immediate tactical task is: *To retreat from the positions of adventurism.* A retreat is in any case inevitable. It is therefore necessary to carry it out as soon as possible, and in the most orderly manner possible.

To call a halt to "wholesale" collectivization, and to replace it with a careful selection based on genuine voluntary desire [of the peasants].

To put an end to record-breaking jumps in industrialization. To reconsider the question of tempos in the light of experience, from the standpoint of the necessity of raising the living standard of the working-class masses.

To abandon the "ideals" of a self-contained economy. To work out a new variant of the plan, calculated on the widest possible interaction with the world market.

To carry out the necessary retreat and then a strategic rearming, without too great damage and, above all, without losing its sense of perspective—this can be done only by a Party clearly cognizant of its aims and strength. This demands a collective criticism of the entire experience of the Party in the post-Leninist period. The fraud and the falsehoods of "self-criticism" must be replaced by honest Party democracy. A general verification of the general line—not of its application but of its leadership—this is where we must begin!

It is impossible to find a way out from the present contradictions without crises and struggle. A favorable change in the relation of forces on a world scale, i.e., important successes of the international revolution, would, of course, introduce a very significant and even decisive factor into Soviet internal affairs. But it is impermissible to build a policy on expectations of some saving miracle "in the shortest possible period of time." To be sure, in the coming period there will be no lack of crucial and revolutionary situations, especially in the countries of Europe and Asia. But this does not yet solve the problem. If the defeats of the post-war years have taught us anything at all, they have taught us that without a strong and self-confident party that has conquered the confidence of the class, victory is unthinkable. Meanwhile, on this decisive point the balance of the post-Leninist period shows a great deficit.

As the foregoing passages show, this Open Letter can be regarded as treasonable only if one accept the position of the Prosecutor, upon which we have had frequent occasion to comment in preceding chapters of this report, that opposition to the policies of the leaders of the Communist Party and the Soviet government is synonymous with criminal activity against the Soviet state and people.

§ 207. Leon Trotsky, testifying before the Preliminary Commission on this charge, said:

My opinion is that now the key to the situation in the Soviet Union is not in the Soviet Union, but in Europe. If the people in Spain are victorious against the fascists, if the working class in France will assure its movement to Socialism, then the situation in the Soviet Union will change immediately, because the workers are very dissatisfied with the dictatorship of the bureaucracy. They, as I say, are in an impasse. They say, "Given choice only between Hitler and Stalin, we prefer Stalin." They are right. Stalin is preferable to Hitler. . . .

FINERTY: I take it that you do not think, from what you say, that it will help the cause for the proletariat to overthrow Stalin by using Hitler as a means.

TROTSKY: This accusation is so absurd! Every time I repeat it, it makes—I am so perplexed that I cannot find arguments against this absurdity—thinking I can use Hitler against Stalin. For what purpose? What can I win by this? Vyshinsky did not explain to me what I can win by this procedure. I must sacrifice all my past, all my friends and all my future, and what can I win? I cannot understand it.

FINERTY: As you see the situation now, Hitler must first be overthrown before Stalin will be overthrown?

TROTSKY: I hope it will be so. All the articles I wrote about this—and I repeat it in dozens of interviews and articles—if a war comes, the first revolution will be in Japan, because Japan is like the old Tsarist Russia, with a most brutally organized authority; and the contradictions of the social body of Japan will burst out. The first revolution will occur in Japan. The second, I hope, in Germany, because Germany, hermetically sealed, will during the war inevitably explode, as during the imperialist war with the Hohenzollerns, because now all of the contradictions, the social contradictions and the economic, remain in more sharp form in Germany. (PC 278–80.)

Concerning his attitude, past and present, on the defense of the Soviet Union, he stated:

> ... With the Left Opposition, we declared many times we will sustain Stalin and his bureaucracy, and we repeat it now. We will sustain Stalin and his bureaucracy in every effort it makes to defend the new form of property against imperialistic attacks. At the same time we try to defend the new forms of property against Stalin and the bureaucracy, against inner attacks against the new form of property. That is our position. (PC 282.)

Trotsky said that he has continuously met with opposition among his own followers to his stand for defense of the Soviet Union; and that he has broken not only with individual members but with organizations on this question:

> There was in Germany the "Leninbund," an organization connected with us; but we separated ourselves in 1929, the beginning of 1929, over this question. Then we have in France a paper of a group which divided from us. One of the editors is Laste, who is our witness, a very important witness. He is my adversary, and attacks me especially on this question. (PC 286.)

Questioned concerning his attitude toward German fascism, he said:

> ... I have many pamphlets, brochures, and articles beginning in 1930. I tried to draw the attention of the Comintern to this tremendous danger [of Hitler's rise to power], and they accused me of being in a panic, that I overestimated the Nazis in Germany, and that the most immediate foe was the Social-Fascists.

STOLBERG: You mean the so-called Social-Fascists?

TROTSKY: The Social Democrats.

STOLBERG: You don't subscribe to that characterization?

TROTSKY: No. I was a Left Social-Fascist, not a genuine fascist but a Left Social-Fascist. The reason was, I insisted upon the necessity of the united front between the Communist Party and the Social Democratic Party, the united front against Hitler. But you know that in Germany the Communist Party concluded a united front with Hitler in Prussia against the Social-Democratic Government on the 9th of August, 1931. It was the famous Prussian plebiscite initiated by Hitler and supported by the Communists. . . .

GOLDMAN: After Hitler took power, what was your attitude toward the relationship between Hitler and the Soviet Union?

TROTSKY: I didn't try to provoke a war. But I showed in my writings how the Soviet bureaucracy in their hopes to remain in good relations with Hitler were absolutely wrong. Then I wrote in the French press in 1933 or 1934—I wrote a series of articles in the bourgeois press denouncing the genuine plans of Hitler. . . . (PC 309–10.)

Of the attitude of the Soviet government after Hitler came to power, he said:

Stalin in the first six months of 1933 hoped to keep in good relations with the fascists in Germany. I can introduce articles, my articles against him on that occasion. I quote from *Izvestia* about the 15th of March, 1933 [March 4, 1933]: "The U.S.S.R. is the only state which is not nourished on hostile sentiments towards Germany and that independent of the form and the composition of the government of the Reich." It was Hitler who repulsed it, not he. Then only did he begin to look in the direction of France, and so on. The first half of 1933, I was an agent of France, the United States and Great Britain. I changed my profession only after the crushing of Stalin's hopes to remain in friendship with Hitler. I can prove it. It was in the *Pravda*. I am represented as "Mr." Trotsky. I am "Mr." Trotsky in spite of my English. (Laughter.) (PC 293.)

Trotsky further testified that after the victory of Hitler and the change of policy by Stalin and the Comintern, and after the Opposition had become convinced that the Comintern was incapable of drawing the necessary conclusions from the defeat of the German proletariat, the Opposition declared that the Comintern was no longer a revolutionary organization or its leading party, the Bolsheviks, a revolutionary party. It had considered the Party the necessary instrument for the peaceful reform of the Soviet state. Now it declared that there must be a new revolutionary party and that the bureaucracy could be removed only through a new political revolution. (PC 271.)

During the hearings of the Preliminary Commission, Mr. Goldman, counsel for Leon Trotsky, quoted, with reference to the arrest of Trotsky in Canada in 1917 as an alleged German agent, an article of Lenin from *Pravda*, No. 34, April 16, 1917. In this article, Lenin said:

Can one even for a moment believe in the trustworthiness of the statement that Trotsky, the chairman of the Soviet of Workers' Delegates in St. Petersburg in 1905—a revolutionary who has sacrificed years to disinterested service of the revolution—that this man has anything to do with a scheme subsidized by the German Government? This is a patent, unheard-of, and malicious slander of a revolutionary. . . . (PC 20.)

Questioned whether this statement of Lenin could be regarded as proof, in view of the fact that Lenin himself had been charged with being a German agent, Trotsky replied:

> ... My proof is not an absolute proof for people who suspect Lenin of having been an agent of Germany. But my accusers, my prosecutors, are sure that Lenin was not an agent of Germany. . . . My proof is that Lenin affirmed that I could not have been a German agent in 1917, before the October Revolution, before the Civil war, before the creation of the Communist International. Now, I think it is an argument in my favor against Prosecutor Vyshinsky and his superior, Stalin. (PC 53.)

Trotsky was also asked whether, in ceding Russian territory through the Brest-Litovsk treaty, the Soviet government had not acted in favor of Germany as a means of obtaining power. In answer, he stated that although the Soviet government did cede territory, it was forced to do so in order to save Socialism. On the other hand, he pointed out, he was accused in the trial of having agreed to make territorial concessions in order to replace Socialism by capitalism. (PC 53–4.)

In his final argument Trotsky dealt with these questions, as follows:

> To bolster up the improbable accusation of an alliance of the "Trotskyites" with Germany and Japan, the foreign attorneys of the GPU are circulating the following versions:
>
> 1. Lenin, with the agreement of Ludendorff, crossed Germany during the war, in order to be able to carry out his revolutionary tasks.
>
> 2. The Bolshevik government did not shrink from ceding enormous territory and paying indemnity to Germany, in order to save the Soviet régime.

Conclusion: Why not admit that Trotsky entered into agreement with the same German General Staff in order to secure, through the cession of territory, the possibility of realizing his aims in the rest of the country? (PC 509.)

Trotsky pointed out that while Lenin did cross Germany by utilizing Ludendorff's false hopes that Russia would disintegrate as a result of the internal struggle, he concealed neither his program nor the purpose of his trip. He called in Switzerland a small conference of internationalists from various countries, who approved his traveling to Russia through Germany; he entered into no agreements with the German authorities and made the condition that no one was to enter his car during his passage through Germany; upon his arrival in Petrograd he explained to the Soviet and the workers the purpose and nature of his trip. Trotsky repeated that although the Bolshevik government did cede large territories to Germany after the Peace of Brest-Litovsk, it did so in order to save the Soviet régime in the rest of the country; that it had no other choice; that the decision was adopted not behind the backs of the people but after open and public discussion; that the Bolshevik government never concealed from the masses that the Brest-Litovsk treaty signified a transitory and partial capitulation of the proletarian revolution to capitalism. On the other hand, he pointed out, the activities ascribed to himself in the January trial have nothing in common with these examples of Lenin's activity because they imply (1) an agreement to renounce socialism in favor of capitalism, (2) an attempt to destroy Soviet economy and exterminate workers and soldiers, (3) concealment of his real aims and methods from the whole world, and (4) that his entire public political activity serves only to fool the working masses about his real plans into which Hitler, the

Mikado, and their agents are initiated.

To be sure, Trotsky said,

> some attorneys of the GPU are inclined to dilute with
> water the over-potent wine of Stalin. It may be, they say,
> that Trotsky agreed only verbally to restore capitalism,
> but in reality was preparing to realize in the remaining
> territory a policy in the spirit of his program. In the first
> place, this variant contradicts the confessions of Radek,
> Pyatakov and others. But, independently of this fact, it is
> just as senseless as the official version given in the indict-
> ment. The program of the Opposition is the program of
> international Socialism. How could an experienced adult
> imagine that Hitler and the Mikado, possessing a complete
> list of his treasons and abominable crimes, would permit
> him to realize a revolutionary program? How could one
> hope, anyway, to achieve power at the price of acts of high
> treason in the service of a foreign general staff? Is it not
> clear in advance that Hitler and the Mikado, after using
> such an agent to the limit, would fling him aside like a
> squeezed lemon? Could the conspirators, headed by six
> members of Lenin's Political Bureau, have failed to under-
> stand this? The accusation is thus internally meaningless
> in both its variants—the official variant, which speaks of
> the restoration of capitalism, and the semi-official variant,
> which concedes to the conspirators a hidden design—to
> fool Hitler and the Mikado. (PC 511.)

§ 208. Several witnesses who appeared before our sub-
commissions made statements bearing upon the charge of
agreements with foreign powers. We have already quoted
(§ 196) Eugene Bauer's testimony on the alleged connection
with the Gestapo. Herbert Solow, journalist, testified before
the New York Sub-Commission that he belonged to the
Workers' Party of the U.S. in 1934 and 1935; that he agrees

with Trotsky on certain questions but on others is in what he considers such fundamental disagreement that he could not belong to the same organization (NY 113). He testified that he visited Trotsky at Prinkipo on August, 1930, after a visit to the U.S.S.R. At that time, he said,

> . . . I had been very much disappointed by what I had seen in Russia . . . and came into that discussion at Prinkipo with an attitude that . . . those who had the slogan of defending the Soviet Union were really sort of half-hearted Stalinists, Trotsky among them. I attempted to characterize him on that basis. He replied by calling me an ultra-Leftist and in a long discussion endeavoring to prove to me that the revolutionary or any progressive must stand on the basis of defending the Soviet Union despite what Stalin was doing, even with Stalin at the head of the government. . . . He made what seemed to us almost like Stalinist speeches because they were so enthusiastic about the potentialities of the Soviet Union. (NY 109–110.)

B.J. Field (identified § 66) testified that during Trotsky's stay in Copenhagen, and also during the preceding four months while Field was working with him at Prinkipo, the question of the attitude of the Trotskyist organization toward Hitler was often discussed by Trotsky in his presence. He said:

> . . . The question of the defense of the Soviet Union in relation to stopping the advance of Hitler, was a very vital issue throughout the whole International Left Opposition. . . . One of the views of Comrade Trotsky regarding the danger of Hitler's coming to power in Germany, was the direct immediate danger to the Soviet Union. He expressed at that time the thought that, if Hitler came to power, his function would be to act as a

super-Wrangel, that is, the spearhead of foreign intervention against the Soviet Union. . . . The Communist
Party, on the contrary, took the position that the question of Hitler's coming to power was a secondary question, that there was little likelihood of Hitler's coming
to power, and if he did come to power he would not last
more than a very few days. . . . The Stalinist organization, in our opinion, was weakening the defense of the
Soviet Union by minimizing the danger of Hitler. Our
tendency, on the contrary, regarded the campaign against
Hitler as the most burning issue for the international
labor movement. (NY 127–8.)

A.J. Muste (identified § 138) questioned about the views expressed by Trotsky during Mr. Muste's conversations with him
at Weksal, near Hoenefoss, Norway, in June, 1936, said:

Both in conversations that I had at Hoenefoss and
throughout the period of my connection with the Trotskyist movement, when there was correspondence with
Comrade Trotsky on the subject, the Opposition constantly had been saying that for one thing, this was not
the period when any important Opposition work could
be done in the Soviet Union because of the severity of
the repression . . . ; that the task of the Trotskyist movement was to build an effective Marxist leadership and
organizations in the capitalist countries. That would
have the result, for one thing, of making it impossible
for these countries to wage war upon the Soviet Union.
The defense of the Soviet Union, regarded by Comrade
Trotsky as a workers' state, should constantly be one of
the dominant aims of the entire movement. Furthermore,
the building up of effective Leninist organizations in the
capitalist countries would eventually make it possible to
have an Opposition within the Soviet Union to change

conditions there in such a way as to secure the defense of the workers' state, and the correction of the evils which, Trotsky holds, exist in that state today. (NY 43.)

§ 209. Among the depositions in our possession there are many references to Trotsky's attitude and that of his followers toward the Soviet Union and toward fascism during those years when he was alleged to have been plotting with the German and Japanese governments for the assassination of Soviet officials and the overthrow of the Soviet government. We quote briefly from typical statements:

Raymond Molinier (identified § 68, 9, a) says that

. . . all the political activity of Trotsky at Copenhagen, his public lectures as well as his speeches for the films had an orientation diametrically opposed to that of the famous terrorist center. . . . At Copenhagen Trotsky called together the principal militants of the international organization who were present. . . . This interview took place, and it is not without interest to recall that the whole axis of the discussion was precisely the menace of Hitler's coming to power in Germany and the need of an energetic propaganda for a united proletarian front in order to block his way. (PC Exh. 16, I/22.)

Erich Kohn, in an affidavit (Oslo), states that as a member of the leadership of the Hamburg organization of the Left Opposition, he was in Copenhagen during the period of Trotsky's stay there and was with Trotsky daily; that since that time he has become widely separated from Trotskyism and the Trotskyist organization. Concerning Trotsky's attitude toward the Soviet Union at that time he says:

In so far as questions concerning the Soviet Union were discussed in the conversations held at that time (which was seldom the case), Trotsky and all his friends held firmly to the point of view of peaceful reform of the Soviet régime and of the Communist Party of the Soviet Union and the unconditional defense of the Soviet Union with the right of political criticism of the ruling faction. (*Ibid.*, I/6.)

H. Sneevliet (identified § 159, 9) states that he visited Trotsky in Copenhagen November 27–29, 1932. Concerning Trotsky's attitude toward the Soviet Union at that time, he says:

Between himself and L.D. Trotsky the existence could be stated of a common opinion about many problems, but the great difference was there, that undersigned and his Dutch friends had already accepted the point of view of the necessity of a new revolutionary party and international in 1929, whereas L.D. Trotsky at the end of 1932 still defended oppositional work inside the parties of the Third International. It seems to him absolutely superfluous to state that L.D. Trotsky strongly stood for the defense of the Soviet Union and in general represented the spirit of revolutionary Marxism which makes it impossible that he, Trotsky, could be responsible for the activities of which he has been accused in the different political "trials" of Moscow. (PC Exh. 18, S VIII, 26.)

Sneevliet states that he also saw Trotsky in Trotsky's house at Royan, France, August 18–20, 1933, and that

The establishment of the Hitler dictatorship in Germany and the responsibility of the German Stalinist Party (KPD) for this greatest defeat of the European proletariat of the later years proved to have pushed L.D.

Trotsky towards recognition of the unavoidableness of
the Fourth International and for that reason also of new
revolutionary parties in the different countries. . . . It
was clear that also at that time L.D. Trotsky maintained
totally the revolutionary Marxist principles and that he
defended revolutionary Marxist practice. *(Ibid.)*

J. Laste (identified § 151; see also § 207) testifies concerning Trotsky's political preoccupations during his stay
at Royan:

> . . . Trotsky was then much absorbed by a change in his
> estimate of the Communist International. . . . He passed
> most of his time writing arguments in favor of his new
> conceptions. . . . Another meeting took place one Sunday
> afternoon with Trotskyist comrades who had come from
> Paris by car. . . . The principal theme of the discussion
> was the creation of the new International and the new
> party; the sabotage of the German revolutionary move-
> ment by the Stalinists appeared to Trotsky as the defini-
> tive bankruptcy of the Communist International. The
> coming of Hitler to power was attributed in large part
> to Stalinism; on this subject Trotsky recalled the united
> front policy he had advocated for Germany, and showed
> how Stalinism, by its political incapacity, was placing the
> U.S.S.R. in danger between the pincers formed by Japan
> and Hitler Germany. (PC Exh. 18, VII/8.)

§ 210. Besides such statements of witnesses as the above,
our exhibits contain various other documents indicating the
nature of Trotsky's political preoccupations during the periods of his visit to Copenhagen and his stay at St. Palais. We
have already cited (§ 199) the sound film which he made in
Copenhagen for Left Opposition propaganda. We have also
the resolutions and manifestos adopted by an improvised

conference of Left Oppositionists held during his visit to Copenhagen, which chiefly concern a proposal for the creation of an Oppositionist international defense organization, and the report of a commission on the situation of the Left Oppositionists in Spain. (PC Exh. 16, III/8.)

We quote the following paragraph from notes made by J. Schwab of the German Socialist Workers' Party, on a series of conversations with Trotsky, August 17–20, 1933 (on the fourth day H. Sneevliet was present and took part in the discussion). These notes were sent to Trotsky by Schwab:

> . . . [Trotsky] was of the opinion that it did not appear possible within a predictable time to bring about a World Labor Congress through the initiative of the parties represented in Paris. But since such a congress would be very useful for the organization of the struggle against the war danger and fascism, especially for the organization of a boycott against Hitler-Germany, the mere propaganda for such a congress would have good results and help the campaign for a new international. (PC Exh. 18, IX/1, a.)

A letter from John Paton (identified § 159, 9) to the *Manchester Guardian* of February 16, 1937, states that at the time he saw Trotsky in Southern France in 1933, Trotsky's objective and entire policy were,

> unless he was playing an elaborate part designed to mislead me and all others in contact with him, including his own followers throughout the world (a meaningless foolery which is inconceivable),

the exact opposite of those attributed to him during that period in the January trial. All Trotsky's main activities in recent years, says Mr. Paton, have been devoted to exposing the dangers for the international working class movement of "collaboration with bourgeois parties and capitalist governments" and to preaching the need for intensification of Communist revolutionary activity as the real bulwark against fascism. (*Ibid.*, VIII/21.)

§ 211. In support of his statement that he had formerly been denounced in the Soviet press as an ally of British, French and American imperialism, Trotsky introduced, among other documents, *Pravda* of March 8, 1929, containing an article by Yaroslavsky, entitled "Mr. Trotsky in the Service of the Bourgeoisie." Yaroslavsky says:

> As a matter of fact *Trotsky in his articles conducts a propaganda against the Soviet Union, the Communist Party and the Comintern.* It is precisely for this that he is being paid by the money-bags of England and America. . . .
> Isn't it strange that Trotsky is being paid tens of thousands of dollars for "propaganda" by the very same English overlords who organized a break with the Soviet Union precisely on account of "propaganda"? . . . (PC Exh. 26.)

Trotsky also introduced excerpts from *l'Humanité*, organ of the official Communist Party of France (July 24, 25, 26 and August 29, 1933) denouncing him as an agent of the French government and the Social Democracy and stating that he has been granted asylum in France in order that he may aid the offensive against the Soviet Union. (PC Exh. 18, X/2–5.) Also *l'Humanité* of August 1, 1933, in which his picture appears as one of "The General Staff of the Counter-Revolution in France," along with those of the Grand Duke Cyril, General Miller, Leon Blum, Rosenfeld,

Kerensky and Tseretelli. (PC Exh. 18, S X/6.)

§ 212. Trotsky's published writings revealing his attitude toward capitalism in general and fascism in particular, and toward the defense of the Soviet Union, are so numerous and so well known that we cite here only two or three. In "What Next? Vital Questions for the German Proletariat," published in 1932, he discusses the rise of fascism in Germany. Fascism, he says, is

> a particular governmental system based on the uprooting of all elements of proletarian democracy within bourgeois society. The task of fascism lies not only in destroying the Communist advance guard but in holding the entire class in a state of forced disunity. (New York: Pioneer Publishers; p. 12.)

He sees Stalin as retarding the proletariat in the struggle against fascism:

> The key to the situation is in the hands of the Communist Party; but the Stalinist bureaucracy attempts to use this key to lock the gates to revolutionary action. (*Ibid.*, p. 40.)

The Stalinist policy, he maintains, is paralyzing the German masses at the very moment when, weak and disorganized as they are, they might still turn Germany from fascism to revolution. He warns that the same Stalinist policy prevented the organization of soviets in China during the period of revolutionary upsurge, and then, when the recession began, urged their formation—too late.

Typical of Trotsky's attitude toward German fascism in his writings after Hitler came to power, is the pamphlet, "What Hitler Wants," copyrighted 1933 and published by the John Day Company, New York. We quote:

... Taken as a whole, the Hitler program for the reconstruction of Europe is a reactionary-Utopian medley of
racial mysticism and national cannibalism. It is not hard
to submit it to an annihilating criticism. . . . (p. 11.)

... Europe needs a new organization. But woe betide it
if this work falls into the hands of fascism. . . . (p. 30.)

His attitude toward Japan is illustrated by the following
excerpt from an article, "Japan Heads Toward a Catastrophe,"
written on July 12, 1933, and published in the *Bulletin of
the Opposition*, No. 38–39, February, 1934:

To summarize. Economically Japan is weaker than
any of its adversaries in a major war. Japanese industry is incapable of assuring an army of several millions
with armaments and equipment over a period of years.
The Japanese financial system which is unable to bear
the burden of militarism in peacetime would completely
collapse at the very beginning of a major war. The Japanese soldier *en masse* does not comply with the require-
ments of new technology and new tactics. The population
is profoundly hostile to the régime. Goals of conquest
would prove incapable of uniting the divided nation. Simultaneously with mobilization hundreds of thousands
of revolutionists or candidates for revolutionists would
flow into the army. . . . The social warp of the country is
ripped, the bolts are loose. In the steel corset of military
dictatorship official Japan appears to be mighty, but war
will ruthlessly dispel this myth.

Trotsky's opinion of the probable effect which imperialist
intervention would have upon the Soviet masses has an
important bearing upon the charges of defeatism, and of
having plotted to bring about such intervention. In "War
and the Fourth International: Draft Theses Adopted by the

International Secretariat of the International Communist League," point 46 reads in part as follows:

> Within the U.S.S.R. war against imperialist intervention will undoubtedly provoke a veritable outburst of genuine fighting enthusiasm. All the contradictions will seem overcome or at any rate relegated to the background. The young generations of workers and peasants that emerged from the revolution will reveal on the battlefield a colossal dynamic power. . . . (New York: Communist League of America, 1934, p. 21.)

§ 213. We have already found, on the basis of the evidence, that the testimony of Radek and Pyatakov is worthless. Therefore, the charge of conspiracy between Trotsky on the one hand and Hitler and the Mikado on the other stands not proved. Moreover this charge seems to us absurd and incredible. If we are to believe the testimony in the Moscow trials, Trotsky and his alleged co-conspirators in Russia were in treasonable relations with Hitler both before and after Hitler came to power. And if we are to believe the official Communist press of the period, both inside and outside the U.S.S.R., he was at the same time an agent of French, British, and American imperialism, and in counter-revolutionary collusion with the Social Democracy. Such indiscriminate conspiratorial activity as all these accusations imply would be more characteristic of a crackpot busybody than of an intelligent man. It would also, one would think, indicate that Trotsky must have had in the Soviet Union a very large and devoted following, ready to accept not only his published program but also its exact opposite, his alleged secret program. It can hardly be assumed that the governments of five great powers would conspire for the overthrow of another great power with a mere individual who could bring nothing more to the bargain than his own personal hatred of its governing group. Yet the indictment in the August trial clearly states that

> Lacking all support in the working class and the toiling masses of the people of the U.S.S.R. . . . the leaders of the Trotskyite-Zinovievite counter-revolutionary *bloc, Trotsky, Zinoviev* and *Kamenev,* sank definitely into the swamp of white-guardism, joined forces and merged with the most inveterate enemies of the Soviet Power. . . . (ZK 12.)

And the indictment in the January trial affirms that

> . . . deprived, as a result of the complete victory of socialism in the U.S.S.R., of all support among the masses of the people, and constituting an isolated and politically doomed group of bandits and spies, branded with universal contempt by the people of the Soviet Union, *L.D. Trotsky* and his accomplices . . . outrageously betrayed the interests of the working class and the peasantry, betrayed their country and became an agency of the German and Japanese fascist forces for espionage, diversive and wrecking activities. (PR 17–18.)

In their testimony, several of the accused stated that they could not count on mass support. The accused Kamenev said:

> It was no use counting on any kind of serious internal difficulties to secure the overthrow of the leadership which had guided the country through extremely difficult stages. . . . Two paths remained: either honestly and completely to put a stop to the struggle against the Party, or to continue this struggle, but without any hope of obtaining any mass support whatsoever, . . . by means of individual terror. (ZK 65.)

The accused Shestov claimed to have told Sedov in 1931 that "we had no support at all among the workers and peasants." (PR 162.) The witness Loginov said he had it from Pyatakov that ". . . this was just how Trotsky thought, that . . . it was impossible to rely on the workers and proletarian masses within the country, . . ." (PR 180.) The accused Sokolnikov said, "We could not count on the support of the masses." (PR 553.) According to Pyatakov, Trotsky told him during their interview in Norway that

> . . . The organization of a mass struggle was impossible, in the first place because the worker masses and the peasant masses were in the main at present under the hypnotic influence of the huge constructive work that was going on in the country, constructive work which they took to be socialist construction. Any attempt on our part in that direction . . . would rapidly lead . . . to the destruction of the comparatively insignificant Trotskyite cadres at present in the country. (PR 61.)

These and similar statements in the records indicate that the accused, and Trotsky too, allegedly sought foreign help precisely because they realized the futility of looking for any support within the U.S.S.R. Even if one assume that Trotsky misrepresented to the governments of Hitler and the Mikado the extent of his influence over the Russian masses, it seems absurd to suppose that they would have taken his word for it if they regarded the overthrow of the Soviet government as a serious business; more especially since, according to the records of both trials, they had their own agents at work in Russia, who might have been supposed to be in a position to inform them correctly about the solidarity of the Russian people behind the existing régime.

If we assume that these Governments knowingly conspired with a "politically doomed group of bandits," then the question arises, what could this group have given them which would merit in exchange the gift of power over the Soviet state? Power, according to the indictments and confessions in both trials, was the stake for which the alleged conspirators risked their heads. But no man of political experience could reasonably expect to attain power by such means under such circumstances; and the principal accused were men of long political experience who had had occasion to learn a great deal about the mechanics of power. One might assume that, blinded by their ambition, they permitted themselves to be duped by the false promises of their alleged foreign allies. But their own testimony concerning the doubts and fears inspired in them by Trotsky's "December directives" indicates conviction that these allies would never permit them to enjoy power; that Trotsky's agreements with Japan and Germany meant that the Soviet state would become "an appendage of fascism." Indeed, the accused Radek, as we have shown, testified to the danger that these agreements would break up the bloc. Moreover, he indicated that Trotsky realized this, too, and therefore forbade the calling of the proposed conference (§ 205). The accused Pyatakov, in telling about his alleged conversation with Trotsky, characterized this "line" as "downright, undisguised high treason" and said that Trotsky warned him that it was not expedient or possible not only to make it public, but even to communicate it to more than a small, restricted group of "Trotsky-ites" (PR 62).

In his final argument, Vyshinsky said:

> But how to "come to an agreement"? Will the fascists be willing to "come to an agreement"? Will they not prefer to act without an agreement, as they act everywhere, all over the world, by grabbing everything, throwing themselves upon, crushing and exterminating the weak? Radek said that it was clear that:

"The masters of the situation would be fascism—German fascism on the one hand, and the military fascism of a Far-Eastern country on the other."

And, of course, Trotsky, their teacher, understood this no less than they did. The whole Trotskyite centre understood it. They accepted it with open eyes. This was the second point of their "remarkable" program. (PR 489.)

This, like many of the Prosecutor's statements, is not quite exact. The accused, as we have seen, had testified that they were alarmed by Trotsky's alleged agreements, and unready to accept them without discussion. As concerns Trotsky, the evidence clearly alleges that he was trying to impose this line on his followers in full knowledge of the risk that it would disrupt them—in other words, that he was following a course which would seem remarkably stupid. Moreover, if Radek had the wit to see that the prospect of "revanche" which Trotsky allegedly set forth was "a prospect from the realm of fiction" it would be a little far-fetched to assume that Trotsky did not himself have the wit to see it.

§ 214. The alternative placed before us in comparing the trial record with the evidence introduced in rebuttal by Trotsky and others is either to assume that Trotsky was plotting to come to power by methods which he knew in advance would be self-defeating—see the above quotation from Vyshinsky's speech—or to believe that his attitude toward German fascism, Japanese imperialism, and the defense of the Soviet Union during the period of the alleged conspiracy was as his own testimony, that of witnesses, the documents cited above, and his published writings represent it. There is no other choice, for the testimony of the accused precludes the assumption that his purpose was to yield a part of Soviet territory in order to carry out a Marxist program in the remainder.

In order to accept the conclusions of the Moscow Court,

one would either have to believe that Trotsky is the most interesting case of split personality in all history, or accept the Prosecutor's contention that his public activity constituted nothing but an elaborate camouflage for his secret counter-revolutionary intrigues. Our study of the trial records convinces us that Trotsky is fully justified in contending that the counter-revolutionary activity ascribed to him is characterized by an extraordinary stupidity. On the other hand, we find that his whole public activity, including his voluminous writings, has followed a consistent theoretical line throughout his long career, and that line is diametrically opposed to the activity ascribed to him in the two Moscow trials. We do not presume to judge the aims to which he has devoted himself, or the methods by which he has pursued those aims. But we can and do state that his career has been that of a man of extraordinary intelligence and ability. To believe that his prodigious public activity was intended merely to cloak conspiratorial enterprises as stupid, inept and feeble as those ascribed to him in the trials, would be to abandon any claim to common sense.

§ 215. We therefore hold the charge of conspiracy with foreign powers to be not only not proved, but preposterous.

25

'The historical connection'

§ 216. As stated in Chapter III of this report, the scope and content of our inquiry was determined by the proceedings in the Moscow trials. In his final argument in the January trial, Prosecutor Vyshinsky defined two categories of

> proofs which in our hands may serve as a test of the assertions of the indictment, of the theses of the indictment. First, there is the historical connection which confirms the theses of the indictment on the basis of the Trotskyites' past activity. We have also in mind the testimony of the accused which in itself represents enormous importance as proof. (PR 513.)

This passage appears at the beginning of the final summary of the Prosecutor's address. That the weight attached to the "historical connection" is not accidental and that it is not wholly a matter of accident that it is placed before the probative value of the "testimony of the accused," is evident from the fact that the speech opens with eleven pages of the Prosecutor's version of the history of Trotskyism in general, followed by as many pages dealing mainly with his version of the past of Pyatakov, Radek and Sokolnikov in particular.

We quote a few of the passages in which Vyshinsky lays special emphasis upon past history:

> Like a reversed cinema reel, this trial has reminded and shown us all the main stages of the historical path traversed by the Trotskyites and Trotskyism, which spent more than thirty years of its existence in preparing for its final conversion into a storm detachment of fascism, into one of the departments of the fascist police. (PR 463–64.)
>
> It is not an accident that the Trotskyites are playing this role of vanguard of the anti-Soviet fascist forces. The descent of Trotskyism into the anti-Soviet underworld, its conversion into a fascist agency, is merely the culmination of its historical development. (PR 466.)

He goes on to say that the alleged terrorism, wrecking and collusion with foreign powers

> merely crowns the struggle Trotskyism has been waging against the working class and the Party, against Lenin and Leninism, for decades. (PR 466.)
>
> We know that at the turning points of our struggle, at the sharp upsurges of our proletarian revolution, the Trotskyite leaders were always, as a rule, found in the camp of our enemies, on the other side of the barricades. (PR 470.)

The importance of the alleged history is summed up in this final quotation:

. . . the history of their fall began long before they organized the so-called "parallel" center, this offshoot of the
criminal Trotskyite-Zinovievite united *bloc*. Organic connection is proved. Historical connection is proved. And
what I have said would be sufficient to remove all doubt
that the principal charge made . . . against the accused
sitting in the dock of attempting to restore in our country
the capitalist system which was overthrown 19 years ago
is fully proved, proved documentarily. (PR 470.)

§ 217. We are not here concerned with these generalizations of past history beyond remarking that all the leading
persons accused in the two trials had occupied for years
positions of great responsibility within the Soviet government and the Party organization; that the trials resulted in
the removal from office and the execution or imprisonment
of every surviving leader of the October Revolution save
Trotsky, who is condemned in exile, and Stalin in power.
Enemies of the Revolution could find no more convincing
ground upon which to condemn it; that is, if they accept the
Prosecutor's version of history.

The Commission does not accept that version, for the
simple reason that it does not accord with the facts. Every one of its members is old enough to have followed the
history of the Russian Revolution in the making; and every one of them was sufficiently interested to do so. We
endorse this statement in the report of our Preliminary
Commission:

> Impartiality in this case does not of course require
> the abandonment by the Commission of its knowledge
> of the simple facts of history. (PC XV.)

We shall not, therefore, make any exhaustive analysis
of the history of the Russian Revolution for the purpose of

determining whether the Prosecutor's sweeping statements about the "historical development" of Trotskyism are true. The mere statement that they are a complete falsification is sufficient; more especially since the history of the Russian Revolution is easily accessible, at least outside the Soviet Union, in sources which have not been subjected to the revision to be found in the speeches of Vyshinsky. On the other hand, the importance attached by the Prosecutor to the alleged evidence which he adduced in support of these generalizations, as *proof* of the charges against the accused in general and Trotsky in particular, requires of us that we establish its historic truth or falsity. This we shall do as briefly as is consistent with accuracy.

§ 218. First, however, it must be noted that the men against whom the Prosecutor inveighed as Trotskyists in his speeches, and identified with

> the struggle Trotskyism has been waging against the working class and the Party, against Lenin and Leninism for decades,

had not, during their political activity, belonged to one same political formation or consistently defended the same conceptions or the same line of conduct. This could be established precisely of each of them. It suffices to consider the cases of two of the most important, Kamenev and Zinoviev. A comparison of their biographies, from official sources, with that of Trotsky in Appendix II to this report clearly shows that during most of their careers they were not his political allies. And it was precisely these two men who, with Stalin, carried on most savagely the fight against Trotsky and the Left Opposition from 1923 to 1926. During Lenin's second illness they formed, with Stalin, the ruling *Troika* of the Party, and together with Stalin they decided to invent "Trotskyism," as they later admitted. ("The Stalin School of Falsification,"* pp. 89–96, New York, Pioneer Publishers, 1937.)

Among our exhibits is the pamphlet "Leninism or Trotskyism" (PC Exh. 5) written by Stalin, Zinoviev and Kamenev during this period. As its title indicates, it is an attack upon "Trotskyism" by the *Troika*. After Zinoviev and Kamenev had broken with Stalin and joined Trotsky in opposition, Zinoviev said at a joint Plenum of the Central Committee and the Central Control Commission (July, 1926) that

> . . . the main nucleus of the 1923 Opposition . . . correctly warned against the dangers of the departure from the proletarian line, and against the alarming growth of the apparatus régime. (Minutes, IV, p. 33. "Stalin School of Falsification," p. 91.)

Together with Trotsky, Zinoviev and Kamenev formulated the program of the Left Opposition (see "The Real Situation in Russia"). But in 1927, during the Fifteenth Congress, at which the Opposition was expelled from the Party, they signed (December 18) the so-called Statement of the Twenty-three, abjuring this program and declaring that Stalin was, and always had been, right. The break with Trotsky was complete; and as the material cited in Chapter VIII of this report indicates, it continued throughout the period of the alleged conspiracy. There is every reason to believe, therefore, that these two men who were tried and condemned in August, 1936, were "Trotskyites" only for the purposes of the prosecution.

---

* Since the documents reprinted in this book have been frequently and widely published, and their authenticity has not been challenged, the Commission considers itself justified in citing the book as a reference. The book was first published in Russian, in Berlin, in 1932. The first part, Trotsky's Letter to the Bureau of Party History, was published in English in 1928 in "The Real Situation in Russia" (cf. § 181), pp. 199–315.

§ 219. The complete shift in the attitude of Stalin toward Zinoviev and Kamenev after they broke with him is worth noting here because of its bearing upon the subject of this chapter. It is clearly shown in two statements of his, the first on November 19, 1924, before the Plenum of the All-Union Central Council of Trade Unions, and the second in the Political Report of the Central Committee to the 15th Congress of the C.P.S.U., on December 3, 1927. In the first speech he defended Zinoviev and Kamenev from attacks by the Opposition. Referring to their votes against the October Insurrection (the other ten votes, including Lenin's and Trotsky's, were in favor of this insurrection), he made light of their opposition to Lenin, remarking that they

> entered the organ of the political leadership of the uprising on a par with the advocates of the uprising. . . . No split took place and the differences of opinion lasted only a few days because and only because Comrades Kamenev and Zinoviev were Leninists, Bolsheviks. ("The October Revolution," by Joseph Stalin. Vol. XXI of the Marxist Library, p. 70. New York: International Publishers. Printed in the U.S.S.R.—in other words, a volume having official approval.)

He made no reference in this speech to Lenin's motion to have them expelled from the Party.

In 1927, however, this opposition to Lenin had become, in Stalin's opinion, the beginning of a "sliding down" toward Menshevism:

> . . . It is obvious to all that the Opposition denies the possibility of the victorious construction of Socialism in our country. And by denying this possibility, it slides down directly and openly to the position of the Mensheviks. Such a line taken by the Opposition to the question

is not new, for *its present leaders, Kamenev and Zinov-*
iev, started with this line when they refused to proceed
to the October uprising. . . . You know that Kamenev and
Zinoviev went to the uprising *only when shown the rod.*
Lenin drove them with a rod, threatening to expel them
from the Party . . . and they were constrained to drag their
feet to the uprising . . . (*Ibid.*, pp. 165–6.) (Italics ours.)

The contradiction speaks for itself. A truly remarkable
change in Stalin's attitude toward political opposition becomes
apparent when one juxtaposes the two documents. In the
speech of 1924, for example, he emphasizes the existence of
disagreements within the Party, and their permissibility:

> Our Party would have been a caste and not a revolu-
> tionary Party had it not allowed certain shades of opin-
> ion in its midst, . . . (*Ibid.*, p. 76.)
> Were there any differences of opinion during that
> period within the Central Committee [before the Octo-
> ber Insurrection]? Yes, there were, and they were of no
> small importance. (*Ibid.*, p. 83.)
> There is talk about measures of repression against the
> Opposition and of the possibility of a split. This is all
> nonsense, comrades. . . . As for repressions, I am decid-
> edly opposed to them. (*Ibid.*, p. 94.)

In 1927, however, differences of opinion on the part of an
Opposition still within the Party

> denotes a spirit of capitulation . . . to the capitalist ele-
> ments in our country . . . to the world bourgeoisie. (*Ibid.*,
> p. 168.)

and furnished the basis for the repressive acts of expulsion
and exile. It is no very long step from this to Vyshinsky's

consistent identification of opposition to the policies of the régime with criminal activity against it, which we have repeatedly had occasion to note in the course of this report.

§ 220. In examining the pronouncements of political leaders in all matters involving historical facts, elementary caution necessitates careful consideration of the current political pressures under which such pronouncements are made, and an equally careful comparison with the historical sources for the period to which they refer. The change, illustrated above, in Stalin's attitude toward Zinoviev and Kamenev is of course explained by the fact that in the period between the two pronouncements they had joined Trotsky in opposing him; and the change in his attitude toward opposition within the Party was possibly due to the strengthening of Opposition forces, and the consequent threat to the supremacy of his faction, which the new oppositional alignment involved. When we turn to the historical sources of the period to which these two documents refer we find that Stalin in 1917, as in 1924, sought to minimize the opposition of Zinoviev and Kamenev to the October Insurrection. Zinoviev and Kamenev had opposed the insurrection in the non-Party press. Lenin, in a letter to the Central Committee, characterized this action as "infinitely vile" and suggested their expulsion from the Party. On the same day, October 20, Stalin, who was one of the editors of *Pravda*, published a "Statement by the Editorial Board" in which the other editor, Sokolnikov, later declared he had had no part. This statement said:

> We on our part express the hope that the matter will be considered as closed with the statement made by Comrade Zinoviev (and also Comrade Kamenev's statement in the Soviet). The sharp tone of Comrade Lenin's article does not alter the fact that we are fundamentally in agreement. ("Stalin School of Falsification," p. 192.)

As a matter of fact, the majority of the Central Committee refused to expel Zinoviev and Kamenev; and Trotsky, testifying on this matter, said that Lenin

> was, two days after the insurrection, very well satisfied with our decision (PC 423)—

a statement borne out by the fact that Zinoviev and Kamenev remained members of the Politburo and close collaborators of Lenin, and held responsible official posts.

To show with what caution one must approach such accusations as Stalin's statement that Zinoviev and Kamenev started sliding down into Menshevism when they opposed the insurrection, we may cite Stalin's own attitude toward Menshevism in the period immediately preceding Lenin's return to Russia, in 1917. One instance will suffice to illustrate. At the Party Conference of March, 1917, during the discussion of a proposal for unification of Bolsheviks and Mensheviks which had been made by the Menshevik leader, Tseretelli, Stalin said:

> We ought to go. It is necessary to define our proposals as to the terms of unification. Unification is possible along the lines of Zimmerwald-Kienthal. (Session of April 1. "Stalin School of Falsification," p. 190.)

It is evident from this passage that if Stalin's attack upon Zinoviev and Kamenev in 1927 was justified, he might himself with equal justice have been attacked on the same grounds.

§ 221. That Lenin himself considered free criticism of the Party's policy a fundamental right of its members becomes clear from even a superficial examination of his utterances on that question—and from this it clearly follows that he by no means regarded opposition to his policies as a counter-revolutionary offense. We could cite many quotations on this point, but one is sufficient in view of the peculiar circumstances which produced it. The Tenth Party Congress, in 1921, adopted as an emergency measure on Lenin's own motion a resolution forbidding fractional groupings and platforms within the Party. At this same Congress Riazanov moved to prohibit the election of delegates to future congresses on the basis of fractional platforms. Lenin opposed him in these words:

> If fundamental disagreements exist on a question we cannot deprive the Party and the members of the Central Committee of the right to address themselves to the Party. . . . The present Congress can in no way and in no form engage the elections to the next Congress. And if, for example, such issues as the Brest-Litovsk peace should arise? It cannot be guaranteed. It is possible that it will then be necessary to elect by platform. (Lenin's Collected Works, Third Russian Edition, 1935. Vol. XXVI, p. 276.)

It is clear from the foregoing that Lenin regarded the authority of the Party Congress as supreme; and that even in a period of emergency he was unwilling to hamper Party members in the exercise of their right to have their views represented in the Congress—even on the basis of fractional platforms; indeed that he even envisaged issues so important as to render fractional opposition to the leadership not only justifiable but necessary.

It would even appear that Lenin considered opposition outside the ruling Party vital to the interests of the proletariat and the state. We quote the following striking passage from his discussion of the trade union issue, on December 30, 1920, before the Party fraction of the Eighth Soviet Congress:

> Comrade Trotsky speaks of the workers' state. Permit me, that is an abstraction. . . . The whole joke is that it is

not quite a workers' state. That is where the basic mistake of Comrade Trotsky lies! . . . Our state is in reality no workers' state but a workers' and peasants' state. . . . From our party program it follows that our state is a workers' state with bureaucratic deformations. . . .

Our present state is such that the organized proletariat must defend itself and we must utilize these workers' organizations for the defense of the workers against their state and for the defense of the state by the workers. (Lenin's Collected Works, Vol. XVIII, Part I, pp. 11–12. Russian Edition. State Publishers, 1925.)

This attitude of Lenin must be borne in mind in examining certain of Vyshinsky's specific "historical proofs" against Trotsky. The Commission wishes to emphasize, before taking up these "proofs," that it does not invoke Lenin as an infallible authority; but since one of the Prosecutor's basic "historical proofs" against Trotsky and several of the accused was their having opposed Lenin in the past, it becomes pertinent to establish Lenin's own attitude toward the authority of the leadership which he exercised and the question of opposition to that leadership by Party members.

§ 222. We shall now proceed to consider, point by point, the Prosecutor's specific historic "evidence" against Leon Trotsky, adduced as proof of his contention that

The conversion of the Trotskyite groups into groups of diversionists and murderers operating on the instructions of foreign secret services and of General Staffs of aggressors merely crowns the struggle Trotskyism has been waging against the working class and the Party, against Lenin and Leninism, for decades. . . . The whole history of the political activities of the Trotskyites represents an uninterrupted chain of betrayals of the cause of the working class, of the cause of socialism. (PR 466-7.)

§ 223. Immediately after the foregoing passage in his summation in the second trial, Vyshinsky says:

> As we know, in 1904 Trotsky came out with a most despicable pamphlet entitled "Our Political Tasks." This pamphlet was packed full of filthy insinuations against our great teacher, the leader of the international proletariat, Lenin, against the great Leninist teaching regarding the paths of the Bolshevik victory, the victory of the toilers, the victory of socialism. In this pamphlet Trotsky squirts venomous saliva at the great ideas of Marxism-Leninism. With it he tried to poison the proletariat, tried to turn the proletariat from the path of irreconcilable class struggle, slandered the proletariat, slandered the proletarian revolution, slandered Bolshevism, slandered Lenin by calling him "Maximilian," after Robespierre, the hero of the French bourgeois revolution, and thereby tried to humiliate the great leader of the international proletariat. (PR 467.)

A copy, in Russian, of this "despicable pamphlet" was submitted to the Preliminary Commission (PC Exh. 4. Published by the Russian Social Democratic Workers' Party. Geneva: Party Print Shop. 1904.) We quote from Trotsky's testimony concerning it:

> It is a theoretical and political pamphlet, and it is not objectionable. I believe it has many errors in it. . . . I can find in this book chapters which are not so bad. There are chapters which are wrong. You know, as a young man I characterized Lenin in . . . a spirit absolutely not found in the relations between him and me. But . . . by my subsequent attitude—I corrected the error. But it is not objectionable, and nothing abominable. (PC 59–60.)

Before discussing this work, we briefly summarize the events which led to its writing. Following the ideological split in the Russian Social Democratic Party at the London Congress of 1903, there was a bitter controversy in the Russian Social Democratic movement over questions of party policy. Lenin stood for strong centralization, which Trotsky and others opposed. Trotsky was not alone in attacking Lenin as a "Jacobin" at this period. Martov and Axelrod had preceded him, and Lenin had answered with the pamphlet, "One Step Forward, Two Steps Back." Part of "Our Political Tasks" deals with this pamphlet, which was also criticized by Rosa Luxemburg in the new *Iskra* (No. 69).

Such, in briefest summary, was the political background of this work of Trotsky, which was written in the harsh polemical style of the period. Trotsky contends that the Party should lead the proletariat, rather than act for it. In speaking of how the Party leadership acts, so to speak, behind the backs of the workers, he quotes as follows from Lenin's pamphlet, "What's To Be Done,"

> "We . . . greeted the illegal Zemstvo convention, encouraging (sic!!!) the Zemstvo workers to fight rather than humbly petition. . . . We encouraged statisticians who protested, and reproved (sic!) statisticians who were scabs" (p.51),

and remarks,

> That's what "we" were doing with Comrade Lenin! Another step and "we" would begin to "encourage" solar and lunar eclipse. (pp. 51–2.)

In the section, "Problems of Organization," Trotsky argues that Lenin's plan of organization would result not in a party but in a Social Democratic factory in which most of the members would be revolutionists, and that further the plan does not provide for the training of leaders. In discussing democracy within the Party, he argues that

> the régime of barracks cannot be the régime of our Party, just as the factory cannot be its model. (p. 75.)

He accuses Lenin of intellectual inconsistency, revolting demagogy, and cynicism. In this connection he says:

> Marxism for him is not a method of scientific investigation which imposes heavy theoretical obligations, but a floor-rag to be used when you must wipe up your traces, a white screen against which to parade your grandeur, a collapsible yardstick when you have to show your Party conscience. (p. 75.)

The third and last section begins with this quotation from Lenin's pamphlet, "One Step Forward, Two Steps Back":

> "A Jacobin closely allied with an organization of the proletariat conscious of its class interests, that is what a Social Democrat is." (p. 90.)

Trotsky argues that a Jacobin is a bourgeois radical, idealistic, rationalist, Utopian. True, he says, the Jacobins

> were intransigent, and so are we. The Jacobins knew a terrible political accusation, which they expressed with the word *moderation*. We know the accusation of *opportunism*. But these intransigencies are qualitatively different: We place between ourselves and opportunism the wedge of the theoretical apparatus of proletarian class ideology, and each full blow of the class struggle drives this wedge deeper and deeper. We purge ourselves in this way of op-

portunism. . . . The Jacobins placed between themselves and moderation the iron of the guillotine. The logic of the class movement was against them and they sought to behead it. Madness! The hydra's heads kept multiplying, while the heads devoted to the ideas of virtue and truth grew fewer with every day. . . . The guillotine was only a mechanical instrument of political suicide, and the suicide itself was the fatal result of their hopeless historical position: the heralds of equality on the basis of private property, the announcers of universal morality within the framework of class exploitation. (p. 94.)

There is no doubt, says Trotsky,

that the entire international movement of the proletariat would have been accused by the Revolutionary Tribunal of moderation—and that Marx's leonine head would have been the first to fall under the blow of the guillotine. Nor is there any doubt that any attempt to introduce the methods of Jacobinism into the class movement of the proletariat is and will be the purest opportunism, the sacrifice of the historic interests of the proletariat to the fiction of temporary success. (p. 95.)

He proceeds to attack Lenin's policies as Jacobin, and says that Robespierre's political axiom,

"Je ne connais que deux partis, celui des bons et celui des mauvais citoyens" is engraved on the heart of Maximilian Lenin. (p. 96)

He refers to Lenin's Jacobinism as the

secret of his failures and the cause of his petty suspiciousness. (p. 98.)

He calls Lenin "the leader of the reactionary wing of our Party" (p. 98), accuses him of "a theoretical attempt upon the class character of our Party" (p. 98), and indirectly refers to him as "a nimble statistician and slovenly lawyer" (p. 100). He charges Lenin's followers from the Urals with preaching not "dictatorship of the proletariat, but dictatorship over the proletariat" (p. 102). Trotsky does not believe that such a policy will succeed,

> for it is all too obvious that the proletariat capable of dictatorship over society will not tolerate dictatorship over itself. The working class, having seized the helm, will undoubtedly have in its ranks many political invalids and in its baggage train much ideological lumber. In the era of dictatorship it will be necessary for it, as it is necessary for it now, to purge its consciousness of false theories, of bourgeois relics, to free its ranks from political phrasemongers and revolutionary diehards. . . . But this complicated task cannot be obviated by placing over the proletariat a well chosen group of people, or better still, one person empowered with the right to dismiss and degrade. (p. 105.)

The attitude of the Ural group, Trotsky believes, is not a local "absurdity" but rather a significant thing:

> Did not the Siberian delegation, long before the appearance of the Ural document, write that, according to the logic of a "state of siege," the hegemony of Social Democracy in the struggle for liberation meant the hegemony of one person over Social Democracy? And again, does not Lenin know who is being groomed for the central rôle in the system of Ural Social Democratic Boulangism? . . . he is silent on these matters so eloquently that it seems to all as if he were savoring his rôle in advance and privately preening himself. (p. 106.)

Such is the content and style of this "despicable pamphlet."
The Commission is not in the least concerned with the question whether Trotsky was or was not justified in his criticisms of Lenin, but only with the question whether or not the pamphlet bears out what Vyshinsky says about it. We note, in the first place, nothing in this pamphlet that could possibly be construed as a slander upon the proletariat or the proletarian revolution. We note that nothing in it can possibly be construed as an attempt to "poison the proletariat" or to turn it "from the path of irreconcilable class struggle." The quotations we have given above sufficiently disprove this charge. Nor is there anything to justify Vyshinsky's statement that Trotsky "squirts venomous saliva at the great ideas of Marxism-Leninism." The book attacks Lenin not on questions of theory but on questions of tactics; it does not attack Marx at all. Trotsky's method of attack upon Lenin, as the above quotations show, was not one of "filthy insinuation" but of harsh and forthright accusation. It was not exceptional in the polemics exchanged at the period among all tendencies in the Russian Revolutionary movement; nor is it likely to shock people today who are accustomed to the rough-and-tumble of political campaigns in democratic countries. And it is positively mild and polite in comparison with "polemics" of the official Soviet press of today as illustrated in several articles among our exhibits.

Lenin was not outdone by Trotsky in this field. Anyone who knows his works at all is aware that he was a master of harsh invective. In illustration we confine ourselves to two quotations cited by the Prosecutor himself, in discussing his next "historical proof," the August bloc:

Lenin wrote that this *bloc* was "built up on lack of principle, on hypocrisy and empty phrases." . . . Concerning Trotsky, Lenin wrote: "Such types are characteristic as the wreckage of yesterday's historical formations, or

systems, of the time when the mass working class movement in Russia was still sleeping." (PR 467.)

We do not know the source of these quotations; but Trotsky,
questioned on the first, said:

> I believe the style is absolutely Lenin's. He was right,
> the bloc was a sterile attempt, and Lenin did not play
> with the thing. He gave serious blows to his adversar-
> ies. (PC 60.)

We could quote even harsher characterizations from Lenin's
writings, but space does not permit. It is sufficient to state
here that between Trotsky and Lenin in the exchange the
honors were at least even.

§ 224. The abortive revolution of 1905 intervened between
the period of the controversy over "Jacobinism" and the
"August Bloc" of 1911–12. Vyshinsky omits all mention of
this revolution in discussing the Trotskyites' "uninterrupted
chain of betrayals of the cause of the working class, of the
cause of socialism" (PR 467). Trotsky, as president of the St.
Petersburg Soviet, led this revolutionary attempt and was
condemned to Siberian exile after it had failed; a chapter in
his political history which stands in sharp contradiction to
the Prosecutor's contention. And we note that Lenin, about
whom Trotsky had used in 1904 the harsh language quoted
above, said that

> the passage of the direction of the Soviet from Khrusta-
> lev to Trotsky will be an immense step forward.

§ 225. According to the Prosecutor,

> . . . In 1911–12, Trotsky also organized a *bloc* as he
> later organized the Trotskyite-Zinovievite *bloc;* he or-

ganized the so-called "August *bloc*" consisting of the
lackeys of capital, of Mensheviks, and those who had
been expelled from the ranks of the Bolshevik Party, of
flabby intellectuals, and the refuse of the working-class
movement. . . . (PR 467.)

We have cited above Vyshinsky's quotations from Lenin on
this bloc, and Trotsky's statement that Lenin was right in
refusing "to play with the thing." According to Trotsky, the
bloc was an attempt to bring together the Bolsheviks and
Mensheviks. He further testified that

> Lenin designated all reformists as lackeys of capitalism,
> and he named in such a manner the Mensheviks who
> participated in the conference. It is a question of political
> appreciation and not of criminal thought. (PC 61.)

The history of the August Bloc is given as follows by Lenin
and Zinoviev, in a pamphlet entitled "Socialism and War,"
written in August, 1915, and first published as a pamphlet in
the autumn of that year by the *Sozialdemokrat,* Geneva:

> The history of those Social-Democratic groups which
> struggle against our party is a history of breakdown and
> degeneration. In March, 1912, all of them, without excep-
> tion, "united" in reviling us. In August, 1912, however,
> when the so-called "August Bloc" against us was creat-
> ed, disintegration set in. Part of their groups split away.
> They were in no position to create a party and a Central
> Committee. What they created was an Organization
> Committee "for the re-establishment of unity." In real-
> ity, this Organization Committee proved an ineffective
> shield for the Liquidationist group in Russia. Through
> the whole period of a tremendous rising wave of the labor
> movement in Russia and of the mass strikes of 1912–1914,

the only group of the August Bloc which conducted work among the masses was *Nashe Zarya*, whose strength is in its liberal connections. At the beginning of 1914, the August Bloc was formally relinquished by the Lettish Social Democrats (the Polish Social Democrats did not belong to it), whereas Trotsky, one of the leaders of Bloc, relinquished it informally, having created his own separate group. (Lenin's Works, Vol. XVIII, p. 256. New York: International Publishers, 1930. "The only edition authorized by the V.I. Lenin Institute, Moscow.")

It is evident in this quotation, from a source by no means favorable to the August Bloc, that its purpose was "the reestablishment of unity"—even though Lenin and Zinoviev call it "a bloc against us." It is also evident that Lenin and Zinoviev, in writing about it in 1915, criticized it as politically ineffectual, not as criminal. It may be noted here that less than two years after the publication of this pamphlet, Lenin and Trotsky began that close collaboration which was to last until Lenin's death.

§ 226. The next "proof" in Vyshinsky's "historical connection" is as follows:

> In 1915 Trotsky came out in opposition to Lenin's doctrine of the possibility of the victory of socialism in one country. Thus he completely capitulated to capitalism over twenty years ago! (PR 468.)

It is impossible to examine this charge without going into the hotly contested question of "socialism in one country." Therefore the Commission wishes to state emphatically that it is not in the least interested in the question of the correctness or incorrectness of the theory that socialism can be built in a single isolated country, or of the opposite theory that socialist revolution in one country can not be successful unless it is supported by socialist revolutions in several of the more advanced countries. And it is certainly not concerned to show that Trotsky either was or was not right on this question or any other in so far as he agreed with Lenin. But since Vyshinsky, not only in the passage quoted but in others as well (e.g., pp. 475–477) imputed to Lenin the idea that socialism can be successfully established in a single country, and represented Trotsky's alleged opposition to Lenin on this question as a link in the chain of historical proofs against him, it becomes necessary to establish by reference to the historical sources (1) what in fact was Lenin's attitude toward "socialism in one country," and (2) whether the charge that Trotsky opposed Lenin on this issue is true or rests upon falsification.

We begin by pointing out that even if Lenin had advanced such a doctrine in 1915 as Vyshinsky attributes to him, and Trotsky had opposed it, the Prosecutor's second sentence would still be a *non sequitur,* and a false *non sequitur* at that. Capitulation to capitalism is by no means a necessary alternative to the acceptance of the idea that socialism is possible in a single country. Moreover, the most superficial examination of Trotsky's voluminous writings on the question shows that he has always opposed to the idea of socialism in a single country the idea that socialism can ultimately triumph only on an international arena. And it is precisely on this ground that Stalin himself attacked him, as will be seen in the subsequent quotations.

This controversy, which had an importance by no means merely theoretical, began in 1924. Involved in it was the whole policy, internal and external, of the Soviet Union. It is no part of our task either to trace its development or judge its merits. Our sole interest, as we have already said, is to establish whether or not Lenin advanced the doctrine of victorious socialism in one country and whether Trotsky "came out against" it.

In December, 1924, Stalin published a pamphlet entitled, "The October Revolution and the Tactics of the Russian Communists," in which he maintained that the building of socialism in a single country was possible, and cited Lenin as authority for this idea. This pamphlet followed one published eight months earlier, in April, under the title "Foundations of Leninism," in which Stalin had said that

> It used to be supposed that the victory of socialism in one country alone would be impossible, the assumption being that the conquest of the bourgeoisie could only be achieved by the united action of the proletarians of all advanced countries, or at any rate in the majority of these. This contention no longer fits the facts. We must now set out by assuming the possibility of such a victory; for the varying speed of social evolution in different capitalist countries (proceeding in some, under imperialist conditions, by leaps and bounds); the development of catastrophic conflicts as the outcome of imperialist rivalries, inevitably culminating in wars; the growth of the revolutionary movement in all countries throughout the world—these factors, working together, make proletarian victories in separate countries not merely possible, but necessary. . . .
>
> But the overthrow of the power of the bourgeoisie and the establishment of the power of the proletariat in one country alone does not, per se, mean the complete victory of socialism. The chief task, the organization of socialist production, still lies ahead. Can this task be performed, can the final victory of socialism be gained, in one country alone, and without the joint efforts of the proletarians in several of the most advanced countries? No, this is out of the question. The history of the Russian Revolution shows that the proletarian strength of one country alone can overthrow

the bourgeoisie of that country. But for the final victory
of socialism, for the organization of socialist production, the strength of one country (especially a peasant
country, such as Russia) does not suffice. For this, the
united strength of the proletarians in several of the
most advanced countries is needed . . . ("Leninism,"
by Joseph Stalin. New York: International Publishers,
1928. pp. 52–53.)

This second paragraph is even stronger in the second edition, where it contains the words:

Does this mean that the workers in one country alone,
unaided, can definitively install socialism, guaranteed
against intervention, guaranteed against a restoration of
the old regime? No, certainly not. For that, the victory
of the revolution, if not everywhere, at least in several
countries, will be requisite. . . . (*Ibid.*, p. 109.)

In "Problems of Leninism," dated January 25, 1926, Stalin
speaks of these two paragraphs as "two formulations of the
problem of the victory of socialism in one country alone,"*
and says that the second formulation (he quotes paragraph
two, first edition)

was directed against some of the critics of Leninism,
against the Trotskyists who declared that the dictatorship of the proletariat "could not be maintained against
conservative Europe" in one country alone, and in the
absence of a proletarian victory in other lands. In view
of its purpose (and only in view of this), that formula-

---

* The interpretation obviously indicated by the text is that Stalin was
dealing with two stages of socialist victory, the initial and the ulti-
mate.

tion was adequate in April, 1924, and doubtless had its uses. (*Ibid.*, p. 53.)

What was wrong with the formulation, he said, was that

it may be interpreted as implying that the organization of a socialist society by the unaided forces of one country is impossible—a manifest error. (*Ibid.*, p. 53.)

Therefore, he says, he rectified it in December, 1924, in "The October Revolution and the Tactics of the Russian Communists."

In this December pamphlet, as we have said, Stalin quotes Lenin as authority for the idea that the victory of socialism is possible in an isolated country. One of the passages upon which he bases himself is to be found in Lenin's article, "The United States of Europe Slogan," first published in Switzerland in the *Sozialdemokrat* (central organ of the Bolshevik Party at the time), August 23, 1915. Before quoting the relevant passage, it is necessary to give the historical background of the article. At a conference in Berne of the Foreign Sections of the Bolshevik Party, February 16–March 4, 1915, the question was raised of adopting "The United States of Europe" as a slogan. But

the discussion took a one-sided political turn and it was decided to postpone the question pending an analysis of the economic side of it in the press. (Lenin, Collected Works, Vol. XVIII, p. 145. New York: International Publishers.)

Lenin's article of August 23 explained why the slogan, in the existing economic conditions, was incorrect; that

. . . if the United States of Europe slogan, conceived in connection with a revolutionary overthrow of the three most reactionary monarchies of Europe, headed by Russia, is entirely impregnable as a political slogan, there still remains the most important question of its economic content and meaning. From the point of view of the economic conditions of imperialism, *i.e.*, capital export and division of the world between the "progressive" and "civilized" colonial powers, the United States of Europe under capitalism is either impossible or reactionary. (*Ibid.*, pp. 269–70.)

After setting forth the reasons for this conclusion, the article goes on to state that the United States of the World (not of Europe alone), is a state form of national unification and freedom envisaged in connection with socialism. Then follows the passage containing the reference to the victory of socialism in one country (italics ours):

. . . we think of [the United States of the World] as becoming a reality only when the full victory of Communism will have brought about the total disappearance of any state, including its democratic form. As a separate slogan, however, the United States of the World would hardly be a correct one, first because it coincides with Socialism, *second, because it could be erroneously interpreted to mean that the victory of Socialism in one country* is impossible; it could also create misconceptions as to the relations of such a country to others.

Unequal economic and political development is an indispensable law of capitalism. It follows that the victory of Socialism is, *at the beginning,* possible in a few capitalist countries, even in one, taken separately. The victorious proletariat of that country, having expropriated the capitalists and organized Socialist production at home, would rise against the rest of the capitalist world, attracting the oppressed classes of other countries, raising among them revolts against the capitalists, launching, in case of necessity, armed forces against the exploiting classes and their states. The political form of a society in which the proletariat is victorious, in which it has overthrown the bourgeoisie, will be a democratic republic, centralizing ever more the forces of the proletariat of a given nation or nations in the struggle against the states that have not yet gone over to Socialism. It is impossible to annihilate classes without a dictatorship of the oppressed class, the proletariat. It is impossible freely to unite the nations in Socialism without a more or less prolonged and stubborn struggle of the Socialist republics against the other states. (*Ibid.*, pp. 271–2.)

From this second paragraph, Stalin, in his December pamphlet, deduces Lenin's

own theory of the proletarian revolution, which is: that socialism can be victorious in one country alone even when that country is in a condition of backward capitalist development. ("Leninism," p. 191.)

We are obliged to note here that this formulation of Lenin's "own" theory of the proletarian revolution is in distinct contrast to Stalin's formulation of that theory in his April pamphlet. We quote from the second edition, from the word "requisite" in the passage quoted on page 337, to the end:

. . . That is why a country in which the revolution has triumphed must not look upon itself as an independent magnitude, but as an auxiliary, as a means for hastening the victory of the proletariat of other lands. Lenin expressed this idea pithily as follows:
"In any country, the victorious revolution must do its utmost to develop, support, and awaken the revolution

in all other countries." (*Works*, Russian edition. Vol. XV, p. 502.) [Citation in original.]

Such, in broad outline, are the characteristics of Lenin's theory of the proletarian revolution. ("Leninism," p. 109.)

In the December pamphlet Stalin maintains that Trotsky's theory of the permanent revolution* conflicts with Lenin's theory of the proletarian revolution as Stalin defines it in that pamphlet. He quotes from Trotsky's pamphlet, "The Program of Peace,"† the following passage:

The only concrete and historical objection to the slogan of the United States of Europe was formulated by the *Sozialdemokrat*. Here we read: "Irregularity in political and economic development is the supreme law of capitalism." From this the *Sozialdemokrat* concluded that socialism may be victorious in one country alone, and that, consequently, it was not necessary to make the dictatorship of the proletariat dependent in each

---

* Trotsky's theory, briefly stated, was that because of the weakness of the Russian bourgeoisie, and the peculiar contradictions in the Russian economy, the bourgeois tasks of the revolution could not be accomplished either under bourgeois leadership or under that of an independent peasant movement, but only under the hegemony of the proletariat; and that the proletariat could not but proceed immediately to undertake the socialist tasks of the revolution; but that the socialist revolution in one country could not succeed unless it was followed by a series of socialist revolutions in other countries. This perspective of the immediate assumption of power by the proletariat without an intervening period of bourgeois capitalism, was labeled "Trotskyism" by Bolsheviks and Mensheviks alike. (See Trotsky's biography, App. 2.)

† Annotation No. 74 concerning this pamphlet in Trotsky's Collected Works, Vol. III, Part I says: "The pamphlet 'Program of Peace' represents an elaboration of articles published by L.D. Trotsky in *Nashe Slovo* [Paris] during 1915 and 1916" (p. 387).

country upon the inauguration of the United States of Europe. It is an indisputable fact that the development of capitalism is irregular. But this irregularity is, itself, irregular! Certainly the degree of capitalist development is not the same in Great Britain, in Austria, in Germany, and in France. Nevertheless, in comparison with Africa or Asia, these countries represent capitalist "Europe" ripe for the social revolution. No country can afford to "wait" for the others to join in the struggle; this is an elementary truth which it is well to reiterate, so that the idea of simultaneous international action be not replaced by the idea of international postponement and inaction. Without awaiting the others, we have to begin and continue the struggle on a national scale, urged on by the conviction that our initiative will set the ball rolling in other lands. Should this not happen, it would be futile to expect (and historical experience no less than theoretical considerations are there to prove the contention), for instance, that Revolutionary Russia could hold its own in face of a conservative Europe, or that a socialist Germany could be maintained in isolation in the midst of a capitalist world. (Trotsky, Collected Works, Russian edition, Vol. III, Part I, pp. 89–90; "Leninism," p. 193.)

Here, says Stalin, we have

. . . the theory that the triumph of socialism must take place simultaneously in the leading countries of Europe. This theory conflicts with the Leninist theory of revolution and the victory of socialism in one country. ("Leninism," p. 193.)

And here, apparently, we have the source of Vyshinsky's charge that

In 1915 Trotsky came out in opposition to Lenin's doctrine of the possibility of the victory of socialism in one country.

It seems to us that the passage Stalin quotes from Trotsky is in very close agreement with Stalin's April version of Lenin's theory of the proletarian revolution. It is also, we think, very close to Lenin's statement of 1915. Lenin says that the proletariat, victorious in one country, "will rise against the rest of the capitalist world, attracting the oppressed classes of other countries, raising among them revolts against the capitalists . . ." Trotsky says that "without awaiting the others, we have to begin and to continue the struggle on a national scale, urged on by the conviction that our initiative will set the ball rolling in other lands." And Stalin, in his pamphlet of April, 1924, says that because the unaided workers of one country can not definitively install socialism, ". . . the fostering of revolution, the support of revolution, in other countries, is incumbent upon the country where the revolution has triumphed."

In that same pamphlet from which Stalin quotes, and which was directed not at Lenin but at the Socialist patriots of the warring countries, Trotsky said that

the unification of Europe . . . through an agreement between capitalist governments is a Utopia.

but that its

economic unification . . . is becoming a revolutionary task of the European proletariat. (Trotsky. Collected Works, Russian edition, Vol. III, p. 85.)

He attacks the "Messianism" of such Socialist patriots as Vaillant (who "to his dying day considered France the promised land of social revolution; . . . stood for national defense to the end") and Lensch. Trotsky says:

> If the victorious revolution were really conceivable within the boundaries of a single more developed nation, this Messianism together with the program of national defense would have some relative historical justification. But as a matter of fact it is inconceivable. To fight for the preservation of a national basis of revolution by such methods as undermine the international ties of the proletariat, actually means to undermine the revolution itself, *which can begin on a national basis but which cannot be completed on that basis* under the present economic, military, and political interdependence of the European states, which was never before revealed so forcefully as during the present war. (*Ibid.*, pp. 90 ff.) (Italics ours.)

We find nothing whatever in this article to bear out Vyshinsky's charge. On the other hand, we find that (1) Lenin's article on "The United States of Europe Slogan" can be taken to mean that socialism can be definitively established in a single country only if one leaves out the crucial phrase "at the beginning" and wrenches the quotation from its context in the matter under discussion; (2) that Trotsky and Lenin are in essential agreement that the socialist revolution can *begin* on a national basis, but that it will be completed internationally; (3) that Trotsky's contention that the revolution, to be successful, must be international was not new in 1915 "in opposition to Lenin," as the Prosecutor's remark might be taken to imply, but goes back to the period before the revolution of 1905; and that Stalin himself indicates that it was not new in his pamphlet of December, 1924, where he quotes from Trotsky's book, "Our Revolution," published in 1906, in order to show that Trotsky's theory of the permanent revolution had nothing in common with Lenin's "own theory of the proletarian revolution" (Stalin's December version). ("Leninism," p. 192.)

Since the Prosecutor, as we have said, lays great stress on Trotsky's alleged opposition to Lenin's alleged doctrine of the possibility of the victory of socialism in one country, it is pertinent here to determine what really was Lenin's conception of the socialist revolution. Since much is made of the early disagreements between Lenin and Trotsky, we begin by quoting from an article, "Social Democracy and the Provisional Revolutionary Government," which was edited and approved by Lenin and published in the Bolshevik paper, *Vpered*, of which he was editor-in-chief, on March 26 and 30, 1905:

> If the democratic revolution succeeds in Russia then the revolutionary conflagration will set fire to Europe.... The European workers will rise in turn ... ; then the revolutionary rising of Europe will have a retroactive effect upon Russia. The epoch of several revolutionary years will become an epoch of several revolutionary decades. ("Leninsky Sbornik," Vol. XXVI, pp. 177–8. Moscow: Gosizdat, 1934. A publication of the V.I. Lenin Institute.)

Upon leaving for Russia in April, 1917, Lenin wrote a "Farewell Letter to the Swiss Workers," in which he said:

> The great honor of beginning the *series of revolutions* caused with objective inevitability by the war has fallen to the Russian proletariat. But the idea that the Russian proletariat is the chosen revolutionary proletariat among the workers of the world is absolutely alien to us. We know full well that the proletariat of Russia is less organized, less prepared, and less class-conscious than the proletariat of other countries. It is not its special

qualities but rather the special coincidence of historical circumstances that has made the proletariat of Russia *for a certain, perhaps very short,* time, the vanguard of the revolutionary proletariat of the whole world. Russia is a peasant country, one of the most backward of Europe. Socialism cannot triumph there immediately. But the present character of the country . . . may make our revolution a *prologue to the world Socialist Revolution,* a step forward in that direction. . . .

The Russian proletariat single-handed cannot bring the Socialist revolution to a victorious conclusion. But it can give the Russian revolution a mighty sweep such as would create most favorable conditions for a Socialist revolution, and, in a sense, start it. . . . The objective circumstances of the imperialist war make it certain that the revolution will not be limited to the *first stage* of the Russian revolution, that the revolution will not be limited to Russia. (Lenin's Collected Works, Vol. XX, Book I, pp. 85–86, and p. 87. New York: International Publishers.) (Our emphasis.)

If it should be said that Lenin changed his position after reaching Russia, the following quotations are decisive.

During the period between the February and October Revolutions of 1917, a resolution (On the Current Moment) written by Lenin and adopted at the April (May) conference of the Bolshevik Party, declared:

The proletariat of Russia . . . cannot set itself the goal of an immediate realization of the socialist transformation. (Lenin's Collected Works, Vol. XX, p. 281. Russ. Ed., 1935.)

In spite of this fact, the resolution continued, the proletariat can not renounce its leading rôle in the coming revolution, or fail to advocate "the urgency of a number of practical mature steps toward socialism" (*Ibid.*, p. 281). In his speech in defense of the resolution Lenin emphasized that

> The principal question taken up in the resolution is what tasks will confront the Russian proletariat in case the world-wide movement brings us face to face with a social revolution. (*Ibid.*, p. 280.)

In September of the same year, in an article "Will the Bolsheviks Be Able to Hold Power," Lenin said:

> There is no power on earth which can prevent the Bolsheviks, *if they do not let themselves be frightened* and succeed in seizing power, from holding it until the triumph of the world-wide socialist revolution. (Lenin's Collected Works, Vol. XIV, Pt. 2, p. 253. Russ. Ed. State Publishers, 1921.)

After the victory of the October Revolution, Lenin repeatedly emphasized the vital need of the Soviet power for the support of revolutions elsewhere. In a "Letter to the American Workers," in 1918, he said:

> We know that circumstances have pushed to the fore *our* Russian detachment of the socialist proletariat, . . . We are in a besieged fortress, until other detachments of the international socialist revolution come to our aid. (Works, Vol. XX, pp. 188–89. Russ. Ed., 1935.)

On March 7 of that year, he said:

> Without a revolution in Germany we shall perish. (Works, Vol. XV, p. 123. Russ. Ed., State Publishers, 1925.)

And again in April:

We will perish unless we are able to hold out until we have the mighty support of the insurrectionary workers of other countries. (*Ibid.*, p. 174.)

In March, 1919:

The existence of the Soviet Republic side by side with imperialist states for any length of time is inconceivable. (*Ibid.*, Vol. XVI, p. 102.)

In November, 1920:

As long as capitalism and socialism exist side by side, we cannot live peacefully—one or the other will triumph in the end. . . . At present we have only a respite in the war. (Works, Vol. XVII, p. 398. State Publishers, 1923.)

In July, 1921, at the third congress of the Comintern, Lenin said, referring to the failure of the German Revolution:

It was clear to us that without aid from the international world revolution, a victory of the proletarian revolution is impossible. Even prior to the revolution, as well as after it, we thought that the revolution would occur either immediately or anyway very soon in other more advanced capitalist countries, otherwise we should perish. Notwithstanding this belief, we did our utmost to preserve the Soviet system under any circumstances and at all costs, *because we knew we were working not only for ourselves but also for the international revolution.* (Works, Vol. XVIII, Part 1, p. 297. State Publishers, 1925.)

These quotations could be multiplied many times over. However, since the position they indicate was a commonplace of the whole movement until the latter part of 1924 (it was reaffirmed by Stalin in his April pamphlet of that year, as the quotations we have given indicate), it is not necessary. We give only two further quotations from Lenin, the first of which is among those cited by Stalin in support of his December version of Lenin's theory of the proletarian revolution:

> In actual fact, all the means of large-scale production are in the hands of the State, and the powers of the State are in the hands of the proletariat; there is the alliance of this same proletariat with the many millions of middle and poor peasants; there is the assured leadership of these peasants by the proletariat; and so on, and so forth. Have we not already, here and now, all the means for making out of the cooperatives (which, in the past, we have treated as trading concerns, and which, even today, we have a certain justification for treating similarly under the new economic policy), out of the cooperatives alone—have we not all the means requisite for the establishment of a fully socialized society? Of course we have not yet established a socialized society; but we have all the means requisite for its establishment. (Lenin, Collected Works, Vol. XVIII, Part II, p. 140. Russ. Ed.)

This article was published after Lenin's death. Therefore, even if it be interpreted as indicating that Lenin at the end of his life changed his position on the question of socialism in one country, it can hardly be adduced in support of the theory of a continuous struggle between Lenin and Trotsky on this question. Since in the same article Lenin refers to "our duty to fight for our position on an international scale," it seems probable that he had no idea of reversing the earlier position defined by Stalin in his April pamphlet—also, it should be noted, published after Lenin's death. Moreover, it seems most unlikely that Lenin would have reversed himself on a question of such fundamental importance casually and by implication only, in an article devoted to another subject—the Cooperatives.

Our last quotation from Lenin on this subject is one which is used by the Prosecutor himself in speaking of Pyatakov's alleged opposition to Lenin in 1918:

> This was the year when Lenin said: "Better suffer and bear and put up with infinitely great national and state humiliation and burdens *and remain at our post as the socialist unit which events had cut off from the main body of the socialist army and which is compelled to wait until the socialist revolution in other countries comes to its aid.*" (PR 476.)

The italics are ours; and we confess to a certain surprise at finding this particular quotation (which sounds authentic) in a paragraph immediately following the accusation that Pyatakov had opposed Lenin's thesis on the possibility of building socialism in one country.

A careful study of the relevant historical material has convinced this Commission that Lenin's actual view on this subject was that while the Socialist revolution could triumph initially in a single country, it could not be ultimately successful without the aid of successful socialist revolutions elsewhere; but that the initial victory of socialism in one country, and the organization of socialist production in that country, would stimulate the oppressed masses of other countries to rise against the class in power, aided by the proletariat of that country in which the revolution had already succeeded. We are not in the least concerned with the correctness of Lenin's view. What does concern us is (1) that the Prosecutor falsified Lenin's position; and (2) that Trotsky, far from opposing Lenin on the question of "socialism in one country" was in essential agreement with him. Obviously, if Trotsky had not held this position he would have opposed instead of vigorously supporting the October Revolution.

§ 227. It is significant that Vyshinsky, in his attempt to establish the "uninterrupted chain of betrayals of the cause of the working class, of the cause of socialism" which he imputed to Trotsky, passed over in silence the universally known facts that Trotsky, as President of the Petrograd Soviet and Chairman of its Revolutionary Military Committee, led the October Insurrection; and that as Commissar of War he organized the Red Army and led it to victory in the Civil War. Since the present Soviet régime owes its existence to the success of the insurrection and the Civil War, and since it also considers itself a Socialist workers' state, it can not take the stand that those events in world history were of no benefit to the workers or to Socialism. Trotsky's rôle in those events may perhaps help to account for the Prosecutor's silence concerning them. The close collaboration of Lenin and Trotsky throughout this period and up until Lenin's death may also have had something to do with it; a supposition which gains weight from the fact that Vyshinsky mentioned Trotsky's relations with Lenin at that time only in such a way as to indicate that he continued his alleged struggle against Lenin. We quote:

> Jointly with Trotsky, Pyatakov rose against Lenin in the stern days of Brest. Jointly with Trotsky, Pyatakov rose against Lenin at the time our Party was effecting the complicated swing toward the New Economic Policy. Jointly with Trotsky, Pyatakov opposed Lenin's plan to build socialism in our country, opposed the industrialization and collectivization of our country . . . (PR 477.)

Since these statements, although mainly directed against Pyatakov in the Prosecutor's summation, nevertheless constitute alleged historical proofs against Trotsky, we are obliged to include them in the specific charges whose truth or falsehood it is our duty to examine.

(1) The facts about Brest-Litovsk are well known. The majority of the Bolshevik leaders strongly opposed signing the terms proposed by the Germans, and the more extreme among them, led by Bukharin, were in favor of continuing the war as a revolutionary war. Both Lenin and Trotsky believed that a revolutionary war was impossible. Lenin favored trying to delay the negotiations, and in case of a German ultimatum, capitulating immediately. Trotsky favored delaying negotiations, and in case of an ultimatum, declaring the war at an end but refusing to sign the peace treaty. On January 22, 1918, the Central Committee adopted Trotsky's proposal. On February 14, the Central Executive Committee approved the action of the Brest-Litovsk delegation, headed by Trotsky, taken in pursuance of this decision. The Germans answered by announcing the resumption of the state of war. Lenin thereupon favored immediate capitulation, while Trotsky favored waiting until an actual German offensive began, in order to demonstrate to the workers of Germany and other countries that the capitulation was forced by German aggression. On February 3, new and extremely humiliating terms were offered by the Germans. Lenin held that they must be accepted, and Trotsky abstained from voting in order that he might secure a majority in the Central Committee. On March 3 the Soviet delegation signed the treaty without reading it. On October 23, Trotsky, in a public speech before representatives of the Soviet government, declared that Lenin had been right in his policy on Brest-Litovsk, and the others wrong. Among these others was Stalin. At the session of the Central Committee, February 1 (January 19), 1918, he said:

> . . . The way out of the difficult situation was provided us by the middle point of view—the position of Trotsky.

(Protocols of the C.C. for the year 1917, p. 214. State Publishers, 1929; "Stalin School of Falsification," p. 193.)

Again, at the session of February 23, after the Germans had resumed hostilities:

> COMRADE STALIN: We need not sign, but we must begin peace negotiations.
> COMRADE LENIN: . . . Stalin is wrong in saying that we need not sign. These conditions must be signed. If you do not sign them, you will sign the death sentence of the Soviet Power within three weeks. (*Ibid.*, p. 249; p. 194.)

That Trotsky disagreed with Lenin concerning Brest-Litovsk is true. That he "rose against" Lenin is no more true of Trotsky than of Stalin, who endorsed Trotsky's position. The fact is that a majority of the Central Committee opposed Lenin's position until the German offensive forced its adoption.

(2) There was no dispute between Trotsky and Lenin on the subject of the New Economic Policy, known as the Nep. This policy was adopted at the Tenth Party Congress, in 1921. Except for the "Workers' Opposition" headed by Shliapnikov and Kollontai, there were no differences of opinion. In fact, Shliapnikov attacked both Lenin and Trotsky indiscriminately as the authors of the Nep. At the Congress, Trotsky emphasized that he not only welcomed the new policy proposed by Lenin, but that he had himself proposed the substance of it a year earlier. (Speech of Leon Trotsky, Minutes of the Tenth Party Congress, p. 146. Russ. Ed. State Publishers, 1921.) At the Third Congress of the Communist International, which followed the Tenth Party Congress, Trotsky and Lenin jointly defended the Nep against the criticism of the Workers' Opposition. Because of Trotsky's opposition to Lenin on the Trade Union question, the world press had reported that he opposed Lenin on the Nep. Trotsky referred to these reports

at the Third Congress of the International and declared his solidarity with Lenin. (*Protokoll des III. Weltkongresses der Kommunistischen Internationale, Moskou, 22 Juni bis 12 Juli 1921.* Hamburg, 1921. pp. 782 ff.)

Since the Nep was adopted at the Tenth Party Congress, it seems useful here to quote the following passage from Lenin's closing speech at that Congress, in summing up the dispute on the trade unions:

> The Workers' Opposition said: "Lenin and Trotsky will unite." Trotsky, taking the floor, replied: "Whoever does not understand that it is necessary to unite is going against the Party; of course we will unite because we are Party men." I supported Trotsky. To be sure, Trotsky and I have differed. When more or less equal groupings arise in the Central Committee, the Party decides, and decides in such a way that we unite according to the will and directives of the Party. That is the announcement with which Trotsky and I went to the Miners' Congress and have come here. . . . (Lenin, Collected Works, Vol. XVIII, Part 1, p. 121. State Publishers, 1925.)

We find that there is no historical basis whatever for Vyshinsky's statement that Trotsky "rose against Lenin at the time when our Party was effecting the complicated swing towards the New Economic Policy." Trotsky did not oppose the Nep. If Vyshinsky's statement, on the other hand, be taken to refer to the dispute over the trade unions, the above quotation from Lenin sufficiently indicates the facts.

(3) The charge that Trotsky opposed the industrialization and collectivization of Russia is without the slightest foundation in fact. Indeed, the precise opposite is true. We refer our readers to Chapter XXIII of this report, and also to the Platform of the Opposition referred to therein ("The Real Situation in Russia").

§ 228. The Prosecutor claimed, as a proof of the progression of "Trotskyism" in the direction of a program of capitalist restoration, that Trotsky

in 1922, proposed that our industrial enterprises, our trusts, be permitted to mortgage our property, including our basic capital, to private capitalists in order to obtain credits, which the Soviet state really needed at that time. (PR 469.)

Here, as in other instances—notably the charge that Trotsky opposed Lenin's alleged doctrine of the possibility of socialism in one country—Vyshinsky cites no documentary evidence in support of his historical "proof." We have queried Trotsky on this matter; and in reply he states that the Prosecutor evidently refers to a letter he wrote to the Politburo during a discussion connected with the inauguration of the New Economic Policy, which was never published, and which no doubt remains in the archives of the Politburo. The question had arisen, What should be the relationship between the industrial enterprises and the banks in the sphere of credit operations? It was proposed that industrial enterprises be permitted to mortgage to the banks only their floating capital. In answer to Trotsky's question, "Why?" Rudzutak (now imprisoned) said that the mortgaging of fixed capital could signify the beginning of the de-nationalization of the means of production. Trotsky pointed out—and the next day put in writing—that the banks and the industries were both state property, and that, since private capital could play only a subordinate rôle limited by the state, the relation between the factories and the banks was a question not of ownership, but of the state's bookkeeping; that the distinction between fixed and floating capital had no importance for nationalization, since both were state property; and also that since in the backward industries fixed capital might represent as little as twenty-five per cent of the total, whereas in important and highly organized industries it might represent as much as seventy to ninety per cent, to permit only floating capital to be mortgaged would be to create an absurd situation in which the most important and modern factories would be able to borrow the least money. He therefore recommended that in this question the distinction between floating and fixed capital be abandoned and that industries be permitted to mortgage their whole capital up to a certain level—say, twenty-five per cent. The matter was never publicly agitated in any way, and the actual later development proceeded largely along the line suggested by Trotsky.

A fact which is of public record, and which shows how little truth there is in the Prosecutor's assertion that

> . . . this proposal of Trotsky's was a step towards the return to the rule of the capitalists (PR 469)

is that in December, 1922, the Central Committee entrusted to Trotsky the responsibility of reporting to the Fourth Congress of the Comintern on the economic development of Soviet Russia and the perspectives of world revolution. In the conspectus of this report, which is to be found in Vol. XII of his Collected Works (Russ. Ed. pp. 346–56), Trotsky showed that the state managed 4,000 enterprises with an average of 207 workers in each, whereas private capitalists had been permitted to lease some 2,000, with an average of seventeen workers; and that whereas 75 per cent of industrial credit was utilized by state enterprises and 20 per cent by the cooperatives, no more than 5 per cent was utilized by private enterprises. He said:

> The affirmation of the Social-Democrats on the "capitulation" of the Soviet state before capitalism presents thus an obvious and brutal deformation of reality. . . . (Paragraph 14)

There is not the slightest reason to believe that the State's accumulation will grow more slowly than that of private capitalists and that private capitalists will thereby issue victorious in the fight. (Paragraph 16)

§ 229. Vyshinsky's statement that in 1926–27 the Trotskyites

carried their struggle against the leadership of our Party, against the Soviet government, into the streets or at least tried to (PR 470)

is so vague that it is hardly worthy of note except for its complete identification of the Stalinist leadership with the government—since Trotsky and the Opposition were quite as much a part of the Bolshevik Party at that time as Stalin and his followers. Presumably Vyshinsky's reference is to the placards, with their slogans, carried by the Opposition in the parade of November, 1927, celebrating the tenth anniversary of the Revolution. The slogans were as follows: "Fulfill Lenin's testament!" "Turn the Fire on the Right—Against the Nepman, the Kulak, and the Bureaucrat!" "For Genuine Workers' Democracy!" "Against Opportunism, against Splits—For the Unity of the Party of Lenin!" "For the Central Committee of Lenin!" (PC 422.) No argument is needed to show that if, and only if, opposition within the Party to its controlling group was "open anti-Soviet crime," was the action of the Oppositionists in attempting to carry their banners in that parade counter-revolutionary.

§ 230. Vyshinsky's statement that

The Trotskyite-Zinovievite *bloc* of 1926 was a *bloc* which turned the edge of its struggle against the cause of socialism in our country and for capitalism has already been dealt with in Chapter XXIII of this report. We refer our readers to that chapter, and repeat that we are not concerned to determine who was right or wrong in the struggle between the majority and the Opposition. It is theoretically possible that in first opposing and later adopting, with an increased tempo, the economic plan offered by the Opposition, Stalin was a better judge of actual conditions than were the Oppositionists. But such speculations have nothing to do with the fact that the very measures proposed by the Opposition and later adopted by the régime were represented in the January trial as "counter-revolutionary"; as "a special form of diversion, a form of destructive acts against the dictatorship of the proletariat and the cause of socialist construction"; as a "special form of struggle against the Soviet state corresponding to the historical situation at that time"; and as a logical prelude to the particular crimes with which the accused were charged.

§ 231. "We must remember," said Vyshinsky, in his final argument in the January trial.

> that ten years ago Trotsky justified his defeatist position in regard to the U.S.S.R. by referring to the famous Clemenceau thesis. Trotsky then wrote: "We must restore the tactics of Clemenceau, who as is well known, rose against the French Government at the time when the Germans were 80 kms. from Paris." . . . it is not an accident that Trotsky and his accomplices advanced the Clemenceau thesis. They reverted to this thesis once again, but this time advancing it not as a theoretical proposition, but as a practical preparation, real preparation, in alliance with foreign intelligence services, for the defeat of the U.S.S.R. in war. (PR 497.)

In the August trial Vyshinsky referred to this same "thesis" as "historical support" of the testimony of David and

Berman-Yurin concerning Trotsky's "defeatism" in their alleged interviews with him in Copenhagen. (ZK 131.)

It is clear that the so-called Clemenceau thesis is advanced as one of the "historical connections" which serve as
"proof" of the charges against Trotsky—in this case proof
that as far back as 1926 he took a "defeatist" position from
which his alleged "practical preparation" for the defeat of
the U.S.S.R. logically followed. The implication is two-fold:
first that Trotsky was a defeatist in 1926, and, second, that
Clemenceau was a defeatist during the World War. Obviously, unless Clemenceau was a defeatist there is no point
whatever in the allegation that Trotsky was a defeatist in
citing his behavior as an example. (Incidentally, although
the Prosecutor put Trotsky's alleged argument in quotation
marks, he made no attempt at verification or documentation
of what Trotsky actually said in referring to Clemenceau.)

We quote from Trotsky's comment on the above passage
from Vyshinsky, in his closing argument before the Preliminary Commission:

> It is hard to believe that the text of this speech was
> printed in foreign languages, including the French. One
> would imagine that the French were not unastonished to
> learn that Clemenceau, during the war, "rose against the
> French Government." . . . The fact is that the Stalinist
> bureaucracy, to justify violence against the Soviets and
> the Party, has, since 1926, appealed to the war danger—
> classic subterfuge of Bonapartism! In opposing this, I
> always expressed myself in the sense that freedom of
> criticism is indispensable for us not only in time of peace
> but also in time of war. I referred to the fact that even in
> bourgeois countries, France in particular, the ruling class
> did not dare, despite all its fear of the masses, completely
> to suppress criticism during the war. In this connection
> I adduced the example of Clemenceau, who, despite the

proximity of the war front to Paris—or rather, precisely because of it—denounced in his paper the worthlessness of the military policy of the French Government. In the end, Clemenceau, as is well known, convinced Parliament, took over the leadership of the Government, and assured victory. Where is the "uprising" here? Where is the "defeatism"? Where is the connection with foreign intelligence services? . . . (PC 575–6.)

The actual facts concerning Clemenceau's opposition to the War government in France are as follows:

(1) Clemenceau refused from the beginning of the war to enter the French Cabinet, because he thought it incapable of achieving victory and wished to be able to criticize it publicly.

(2) He did vigorously criticize the Cabinet and its conduct of the war; and his articles were often suppressed by the government censor and his paper forbidden to publish for several days.

(3) His criticisms were reproduced by the press of Germany and its allies, and he was denounced as a defeatist by the supporters of the Cabinet in France.

(4) In fact, Clemenceau was attacking the government in the interests of victory. He finally succeeded in overturning it, not by arms but in conformity with parliamentary procedure.

(5) The coming to power of Clemenceau was followed by a more vigorous prosecution of the war, and by the defeat of the enemy.

These facts are so much a matter of public knowledge that we should be obliged to apologize for mentioning them, were it not for the Prosecutor's absurd falsification, which is only a repetition of earlier falsifications against which Zinoviev, Radek and others vainly protested. Trotsky's real attitude toward the defense of the Soviet Union at the time when this falsification was being circulated, is clearly stated in the following passage from his speech at the Joint Plenary Session of the Central Committee and the Central Control Commission on August 1, 1927, on "The War Danger—the Defense Policy and the Opposition":

> Do we, the Opposition, cast any doubts on the defense of the socialist fatherland? Not in the slightest degree. It is our hope not only to participate in the defense, but to be able to teach others a few things. Do we cast doubts on Stalin's ability to sketch a correct line for the defense of the socialist fatherland? We do so and, indeed, to the highest possible degree. . . . Every Oppositionist, if he is a genuine Oppositionist and not a fraud, will assume in the event of war whatever post, at the front or behind the lines, that the Party will entrust to him, and carry out his duty to the end. But not a single Oppositionist will renounce his right and his duty, on the eve of war, or during the war, to fight for the correction of the party's course—as has always been the case in our party—because therein lies the most important condition for victory. To sum up: For the socialist fatherland? Yes! For the Stalinist course? No! ("Stalin School of Falsification," pp. 175–7.)

From this passage it clearly appears that Trotsky in Russia, as Clemenceau in France, criticized the ruling group not in the interest of defeatism but in that of national defense.

§ 232. We regret having been obliged to dwell at such length on matters which are almost entirely of public record and therefore easily accessible to anyone outside Russia who is interested in ascertaining the reliability of Vyshinsky's "historical proofs." But Vyshinsky's falsifications, presumably designed mainly for home consumption, have left us no other course; particularly in view of the importance which he himself attached to them. In our opinion, such whole-sale falsification as our examination of this material reveals fully justifies the presumption of falsification in all details of this evidence which, according to Vyshinsky, "confirms the theses of the indictment on the basis of the Trotskyites' past activity." And the fact that he resorted to such falsification inevitably reflects back upon the entire conduct of the trials, justifying the suspicion that their purpose was to discredit a political opposition, past and present, rather than to establish the actual truth through a fair procedure.

Part 5

Final considerations

26

The question of confessions

§ 233. A careful examination of the trial records and other evidence adduced in previous sections of this report has convinced this Commission that the confessions of the accused and witnesses in the Moscow trials were false in so far as they implicated Leon Trotsky and Leon Sedov in the criminal activities to which they confessed. But since the charges against Trotsky and Sedov were crucial in both trials, the discrediting of the testimony purporting to convict Trotsky and Sedov inevitably discredits the trials as a whole. The Commission does not pretend to know whether or not the accused were guilty, or if guilty what crimes they had committed. We can, and do, state in the most categorical fashion that on the basis of all the evidence we find them not guilty of having conspired with Leon Trotsky and Leon Sedov for any purpose whatever. We repeat, moreover, that it is impossible for any honest person, on the basis of records so full of contradictions and deliberate falsifications as the records of both trials, to come to any conclusion concerning their guilt or innocence of other charges, or the nature of their crimes if any.

The question naturally arises, If the accused were innocent of having conspired with Leon Trotsky and Leon Sedov for the criminal purposes stated in the charges and the testimony, then why did they confess? We do not know; and since our inquiry is concerned with the truth or falsity of their confessions in so far as they implicate Trotsky and Sedov, our report is conclusive irrespective of any theory as to the reasons why they confessed. But material in our hands bears directly upon the important question whether the extortion of false confessions, and their use to inculpate those confessing and other persons, is a common practice of the Soviet police. Because of the historic significance of this question, we judge it proper to present this material.

§ 234. We quote, first, from an article by Anton Ciliga (identified § 290) in *La Révolution Prolétarienne*, January, 1937, entitled "Judicial Investigation in the U.S.S.R., as I Saw It." This article, to which Dr. Ciliga refers in his statement to the *Comité pour l'Enquête sur le Procès de Moscou*, has been sent to us with that statement. Ciliga says:

> The [Zinoviev-Kamenev] trial was only the latest and most sensational of a whole series of *trials of a political nature* which I had the opportunity to witness on the ground. The means of preparation and presentation of the preceding trials (against the engineers in 1929 and 1930, against the Russian Social Democrats in 1931) were simply perfected and carried to the point of absurdity in the latest trial. (Com. Exh. 5, 2.)

Ciliga was arrested on May 21, 1930, in the night. It is a general rule, he says, to make searches and arrests at night, furtively as it were, and without commotion.

The purpose of this method of acting *secretly* is to weaken the arrested person's will to resist. On the order of arrest which was shown to me, not the slightest reason for the arrest was indicated. Nor was this detail accidental; it is the general rule.

He was conducted to prison in a private vehicle, he says, this "privilege" being due to the fact that he was living in a Leningrad palace in which resided Kirov and the other high party officials.

. . . The appearance of a closed police-wagon before the "House of the Party" would have made too great a sensation. All that I was able to see in Russia has brought me to the conviction that the fundamental *tactical* rule of bureaucratic justice is as follows: all sorts of vexations, lies and violence are permitted, but everything must be done quietly, without scandal; appearances must be saved. (*Ibid.*)

On the third night after his arrest he was taken before the examining judge.

It is a general rule of the GPU to call arrested persons for examination during the night; a sleepy man is less concentrated, less prepared to resist. Psychology is the favorite science of the policemen of the GPU.

"You know why you have been arrested? No, you don't know? Well, then, why do you suppose?"

Such were the first questions. Some time later I read in prison a work on the Spanish Inquisition, and to my great astonishment I learned that these were also the classical first questions of the Inquisitorial examiners. (*Ibid.*)

Ciliga says that he was later informed that he had been arrested as an Oppositionist; and that he was offered his liberty at the price of a declaration renouncing the Opposition and condemning Oppositional activity. At that time, he states, the GPU and the Party did not demand that one change one's point of view, but were content with a simple *declaration*. They even admitted privately that the Opposition might be right "in some things." But they were all the more insistent that the declarations should affirm that the majority was 100 per cent right, and the Opposition 100 per cent wrong. This was demanded in the name of safeguarding and reinforcing the authority of the Party.

> This fact is of great importance to an understanding of the mechanism of social and political life in the U.S.S.R. The Russian Communists are absolutely impregnated, more exactly infected, with this theory of two truths: one, the real truth, for the initiates, for a small governing circle; the other, the lie-truth, for the non-initiates, the great mass of the people. In its ultimate development this philosophy of two truths has led to the lie which permeates the whole social life to the point of hypocritical and lying declarations and testimony and the monstrous trials of the "penitents." *(Ibid.)*

He states that at the time of his arrest he did not believe that torture was employed by the Soviet government to obtain false depositions:

> Are tortures and false depositions, so shameful to the revolution, employed in the Soviet Union? are they employed systematically? each of you will ask in painful perplexity. Before being imprisoned not only did I doubt these facts, but I believed that all statements to this effect were wicked calumnies against Russia, even against the Russia of Stalin! . . .
> One evening, my cell-mate pricked up his ears. "What's

the matter?" "Don't you hear a muffled noise?" he replied. And, indeed from the end of the corridor came muffled sounds. "What can it be?" I asked. "They are torturing someone." I was indignant. "That people abroad believe all these petit-bourgeois tales circulated against the GPU may be understandable, but to believe such stories here, in Russia, is shameful! Come now, the GPU is not the Tsarist Okhrana! Evidently the GPU kills, annihilates, when it is necessary; but it does not torture." My companion looked at me uneasily, not knowing what to think of me. Then he said, "I wish you a long stay in the hands of the GPU; then you will come to understand what it is. You foreign Communists really know nothing. If a Russian Communist had said such a thing to me I would simply have stopped talking to him." *(Ibid.)*

The prison at that time, says Ciliga, was full of engineer "saboteurs." Among them were several who had "confessed."

Little by little, with great difficulty, I was able to learn the history of their affairs, the history of their connection with "sabotage." "They kept me five months in isolation," said one of them who had "confessed," "without papers, without anything to read, without mail, without contact with the outside world, without visits from my family; I was hungry, I suffered from solitude; they demanded of me that I confess having committed an act of sabotage that never took place; I refused to take upon myself crimes that had never been committed, but they told me that if I was really for the Soviet power, as I said I was, I ought to confess in this affair, for the Soviet power needed my confession; that I need have no fear of the consequences; the Soviet régime would take into consideration my open-hearted confession, and would give me the opportunity to work and to make good my mistakes through work. At the same time I would have visits from my family, letters, walks, newspapers. But if I persisted in maintaining silence I would be subjected to pitiless repression, and not myself alone, but my wife and children also. For months I resisted; but my situation became so intolerable that nothing, it seemed to me, could be worse; in any case I had become indifferent to everything. And I signed everything the examining judge demanded of me. . . ."

After having spent several months side by side with these engineer "saboteurs," I realized that this was no case of an honest although pitiless terror; it was a lugubrious terror, combined with the most detestable blackmail. . . . It was as if the state said to its adversaries: "Do what we demand of you, sell your conscience and your honor, take upon you crimes which you have never committed, and you will receive in recompense all the good things of this earth." *(Ibid.)*

Ciliga tells of a young sailor who was brought into the overcrowded cell in which he was confined.

. . . During his detention in an isolated cell the GPU had tried to extort from him a confession to his participation—fictional—in a plot—fictional—against Stalin. The GPU tried to get this result by inquisitorial means. They summoned him from his cell several times during the evening; they told him they were going to shoot him because of his criminal obstinacy; they led him into the court, stood him against the wall, and afterwards—led him back to his cell. "After all, you are a worker. We don't want to shoot you like some white guardist. As a worker you ought to confess honestly." The sailor, in spite of everything, did not confess; but after these tortures he became half-crazy; then they let him alone. The most important point of this story is—perhaps—that this did not happen after the assassination of Kirov, in 1934, but long before, in 1930. In the story of this sailor there is another circumstance to which I did not attach any importance at the time, but which takes on today, after the three trials against Zinoviev, a symptomatic significance: They tried—but without results—to extract from this sailor the false confession that he belonged to the Trotskyist Opposition. In reality he was a non-political worker. Employed on one of the Soviet ships in the foreign trade, he had become guilty of contraband—the only crime of which he could justly be accused. *(Ibid.)*

§ 235. We shall return later to this article by Ciliga. Another eye-witness to the methods employed by the GPU, the Franco-Russian writer, Victor Serge, testified before the *Commission Rogatoire* that he belonged to the Left Opposition from 1923 to 1936; that he was arrested twice: In 1928 on the eve of May 1, and in 1933 on March 7 or 8. The first time, he was in prison only about six weeks and his treatment was not particularly severe. The second time he did not fare so well. No accusation, either oral or written, was ever brought against him, and even the people who questioned him began by declaring that they were not, in the strict sense of the word, functionaries of the judiciary but armed representatives of the Party—in other words, that it was not primarily a question of discussions of fact and law of a juridical character, but of a political discussion. He was held incommunicado, without correspondence, without books or exercise, for three months.

During those three months I was questioned about ten times. Except twice, when they took place during the day, the interrogations took place at night . . . after we had been obliged to go to bed at the prescribed hour, that is at 9:00 P.M., we were brusquely awakened—at least they awakened me brusquely, after eleven o'clock, ordering me to get up to go to be questioned. . . .

The questioning, in the beginning, assumed the aspect of psychological conversation much more than of a judicial examination; that is to say, not only did they not give any information about the accusations, but they tried to establish an atmosphere now of confidence, now of menace, not in order to establish such or such a fact but in order to lead me in a very general discussion of my life and my ideas. They would say, "Describe your life in such a way that it will be possible to establish the truth regarding you." Naturally, when I resisted such a procedure, they reached the point of trying to excite my pity for the situation of those dear to me, or of threatening me. But I wish to emphasize that never, during these interviews, did I have counsel at my side; never did I see a clerk take down a verbatim report. There was no clerk—a fact which probably does not preclude the probability that either in an adjoining room or elsewhere some one took very precise notes, for on one occasion the judge was able to remind me in detail of a previous interrogation.

. . . Once, after other functionaries, I had to do with Rudkovsky, who greeted me by saying without mincing words that I was lost, but that he wished nevertheless to save me and offer me a life preserver. The life preserver consisted of this: He began to read a pretended statement of my sister-in-law, Anita Russakova, in which she, in the most nonsensical fashion, had purportedly enumerated a whole series of persons with whom I was supposed to be in contact, although I did not know any of them. Knowing my sister-in-law, and hearing what I heard, I understood at once that it was a question of a forgery. But at one point I was struck by the fact that among the persons with whom I was supposed to be in contact was one who lived in a military city. This detail, as false as the rest, made me think that they were trying to arrive at a capital verdict either against me or against my sister-in-law. It was then, restraining myself no longer, that I allowed my indignation to burst forth in harsh terms, refusing even to listen to any further reading of this pretended examination. On the contrary, I demanded to be confronted with my sister-in-law. Rudkovsky understood that there was nothing to be got from me, offered me a glass of water, and urged me to calm myself. The questioning ended. (CR 41.)

The false deposition having failed of its intended effect, said Serge, it was abandoned. His sister-in-law was liberated, and he himself was deported to Orenburg. However, he was never able to question his sister-in-law concerning the matter, for when he was passing through Moscow and could have seen her, he learned that she had just been deported to Verka, where she is still serving out five years of exile.

Serge described several episodes of his imprisonment which, he said, indicate "how things are done in the judicial domain in the U.S.S.R." In a Leningrad prison where he spent a night he met one P., who had been in solitary confinement for several months,

. . . and he told me that they always tried to make him confess by the same method; that is to say, by making him believe that friends of his had confessed, and that there was nothing he could do henceforth but ratify these confessions. Naturally he did not fail to tell me that he was perfectly convinced that these confessions did not exist, and for my part I did my best to strengthen his morale. (CR 42.)

In the Lubianka prison in Moscow, said Serge, he was placed in a cell with some thirty other prisoners. One of them, he learned, was a professor who had been undergoing a long investigation,

> in the course of which he had finally confessed to everything they wished and even more, in such a way that the judge himself had ended up by no longer understanding anything about it. And so they had finally sent him with the judge and another of the accused to Moscow to try to untangle the imbroglio of complicated and implausible confessions that both he and his co-defendant had ended by making. Travelling for this purpose, and with his judge, he had had the best treatment in the world; had been well-lodged and well-fed. And the funniest thing was that on one of the following days I met the other of the co-defendants, a veterinary who also confirmed with enormous amusement having made confessions so improbable as to be ridiculous. He laughed especially over having confessed to spreading epidemics, a thing in his opinion completely impossible; which confirms my belief that the system of confessions that are not confessions was practiced at that time (1933), well before the two trials in question at present. (CR 42–3.)

§ 236. The Russian refugee, A. Tarov (identified § 30), also testified to the methods of the GPU in extorting confessions. Under the heading, "How the GPU Manufactures 'Cases' and Tortures Prisoners," Tarov says:

> The ordinary procedure is as follows: A list of people, handed down from above with the instructions to arrest them, manufacture such and such a case against them, extort a confession, sentence and shoot them. At the same time, the examining magistrate is supplied with

a prepared draft of the case by the highest authorities. (Com. Exh. 6.)

In 1931, says Tarov, during the night of January 21–22, the GPU carried out mass arrests of Oppositionists in different cities and places of exile. He was among a colony of exiles at Akmolinsk who were arrested on that night.

> . . . They accused me of having tried to construct a short-wave radio broadcasting station in order to establish communication with Trotsky, abroad. This was recorded in my indictment. I knew nothing about a radio broadcasting station, short wave or any other kind. If it were not for the arrest, it would have been comic. In Kazakhstan, at Akmolinsk, a place where there was not yet a railway, a man trying to construct with bare hands a broadcasting station to communicate with Trotsky abroad! But the GPU had "located" a witness who declared that we had attempted to build this station together. They even found material proof at the "witness's" house, that is, parts of radio apparatus. This witness was a direct agent of the GPU. He was incarcerated together with us during the preliminary investigation and "accompanied" us to the Verkhne-Uralsk isolator. There, after three days, he handed in a "declaration of recantation" and was set free so that he could continue his work elsewhere.
>
> From Akmolinsk we were transferred to Petropavlovsk. The investigation of our case was carried on in the inner prison of Petropavlovsk. We were isolated from each other at the start. After a preliminary questioning I was placed with ordinary criminals. In a cell intended for two or three men, there were from twenty-six to twenty-eight prisoners. We could only sit down. To stretch out, it was necessary to ask the only one lying under the bench to yield his place. We suffered excruciating torture from the lack

of ventilation in the cell. It was well-nigh impossible to breathe. It was hot, stifling; bathed in sweat, we felt ourselves suffocating. Our lungs seemed compressed. Even the tiny peep-hole was barred from the outside. I shall never forget these days of terrible torture. The prisoners organized demonstrations, demanding air, but not a sound came from the corridor; the guards were under orders to maintain absolute silence. They had placed me among the ordinary criminals to force me to give false testimony. But after the questioning, I wrote on the pages of the record: "I consider the entire testimony of the witness, agent of the GPU, to be provocative insinuations of the GPU." The examinations were terminated. I was sentenced to three years hard labor, with Jantiev, Khudaev, Peter Popov, Zalaev, and two local workers whom they had mixed into our case. The rest were deported to the depths of Siberia.

According to Tarov,

When the GPU men arrest anybody in the street or at home, they never say, "Hands Up!" or "Don't move!" but shout, "Lie down!" I first discovered this in Petropavlovsk prison in 1931. The one-eyed executioner of the GPU (well-known in the city; of German origin; I forget his name) thus arrested kolkhoz and worker "wreckers." In the beginning, there were very few who consented to lie down before the GPU agent. But the régime ruthlessly destroyed men, and it taught the Soviet citizen to lie down before the GPU agent whenever he demanded it. Thus are Soviet citizens treated from the moment of arrest, that is, when it is not yet established whether they are guilty or not. *(Ibid.)*

Tarov tells of a peasant in the Akmolinsk district who was arrested in 1930 and accused of "non-delivery of wheat to the state." He had been denounced to the GPU, says Tarov, by the kulaks in the village soviet.

> The GPU . . . subjected him to unheard-of tortures to make him reveal the spot where the wheat was supposed to be hidden. The tortures were so intolerable that the poor peasant, who had no wheat, falsely confessed that he had. The GPU demanded that he show them the place. The peasant agreed. He conducted the GPU agents through the streets, as if he were going to point out the hiding place. He sought only to escape, if but for a few hours, the terrible torture. In the end, he could obviously show nothing, and the GPU men, beside themselves, believing he was still deceiving them, threw him into a ditch and poured water over him. It was the dead of winter, with the thermometer far below zero. The local poor peasants and agricultural laborers, aroused by this bestial treatment of their comrade, expressed their indignation in strong agitation. Then the official press insincerely undertook the defense of the poor peasant who had been turned into an icicle three months previously. A few "minor" shifts were made in the lower ranks of the GPU personnel. But if this case reached the press, how many thousand similar cases remained unpublicized! *(Ibid.)*

Tarov testifies to other means of intimidation than physical torture or mental torture of the kind described by Serge and Ciliga:

> In the inner prison of Petropavlovsk, where the author of these lines remained for six months waiting for the sentence pronounced in contumacy in Moscow, the GPU shot the condemned in a special structure erected exactly in the center of the courtyard where the prisoners took their daily walks. Generally when at night they

dragged the victim along the corridors to the "slaughter-house"—as the prisoners called this place—they gave him the opportunity to cry out, howl, implore, beg for mercy, etc. This was done with the purpose of frightening the other prisoners. It was not until they reached the courtyard that they gagged the condemned man and the cries ceased. We knew, by counting the shots, the number of bullets it took to finish the victim. The next day, while walking in the courtyard around this strange structure that reeked of blood, we could learn which of us was missing. *(Ibid.)*

He tells the story of an Oppositionist who was arrested in 1928 for distributing Opposition literature, and tortured in the effort to make him reveal its source. Since the work was arranged in such a way that even those who distributed the literature did not know where it came from, he could not tell. The examining magistrate, says Tarov,

was not satisfied with an explanation that corresponded to the truth. They put Andrusha in a cell. There he was tied to the cot, so arranged that water dripped constantly on him. At night, he was transferred to an even more terrible place, he was undressed, the barrel of a loaded revolver was pressed against his belly, and they threatened him: "We are going to fire all seven shots if you do not confess." The Young Communist Leaguer gave in, but he did not know whom to name. The GPU gave him time to "regain his senses." The YCL'er "regained his senses" and remembered me, for he knew that I belonged to the Opposition (he knew nothing else). He decided then to tell the GPU that it was I who had given him the propaganda material. But he could not remember my name and exact address. He therefore undertook to conduct the GPU agents to my lodging. *(Ibid.)*

One more quotation from Tarov, and we are through for the moment with this depressing evidence:

> It must be stressed that the GPU carries on its operations at night, unexpectedly, when the victim is in bed. The GPU behaves toward the prisoner in such a way that he feels himself to be constantly on the brink of the grave. In the GPU, they torture a man, but they do not let him die, in order to continue to torture him. After all, death is sometimes a welcome deliverance from intolerable torture. In the hands of the GPU the tortured man is deprived even of this means of "salvation." Many cry out, begging to be shot. But the orders provide only for torture. (Ibid.)

§ 237. This Commission holds that the testimony cited above, given from first-hand knowledge on the part of the deponents, indicates that the extortion of confessions through torture, both mental and physical, is a common practice of the Soviet police today. We find that this testimony, taken in connection with the fantastic discrepancies which we have pointed out in the confessions of the accused and witnesses in the two Moscow trials, and the demonstrated falsity of the testimony implicating Leon Trotsky and Leon Sedov, justifies the presumption of duress in the obtaining of these confessions. We find, moreover, that duress in the cases of several accused is indicated in the records themselves. Before adducing illustrations on this point, we quote once more from Strogovich-Vyshinsky on the principles of Soviet criminal procedure:

> . . . The accused has the right to give evidence but he is not obligated to do so. For refusing to give evidence, just as for giving false evidence, in contrast to the witness, he does not bear criminal responsibility. It is prohibited

to force the accused to give evidence and in those cases where, during examination, illegal methods for forcing the accused to give evidence are applied (violence, threats, terrorization, tricks, etc.) the person in charge of the investigation is criminally liable according to Section 2, Article 115, UK. (P. 73.)

Prosecutor Vyshinsky, under whose editorship the foregoing passage was written, himself made it clear (if he spoke the truth) in his final speech in the August trial that the refusal of the accused Smirnov to give evidence was by no means accepted by the examining officials. Smirnov, at first, says Vyshinsky,

denied everything; he denied the existence of a Trotskyite organization, he denied the existence of a center, he denied his participation in the center, he denied connection with Trotsky, he denied that he gave any secret instructions, even those which he gave in 1936. . . . He denied everything—he denied the existence of a Trotskyite center in 1931, he denied the existence of such a center in 1932. He denied everything. The whole of his examination of May 20 consisted solely of the words: "I deny that, again I deny, I deny." That is the only thing left for him to do.

Accused Smirnov, your experience, your skill in deceit, has betrayed you. Exposed by the evidence of Safonova, Mrachkovsky and Ter-Vaganyan, you were compelled to admit that there was a center, that you were a member of this center. Your denials were of no avail. You denied that you had received any instructions on terrorism, but you were exposed on this matter by Gaven, and you confessed; you were exposed by Holtzman who received instructions from Trotsky . . . Smirnov was exposed as a terrorist by Holtzman, by

Mrachkovsky, by Safonova and by Dreitzer.

On July 21, you, Smirnov, gave somewhat different evidence, that is to say, at first you denied that you had received any instructions from Trotsky to organize terrorism, but here you admitted that you did receive them. Your denials came to naught.

When confronted with Mrachkovsky, you continued to deny that you had received from Trotsky and conveyed to Mrachkovsky instructions to organize a terrorist group. Mrachkovsky put you to shame by saying: "Why, Ivan Nikitich, you want to get out of a sordid bloody business with a clean shirt?" ... In reply to Mrachkovsky you said: "Invention and slander," but later you did confess to something. . . .

I want to remind you that the confrontation with Safonova during the preliminary investigation, which, in the main, reproduced what we saw in this Court, was very characteristic. Smirnov does not venture to deny Safonova's evidence. He invents an elastic form of lies. He knows that Safonova will not slander him, Safonova was formerly his wife, and has no personal grudge against him; therefore, he cannot plead a personal grudge. He says: "I do not remember," "evidently such a conversation may have taken place." He is asked: Was there any talk about organizing terrorism? He replies: "There was not, but there might have been." When now, masking himself, he says: "I have nothing to reply to that," he is guided by the same animal cowardice. But on August 13 he was compelled to admit that this conversation did take place in 1932, that he, Smirnov, bears full responsibility for this, and that now he does not intend to evade responsibility. (ZK 158–60.)

We have quoted Vyshinsky at length because his account of the methods by which Smirnov—who under Soviet law was not under the slightest obligation to give evidence against himself—was forced to confess tallies remarkably (except that Vyshinsky does not mention physical torture) with the evidence we have cited above concerning GPU methods of extorting confessions. And his corroboration of that testimony lends strength to the supposition that for once he was telling the truth. It will be noted that according to Vyshinsky, Smirnov's preliminary examination lasted at least from May 20 to August 13 (only six days before the opening of the trial), when he finally "did confess to something."

Speaking of the accused Ter-Vaganyan, Vyshinsky says:

> He, too, at first adopted a position of denial; but on August 14 he gave more truthful evidence. (PR 160.)

He does not, however, indicate the length of Ter-Vaganyan's ordeal; we only learn that his confession was obtained five days before the trial opened.

In view of the Prosecutor's own revelation of the methods used to obtain the confession of Smirnov, this Commission does not find particularly convincing the statements which he elicited from several accused in the January trial to the effect that they were well treated and that no pressure was brought upon them to make them confess; more especially since there is evidence in that trial also that various accused were questioned for several months before they finally consented to testify against themselves, and that there, too, the system of "confrontations" was employed. Muralov, for example, according to his own testimony, held out for eight months before he finally agreed to confess, and finally

> said to myself, almost after eight months, that I must submit to the interests of the state for which I had fought actively in three revolutions, when my life hung by a thread dozens of times. (PR 233.)

Radek stated that he was first questioned on September 22, 1936, and "denied everything" until December 4 (PR 133–5). In his last plea he said that

> When I found myself in the People's Commissariat of Internal Affairs, the chief examining official . . . said to me: "You are not a baby. Here you have fifteen people testifying against you. You cannot get out of it, and as a sensible man you cannot think of doing so. If you do not want to testify it can only be because you want to gain time and look it over more closely. Very well study it." For two and a half months I tormented the examining official. . . . For two and a half months I compelled the examining official, by interrogating me and by confronting me with the testimony of other accused, to open up all the cards to me, so that I could see who had confessed, who had not confessed, and what each had confessed. . . . And one day the chief examining official came to me and said: "You are now the last. Why are you wasting time and temporizing? Why don't you say what you have to say?" And I answered: "Yes, tomorrow I shall begin my testimony." (PR 549.)

The accused Norkin stated that he refused to testify for two months; and that although there were "confrontations" no "outward pressure" was brought to bear upon him. Pyatakov in his final speech said that

> of course no measures of repression or suasion have been employed in regard to me. (PR 540.)

We repeat that it is impossible to pronounce upon the motives which prompted the accused and witnesses to confess. But we repeat also that in the light of the evidence cited above, their denials of duress are not convincing, since it may logically be assumed that the same pressure which forced them to confess was exercised to force them to deny duress. We note, moreover, that the testimony to repeated questionings and confrontations corroborates that of Serge, Ciliga, and Tarov; and if true it indicates that several of them were questioned over long periods during which they refused to state what was demanded of them; that they were confronted with confessions by other people incriminating them; and that only after such repeated interrogations and confrontations did they consent to make the confessions which cost all but four of them their lives. We note that this procedure is in direct violation of Soviet law as defined by Strogovich-Vyshinsky in the quotation cited above. In our opinion, such a procedure, in violation of the immunity conceded to accused persons under Soviet law as stated in that quotation, itself constituted duress, irrespective of any other possible means that may have been employed; and the use of duress in the cases of Smirnov, Muralov, Radek, and others constitutes presumptive evidence that it was used in the cases of all accused.

27

The real historical connection

§ 238. The indication of duress in those cases on which the records are explicit, and the presumption of duress in other cases, again taken in connection with the character of the charges and the evidence in both trials, constitutes, in our opinion, strong presumptive evidence that the trials were frame-ups. We have repeatedly noted the Prosecutor's contention that the alleged criminal activities of the accused in the two trials followed logically from their opposition to the policies of the Communist Party in 1926–27, and even earlier; and we have pointed out that the Prosecutor deliberately identified political opposition to the régime with criminal activity against it. We shall now examine Trotsky's counter-charge that the trials of August, 1936, and January, 1937, were the logical culmination of a series of frame-ups by the ruling majority of the Party, directed against the Left Opposition.

First, we would remind our readers of the change in Stalin's attitude toward opposition, even within the Party, between 1924 and 1927 (§ 219). The Opposition was expelled in December, 1927, and the wholesale arrests and exile of Oppositionists followed shortly after. The testimony of Serge, Ciliga, and Tarov contains much information, part of which we have cited in Chapter VIII, concerning the treatment to which Oppositionists were subjected in exile and in Soviet prisons. Serge and Tarov were first arrested in 1928, and Ciliga in 1930. Serge informed the *Commission Rogatoire* that at Orenburg he met two militants of the Trotskyist movement who were there to serve sentences of four and five years in exile. These men, he said, were in no position to do anything that should have led to their being accused in connection with the Kirov assassination. Nevertheless they were both arrested and tried after the assassination of Kirov, and were both sentenced to five years more of imprisonment. Another Trotskyist, Eleazar Solntsev, was sentenced by the same methods.

> This militant, after having had a three-year sentence, saw his penalty increased by two more years when the former sentence was completed, and without trial. After which he was deported, and at the time of the Kirov assassination he was again arrested and again sentenced to five years in prison, which he did not serve for the very simple reason that he preferred a hunger strike, from which he died. And it should be known that they took care to deport his wife and son to another place. (CR 43.)

The testimony already quoted from Tarov (§§ 30, 236) deals largely with the treatment of Oppositionists in Soviet prisons, in the attempt to extort denunciations of their comrades, or false confessions to criminal activity. Tarov says that

> The extortion of false testimony under the threat of cruel measures began a long time ago, at least ten years

ago. If that is now being done in the cells of the GPU prisons, in 1924–1927 it was done in the offices of the Party committees and control commissions. (Com. Exh. 6.)

He describes the tortures of an Oppositionist worker, Gassanov, who was arrested in Baku in 1929 and deported to Siberia. There he was arrested again, and driven into insanity in the attempt to force him to renounce the Opposition and name the Oppositionists of the Baku organization.

His renunciation of the Opposition would have been very important for the Stalinist apparatus, for Gassanov was very popular among the Baku workers. As a result of these tortures, Comrade Gassanov's nervous system was shattered. The GPU transferred him to Akmolinsk, to our colony, in a state of dementia. In spite of that, the GPU arrested him with us in 1931 and shut him up also in the Petropavlovsky prison. Repeatedly we sent protests to Moscow, to the GPU, the Central Executive Committee of the Soviets, but we received no reply. Mentally ill, Gassanov was kept in prison. Only when his malady assumed a violent character did they send him under convoy to the psychiatric clinic at Omsk. *(Ibid.)*

He tells of an Oppositionist, Guloyan, now chairman of the Central Executive Committee of one of the Soviet republics, who was expelled from the Party and dismissed from his job on the charge of having stolen 500 rubles from the treasury of the local committee, of which he was secretary; and who was reinstated and promoted after having capitulated and betrayed his comrades. But, says Tarov,

hundreds and thousands of Oppositionists who did not yield to this kind of "training" had to suffer in prisons and concentration camps; their wives and children were doomed to hunger and death. From among these thousands of men I should like to mention the following Oppositionists: Krapivsky, Popov, Boltoboy Vanush, the machinist Tatekhsian, the locksmith Gornilov, and thousands of others who had three, four, or five, and sometimes more, small children. Each of these was the sole support of his family. After arresting them, the Stalinist apparatus deprived their wives and children of all civil rights.

According to Ciliga,

> After the assassination of Kirov in December, 1934, the whole Leningrad Opposition was deported to Siberia—as many as thirty thousand families, mostly workers. . . .
>
> In July, 1933, at Yeniseisk, they arrested a group of ten Communist Oppositionists; the Trotskyist Maximov, the Detzists [DTZists] Davidov and Boiko, and two Zinovievists, Lifshitz and another whose name I no longer remember. The first three were accused of having tried to propagandize among the arrested Zinovievists, that is, Lifshitz and the other. The charge was invented in toto, and the Trotskyists as well as the Detzists categorically rejected it. The GPU was forced to attempt to persuade the Zinovievists to give false testimony. This time they did not succeed. So far from that: Lifshitz and the one whose name I do not recall sent the Prosecutor, Vyshinsky, a written statement on the subject of the GPU's methods of extortion and provocation. (Com. Exh. 5, 1.)

This testimony indicates that as far back as 1928 the identification of political opposition with crime which characterized the attitude of Vyshinsky in the two Moscow trials was the common practice of the Soviet régime; that provocative and repressive measures, often of the most revolting kind, were employed against Oppositionists; and that their families were often included in the repressive measures against them.

§ 239. Among the exhibits introduced before the Preliminary Commission is a compilation of quotations from statements to the C.C. of the C.P.S.U. and to the Party members, letters, and articles from the Left Opposition press, showing that the attempts of the majority to inculpate the Left Opposition began in 1927 and culminated in the two Moscow trials. These quotations corroborate the testimony of Tarov, Serge, and Ciliga. They also show that the leaders of the Opposition predicted and warned the Communist Party against those very developments which afterward took place. The first attempt was an effort to link the Left Opposition with a counter-revolutionary military conspiracy. (Leon Trotsky, in his testimony before the Preliminary Commission, told about the effect of this attempt upon the Central Committee—PC 326.) We quote from a letter to all members of the Communist Party of the Soviet Union, dated Moscow, October 4, 1927, and signed by Trotsky, Zinoviev, Bakayev, Evdokimov, Peterson, and Smilga:

> . . . On September 13, the GPU sent a communication to the C.C.C. to the effect that Bolsheviks working in an Opposition "printing plant" had been shown to be connected through a non-party member with a Wrangel officer, who, on his part, had been shown to be connected with a military conspiracy aiming to organize an overturn in the Soviet Union "in the near future." The Secretariat of the C.C.C. approved the action of the GPU in conducting raids on Communists who had allegedly joined the "counter-revolutionary organization." The Political Bureau of the Central Committee and the Praesidium of the C.C.C., on September 22, sent out to the entire Party a special communication to the effect that

members of the Opposition, who printed our platform destined for the Party Congress, were connected with a counter-revolutionary conspirator. This communication was and is being read in all the nuclei, even in the most forsaken parts of the country. The rumor about the "connection" between the Opposition and the military conspiracy is spreading among ever wider circles of non-party members. On what is this unheard-of accusation based? On the fact that one of the members of the Opposition "printing plant" had an alleged conversation about a mimeograph machine with some Wrangel officer. That is the version of the GPU.

On September 23, comrades Zinoviev, Smilga and Peterson (Oppositionists) addressed themselves to the C.C. and to all party organizations with the following letter of inquiry:

"Who is this Wrangel officer? What is his name? Why is it concealed? Has he been arrested?"

Only under the whip of these questions did *the chairman of the GPU communicate by letter that the so-called Wrangel officer was simply an agent of the GPU,* who had more than once helped to discover White Guard conspiracies. In this way the whole communication about the Wrangel officer and about the connection between the "printing plant" and the military conspiracy was shown to be false. . . .

The affair of the military conspiracy has no connection whatever with the printing of the Opposition platform of the Bolshevik-Leninists. This was completely proved at the trial of the participants in the so-called Opposition printing plant. Not one of the accusers from among the Central Control Commission referred by so much as a single word to any connections with the military conspiracy. This is a lie based on this, that a GPU agent has been passed off on the Party as a conspirator.

. . . What is the essence of the deposition of Tverskoi about the preparation of "the military overturn in the Soviet Union in the near future"? Referring to some citizeness, who refers to another citizen, etc., Tverskoi says:

"In military circles there was a movement on foot, headed by comrades Trotsky and Kamenev, obviously the military one, and . . . this organization is active. No mention was made that this organization intended to perpetrate an overturn, but that was self-understood."

It follows from the communication of the GPU itself that Tverskoi on his own initiative told a GPU agent that he had heard at third or fourth hand about the existence of a military "movement" headed, you see, by Trotsky and Kamenev. Who were the Communists that entered into the counter-revolutionary organization? Those who printed the platform? No, the Praesidium of the C.C.C. itself categorically rejected this accusation. Who, then, are the Communists referred to? Perhaps Trotsky? Tverskoi names Trotsky and only Trotsky. But the concocters of this abominable business apparently dare not as yet to put in circulation this second and much more peppery dish concerning a military conspiracy headed by Trotsky. They manifestly think that the hour has not yet struck. . . .

. . . All threads lead to Stalin. Without his consent, without his sanction, without his encouragement, nobody would have ever dared to launch accusations, based on a frame-up, in the Party ranks against Opposition Communists about their participation in a counter-revolutionary organization. . . . (PC Exh. 33, 2.)

The following extract from a statement to the Joint Plenum of the C.C. and the C.C.C. in reply to a speech by Molotov on the "insurrectionism" of the Opposition indicates

that the accusation of "defeatism" is not new. It is signed by
Kamenev, Zinoviev, Pyatakov, Smilga, Soloviev, Muralov,
Trotsky, Bakayev, Avdeyev, Rakovsky, Evdokimov, Lisdin,
and Peterson:

> . . . By using the term "insurrectionism" in referring
> to the Opposition, the nucleus of the Stalinist fraction
> intends to accustom the Party to the idea of the destruc-
> tion of the Opposition.
> . . . It is not correct that the Opposition holds the view-
> point of "conditional defensism."
> . . . It is not correct that the path of the Opposition
> *leads to the insurrection against the Party and the So-*
> *viet power.* On the contrary, it is an incontestable fact
> that the Stalinist fraction is cold-bloodedly planning to
> place the emphasis on our physical destruction in order
> to attain its goals. From the side of the Opposition there
> is no trace of a threat of insurrectionism. On the con-
> trary, from the side of the Stalinist fraction there is a
> real threat of a further usurpation of the supreme rights
> of the Party. Through the mouth of Molotov this threat
> has been pronounced openly. While preparing *in fact,*
> step by step, the destruction of the Opposition on the
> pretext of its "insurrectionism" the Stalinist tops soothe
> the hesitating members of the Central Committee and
> the Central Control Commission with verbal assurances
> that matters will never go so far, but that it is merely
> necessary to *frighten* the Opposition. In this way the
> Stalin group gradually draws into its orbit wider circles
> and accustoms them to its plan which in its pure form
> would repel them today. . . .
> . . . At the same time, we declare again that we are
> ready to accept every proposal that can ameliorate the
> internal relations, allay the internal struggle, facilitate
> for the Party and the Central Committee a more efficient

utilization of all the forces—in any work—for the needs of the Party and the Soviet government, so as to create ultimately the conditions which will assure a general examination of the real differences by the Party and the elaboration of a correct line at the Fifteenth Congress of the Party. (*Ibid.*, 3.)

The following excerpt from a private letter by a Russian Communist on the exile of Trotsky and other Oppositionists in 1928, is quoted from page 353 of "The Real Situation in Russia":

As the Government gets deeper into the economic difficulties of which the Opposition forewarned them, *they try to blame these difficulties upon the Opposition.* Will it be long, at this rate, before they frame up a prosecution that will end in executions? (*Ibid.*, 5.)

On January 18, 1929, Leon Trotsky, then in exile at Alma Ata, was condemned to exile beyond the borders of the Soviet Union on the ground of

counter-revolutionary activity expressing itself through the organization of an illegal anti-Soviet party, activity which during the last period was directed toward the provocation of anti-Soviet demonstrations and toward preparation of the armed struggle against Soviet power. (From the Minutes of the Special Committee of the Collegium of the GPU, January 18, 1929.) (*Ibid.*, 6.)

On March 4, 1929, Trotsky wrote as follows:

There remains only one thing for Stalin: to try to draw a line of blood between the Party and the Opposition. He must absolutely *connect the Opposition with terrorist attempts, preparation for armed insurrection,* etc. . . . (Published in the *Bulletin of the Opposition,* Nos. 1–2, July, 1929.) (*Ibid., 7.*)

The following quotations are from a declaration of Oppositionist deportees at Kansk to the 16th Congress of the C.P.S.U. (excerpts were published in *The Militant,* New York, of February 15, 1931):

> For two and a half years the vanguard of the Bolshevik Party has been subjected to merciless repressions, . . . calumny and provocation, raids and arrests, deportations and solitary confinement, up to assassination itself. . . .
> The most monstrous and absurd accusations have been flung at the Opposition, and continue to be flung without being supported by any proof. . . . Very often the prisoners are subjected to icy douches (Upper Urals), to the threat of being shot, which fortunately was not carried out thanks to the revolutionary consciousness of the Red soldiers (Tobolsk). They had medical assistance refused to the very ill (Tomsk, Uralsk, etc.), suffered imprisonment under conditions which condemned them to physical extermination (for example, at Upper-Uralsk, where the prisoner does not have a space equal to that of a tomb), continual raids applied to the Mensheviks, the Social Revolutionists, the White Guards, until the arrival of our comrades in solitary (Suzdal). . . .
> . . . Provocation serves as a mask for a shameful repression; slander encourages the criminal method of struggle. With this object, the apparatus blackmailed the Party on the eve of the Fifteenth Congress with the aid of the "Wrangel officer," allegedly connected with the Opposition. . . . With this object, criminal and charlatanist, Yaroslavsky, on the eve of the Sixteenth Congress, attributes to the Opposition the intention of

"putting itself at the head of peasant uprisings"; and to the Bolshevik-Leninists who are arrested in deportation the false accusation is presented "of creating anti-Soviet organizations on the U.S.S.R. scale" (Kansk). We warn the Sixteenth Congress that the Stalinist faction, in the struggle against the Opposition, is employing an ever-increasing system of repression. . . . (*Ibid.*, 13.)

A letter from the U.S.S.R., in the *Bulletin of the Opposition*, No. 25–26, November–December, 1931, says:

> . . . Before the Sixteenth Congress, the Rights displayed a very energetic activity. At that time, Stalin decided to present them with a remodeled "Wrangel officer." A series of meetings of the Rights took place in the apartment of Kozelev. Among the participants at these meetings was an *agent provocateur* who expressed himself to the effect that the only way out was the physical extermination of Stalin. The next day Kozelev was accused of "failing to denounce" an "attempt" against Stalin (by Stalin's own agent!). The question was immediately taken up in a session of the Politburo. In this session Rykov, Bukharin and Tomsky participated. Mikoyan moved: "to shoot Kozelev." Stalin replied that it was enough for the time being to expel him from the Party. (*Ibid.*, 16.)

After the Kirov assassination, Trotsky wrote an "Answer to Some American Friends," which appeared in the *Bulletin of the Opposition*, No. 42, February, 1935:

> . . . As far as I can see from a distance, as an isolated observer, the strategy developed around the corpse of Kirov has not brought Stalin any greater laurels. But precisely for this reason he can neither stop nor retreat. *Stalin will be forced to cover up the unsuccessful amal-*

gams with new, broader and . . . more successful ones.
We must meet them well-armed. (*Ibid.,* 23.)

After the assassination of Kirov, Zinoviev and Kamenev
were arrested and confessed to "moral responsibility." They
were sentenced to prison. The following letter from Anton
Ciliga, then in prison in Russia, dated December 9, 1935,
which appeared in the *New Militant* of January 25, 1936,
tells about a second trial of Kamenev:

> . . . Kamenev has received as the outcome of a new trial
> a sentence which runs to ten years. The second trial was
> based on the charges of a plot against "himself" (that is
> to say, Stalin). The principal hero of the accusation was
> Kamenev's own brother, the painter Rosenfeld. There
> were 36 indicted, a mixed and very suspicious collec-
> tion. . . . Kamenev denied categorically that he knew
> anything about this affair and insisted that he saw the
> principal accused individuals for the first time in his life
> during the trial. . . . For his categorical refusal to know
> anything about this affair, Kamenev received not only
> an increase of about ten years, but was sent to a com-
> mon cell (No. 57, third tier, north isle of the penitentiary,
> with 12 men in a large cell). (PC Exh. 33, 24.)

§ 240. In connection with the conclusions inevitably
flowing from the mass of material on which previous sections of this report are based, we find that this compilation,
largely corroborated by the evidence of such eye-witnesses
as Tarov, Ciliga and Serge, substantiates the argument that
the Moscow trials of August, 1936, and January, 1937, were
the culmination of a series of repressive measures against a
political opposition. We have noted in previous sections of
this report that the men actually tried were not Trotskyists.
They were, however, accused as Trotskyists, and confessed

as such; and the effect of their confessions was to discredit the Trotskyist Opposition as surely as if they had actually belonged to it, and to discredit them in the eyes of opponents of Trotsky by linking their names with his. We quote again from Ciliga on the Zinoviev-Kamenev trial:

> In the measure that the GPU did not succeed in pushing into false confessions for the Moscow trial Trotskyists who remained loyal to their organization, it had to be satisfied with the false confessions of former Trotskyists who had capitulated four or five years before and who had been in prison three or four years. The mechanism of the ordeal that they endured and of the staging of the trial was prepared—as I have said—by the previous trials, by the methods and by the means which have become common in Russia in the last few years. The application of those methods on a vast scale gave me the opportunity to meet in the Stalinist prisons how many men, how many victims, broken physically and morally! (Com. Exh. 5, 2.)

After the Zinoviev-Kamenev trial, Trotsky wrote from his Norwegian internment a letter to his lawyer, Puntervold, dated September 15, 1936, in which he predicted that Stalin would try to bolster up the charges against him by "uncovering" new "attempts" and "treasons," and would remove the base of the "terrorist activities" from Copenhagen to Oslo. (PC Exh. 19, III/2.) The January trial, with Pyatakov's testimony about his flight, bore out this prophecy. In his final argument before the Preliminary Commission, Trotsky prophesied once more:

> Tomorrow we shall hear about new misdeeds of the Trotskyists in Spain, of their direct or indirect support of the fascists. Echoes of this base calumny, indeed, have

already been heard in this room. Tomorrow we shall hear how the Trotskyites in the United States are preparing railroad wrecks and the obstruction of the Panama Canal, in the interests of Japan. We shall learn the day after tomorrow how the Trotskyites in Mexico are preparing measures for the restoration of Porfirio Diaz. You say Diaz died a long time ago? The Moscow creators of amalgams do not stop before such trifles. They stop before nothing—nothing at all. Politically and morally, it is a question of life and death for them. Emissaries of the GPU are prowling in all countries of the Old and the New World. They do not lack money. What does it mean to the ruling clique to spend twenty or fifty millions of dollars more or less, to sustain its authority and its power? These gentlemen buy human consciences like sacks of potatoes. We shall see this in many instances. (PC 584.)

Time alone will show whether or not Trotsky has correctly forecast events here too. In our opinion the trial records themselves warrant expectation of a new trial, that of the "Rights." In both trials Rykov, Bukharin, and Tomsky (who had committed suicide) were implicated by the accused. We refer our readers especially to §§ 119 and 120 of this report. We refer them also to § 205 concerning the reasons given by Radek for his failure to call a conference about Trotsky's alleged agreements with foreign powers. In his testimony, Radek referred to his attempts to get Dreitzer to come to Moscow at all costs, and said:

> I will tell why—it is perhaps the most important thing in this case. (PR 121.)

Either he did not tell why, or his testimony was not printed. He turned to the subject in his final speech, saying,

... why did I not tell about the December instructions and about Pyatakov's meeting with Trotsky even to a man so close to me as Bukharin, who knew about the contacts with the representatives of the West-European and Eastern powers? I shall speak about this because it may later have a practical significance and supply the answer to the question whether something *still remains undisclosed.* I think it does; that *something remains hidden both from us and from the authorities and could be disclosed.* . . . (PR 547.) (Our emphasis.)

Then follows Radek's confused statement (§ 205) of his reasons for assuming that Trotsky

was creating some other devilish business in addition to the parallel center. (PR 548.)

Since our inquiry has established the fact that all testimony implicating Trotsky in the alleged conspiracy is false, it is obvious that these insinuations of Radek are also false. And since, as we have shown in Chapter XXVI, there is reason to believe that the accused confessed falsely under duress, we hold that there is reason also to believe that the statements of Radek, quoted above, were put into his mouth by the prosecution in order to prepare the public mind for a subsequent trial of Bukharin, Rykov, and others implicated by the accused in the August and January trials.*

---

* The trial predicted took place on March 2–13, 1938, in the interval between the transmission of the final revision of this report to members of the Commission and the receipt of their approval. There were twenty-one accused, among them N.I. Bukharin, A.I. Rykov and K.G. Rakovsky. Our investigation of the two preceding trials, and our conclusions, have made an investigation of the Bukharin-Rykov trial unnecessary.

It suffices to state that we were able to offer to the Soviet ambassa-

In the light of this evidence, and of the long series of forewarnings subsequently justified by the events which we have cited above, Trotsky's prediction of future amalgams directed against opponents of the Soviet régime appears justified.

§ 241. In his final speech in the January trial, the Prosecutor referred to

> other detachments of capitalist agents in our country: the "Industrial Party," Kondratyev's "Toiling Peasants' Party," a kulak party, the "Union Bureau of the Mensheviks," the activities of which were examined by the Supreme Court—all these organizations exposed as organizations of wreckers and groups of diversionists who welcomed Trotsky's struggle against our Party, against the Soviet government. . . . (PR 465.)

This statement, used as proof of the "historical connection," leads us to consider some aspects of trials previous to August, 1936, and January, 1937, as indicating an historical connection of a kind quite the opposite of that alleged by Vyshinsky.

In the first place, an examination of the records of previous trials reveals that political motivation on the part of the Prosecution is not exceptional. The whole pattern—charges, confessions, procedure, even the language—is in each case so nearly identical with the trials of August and January as to engender a disturbing suspicion that the accused were not so much "exposed" as selected to fit into a prearranged scheme for discrediting current enemies of the régime or whitewashing its leading officials by shifting to other shoulders the responsibility for their mistakes. And this suspicion

---

dor in Washington, for transmission to his government, evidence from our files impugning in vital points the testimony of certain accused against Leon Trotsky.

receives ample warrant from the evidence we have cited above;
as also from such universally known facts as that Professor
Ramzin, the leading "traitor" of the Industrial Party (Promparty) trial in 1930, was almost immediately liberated and
reinstated in his professional work (see Ciliga, § 234, on the
engineer "saboteurs"), and that two of his alleged co-conspirators, Riabushinsky and Vishnegradsky, had died some
time before he conspired with them; also that Abramovich,
the well-known Menshevik exile who was accused in the
Menshevik trial of 1931, was able to establish photographi-
cally that the testimony implicating him was false.

We shall briefly consider the records of these two previous trials.

§ 242. In each case the accused (eight in the first trial,*
fourteen in the second) were charged with having formed
an anti-Soviet center for the purpose of bringing about the
overthrow of the Soviet régime and the restoration of capitalism through wrecking activities, disruptive work in the
army, and the furthering of armed intervention against the
Soviet Union. According to the indictment in the trial of the
"Promparty," the

> Industrial Party or the "Council of the Allied Engineers'
> Organizations" . . . united in a single organization all the
> different wrecking organizations in the various branches

---

* One member of the alleged "center," L.G. Rubinovich, had been sentenced in the Shakhty trial. He was not "implicated" and tried in this
trial because, in the words of the indictment, he "did not participate
in the work of the counter-revolutionary organization during the last
two years of its existence when the gravest crimes were committed."
(A similar situation did not save I.N. Smirnov in the August trial.) Another member, P.A. Palchinsky, had been previously shot by the GPU
in connection with the alleged wrecking in the gold and platinum industry. A third, the engineer Khrennikov, "died during the preliminary investigation."

of industry and acted not only in accordance with the orders of the international organizations of former Russian and foreign capitalists, BUT ALSO IN CONTACT WITH AND UPON DIRECT INSTRUCTIONS OF THE RULING CIRCLES AND THE GENERAL STAFF OF FRANCE IN PREPARING ARMED INTERVENTION AND ARMED OVERTHROW OF THE SOVIET POWER. (*Pravda*, November 11, 1930.)

The indictment was outspoken on the alleged connections with foreign imperialism, as the following headings show:

(a) THE FRENCH GOVERNMENT AND ITS RÔLE IN PREPARING THE INTERVENTION.
(b) PRIVATE NEGOTIATIONS OF POINCARÉ AND BRIAND WITH THE TORGPROM.*
(c) THE JOINT ACTIVITIES OF THE TORGPROM, THE WRECKERS AND THE FRENCH GENERAL STAFF.
(d) THE TIES WITH THE ENGLISH GENERAL STAFF. *(Ibid.)*

It was charged and held proved that France and Great Britain were extending help to the conspirators in return for territorial and other concessions. According to the accused Fedotov:

A secret communication was received from Ramzin that during his stay in Paris he had been compelled in the name of the Allied Wrecking Organizations to agree to the concessions which the Torgprom had made at the expense of Russia, to wit: a section of the Caucasus, primarily the oil-bearing regions, to be ceded to England;

---

* An alleged Commercial-Industrial Committee abroad, composed of emigré capitalists. This was the "native" counter-revolutionary organization with which Ramzin and his colleagues allegedly maintained contact.

and a section of the right shores of the Ukraine to Poland and France. *(Ibid.)*

We note a remarkable similarity between this passage and the testimony of Radek and Pyatakov concerning the territorial concessions allegedly agreed to by Trotsky. In 1930, it appears, not Trotsky but Poincaré was the arch-enemy and impatient moving spirit of the alleged plot. According to the indictment:

> ... As a matter of fact the French ruling circles, through the person of Poincaré, merely used the Torgprom as a tool for their aims. It was not for nothing that Poincaré INSISTED ON THE URGENT NEED OF INTENSIFYING THE ACTIVITIES OF THE WRECKING ORGANIZATION WITHIN THE U.S.S.R. *(Ibid.)*

The accused who were tried confessed to everything: to wrecking activities in the principal industries; to espionage; to diversionist activity in the war industries, power stations, and railways—which was to coincide with intervention; to treasonable activities in the Red Army. Exhaustive accounts of the trial appeared in *Pravda* of November 25 to December 10, and for several issues thereafter; preceded, in the interval between the publication of the indictment and the beginning of the trial, by a campaign stressing the danger of intervention and the rôle of the imperialists, especially of France. No evidence was introduced except the confessions of the accused. The Prosecutor, Krylenko, said in this connection:

> What evidence can there be? I have cross-examined [the accused] on this point. It transpires that in all those instances where documents did obtain, they were destroyed. *(Pravda,* December 8, 1930.)

§ 243. In the indictment of the "Menshevik counter-revolutionary organization of Groman, Sher, Ikov, Sukhanov et al." the accused were charged with a series of alleged crimes against the state; and the charges were buttressed by lengthy quotations from the political program of the Mensheviks. The accused were charged with plotting

> to restore the capitalist system through the armed assault of foreign imperialist gangs upon the U.S.S.R. (Official Minutes of the trial, Moscow: *Sovietskoye Zakonoizdatelstvo*, 1931.)

The foreword to the trial record states that the trial has proved to the hilt

> on the one hand the close tie between the Russian Mensheviks and the émigrés abroad, and through the latter with the Second International; and on the other hand a close tie with the Promparty and through the latter with the Torgprom, through which in turn they were connected with the French General Staff and the ruling circles of the imperialist French bourgeoisie—in the common cause of preparing the armed overthrow of the Soviet power and the armed restoration of capitalism in the U.S.S.R. (*Ibid.*, p. 5.)

The platform of this "alliance" is specified in the indictment as follows:

> (a) The restoration of capitalist relations in the U.S.S.R. was the common aim in [plotting] the counter-revolutionary *coup d'état*.
> (b) They banked on intervention as the sole feasible and quickest method for the overthrow of the Soviet power.

(c) Wrecking as the principal method of counter-revolutionary work within the U.S.S.R. together with carrying on disruptive work in the army.

(d) Receipt of material means, in particular from one source, the Torgprom.

(e) Organizational connection with the ruling circles of Western Europe, in particular that of the Mensheviks with the leading circles of the Second International. (*Ibid.*, p. 11.)

All the defendants confessed their guilt of the charges; and their confessions, like those in the trials of August, 1936, and January, 1937, contained remarkable discrepancies. In this trial Krylenko had some documentary "evidence" to introduce. Two letters which the accused Ikov had attempted to smuggle abroad, forewarning against and denouncing the impending "frame-up," were introduced as "exhaustive proof" of the fact that there was

direct contact between the accused and the center abroad. (*Ibid.*, p. 45.)

Krylenko also introduced as exhibits two speeches by the accused Petunin, member of the directorate of the Tsentrosoyus, one of which had been delivered at a session of the praesidium of that directorate on April 23, 1929, and the other at a session of the People's Commissariat of Workers' and Peasants' Inspection on July 13, 1929. Also the Menshevik program and the publication of the Mensheviks abroad, *Sotsialisticheski Vestnik*. One of the accused, Rubin, confessed that there were incriminating documents which established the link between the "wreckers" and the imperialists. All he could recall, however, was that they were "on thin paper and began with the words, Dear Comrades." (*Ibid.*, p. 29.)

§ 244. The similarities between these two trials and those

of August, 1936, and January, 1937, are too apparent to need pointing out. The only significant difference, indeed, is in the names of the foreign powers and interests which the accused were alleged to be serving—and in the comparative mildness of the punishment (five to ten years imprisonment) meted out to the accused.

The nature of the foreign alliances to which the accused confessed seem to us more explicable in terms of Soviet foreign relations than of their uncorroborated confessions. The years 1930 and 1931 were part of the famous "third period" in which the Soviet government regarded British and French imperialism as its main enemies, and the Second International as the ally of those imperialisms. In 1936, however, the Soviet government was in alliance with French "imperialism" and courting British "imperialism"; and the sections of the Communist International were united in a "popular front" with the Social Democracy. German fascism on the West and Japanese imperialism on the East had become the most menacing enemies of the Soviet Union; and the pattern of the Moscow trials of August, 1936, and January, 1937, reflected this shift in Soviet foreign relations—even to the point of dating the alleged alliance of the "Trotskyists" with Hitler's Gestapo back to a period before the Gestapo existed.

Within Russia, in 1930–31, the agitation over the danger of foreign intervention, and the punishment of alleged wreckers and diversionists in the employ of interventionist powers must have had—irrespective of the question whether or not it was justified in fact—the effect of rallying the population to the support of the régime during the period of strains and stresses due to the rapid tempo of collectivization and industrialization, and of convincing the Russian masses that the ills from which they suffered were due to deliberate sabotage in the interests of foreign powers.

We quote again from Ciliga. Referring to the practice of eliciting false confessions from engineer "saboteurs" he says:

If you ask me what was the reason for *such* a method, I can answer in a few words that it was a specific act in the political fight of the bureaucracy of the Party against the non-Party specialists. It had to do with rather important matters: The specialist intellectuals dreamed—and this dream then had a chance to be realized—that the peasants, in revolt against forced collectivization, would overthrow the power of the "Communist" bureaucracy; this overthrow of the existing power might lead—according to them—to a government of engineers, of specialists. The Stalinist government, on its part, meant not only to destroy its enemies physically, but also to compromise them morally and to disunite them—all this with the aid of show trials and false confessions. The Stalinist government hoped, at the same time, to place upon its political enemies the whole responsibility for the economic and political difficulties which were upsetting the country. (Com. Exh. 5, 2.)

Ciliga points out the evident absurdity of the charges and confessions in the Menshevik trial, and says:

If in the trial against the engineers most of the accusations were lies, here, in the trial against the Mensheviks, all the accusations and self-accusations were 100% false. From this point of view that trial was like a dress-rehearsal of the future trial of Zinoviev and his associates. *(Ibid.)*

The men sentenced in this trial, he says, were brought to the political prison at Verkhne-Uralsk, where he was imprisoned.

The new prisoners were distributed in the prison in such a way that they could not communicate either with the earlier prisoners or with one another. Manifestly the GPU feared something. But in spite of that we found ways of communicating. In a letter to them I put the question: How could they have made such monstrous confessions? "We ourselves do not understand," they answered, "how such a nightmare could have taken place." Victor Serge has now brought out of Russia more complete information concerning this group. Permit me to repeat here one of his observations: "One of the principal accused, the well-known historian and publicist Sukhanov, circulated in the isolator a copy of his protest to the Soviet government, in which he demanded that it fulfill its promise to set him free after he had consented to make false confessions." *(Ibid.)*

The political trials of 1929–31, says Ciliga, were staged by the régime because of the economic crisis due to the difficulties involved in the Five-Year Plan. That of August, 1936, was due to the social and economic bankruptcy of the Plan. The masses feel that they have been duped by these five-year plans—that the fruits of their sacrifices have been appropriated by others. New trials were needed to dull their minds and smother their discontent.

The trial of the Sixteen was above all a trial against Trotskyism. But not only against Trotskyism. Along with the Trotskyists they accused all oppositionist Communist groups, among others the Right opposition also. . . . In the latest trial of Novosibirsk they accused, alongside the alleged Trotskyists, engineers belonging to no party. This proves that the slogan "Against Trotskyism" serves Stalin as a pretext—like Hitler's slogan, "Against Communism"—for a fight against all discontented social strata, as against all the oppositional political groups in the country. *(Ibid.)*

§ 245. In our opinion the analysis of the records of the August and January trials, in previous chapters of this report, and the mass of evidence which, with that analysis, has formed the basis of our previous conclusions, furnish, when taken together with the material in the present chapter, convincing corroboration of these statements of Ciliga. In the light of all this evidence the conclusion appears inevitable that the indictments and confessions in the widely publicized series of trials of alleged plotters against the Soviet régime were determined in each case—including the trials of August, 1936, and January, 1937—by the current internal difficulties, economic and political, and by the current situation in the foreign relations, of the Soviet régime. In other words, we find that the trials have served not juridical but political ends.

§ 246. On the basis of all the evidence herein examined and all the conclusions stated, we find that the trials of August, 1936, and January, 1937, were frame-ups.

§ 247. On the basis of all the evidence herein examined and all the conclusions stated, we find Leon Trotsky and Leon Sedov not guilty.

John Dewey, Chairman
John R. Chamberlain
Alfred Rosmer
E.A. Ross
Otto Ruehle
Benjamin Stolberg
Wendelin Thomas
Carlo Tresca
F. Zamora
Suzanne La Follette, Secretary
John F. Finerty, Counsel, Concurring.

Appendix 1

Preliminary commission of inquiry
(Hearings in Coyoacan, Mexico, April 10–17, 1937.)

Members

Dr. John Dewey, Professor Emeritus of Philosophy, Columbia University (New York City), Chairman.

Carleton Beals, author and lecturer (California). (Resigned.)

Suzanne La Follette, author and former editor of the *New Freeman* (New York City), Secretary.

Otto Ruehle, former member of the German Reichstag and Biographer of Karl Marx (Mexico City).

Benjamin Stolberg, author and journalist (New York City).

Counsel

John F. Finerty, former counsel for Sacco and Vanzetti and counsel for Tom Mooney, acting as counsel for the Preliminary Commission of Inquiry (Washington, D.C.).

Albert Goldman, Labor attorney, acting as counsel for Leon Trotsky (Chicago).

Witnesses

Leon Trotsky, Jan Frankel.

Commission Rogatoire
(Hearings in Paris, May 12–June 22, 1937.)

Members

G.E. Modigliani, lawyer, member of the Executive Committee of the Labor and Socialist International, leader of the Italian Socialist Party, Chairman.

Mme. César Chabrun, Chairman of the Committee for Aid to Political Prisoners.

Maurice Délépine of the Paris Bar, member of the Permanent Administrative Committee of the Socialist Party of France, president of the Socialist Lawyers' group.

Jean Galtier-Boissière, writer, editor of *Crapouillot*.

Professor Jacques Madaule.

Jean Mathé, former secretary of the National Union of Postmen.

Counsel

Gérard Rosenthal, counsel for Leon Sedov.

Witnesses

Leon Sedov, Victor Serge, Eugene Bauer, Franz Pfemfert, Alexandra Pfemfert.

New York Sub-Commission
(Hearings in New York, July 26–27, 1937.)

Members
(The New York Sub-Commission was composed of those members of the Commission who were present in New York at the time of the hearings.)

Suzanne LaFollette, Secretary.
Alfred Rosmer.
Benjamin Stolberg.
Carlo Tresca.
Wendelin Thomas.

Counsel

John F. Finerty, Counsel for the Sub-Commission.
Albert Goldman, Counsel for Leon Trotsky.

Witnesses

Esther Field, B.J. Field, A.J. Muste, Sara Weber, Max
Shachtman, Herbert Solow, Max Sterling, Davis Herron,
Harold Isaacs, Viola Robinson.

Appendix 2

BIOGRAPHICAL INDEX OF THE ACCUSED

Note: The information given below concerning the accused in the Moscow trials of August, 1936, and January, 1937, has been compiled from official Soviet sources where such sources were available. An asterisk before the name of an accused indicates that the information concerning him is neither official nor vouched for as authentic by the Commission, although we have reason to believe that it is accurate.

The trial in which each accused was involved is indicated by the initials, ZK (Zinoviev-Kamenev) or PR (Pyatakov-Radek), following his name.

Accused, tried, and convicted

Arnold, Valentin Volfridovich (PR), 1894– .

Bakayev, Ivan Petrovich (ZK), 1887–1936. Old Bolshevik. In revolutionary movement from 1905. Member of Bolshevik Party from 1906. One of the organizers of the armed uprising in Kamyshin, 1906. Participated in October Insurrection in Petrograd. Commissar, Third Division (Ural front) and Second Division (Petrograd front). Chairman, Petrograd Division of the Cheka, 1919–20. Member, Leningrad Soviet and District Executive, 1917. Held other important posts. Follower of Zinoviev. Expelled from C.P.S.U., and capitulated, at 15th Congress. Arrested December 16, 1934. First trial January 15–16, 1935.

*Berman-Yurin, Konon Borisovich (Hans Stauer) (ZK), 1901–1936. Russian. Member, C.P.S.U. Went to Germany, 1923, as correspondent of Soviet Communist Youth League papers. Member, Communist Party of Germany (K.P.D.). Disagreed with ultra-left policy adopted 1929, and from that time held no official position. During last years in Germany not regular correspondent of Soviet papers but wrote only occasionally as free lance. Returned to U.S.S.R. March or April, 1935, on order of the Russian Party representative. Arrested end of May, 1936. Posthumously expelled from K.P.D.

Boguslavsky, Mikhail Solomonovich (PR), 1886–1937. Old worker-Bolshevik. In revolutionary movement from 1904, when he was arrested in Kharkov. Participated in October strikes, 1905. Member of the first C.E.C. and first Soviet government in the Ukraine. In 1919, elected secretary of All-Ukrainian C.E.C. of Soviets, and also of Council of People's Commissars in the Ukraine. Transferred to Moscow, and in 1921 elected to Moscow Executive Committee. Member, "Democratic Centralist Group." Expelled from C.P.S.U. at 15th Party Congress and exiled to Novosibirsk; capitulated, 1929, and was assigned to work in Novosibirsk where he remained until his arrest, August 5, 1936.

*David, Fritz (Ilya-David Israilevich Kruglyansky) (ZK), 1897–1937. Polish Russian. Member and minor official K.P.D. In 1931 became trade-union editor of the *Rote Fahne* (organ of the K.P.D.). Author of "The Bankruptcy of Reformism," theoretical justification of the ultra-left trade-union policy. Went to Russia in March, 1933, and began to write articles for Soviet press as free lance. Became secretary to Pieck (K.P.D. leader and German representative in the E.C.C.I.). Posthumously expelled from the K.P.D.

*Dreitzer, Ephim Alexandrovich (ZK), 1894–1936. Officer in the Red Army during Civil War. Twice decorated with order of the Red Flag. Fought against Kolchak and in the Polish campaign. Left Oppositionist; member of Trotsky's volunteer body-guard, 1927. Expelled from C.P.S.U. at 15th Party Congress. Capitulated, 1929.

Drobnis, Yakov Naumovich (PR), 1890–1937. Old worker-Bolshevik. Entered movement in 1905, at age of 15. During 1918 assigned to the most dangerous and responsible work in the Ukraine, where he functioned in the underground organization, mobilizing partisan detachments against Petlura and the Germans. Served on the Denikin front, 1919–1920. Twice condemned to death by The Whites, and once shot and left for dead. Member of "Democratic Centralist Group"; expelled at 15th Party Congress; capitulated, 1929; reinstated and assigned to work in Siberia. Assistant Chief, Kemerovo Combined Works Construction. Arrested August 6, 1936.

Evdokimov, Grigori Eremeyevich (ZK), 1884–1936. Old worker-Bolshevik. Sailor from age of 15. Joined party in 1903; arrested in 1908; carried on Party work in Omsk 1908–13. From 1913 worked in Petersburg, where he was arrested and exiled. Escaped in 1916 and was rearrested. After February (1917) revolution an agitator in Petrograd. Head, political department, Seventh Army; participated in defeat of Yudenich. Chairman, Petrograd Council of Trade Unions, 1922; Deputy Chairman, Petrograd Soviet. Secretary of the Leningrad Committee, 1925. Member, 8th, 12th, 13th and 14th Party Congresses. Official Party speaker at Lenin's funeral. Follower of Zinoviev. Member, Left Opposition bloc. Expelled from C.P.S.U., and capitulated, at 15th Party Congress. Appointed to minor post in the grain and cattle center, 1931. Arrested December 16, 1934. First trial, January 15–16, 1935.

*Holtzman, Edouard Solomonovich (ZK), 1882–1936. Old Bolshevik administrator. Left Opposition sympathizer, 1926–27. Never a member of the Opposition.

Hrasche, Ivan Yosifovich (PR), 1886–1937. Member, C.P.S.U. from 1917. Head of the foreign bureau, Soviet Nitrogen industry, 1932. In same position, Central Administration of the Chemical Industry, from spring, 1934.

Kamenev, Lev (Leon) **Borisovich** (ZK), 1883–1936. Old Bolshevik. Joined Social Democratic Party in 1901 as a student in Moscow Institute. Arrested at a demonstration, March, 1902, expelled from university and placed under police surveillance. Went to Paris, autumn, 1902. Joined Bolsheviks after the split, 1903. Returned to Russia. Worked in St. Petersburg, 1905–07; after arrest in 1908 emigrated again. Ordered back to Russia by the C.C., 1914, to serve as editor of *Pravda* and guide work of Party faction in the Duma. Arrested with

Duma faction, 1914, and exiled, 1915. Member, C.C., from April Conference, 1917 to 1927. At second Soviet Congress elected Chairman of the C.E.C. of the Soviets, in which post he was replaced by Sverdlov. Lenin's deputy as Chairman of Party Politbureau. Member, Brest-Litovsk delegation. Chairman, Moscow Soviet, 1918–26. Deputy Chairman, Council of People's Commissars, 1922; Ambassador to Italy, 1927. Member, Left Opposition bloc. Expelled from C.P.S.U., and capitulated, at 15th Congress, December, 1927; reinstated, 1928. Expelled from Party and exiled, October, 1932; capitulated and returned to Moscow, May, 1933. Arrested, December 16, 1934. First trial, January 15–16, 1935; second trial, July, 1935. Editor of Lenin's works.

Knyazev, Ivan Alexandrovich (PR), 1893–1937. Member of C.P.S.U. from 1918. Went to work on railways at age of 20. Chief of the South Urals railway; Assistant Chief of the Central Traffic Division, People's Commissariat of Railways.

Livshitz, Yakov Abramovich (PR), 1896–1937. Member, C.P.S.U. Assistant People's Commissar of Railways.

Lurye, Mossei Ilyich (Alexander Emel) (ZK), 1897–1936. Opponent of Trotskyist movement in Germany. Contributor to *Inprecorr* (official organ of C.I.). Went to Russia in March, 1933.

Lurye, Nathan Lazarevich (ZK) 1901–1936. Polish Russian. Member, K.P.D. Went to U.S.S.R., 1932, after foreigners were deprived by governmental decree of the right to work in Germany.

***Mrachkovsky, Sergei Vitalevich** (ZK), 1883–1936. Member, Bolshevik Party, from 1905. Organized the workers' insurrection in the Urals, 1917, and became commander of the Urals military district after the victory of the Soviets. Active Left Oppositionist. Expelled from the C.P.S.U. at the 15th Party Congress, 1927. Capitulated, 1929. Exiled at beginning of 1933.

Muralov, Nikolai Ivanovich (PR), 1877–1937. One of the oldest worker-Bolsheviks. One of the leaders, Moscow insurrection, October, 1917; legendary hero of Civil War. Commandant Moscow Military District; member, Central Control Commission. Left Oppositionist; expelled from C.P.S.U. at 15th Congress and exiled to Western Siberia. Left the Opposition and politics without formally capitulating. Arrested April 17, 1936.

Norkin, Boris Osipovich (PR), 1895–1937. Chief of the Kemerovo Combined Works Construction. Member of West Siberian Territory Committee, C.P.S.U., and member of Bureau of the City Committee. Arrested September 30, 1936.

Olberg, Valentine Pavlovich (ZK), 1907–1936. Latvian. Went to Berlin, 1927. Worked for *Inprecorr*. Joined Left Opposition in Berlin as member of Landau group, 1930; expelled with same group, 1931. Applied for readmission as individual and was refused. Went to Russia, 1933, because Hitler government was about to deport him as undesirable alien. Obtained position as teacher of history in Stalinabad. Left Russia July, 1933, and went to Prague, where he obtained Honduran citizenship. Returned to Russia, 1935, and obtained position as teacher of history in Gorky. Arrested during or after January, 1936.

*Pickel, Richard Vitoldovich (ZK), 1896–1936. Man of letters. Former secretary of Zinoviev. Expelled and capitulated at 15th Congress.

Pushin, Gavriil Yefremovich (PR), 1896–1937. Member, C.P.S.U. Employed in Central Administration of the Chemical Industry. Arrested October 22, 1936.

Pyatakov, Yuri (Georgi) **Leonidovich** (PR), 1890–1937. Participated in revolutionary movement from 1904. Arrested, 1912; exiled, 1913; escaped abroad (through Japan), 1914. Participated in Berne Conference of Bolsheviks. After February revolution Chairman, Kiev Committee of the Bolsheviks. After October Assistant Commissar and then Chief Commissar of State Bank. During Civil War served in the Ukraine. Chairman, first Soviet government in the Ukraine, December, 1918. Chairman, Military Revolutionary Committee of Thirteenth Army. Commissar of the Military Academy, 1920. Member, Revolutionary Military Committee of the Sixteenth Army at Polish front, May, 1920; then of the Sixth Army at Wrangel front. Head of management of coal industry in the Don Basin, 1921. Vice-Chairman, Supreme Council of National Economy, 1923. Member, Left Opposition; expelled from

C.P.S.U. at 15th Party Congress; capitulated and reinstated, 1928. From that time held various high posts, the last being that of Vice-Chairman, People's Commissariat of Heavy Industry. His name was among six mentioned by Lenin in his so-called "testament," bracketed with that of Bukharin as one of the "two ablest young men in the Party."

Radek, Karl Berngardovich (PR), 1885– . In revolutionary movement from age of 14. First worked in Austrian Poland and Galicia (1904–8). In 1908 went to Germany where, with Rosa Luxemburg, he formed the left wing in the German Social Democracy around the newspaper *Bremer Arbeiterpolitik*. Internationalist during World War. Participated in Zimmerwald and Kienthal Conferences. On Bureau of Zimmerwald Left. Went with Lenin to Stockholm in 1917 but was prevented from entering Russia. Arrived in Moscow after October Revolution. After Brest-Litovsk peace, in charge of Central European section, Commissariat of Foreign Affairs. After revolution of 1918 in Germany went there illegally; participated in organizing first Congress of German Communist Party ("Spartacists"); arrested in Germany, February 15, 1919; released December, 1919, and returned to Russia. One of the most active participants in work of the C.I. under Lenin. In 1920, secretary, E.C.C.I. Member, Left Opposition; expelled from C.P.S.U. at 15th Congress; capitulated 1929; reinstated 1930, and served on *Izvestia*. Arrested after Zinoviev-Kamenev trial.

Rataichak, Stanislav Antonovich (PR), 1894–1937. Former worker. Member, C.P.S.U. Chief of the Central Administration of the Chemical Industry.

*Reingold, Isak Isayevich (ZK), 1897–1936. Former Assistant People's Commissar of Finance. Connected politically with Kamenev. Expelled from C.P.S.U., and capitulated, at 15th Congress.

Serebryakov, Leonid Petrovich (PR), 1890–1937. Old Bolshevik; began factory work as a metal worker at age of 9; entered revolutionary movement in 1904. Arrested, 1905. Professional revolutionist from 1909; participated in Prague Conference of Bolsheviks. Arrested, 1912, in Samara and exiled to Narym;

escaped, 1914, and returned to Moscow, where he organized May-day demonstration. Rearrested and sent back to Narym; after serving term of exile went to Tomsk, 1916. After February revolution organized the Komstromsky Soviet. In middle of 1917 went to Moscow, where he served on Moscow Central Committee. After October, member, Praesidium, Moscow Soviet, and secretary, Moscow Committee. Secretary of the C.C. (C.P.S.U.) 1919–20; Secretary of All-Russian C.E.C. of Soviets. Active participant in Civil War; member, Military Revolutionary Committee of the Southern Front, 1921; then Commissar of Communications. Member, Left Opposition; expelled from C.P.S.U. in October, 1927; capitulated June, 1929; reinstated January, 1930. Since served in various high posts, the last being that of Assistant Commissar of Communications.

Shestov, Alexei Alexandrovich (PR), 1896–1937. Old worker-Bolshevik. Member of Board, Eastern and Siberian Coal Trust.

Smirnov, Ivan Nikitich (ZK), 1881–1936. Old worker-Bolshevik. Professional revolutionist. In revolutionary movement from 1898; party member from 1899; joined Bolsheviks after the split, 1903. Arrested, 1899, then exiled; escaped, 1903; arrested, 1904. Participated in Moscow armed uprising, 1905. Arrested, 1910, and exiled to Narym; escaped, 1912; arrested, 1913, and again exiled to Narym; escaped, rearrested, and returned to Russia (from Siberia). Mobilized into army, 1916. One of prominent figures in Civil War. Member, Revolutionary Military Committee of the East. Leader of Siberian forces; insured victory of Fifth Army over Kolchak. After Kolchak's defeat Chairman, Siberian Revolutionary Committee. People's Commissar of Communications, 1923–27. Member, Left Opposition; expelled from C.P.S.U. at 15th Congress; capitulated, 1929; reinstated and appointed director of automobile plants at Nizhni-Novgorod. Arrested January 1, 1933, and sent to prison, where he remained until trial of August, 1936.

Sokolnikov, Grigori Yakovlevich (PR), 1888– . Old Bolshevik. In revolutionary movement from 1903; member of Party from 1905. In 1905–07 agitator-propagandist and organizer in Moscow. Participated in Moscow armed uprising, 1905. Arrested, 1907; exiled, 1909, and escaped. In emigration, 1909–1917. Internationalist during World War. Member, Moscow Committee of Party, April, 1917. After October Revolution directed nationalization of banks; Chairman Soviet Peace Delegation at Brest-Litovsk, 1918; signatory of treaty. Member, Revolutionary Military Committee of Second, Eighth, Ninth and Twelfth Armies, 1918–20. Assistant Commissar of Finance, 1921; Commissar of Finance, 1922. Deputy Chairman, State Planning Commission, 1926; Chairman, Oil Syndicate, 1928. Ambassador to Great Britain, 1929. Member, C.C. of C.P.S.U., 1917–19, 1922–30. Sent to Hague Conference, 1922. During 1925–6 supported "United Opposition" but left it, shortly after capitulating to Stalin-Bukharin. At 16th Party Congress elected candidate to C.E.C. Assistant Commissar of Foreign Affairs, 1934. Arrested summer of 1936.

Stroilov, Mikhail Stepanovich (PR), 1899– . Non-Party engineer; Chief Engineer, Kuzbas Coal Trust. Decorated with Order of the Labor Red Banner, July 7, 1935. Decorated again at session of C.E.C., October 7, 1935, for raising coal output in mines under his direction. Alternate member, All-Russian C.E.C.

*Ter-Vaganyan, Vagarshak Arutyunovich (ZK), 1893–1936. Old Bolshevik. Leader of Armenian Communists and of Soviet revolution in Armenia. Author of numerous works on the national question and other problems of Marxism; founder and first editor, under Lenin, of the Party's principal scientific review, *Pod Znameniem Marxisma* (Under the Banner of Marxism). Member, Left Opposition; expelled from C.P.S.U. at 15th Congress; capitulated 1929; exiled at beginning of 1933.

Turok, Yosif Dmitrievich (PR), 1900–1937. Member, C.P.S.U. for twenty years; participated in Civil War. Assistant manager, traffic department, Perm and Urals Railway.

Zinoviev, Grigori Evseyevich (ZK), 1883–1936. Old Bolshevik. Member of Party from 1901; Bolshevik from the split in 1903. Emigrated, 1902; returned to Russia, 1905; worked in Petrograd; arrested, 1908, and forced to emigrate again. Internationalist during World War. Closest collaborator of

Lenin; participant in Zimmerwald and Kienthal Conferences. Returned to Russia with Lenin, 1917. During July days forced to hide out with Lenin in Finland. After October Revolution, Chairman, Petrograd Soviet. Chairman, E.C.C.I., 1919–26. Member, Central Committee of Party, 1907–27. Member, Left Opposition bloc. Expelled from C.P.S.U., and capitulated, at 15th Congress, December, 1927; reinstated, 1928; expelled and exiled, October, 1932; capitulated and returned to Moscow, May, 1933. Arrested December 16, 1934; first trial, January 15–16, 1935.

Accused and declared convicted, but not tried

Sedov, Lev (Leon) **Lvovich** (ZK, PR), 1906–1938. Son of Lev (Leon) Davidovich Trotsky and Natalia Ivanova Sedov-Trotsky. Born in Russia. Shared exile of his parents in Austria, Switzerland, France, the United States; returned with them to Russia, 1917. Active in Communist youth movement. Accompanied parents to exile in Alma-Ata, 1928, and Turkey, 1929. Closest collaborator of Leon Trotsky. Studied engineering, *Technische Hochschule*, Berlin, 1931–33 and edited *Bulletin of the Opposition*. Forced to leave Germany after Hitler's rise to power, went to Paris, March, 1933; studied at Sorbonne; continued editing *Bulletin* until his death, February 16, 1938.

Trotsky, Lev (Leon) **Davidovich** (ZK, PR), 1879– .

"L.D. Trotsky, born in 1881 [1879], active in the workers' circles in the city of Nikolayev; in 1898 exiled to Siberia; soon after escaped abroad and participated in the *Iskra*. Delegate from the Siberian League at the Second Congress of the Party. After the split in the Party, adhered to the Mensheviks. Even prior to the revolution, in 1905, he advanced his own and today particularly noteworthy theory of the permanent revolution, in which he asserted that the bourgeois revolution of 1905 must pass directly into the socialist revolution, being the first of the national revolutions; he defended his theory in the newspaper *Nachalo*, the central organ of the Menshevik faction published during November–December, 1905, in Petersburg. After the arrest of Khrustalev-Nossar, he was elected Chairman of the First Petersburg Soviet of Workers' Deputies. Arrested together with the Executive Committee on December 3, 1905, he was sent into life exile to Obdorsk, but escaped en route and emigrated abroad. Trotsky chose Vienna to live in, and there he issued a popular labor newspaper, *Pravda*, to be circulated in Russia. He broke with the Mensheviks and attempted to form a group outside of all factions; however, during the factional struggle abroad he made a bloc with the Mensheviks and the *Vpered* group against the bloc between Lenin and Plekhanov who fought the liquidators. From the very beginning of the imperialist war he took a clear-cut internationalist position, participated in the publication of *Nashe Slovo*, in Paris, and adhered to Zimmerwald. Deported from France, he went to the United States. On his return from there after the February revolution, he was arrested by the English and set free only on the demand of the Provisional government, which was forced to intervene under the pressure of the Petersburg Soviet. In Petersburg he entered the organization of the *'Mejrayontsi,'* together with whom he joined the Bolshevik Party at the Sixth Party Congress in July, 1917, in Petersburg. After the July days, he was arrested by the government of Kerensky and indicted for 'leading the insurrection,' but was shortly freed through pressure from the Petersburg proletariat. After the Petersburg Soviet went over to the Bolsheviks, he was elected Chairman, and in this capacity he organized and led the insurrection of October 25. Standing member of the C.C. of the C.P.S.U. since 1917; member of the Council of People's Commissars, first holding the post of People's Commissar of Foreign Affairs up to the signing of the Brest Treaty, then People's Commissar of War."[*]

Member, Political Bureau, C.C. of C.P.S.U., 1917–27. Active in formation of C.I. Organizer and leader of the armed forces in the Civil War. Leader, Left Opposition, from 1923.

---

[*] Note to the first edition of Lenin's Collected Works, Volume XIV, part 2, page 481–2. Moscow: State Publishers, 1921.

Expelled from C.P.S.U. at 15th Congress, 1927; exiled to Alma-Ata, 1928, and Turkey, 1929; deprived of Soviet Citizenship, 1932. Removed to France, July, 1933; to Norway, 1935; deported to Mexico, December, 1936. Author of many works on theoretical and historical subjects.

Appendix 3

MEMORANDUM TO AMBASSADOR KOBETZKY
BY WINDFELD-HANSEN

MOSCOW, 7 AUGUST, 1932.

Dear Mr. Kobetzky:

In compliance with your wish I hereby beg to submit a summary of the technical research-work and projecting performed here with the object of utilizing the extensive deposits of low-grade, impure phosphates existing in great parts of Central Russia, as for instance in the Governments of Vjatka and Kjäsan, as well as in Kazakhstan (Aktjubinsk). Great importance is attached here to the utilization of these phosphates, as the phosphate fertilizers produced from them may be used in the same districts and thus mean a great saving in carrying expenses. To be sure, the Soviet Union possesses some of the richest phosphate deposits in the world, namely, the enormous deposits of apatite at Chibin in the peninsula of Kola. But the long railway haul to the middle and southern localities of the Union nevertheless makes the utilization of the lead phosphates in Central Russia most desirable. It is now the intention to use the Chibin apatite principally for the production of superphosphate, as the apatite is very high-grade—35–40 per cent. of P_2O_5—and therefore will yield a very high-grade superphosphate, which can bear the expense of bagging and transportation. Consequently, it is necessary first to make a solution of phosphoric acid from these phosphates, and same may then be used—after evaporation, if necessary—for the production of different high-grade phosphate fertilizers, especially for double superphosphate by mixing it with a suitable quantity of raw phosphate, or ammonia phosphate by saturating the phosphoric acid with ammonia.

The production of phosphoric acid is effected by treating the phosphate with sulphuric acid, by which process phosphoric acid and gypsum are formed. The main problem consists in precipitating gypsum so coarse-grained that it may easily be extracted from the phosphate solution, where after it is washed free of phosphoric acid. If the gypsum has been separated in a bad form (small or needle-shaped crystals) great quantities of the solution will adhere, and a lot of water is required to wash away the adherent solution. The acid thus produced will be correspondingly diluted, however, and a corresponding quantity of water has to be evaporated later on.

Now the production of phosphoric acids from these [low-grade] phosphates is rendered difficult by their great content of iron oxide (Fe_2O_3), the solution of phosphoric acid becoming very ferruginous, and thus more sulphuric acid will be used. The iron contents in the acid have the effect that a corresponding quantity of phosphoric acid in the finished fertilizers will be insoluble in water, and when producing ammonia phosphate, too great a quantity of sludge will be formed, which will make difficulties.

When I was working in the branch of the Dorr Company in Berlin, the Russian Trade Delegation there asked us to devise a process for the production of ammonia phosphate from these low-grade phosphates, and our research laboratory worked most intensively with this task for several months, and I participated in this work. We succeeded in producing without difficulty an excellent gypsum, and we further found out that the iron oxide in the phosphate became practically insoluble, when first calcinating the phosphate. We devised an efficient process and a great project in the spring of the year 1931, but it did not come to business with the Soviet Union.

However, I here beg to point out that the Dorr Company kept the process secret, demanded a very large engineering fee, and refused to give any binding guarantees.

The gypsum obtained in the production of the phosphoric acid may be utilized for the manufacture of ammonia sulphate without employment of sulphuric acid, in this manner utilizing again the sulphuric acid already used for the production of the phosphoric acid. This process is used in many places abroad, and it is also planned to use it here in the Soviet Union, both with regard to natural gypsum and gypsum obtained in the production of phosphoric acid. From my work in the Dorr Company I have had thorough experience with regard to this process, which we succeeded in developing so well.

I will now account for the work done here to solve the said problems.

The experimental work has been performed by the Technical Department at the Fertilizer Institute [NIU] in Moscow under the management of Mr. Volfkovich, the Head of the Department, and the projects were prepared in "Giprokhim" [the State planning organization for the chemical industry] under the management of the engineer, Mr. Vogt, the head of the Phosphate Department.

Up to date the Fertilizer Institute have not succeeded in producing a serviceable gypsum, which they also admit. Consequently they are able to produce only a highly diluted phosphoric acid. Further, they had arrived at the definite conception that it was impossible to evaporate phosphoric acid from these phosphates in the usual manner in evaporators by means of steam, and they neglected to make reasonable tests to this end. They further neglected to make tests with calcinated phosphates, although aware of the fact that this would make the iron oxide insoluble. They contended that in such a case the gypsum would be of an inferior quality, which is absolutely incorrect.

Being unable to solve these three fundamental problems, they encountered difficulties of a secondary nature; and in this manner the total experimental work got onto the wrong track. In their calamity they therefore resorted to three different processes, which are to be considered impossible from an engineering point of view, but by which they avoid the evaporation of the solution of phosphoric acid.

It is now the intention to try out two of these processes in a rather large test plant in the Chemical Works at Tschernoretsche. I estimate that this plant will cost 200,000 Rmk. according to German conditions. The running of this plant is now being started. A reconstruction of this plant to a rational process will be so expensive that a new plant probably could be erected at the same cost.

The third process consists in precipitating the phosphoric acid again by means of a great quantity of ground limestone and burnt lime, thus obtaining a fertilizer which is called precipitate and contains about 35 per cent. of P_2O_5. However, this process consumes about 30 per cent. more sulphuric acid per kg P_2O_5 as compared with the figure in the production of double superphosphate. Though the responsible men notoriously were aware of this fact, they resolved to construct a large plant in Voskressensk according to this process. In a plant of this size the additional consumption of sulphuric acid will amount to about fifty tons per twenty-four hours, apart from the great quantity of chalk; this waste of raw materials having no evident advantages, apart from the fact that they believe they are able to handle this process.

On June 13 I informed Mr. Vogt of my objections and handed him a calculation of the consumption of sulphuric acid. I suggested to him to stop the construction of the plant and possibly to change it to double superphosphate. But he declared that this was absolutely out of the question. His other arguments in favor of this project were so peculiar that I considered them an attempt to veil the matter and set me wrong. He has never brought the matter up since. I was later told by a leading engineer in the Fertilizer Institute that, when the project was considered, he advanced exactly the same view as mine in a written report, but it was ignored.

With regard to the production of ammonia sulphate from gypsum the results achieved are no better. For this purpose a process has been resorted to which will hardly do in practice, this process not having been first tested on a small scale before constructing a large test plant in Tschernoretsche. I estimate the cost of this plant at 300,000 Rmk. according to German conditions. It comprises a large evaporating plant for the solution of ammonia sulphate, which will hardly be able to operate on account of choking up, and which is far too complicated. In this case also, they have failed to make tests on a small scale. In all three plants an immense number of structural faults of a more or less serious nature have been committed.

As early as May and the beginning of June, I submitted a number of memoranda on all the above-mentioned subjects, which memoranda also contain concrete proposals for the solution of the problems on the basis of my experience, and are accompanied by drawings and calculations. I have likewise proposed to start new tests on a semi-technical scale in the experimental plants of the Fertilizer Institute. But to date practically nothing has been done in this respect.

Summing up the above statements, it may be said that the work in these fields practically has to be begun again from the beginning. Consequently, great delays in the industrial development in this field are unavoidable, even if the necessary energetic measures be taken within the near future. If such measures are not taken, I see no possibility of starting production within a measurable period.

Translation certified and notarized, Copenhagen, April 1, 1937.

Index

Abramovich, 491

Adelante (Barcelona), 70–71

Adolphe, 265, 266, 267, 270, 272, 371; testimony, 280, 284–85

Adunskaya, Esther, 176

Adunskaya, Nekha, 175–76

Aftenposten (Oslo), 242, 244

Aktjubinsk, chemical fertilizer plant, 349, 515

American Committee for the Defense of Leon Trotsky, 27

André, Hervé, testimony, 281–82

Antonov-Ovseyenko, V.A., 303n

Arbeiderbladet (Copenhagen), 129

Arbeiderbladet (Oslo), 240, 241–42

Arnold, V.V., 209, 315

August Bloc, 421–24

Avdeyev, 482

Axelrod, 417

Bakayev, I.P., 67, 89–90, 138, 142, 190, 250, 315, 479, 482

Bardon, Albert, testimony, 282–83

Batalla, La, 71

Bauer, Eugene, 121n, 156, 167, 284; testimony, 116–17, 142–43, 149, 152, 153, 164–65, 174–75, 177–78, 216, 222–23, 366, 371, 389

Beaussier, Jean, 267, 284

Beaverbrook, Lord, 71, 307

Berliner Tageblatt, 70

Berman-Yurin, K.B. (Stauer, Hans), 22, 81, 125, 159–71, 370; alleged instructions from Trotsky, 22, 81–82, 159, 160–62, 168–69, 171, 365, 368, 370; alleged relations with Sedov, 159–61, 162, 163, 166–68; testimony, 159–63, 167, 168, 169–70, 365, 372, 448–49

Biline, 246

Birney, Earle, 238

Blancan, Agence, 277

Blum, Léon, 396

Blume, Maria, testimony, 175–76

Blumkin, 62, 69–70, 94, 218

Boeggild, 114

Bogstad Airport, 244

Boguslavsky, M.S., 66, 67, 92, 208, 213

Bolshevik government, 387–88 (*See also* Soviet government)

Bolshevik-Leninists (*See* Left Opposition)

Bolshevik Party, 65, 73, 75, 113, 128, 255, 323, 386, 413, 428, 436, 437, 447 (*See also* Communist Party of the Soviet Union)

Borsig, 212, 214, 220, 222, 223–24, 225, 300

Brandler, 71

Brest-Litovsk, 257, 387–88, 414, 442–43

Breton, André, 40

Briand, Aristide, 492

Bristol Café (*See* Bristol Confectionery)

Bristol Confectionery, 115–16, 119, 129–30, 131–34

Bristol Hotel, 112, 115, 128–30, 131–33

Britzke, Professor, 344, 350, 354

Brockway, Archibald Fenner, 287

Brodsky, Joseph, 32

Bruening, Heinrich, 300

209, 210, 213, 293–302; alleged
interviews: with Pyatakov, 220,
221, 294, 297, 298, 299–300; with
Sedov, 207, 221, 225, 294–95, 296,
297–300, 302; with Smirnov, 220–
21, 294, 296–97, 299–300; alleged
letters for Muralov and Pyatakov,
181–82, 207, 225, 226, 297, 300–301,
302; testimony, 22, 207, 293–97,
298–300, 301–2, 305, 401; Novosibirsk trial, 298, 299, 302
Shkiriatov, 72
Shliapnikov, 443
Sinot, 355
Slomovitz, 138, 365, 366–67
Smilga, 192, 208, 479, 480, 482
Smirnov, I.N., 56, 66, 73, 84–86, 87–
88, 92–94, 99–100, 107–8, 109–10,
138, 142, 160, 167, 208, 219, 252,
294, 299–300, 304, 305, 308, 309,
314–15, 471–72, 491n; alleged
communication with Sedov, 56,
92; alleged codes, 83, 87–88, 92,
95, 97; alleged go-between: for
Sedov and Pyatakov, 211, 212, 215,
219, 220–21, 224, 302; for Sedov
and Shestov, 215, 294, 295–97,
299–300, 302; alleged interviews:
with Muralov, 304, 309; with
Pyatakov, 211, 213, 215, 216, 217,
220–21, 252; with Shestov, 220–
21, 294, 295–97, 299–300; alleged
instructions: from Trotsky, 21,
83, 84–85, 86, 89, 91, 93, 95, 98,
99, 100–102, 106–7, 108, 112, 131,
224; to Dreitzer, 83, 85–86, 87, 98,
103–4, 106; alleged letter from
Trotsky, 84, 86, 88n, 91, 101–2,
109; alleged meeting with Sedov
and Pyatakov, 213, 215, 216–17,
218, 220–21; denials, 86, 95–96,
98, 99; interview with Sedov, 83,
87, 91, 93–94, 95, 99, 101, 215,
220–21; letter for Trotsky, 86, 87,

88, 92, 93–94, 96–97, 100, 107–8;
on Trotsky, 100–101; testimony,
22, 83, 84–85, 91–92, 95–96, 99,
101–2, 104, 220, 224; Vyshinsky
on, 96, 97, 470–72
Smith, Charles Andrew, 284; testi-
mony, 286–87, 288n, 289
Sneevliet, H., 284, 395; testimony,
286, 393–94
Sobolevich (See Senin)
Sobolevitzius (See Senin)
Social Democracy, 177, 496 (See also
Second International)
Social Democratic Party, Danzig, 367;
Germany, 255, 384–85; Poland,
255n; Russia, 255, 416, 417, 456
Social Revolutionaries, 317, 484
"Socialism in One Country," 248,
424–41
Socialist Party, U.S., 235
Socialist Workers' Party, Germany,
116, 395
Sokolnikov, G.Y., 59, 63, 66, 81, 179, 180–
81, 183, 186, 189, 190–91, 196–98,
201, 202, 204, 205–6, 208, 372, 377,
406, 412; testimony: on "reserve
center," 191, 192–94, 196, 199–200;
on "parallel center," 197, 199–201;
on Trotsky, 190, 191, 192
Solntsev, Eleazar, 476
Soloviev, 482
Solow, Herbert, testimony, 389–90
Sosnovsky, 303n
Sotsialisticheski Vestnik (Paris),
495
Soulard, M., testimony, 281–82
Souvarin, Boris, 71
Soviet government, 28, 30, 60, 82,
83, 171n, 180, 212, 225, 234, 267,
290, 315, 316, 365, 380, 382, 385,
387, 392, 401, 407, 442, 458, 483,
496, 498; execution of defendants,
30, 132; non-cooperation, 30, 32,
37, 131

Cuba and the Coming American Revolution

JACK BARNES

This is a book about the struggles of working people in the imperialist heartland, the youth attracted to them, and the example set by the Cuban people that revolution is not only necessary—it can be made. It is about the class struggle in the U.S., where the political capacities and revolutionary potential of workers and farmers are today as utterly discounted by the ruling powers as were those of the Cuban toilers. And just as wrongly. Second edition, with new foreword by Mary-Alice Waters. $10. Also in Spanish and French.

Our History Is Still Being Written

The Story of Three Chinese–Cuban Generals in the Cuban Revolution

Armando Choy, Gustavo Chui, and Moisés Sío Wong talk about the historic place of Chinese immigration to Cuba, as well as over five decades of revolutionary action and internationalism, from Cuba to Angola and Venezuela today. Through their stories we see the social and political forces that gave birth to the Cuban nation and opened the door to socialist revolution in the Americas. $20. Also in Spanish.

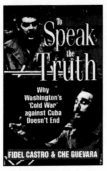

To Speak the Truth

Why Washington's 'Cold War' against Cuba Doesn't End

FIDEL CASTRO, ERNESTO CHE GUEVARA

In historic speeches before the United Nations and UN bodies, Guevara and Castro address the peoples of the world, explaining why the U.S. government so fears the example set by the socialist revolution in Cuba and why Washington's effort to destroy it will fail. $17

www.pathfinderpress.com

THE RUSSIAN REVOLUTION

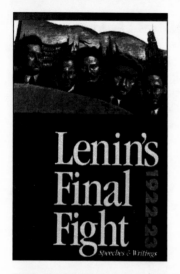

LENIN'S FINAL FIGHT
Speeches and Writings, 1922–23
V.I. LENIN

In the early 1920s Lenin waged a political battle in the leadership of the Communist Party of the USSR to maintain the course that had enabled the workers and peasants to overthrow the tsarist empire, carry out the first successful socialist revolution, and begin building a world communist movement. The issues posed in Lenin's political fight remain at the heart of world politics today. $21. Also in Spanish.

THE CASE OF LEON TROTSKY
Report of Hearings on the Charges Made against Him in the Moscow Trials
LEON TROTSKY

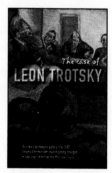

Was the regime of Joseph Stalin and his heirs a continuation of the Bolshevik-led workers and peasants government established by the October 1917 Revolution? No! says Bolshevik leader Leon Trotsky in testimony before a 1937 international commission of inquiry into Stalin's Moscow frame-up trials. Reviewing forty years of working-class struggle in which Trotsky was a participant and leader, he discusses the fight to restore V.I. Lenin's revolutionary internationalist course and why the Stalin regime organized the Moscow Trials. He explains working people's stake in the unfolding Spanish Revolution, the fight against fascism in Germany, efforts to build a world revolutionary party, and much more. $30

BOLSHEVISM AND THE RUSSIAN REVOLUTION
V.I. LENIN, DOUG JENNESS, ERNEST MANDEL

A discussion on the political contributions of V.I. Lenin and the Bolshevik Party in the decade and a half prior to the October 1917 revolutionary victory in Russia. $8

THE HISTORY OF
THE RUSSIAN REVOLUTION
LEON TROTSKY

A classic account of the social, economic, and political dynamics of the first socialist revolution as told by one of its central leaders. "The history of a revolution is for us first of all a history of the forcible entrance of the masses into the realm of rulership over their own destiny," Trotsky writes. Unabridged edition, 3 vols. in one. $36. Also in Russian.

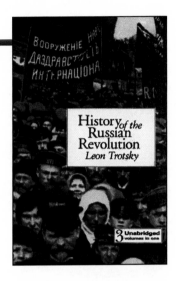

TO SEE THE DAWN
Baku, 1920—
First Congress of the Peoples of the East

How can peasants and workers in the colonial world achieve freedom from imperialist exploitation? By what means can working people overcome divisions incited by their national ruling classes and act together for their common class interests? These questions were addressed by 2,000 delegates to the 1920 Congress of the Peoples of the East. $22

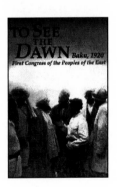

THE REVOLUTION BETRAYED
What Is the Soviet Union and Where Is It Going?
LEON TROTSKY

In 1917 the working class and peasantry of Russia carried out one of the most profound revolutions in history. Yet within ten years a political counterrevolution by a privileged social layer whose chief spokesperson was Joseph Stalin was being consolidated. This classic study of the Soviet workers state and its degeneration illuminates the roots of the social and political crisis in Russia and other countries that formerly made up the Soviet Union. $17. Also in Spanish.

Building a **PROLETARIAN PARTY**

The Changing Face of U.S. Politics
Working-Class Politics and the Trade Unions
JACK BARNES

Building the kind of party working people need to prepare for coming class battles through which they will revolutionize themselves, their unions, and all society. A handbook for those seeking the road toward effective action to overturn the exploitative system of capitalism and join in reconstructing the world on new, socialist foundations. $23. Also in Spanish, French and Swedish.

Their Trotsky and Ours
JACK BARNES

To lead the working class in a successful revolution, a mass proletarian party is needed whose cadres, well beforehand, have absorbed a world communist program, are proletarian in life and work, derive deep satisfaction from doing politics, and have forged a leadership with an acute sense of what to do next. This book is about building such a party. $15. Also in Spanish and French.

The History of American Trotskyism, 1928–38
Report of a Participant
JAMES P. CANNON

"Trotskyism is not a new movement, a new doctrine," Cannon says, "but the restoration, the revival of genuine Marxism as it was expounded and practiced in the Russian revolution and in the early days of the Communist International." In twelve talks given in 1942, Cannon recounts a decisive period in efforts to build a proletarian party in the United States. $22. Also in Spanish and French.

What Is To Be Done?
V.I. LENIN

The stakes in creating a disciplined organization of working-class revolutionaries capable of acting as a "tribune of the people, able to react to every manifestation of tyranny and oppression, no matter where it appears, to clarify for all and everyone the world-historic significance of the struggle for the emancipation of the proletariat." Written in 1902. In *Essential Works of Lenin*, $12.95

In Defense of Marxism
The Social and Political Contradictions of the Soviet Union on the Eve of World War II
LEON TROTSKY

Writing in 1939–40, Leon Trotsky replies to those in the revolutionary workers movement beating a retreat from defense of the Soviet Union in face of the looming imperialist assault. Why only a party that fights to bring growing numbers of workers into its ranks and leadership can steer a steady revolutionary course. $25. Also in Spanish.

The Struggle for a Proletarian Party
JAMES P. CANNON

"The workers of America have power enough to topple the structure of capitalism at home and to lift the whole world with them when they rise," Cannon asserts. On the eve of World War II, a founder of the communist movement in the U.S. and leader of the Communist International in Lenin's time defends the program and party-building norms of Bolshevism. $22

Revolutionary Continuity
Marxist Leadership in the U.S.
FARRELL DOBBS

How successive generations took part in struggles of the U.S. labor movement, seeking to build a leadership that could advance the class interests of workers and small farmers and link up with fellow toilers around the world. Two volumes: *The Early Years, 1848–1917*, $20; *Birth of the Communist Movement 1918–1922*, $19.

Also from Pathfinder

CAPITALISM'S WORLD DISORDER

Jack Barnes

The social devastation and financial panic, the coarsening of politics, the cop brutality and acts of imperialist aggression accelerating around us—all are the product not of something gone wrong but of the lawful workings of capitalism. Yet the future can be changed by the united struggle and selfless action of workers and farmers conscious of their power to transform the world. $24. Also in Spanish and French.

Jack Barnes

CAPITALISM'S WORLD DISORDER

WORKING-CLASS POLITICS AT THE MILLENNIUM

THE COMMUNIST MANIFESTO

Karl Marx and Frederick Engels

Founding document of the modern working-class movement, published in 1848. Explains why communism is not a set of preconceived principles but the line of march of the working class toward power, "springing from an existing class struggle, a historical movement going on under our very eyes." $7. Also in Spanish.

TEAMSTER REBELLION

Farrell Dobbs

The 1934 strikes that built the industrial union movement in Minneapolis and helped pave the way for the CIO, recounted by a central leader of that battle. The first in a four-volume series on the class-struggle leadership of the strikes and organizing drives that transformed the Teamsters union in much of the Midwest into a fighting social movement and pointed the road toward independent labor political action. $19. Also in Spanish.

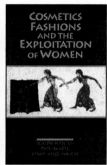

IS SOCIALIST REVOLUTION IN THE U.S. POSSIBLE?

A NECESSARY DEBATE

Mary-Alice Waters

Not only is socialist revolution in the U.S. possible, says Waters. Revolutionary struggles by working people are *inevitable*—initiated not by the toilers, but by the crisis-driven assaults of the propertied classes. As a fighting vanguard of the working class emerges in the U.S., the outlines of these coming battles—whose outcome is *not* inevitable—can already be seen. The future depends on us. $5. Also in Spanish and French.

MALCOLM X TALKS TO YOUNG PEOPLE

"The young generation of whites, Blacks, browns, whatever else there is—you're living at a time of revolution," Malcolm told young people in the United Kingdom in December 1964. "And I for one will join in with anyone, I don't care what color you are, as long as you want to change this miserable condition that exists on this earth." Four talks and an interview given to young people in Ghana, the UK, and the United States in the last months of Malcolm's life. $15. Also in Spanish.

COSMETICS, FASHIONS, AND THE EXPLOITATION OF WOMEN

Joseph Hansen, Evelyn Reed, Mary-Alice Waters

How big business plays on women's second-class status and social insecurities to market cosmetics and rake in profits. The introduction by Mary-Alice Waters explains how the entry of millions of women into the workforce during and after World War II irreversibly changed U.S. society and laid the basis for a renewed rise of struggles for women's emancipation. $15

THE WORKING CLASS AND THE TRANSFORMATION OF LEARNING

THE FRAUD OF EDUCATION REFORM
UNDER CAPITALISM

Jack Barnes

"Until society is reorganized so that education is a human activity from the time we are very young until the time we die, there will be no education worthy of working, creating humanity." $3. Also in Spanish, French, Icelandic, Swedish, Farsi and Greek.

IMPERIALISM, THE HIGHEST STAGE OF CAPITALISM

V.I. Lenin

"I trust that this pamphlet will help the reader to understand the fundamental economic question, that of the economic essence of imperialism," Lenin wrote in 1917. "For unless this is studied, it will be impossible to understand and appraise modern war and modern politics." $10. Also in Spanish.

AMERICA'S REVOLUTIONARY HERITAGE

George Novack

A materialist history of the genocide against Native Americans, the American Revolution, the Civil War, the rise of industrial capitalism, the first wave of the fight for women's rights, and more. $25

WORKERS OF THE WORLD AND OPPRESSED PEOPLES, UNITE!

PROCEEDINGS AND DOCUMENTS OF THE SECOND CONGRESS OF THE COMMUNIST INTERNATIONAL, 1920

The debate among delegates from 37 countries takes up key questions of working-class strategy and program—the fight for national liberation, the revolutionary transformation of trade unions, the worker-farmer alliance, participation in elections and parliament, and the structure and tasks of Communist Parties. The reports, resolutions, and debates offer a vivid portrait of social struggles in the era of the Bolshevik-led October Revolution. 2 vols. $65

FIGHTING RACISM IN WORLD WAR II

C.L.R. James, George Breitman, Edgar Keemer, and others

A week-by-week account of the struggle against lynch-mob terror and racist discrimination in U.S. war industries, the armed forces, and society as a whole from 1939 to 1945, taken from the pages of the socialist newsweekly, the Militant. These struggles helped lay the basis for the rise of the mass civil rights movement in the subsequent two decades. $22

MARIANAS IN COMBAT

TETÉ PUEBLA AND THE MARIANA GRAJALES WOMEN'S PLATOON IN CUBA'S REVOLUTIONARY WAR, 1956–58

Brigadier General Teté Puebla, the highest-ranking woman in Cuba's Revolutionary Armed Forces, joined the struggle to overthrow the U.S.-backed dictatorship of Fulgencio Batista in 1956, when she was fifteen years old. This is her story—from clandestine action in the cities, to serving as an officer in the victorious Rebel Army's first all-women's unit—the Mariana Grajales Women's Platoon. For nearly fifty years, the fight to transform the social and economic status of women in Cuba has been inseparable from Cuba's socialist revolution. $14. Also in Spanish.

MAURICE BISHOP SPEAKS

THE GRENADA REVOLUTION AND ITS OVERTHROW, 1979–83

The triumph of the 1979 revolution in the Caribbean island of Grenada had "importance for all struggles around the world," said Maurice Bishop, its central leader. Invaluable lessons from that workers and farmers government, overturned in a Stalinist-led coup in 1983, can be found in this collection of Bishop's speeches and interviews. $25

New International

A MAGAZINE OF MARXIST POLITICS AND THEORY

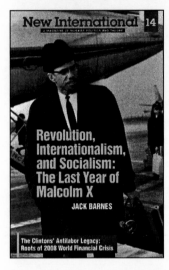

NEW INTERNATIONAL NO. 14

REVOLUTION, INTERNATIONALISM, AND SOCIALISM: THE LAST YEAR OF MALCOLM X

Jack Barnes

"To understand Malcolm's last year is to see how, in the imperialist epoch, revolutionary leadership of the highest political capacity, courage, and integrity converges with communism. That truth has even greater weight today as billions around the world, in city and countryside, from China to Brazil, are being hurled into the modern class struggle by the violent expansion of world capitalism."—Jack Barnes

Issue #14 also includes "The Clintons' Antilabor Legacy: Roots of the 2008 World Financial Crisis"; "The Stewardship of Nature Also Falls to the Working Class: In Defense of Land and Labor" and "Setting the Record Straight on Fascism and World War II." $14

NEW INTERNATIONAL NO. 12

CAPITALISM'S LONG HOT WINTER HAS BEGUN

Jack Barnes

and "*Their Transformation and Ours*,"
Resolution of the Socialist Workers Party

Today's sharpening interimperialist conflicts are fueled both by the opening stages of what will be decades of economic, financial, and social convulsions and class battles, and by the most far-reaching shift in Washington's military policy and organization since the U.S. buildup toward World War II. Class-struggle-minded working people must face this historic turning point for imperialism, and draw satisfaction from being "in their face" as we chart a revolutionary course to confront it. $16

ALL THESE ISSUES ARE ALSO AVAILABLE IN SPANISH AND MOST IN FRENCH AT
WWW.PATHFINDERPRESS.COM

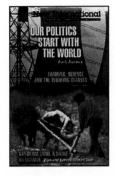

NEW INTERNATIONAL NO. 13
OUR POLITICS START WITH THE WORLD
Jack Barnes

The huge economic and cultural inequalities between imperialist and semicolonial countries, and among classes within almost every country, are produced, reproduced, and accentuated by the workings of capitalism. For vanguard workers to build parties able to lead a successful revolutionary struggle for power in our own countries, says Jack Barnes in the lead article, our activity must be guided by a strategy to close this gap.

Also includes: "Farming, Science, and the Working Classes" *by Steve Clark* and "Capitalism, Labor, and Nature: An Exchange" *by Richard Levins, Steve Clark.* $14

NEW INTERNATIONAL NO. 11
U.S. IMPERIALISM HAS LOST THE COLD WAR
Jack Barnes

Contrary to imperialist expectations at the opening of the 1990s in the wake of the collapse of regimes across Eastern Europe and the USSR claiming to be communist, the workers and farmers there have not been crushed. Nor have capitalist social relations been stabilized. The toilers remain an intractable obstacle to imperialism's advance, one the exploiters will have to confront in class battles and war. $16

NEW INTERNATIONAL NO. 8
CHE GUEVARA, CUBA, AND THE ROAD TO SOCIALISM
Articles by Ernesto Che Guevara, Carlos Rafael Rodríguez, Carlos Tablada, Mary-Alice Waters, Steve Clark, Jack Barnes

Exchanges from the opening years of the Cuban Revolution and today on the political perspectives defended by Guevara as he helped lead working people to advance the transformation of economic and social relations in Cuba. $10

NEW INTERNATIONAL NO. 7
OPENING GUNS OF WORLD WAR III: WASHINGTON'S ASSAULT ON IRAQ
Jack Barnes

The murderous assault on Iraq in 1990–91 heralded increasingly sharp conflicts among imperialist powers, growing instability of international capitalism, and more wars. *Also includes:* "1945: When U.S. Troops said 'No!'" *by Mary-Alice Waters* and "Lessons from the Iran-Iraq War" *by Samad Sharif.* $14

PATHFINDER AROUND THE WORLD

Visit our website for a complete list of titles and to place orders

www.pathfinderpress.com

PATHFINDER DISTRIBUTORS

UNITED STATES
(and Caribbean, Latin America, and East Asia)

> *Pathfinder Books, 306 W. 37th St., 10th Floor,*
> *New York, NY 10018*

CANADA

> *Pathfinder Books, 7105 St. Hubert, Suite 106F,*
> *Montreal, QC H2S 2N1*

UNITED KINGDOM
(and Europe, Africa, Middle East, and South Asia)

> *Pathfinder Books, First Floor, 120 Bethnal Green Road*
> *(entrance in Brick Lane), London E2 6DG*

SWEDEN

> *Pathfinder böcker, Bildhuggarvägen 17, S-121 44 Johanneshov*

AUSTRALIA
(and Southeast Asia and the Pacific)

> *Pathfinder, Level 1, 3/281-287 Beamish St., Campsie, NSW 2194*
> *Postal address: P.O. Box 164, Campsie, NSW 2194*

NEW ZEALAND

> *Pathfinder, 7 Mason Ave. (upstairs), Otahuhu, Auckland*
> *Postal address: P.O. Box 3025, Auckland 1140*